PENGUIN ENTERPRISE
SPEAKING FOR MYSELF

Sukrita Paul Kumar, born and brought up in Kenya, is a poet and critic, currently teaching literature in Delhi. Formerly a fellow of the Indian Institute of Advanced Study, Shimla, she is an honorary fellow of the International Writing Programme, University of Iowa (USA), Hong Kong Baptist University and Cambridge Seminars. She is also honorary faculty at the Durrell Centre at Corfu (Greece). She has published several collections of poems and many critical books including *Without Margins*; *Folds of Silence*; *Narrating Partition*; *The New Story*; *Man, Woman and Androgyny* and *Ismat: Her Life, Her Times*. As director of a UNESCO project, she edited a volume of Urdu short stories in English, *Mapping Memories*. In 2006, she published, as its chief editor, *Cultural Diversity in India*, prescribed in Delhi University. While her latest co-edited volume is *Interpreting Homes*, she has also recently published *Rowing Together*, a bilingual book of poems with a fellow Hindi poet. A recipient of many prestigious fellowships, she has lectured in several universities in India and abroad.

Malashri Lal is a professor in the Department of English, and the current joint director of the University of Delhi, South Campus. With a specialization in literary studies, Malashri Lal has written and lectured extensively in India and abroad on women's socio-cultural positioning and women's writing. As a Fulbright scholar and recipient of several fellowships from the Rockefeller Foundation, the Shastri-Indo Canadian Institute and the British Council, she has conducted research in prestigious institutions such as Harvard University, USA. Malashri Lal's books include *The Law of the Threshold: Women Writers in Indian English*; and the co-edited volumes *At Home in the World: A Window on Contemporary Indian Literature*, *Interpreting Homes in South Asian Literature* and *The Indian Family in Transition*. She is a former Fellow of the Indian Institute of Advanced Study, Shimla, and has served on the international jury for the Commonwealth Writers' Prize, London.

Speaking for Myself

An Anthology of Asian Women's Writing

Edited by

Sukrita Paul Kumar and Malashri Lal

PENGUIN ENTERPRISE
Published by the Penguin Group
Penguin Books India Pvt. Ltd, 11 Community Centre, Panchsheel Park, New Delhi 110 017, India
Penguin Group (USA) Inc., 375 Hudson Street, New York, New York 10014, USA
Penguin Group (Canada), 90 Eglinton Avenue East, Suite 700, Toronto, Ontario, M4P 2Y3, Canada (a division of Pearson Penguin Canada Inc.)
Penguin Books Ltd, 80 Strand, London WC2R 0RL, England
Penguin Ireland, 25 St Stephen's Green, Dublin 2, Ireland (a division of Penguin Books Ltd)
Penguin Group (Australia), 250 Camberwell Road, Camberwell, Victoria 3124, Australia (a division of Pearson Australia Group Pty Ltd)
Penguin Group (NZ), 67 Apollo Drive, Rosedale, North Shore 0632, New Zealand (a division of Pearson New Zealand Ltd)
Penguin Group (South Africa) (Pty) Ltd, 24 Sturdee Avenue, Rosebank, Johannesburg 2196, South Africa

Penguin Books Ltd, Registered Offices: 80 Strand, London WC2R 0RL, England

First published in Penguin Enterprise by Penguin Books India and India International Centre 2009

10 9 8 7 6 5 4 3 2 1

ISBN 9780143065333

Typeset in Venetian by Mantra Virtual Services, New Delhi
Printed at Pauls Press, New Delhi

Dedicated to Sarojini Naidu (1879–1949)
'Bharata Kokila' (The Nightingale of India)

My proud soul shall be unforgiven
For a passionate sin it will ne'er repent,
And I shall be doomed, O Love, and driven
And hurled from Heaven's high battlement, . . .
My outlawed spirit shall crave no pardon . . .

From 'Love Transcendent'

Contents

SOUTH ASIA

Foreword

There has been a fairly sustained and continuous debate on whether there is a specific entity called 'Asian civilization and culture'. While some scholars have clearly identified a coherent body of thought—philosophy, political theories and cultural expressions—called 'western civilization', there have been doubts in regard to Asia. The geographical span of Asia is vast—extending across Central Asia, West Asia, South Asia, Southeast Asia, East Asia and the Asia-Pacific. Each of these nomenclatures is an indicator of some natural boundaries, but is recognized today as a political unit comprising many nation states. The dominant discourses in regard to these nation states or countries have largely been in the context of socio-economic developments and sometimes in regard to political affiliations. Seldom has there been a serious effort to identify the diverse roots of communication between and amongst these countries for centuries.

Today, understandably but not necessarily convincingly, these countries are grouped as either the developing world or members of the developed world. There is scope for reinvestigating the socio-cultural fabric of the groups as also the countries within these groups. Has there been a continuity of dialogue transcending political boundaries? Has there been communication across borders at the very moments of war and conflict or peace?

It was with a view to exploring these dimensions outside the forums of international organizations where these countries are represented as member-states that the India International Centre (IIC) launched a modest project called the IIC-Asia Project. The project did not address itself to answering the major question whether there is an 'Asian civilization' or not; rather it focussed in the first phase, under the leadership of Dr Karan Singh, on India's relationship with Central Asia, West Asia, countries of South Asia, Southeast Asia, East Asia and the Asia-Pacific. The seminars brought together eminent scholars and specialists on current affairs, and six volumes based on the discussions have been published. They have been well received.

In the second phase of the project, a different approach was followed. This time it was thematic, transcending groupings such as Central Asia, West Asia and East Asia; it endeavoured to discriminatingly identify movements which crossed borders, political or national. One of the first priorities was to explore the manner and method of transmission of knowledge within each unit and its transmission across borders.

Seminars and workshops were held to identify the very distinctive methodologies of transmission of knowledge through intra-generational dialogue, especially between mother and child. This brought forth the importance of oral transmission distinctive to Asia. Also, it made visible the importance of visual and aural literacy, known and refined in the region. This was true of communities lying as far apart as Kyrgyzstan, Uzbekistan, China and Korea, and even further, of communities in Australia and New Zealand.

This initiative of identifying the distinctive methodologies had far-reaching implications for evolving a more relevant pedagogy for education. The results of these deliberations were brought to the forums of international organizations, especially UNESCO. As a result a major international conference, 'Education through Art', was held in Lisbon. The conference discussed the many complex questions of introducing visual and aural literacy, as also involvement of the highly cultured, but not necessarily literate, sections of the Asian and African continents.

Over the millennia, there has been dialogue at the level of both conception and visualization which has manifested itself in the architectural monuments of Asia. Here too, there are shared trajectories, distinctive expressions and multiple histories. An important seminar was held to explore these aspects of the Asian dialogue. Resultantly, a volume entitled *Sacred Landscapes in Asia: Shared Traditions, Multiple Histories* has been published. This is a beginning, and it is hoped that departments of art history in India and elsewhere will carry forward the exploration of not only the unilinear chronological trajectory but also the multilayered histories of many of these architectural edifices.

Complementary and as significant is the pervasive, cherished but humble art of the needle and the thread. Hardly ever has there been a serious, academic discussion on the role of women's embroidery in creating and sustaining a vibrant cultural dialogue. The products—be it the white on white embroidery of Afghani women or Vietnamese women, or the more familiar *chikan* of India—do they not speak of the concurrency, transmission and distinctiveness of local space and time? Besides, there is the *sujani* of Central Asia, which has travelled to Pakistan and India through the woman's dowry. The much-coveted *phulkari* has tales to tell beyond the skilfully crafted geometrical patterns of crafts specialists and designers. Whether Pakistan or India, the embroidery of the phulkari is intrinsically woven into the life of the woman from birth to death. Each pausation is inscribed into the particular design of the embroidery. The needle and the thread are the instrumentalities of memory as also expression of joy and sorrow.

Other embroideries, such as the *kantha*, is the piecing together of fragments into a whole through that needle and thread, whereby the stories of life and death, of ritual, of obedience and dissent, are stitched together to speak a language of beauty, a language that crosses borders. *Sui-dhaga*, needle and thread, and the embroideries were the creative expression of emotion through the language of the hands and the finger. Tradition and contemporaneity worked hand-in-hand in the oral narratives, which accompanied the making of these embroideries. It was and is important.

Running parallel to this is the impressive output of Asian women through the modern medium of films. For four years now, 2005–08, there's been a film festival of young Asian documentary filmmakers in conjunction with the International Association of Women in Radio and Television (IAWRT). This is evidence of the new challenges, fears and hopes, defeats and aspirations of a young generation of Asian women. Some remarkable short films screened at these festivals are convincing proof of the ability of Asian women to make technological transitions smoothly into a modern world.

But the most challenging and difficult task in our endeavour to understand the transmission of knowledge across boundaries was the putting together of this anthology of women's writing in Asia, especially contemporary writing, which is linked to the oral tradition and also to a heritage of scripted literature. At first glance it appeared that this may be an easy task for teachers of literature, Sukrita Paul Kumar and Malashri Lal, both known for their abilities as writers, editors and teachers. They were invited to take on this assignment. They responded graciously and selected bright research assistants to help them. All of us thought that the anthology would come together smoothly. This was not to be. As the editors have pointed out in their introduction, libraries of colleges and universities here do not have much material. Bookstores do not carry literature of Asian countries, translations are few and far between, while of necessity the anthology has to be in the English language. Both the editors and their researchers have persevered with patience and courage. The difficulties and the challenges that they faced have been enumerated by them. These point to the woeful lack of direct channels of communication between and amongst Asian countries. A detour route had to be adopted through foreign lands to identify publishers and locate source material.

The extensive scope of the anthology is evident—ranging from Uzbekistan, Kazakhstan and Afghanistan to China, Korea and Japan; from Tibet and Nepal to Sri Lanka and India; from Indonesia and Thailand to Vietnam and Cambodia. What are these voices of women, from where do they come, and to whom do they reach out? Are these cries for emancipation, or are they the voices of strength and resolute courage in moments of crisis, despair and oppression? Further, are these the voices that originate in the recent histories of dislocation and enforced re-location? Or, are these the poignant expressions of human love—mother and child, sister and friend, grandmother and grandchild? This anthology provides a window to witness and hear these voices, different and distinct, but orchestrated together in what one may call a characteristic Asian sensibility which has sustained its identity through many centuries.

New Delhi
October 2008

Dr Kapila Vatsyayan

Introduction

Sukrita Paul Kumar and Malashri Lal

Why writings? Why Asian? And then, why women?

We began with an exercise in self questioning. We dwelt on these philosophical enquiries if only for ourselves, to understand rationally the spontaneous impulse with which we were undertaking the 'natural' task of creating this book. A simple and outright response could have been: we were both Asian, both in the business of writing and reading literature, and that indeed we were both women, deeply engaged with issues pertaining to women's history, culture and literature. We had tried at various forums to understand the plight of women and the neglect heaped upon them by patriarchal generations. Like the proverbial tales of Scheherezade, there was always more recounting and reflection possible on such a subject.

But we paused to ask why there was such little familiarity with the writings of women except in our immediate region. Had the historical act of silencing women cut out the possibility of reading their words and hearing their voices across Asian countries? There seemed a troubling yet enticing void where their untold stories may have been waiting for articulation, or so we surmised. In our fervent search we made exploratory journeys to major libraries and book shops in the city, looking for stories and poems from Bangladesh, Iraq, Macau or Cambodia, and other countries in Asia. Perhaps it is a truism to report that the bookstores and libraries abound in publications from the West, in general, and the market readily offers to obtain more such material on demand. Canonical literature in the universities too seems to stress theoretical texts from Western academia. We found neither agents nor distributors willing to bring in books from Asian sources. As for women's writing, we had no bibliographies and references to guide us to a possible stockist. Too near, therefore inaccessible?! World politics dominating the book trade? Was thoughtless media hype responsible for the easy selling and buying of Western literature and the near-total indifference to the richness of literatures from the East? Or was it the constant lure of the Occident, the glamour of the language and literature of the so-called 'first world' that kept the market moving lucratively?

But then, it could also be an expected consequence of the oft-repeated lament that translation work in English, based on literatures in different Asian languages, is simply not undertaken adequately in most Asian countries. Is it then the lack of local interest in such material or the neglect of translations that makes Asian writing so difficult to come by? On such matters, our curiosity was aroused. As for the university libraries, it is quite understandable that Asian literature is often not on the shelves since most academic programmes in India do not include it in their curricula. All these factors reinforced our initial thought about compiling a single volume that would provide glimpses of the powerful writing by women in Asia. It is our hope that a book such as this one will encourage the academic world to make space for the inclusion of writing from Asia and provide an opportunity to think about cultural affinities and crossovers.

During the time we were researching and collecting material for this book, a couple of fortunate academic visits to some institutions in Asia made us wiser to the limited availability, mostly local, of English translations of several stories and poems from the original Asian languages. We fail to understand why this literature does not enter the Indian markets and of course vice versa too, English translations of Indian writings are not visible in the markets of other Asian countries. Perhaps the creation of their demand will result in their supply. This book is only going to whet the taste for literature from Asia. The selections here are not necessarily representative writings from different Asian countries but it is hoped that they will serve as a take-off point for further explorations.

With no intention of constructing an alternative to the notion of 'Orientalism' which justifiably received a devastating critique from Edward Said, we bring Asian voices together in this volume, for one, to offer an opportunity to understand each other more through literature and also to suggest the range of affinities existent in the quality of the sensibility of Asian writers. Large regions of Asia share a common repertoire of myths and legends, epics and religions as well as similar traditions of storytelling. Physical proximity, many historical and cultural movements and socio-political contexts have contributed in creating a similar philosophical strain and temper in the peoples of various countries of Asia, while modernity and a pragmatic approach to the idea of progress and development have kept the West on a somewhat separate track.

In his book, *Culture and Imperialism,* Edward Said puts it very succinctly: '... studying the relationship between the "West" and its dominated cultural "others" is not just a way of understanding an unequal relationship between unequal interlocutors, but also a point of entry into studying the formation and meaning of Western cultural practices themselves.' (p. 230). Moreover, the 'West' is also equated with imperialism and a stubborn repository of economic and political power, causing simmering resentment amongst its erstwhile colonies. Western sensibility stands differentiated if placed against the Other. This 'other' includes a composite whole of the peoples of Asian countries, which unfortunately has not made sufficient efforts to get all its resources together to evolve a balance of power in the world. The first step towards this end is to get to know each other by sharing and reading each other's stories and poems, the language of the heart and mind! Undoubtedly, differences among cultures, faiths and beliefs, behaviour patterns and styles of communication surface significantly; but bridges of understanding are also constructed through empathy and points of identification.

There is no denying the tremendous heterogeneity of experiences, contexts and modes of articulation clearly evidenced in the writings from Asia. Literary representation as we understand it emerges from very specific and rooted experience and reaches out to the 'Other' by transcending into the realm of essential questions related to human existence. In that sense, any categorization, even that of 'Asian literature', appears quite meaningless. But then, we also realize, that unless the specifics are comprehended, the essence of the 'larger questions' of existence cannot be realized. For example, the anguish of the Cambodian protagonist in a story will inevitably have its roots in a specific socio-political context at a particular point of history; and, without the knowledge of that context, the nature of the experience of that anguish cannot be fully realized. Also, how a character copes with her existential predicament will have plenty to do with the society and culture she has been nurtured in. Even in her posture of rebellion, her social backdrop gets manifested.

Invisibility of literatures from each other's countries within Asia is a phenomenon that pains one all the more, when confronted with the much greater visibility of these literatures in the English dominated 'West', in the bookstores and libraries of the US and the UK. This maybe so perhaps because of the departments and centres of Asian Studies present in most universities in the West. This does get to be a matter of concern. Such studies, when wrenched away from their own physical and sociological contexts, have the danger of getting essentialized. Without an ongoing dialogue with the living complexity, the heterogeneity of the ground reality could get sacrificed dangerously if there is an inadequate ongoing dialogue with those who are actually living the reality of the cultures being studied. This way the Oriental faces the threat of getting more orientalized! For the day-to-day dynamism of our cultures to be theorized upon, a day-to-day contact is necessary. Literature serves as a good medium for the articulation of vibrant reality and our volume is one small and modest attempt to bring the variety of lives in Asia together.

To come to the third and a very vital question regarding this volume: Why women? While on the one hand we certainly do not believe in 'ghettoizing' the voices of women and do not wish to suggest here a separatist world of women, we do want to present women's experiences in different regions of Asia as a perspective in this book. There is a conscious exclusion of male writers to allow the writer's 'experience' of being a woman to authenticate the presentation of female experience. Undoubtedly, the woman too, more often than not, gets to be an accomplice and a consenting agent of patriarchy, being herself very much a product of patriarchal socialization. It is certainly not enough just to be a woman biologically to speak as a woman. But for 'speaking as a woman', the required unlearning of male-centred institutionalized thinking is more possible for a woman as she is herself a victim of patriarchal oppression and may thus feel a greater compulsion to reinvent both, the language as well as the content of creative expression. It is not easy to break out of the unconscious imbibing of structures of gender identity set up over centuries. For a woman the need to do so would be inevitably greater. If the aesthetics of women's writings include the revelation of suppressed histories of gender exploitation, they are bound to also include stories of the heroic struggles and triumphs of women in engaging with life.

In this volume the literature selected suggests that women are not mere objects for commodification: even in the demure and feminine female character, there is a self-reflexive strain which ultimately informs her sense of being. Many women writers here tend to present a case for the re-visioning of women, showcasing the varied dimensions of women's lives in their respective cultures. The received stereotypical image of Asian women upheld generally by the rest of the world as passive, impoverished or anaemic, needs to be questioned and revised. The stories and poems in this volume tend to serve such a purpose, sometimes overtly and at times, subtly. There are occasions when storytelling and sharing in itself is empowering and as Geyang, the Tibetan writer puts it in her narrative 'An Old Nun Tells Her Story': 'We tell each other stories of our lives, and everything we have suffered becomes something beautiful.' Sharing and finding speech for the articulation of 'suffering' is empowering in itself; it is a demonstration of strength acquired through self-reflection. It counters the common notion of a woman's passive acceptance of victimization.

Men act and women, says patriarchy, are acted upon! As we reviewed more and more stories and poems by women of Vietnam or Iran, Pakistan or China, we came across strong, courageous, dignified and energetic representations of women, not just as secondary characters but as complex human beings in positive roles. Liang Xia of the Chinese story 'Melody of Dreams' by Zong Pu, for instance, speaks up with all the daring possible when she says, 'I don't want to hide anything from you. But we must speak out and let these bastards know we are still living. As you know, I'm not afraid of anything.' In the backdrop of the persecution of the intellectuals during the Cultural Revolution in China, she identifies with the heroic young people who protested at Tiananmen Square. The concern for speaking out is equally strong in Fadwa Tuqan of Palestine when she says: 'The time has arrived for this daughter to speak and, when a truthful woman speaks, it is life that is speaking.'

The debunking of negative notions of female identity in literature seems to happen more through a conscious feminist thrust by the woman writer, but she also participates in the expression of social critiquing. The powerful voice of protest in the Pakistani poet, Kishwar Naheed, calls for attention in this context: 'I am the one you hid beneath/the weight of traditions/for you never knew/that light can never fear pitch darkness.' When the writer's imagination gets rebellious and creates greater space for speech and heroic action for the female characters, society gains in its capacity to offer more possibilities of freedom to its women.

Women's movements in different countries have been marked by dynamism and change. The last quarter of a century has ushered in new perspectives on gender issues as well as fresh paradigms of development to empower women. Undoubtedly, women are far more visible and articulate in the public arena now but even today they occupy a limited space between tradition and modernity. 'These voices, they continue to follow me./They try to harm me, but I will not stop. I will stand in their midst and I will face them down./Yes, my executioners .../... But I am not afraid, and I will not stop.' This voice is that of Marsinah, murdered as an activist, and one who wishes to come back to the Earth and assert herself. Ratna Sarumpaet of Sumatra stages her anxious assertions in her play *Marsinah Accuses*, bridging the past with the present that is full of the spirit of vengefulness and one that demands justice. After all, it is a matter of locating the opportunities that have opened up for women in some societies that, in turn, have also impacted redefinitions of female selfhood.

While there are many artistic portrayals of women in whom the strong force of cultural conditioning is shown as a subtle blockage to individual and professional growth, at the same time, there are icons such as the figure of 'Shakti' in India that has been used as an emblem for feminist power. Mahasweta Devi's story 'Draupadi' (not included here) is an unambiguous rendering of the spontaneous expression of female energy told from the viewpoint of the 'disadvantaged' woman. The story takes forward the culturally established and iconic figure of Draupadi echoed through the title of the story and projects the inner source of a woman's *shakti* (power) in her posture of challenge and defiance. We have selected for this volume another story by Devi, 'Giribala', where the strength of a woman's affirmative choice stands endorsed. Indian female writers often revisit mythology in order to upturn the power equations and substantiate the woman's posture of challenge and defiance. How do women reinforce traditional icons or symbols when needed or at times negotiate the persistence of regressive cultural images, many of them drawn from powerful and ancient practices? How do they negotiate unstated new boundaries? Such questions as these helped determine our choice of literature presented in this volume in which writers are engaged in looking at women's choices, their dreams, interrogating set notions of 'honour' and morality, reviewing the construct of female beauty and culture, women's achievements as well as 'failures', women in relation to the workplace, other women, men, community and family.

In her inimitable style, writing originally in Azeri, Afagh Masud of Azerbaijan resists the social constructs that come in the way of the self-confirmation of a woman's identity. In her story, 'Sparrows', the mother wrenches herself away from the observant and alert daughter quietly and firmly and almost heartlessly departs, taking a heroic flight, like the sparrows, to be able to perhaps discover her own self outside the family structure. This story does not at all conform with the much propagated belief that with Asian women, 'motherhood' is sacrosanct to the extent of their total submission of the self. The story is told through the consciousness of a daughter as in the case of Luo Ying's poem from Taiwan, 'Daylily's Journey' (not included here). The difference lies in the tone as well as treatment of the theme. In the latter piece, the poem is a celebration of the mother's flights: the mother who is '... the well in front of the door/a stone inside the well ..../' is also one who 'always flies/without direction, without a way back/She's always flying/scattering bits of feather-shaped/love, non-love, nostalgia, non-nostalgia/ ... she flies, and keeps/flying'. The poet celebrates different dimensions of the mother's being in the poem, and offers her the whole of the sky to fly! The fact that motherhood falls within the ken of several writers in this volume is perhaps an acknowledgement of its significance in the cultures and societies of Asia. From taking flights of freedom from the 'captivity' of motherhood, to a self-conscious commitment to the role of being a mother, different writers choose to explore the complexity of a mother's 'being' differently. We would like to emphasize a variety of perspectives and the occasional ambivalence of the writers on the subject rather than highlight any one authoritative or uni-dimensional representation of motherhood.

Whether it is through subversion of mythology and legends or the use of metaphors, there is a definite concern on the part of most women writers in this volume to seek a sense of justice for the exploited woman, when for instance she gets commodified in such stories as 'A Girl called Apple' by Hanan al-Shaikh from Lebanon or Mey Son Sotheary's story 'My Sister' from Cambodia. There is a definite subtext permeating this literature which celebrates and venerates the dignity and strength of the enlightened woman and represents a critique of the regressive ideals of patriarchy.

As editors, we have consciously avoided the strong temptation to categorize this literature thematically for a neat organization of the material collected for this book since this neatness, we realize, would have been at the cost of the rather nuanced reality of the woman's complex contexts and experiences in different cultures in the expansive continent of Asia. To reduce their stories to either essentialized concepts or confine them to restricted themes would be naive. The multiple positions of the women protagonists, as heroes or victims, or both, do not conform to any specific point of view of the editors. We want the narratives to speak for themselves and the readers to come to their own understanding about any specific theme in each of the stories or poems given here.

Earlier we thought of slotting the stories or poems country wise, but we soon saw that that too would not be convincing since the flow of cultural streams, myths and symbols easily crossed national and political borders, transmuting themselves gradually into newer shapes with time and distance. Physical boundaries become mere shadow lines for tales and songs to travel across, without any constraints specially when there are languages that are shared by some countries. In South Asia, for instance, languages such as Punjabi, Urdu, Bengali, Tamil, Sindhi and some others, are spoken in more than just one country. The technique of *dastaangoi* (long narratives) travelled to

India from West Asia and thrived for centuries. It was for this reason that we decided eventually to let the geographical borders collapse and just have clusters of countries clubbed together as East Asia, Central Asia, South Asia, West Asia and South-East Asia. This is not to deny the differences present within each of the clusters but merely to facilitate the reader to discern the similarities and differences of cultural co-ordinates within and across each one of them.

Most of the literature collected in this volume is translated from different languages of Asia. Unfortunately, therefore, we are not able to identify the linguistic innovation on the part of the writer. It would be very pertinent to study the 'language of women writers' if only to see how women re-invent language to articulate the range of their experiences, so different from those of a man. Ismat Chughtai, an Urdu short-story writer from India, not included in this book, wrote brilliantly in what is called *begumati zubaan* (the language of the upper middle class women). Such a feature is totally lost in translation!

This collection of stories and poems has a deliberate eclecticism about it. The stories and poems are neither representative pieces *vis à vis* their countries, nor of their writers. There is no dominating viewpoint of the editors imposed on the selection. Mainly accessibility and aesthetic appeal have governed our preferences and if we may add, in general what we modestly offer in this book is a posse of women's writings that insists on the dignity of Asian women shown by the sheer strength of women's identities lived in a variety of roles, with many of them breaking the stereotype and seeking to come into their own. There may not be easy resolutions suggested in these creative pieces but that is also because literature does not really propound resolutions, though it may inevitably carry the tone of interrogation and a subtle and sometimes not-so-subtle expression of resistance to fixed notions and beliefs.

This book would not have come into being but for the invitation that we received from Dr Kapila Vatsyayan, Chairperson of the IIC-Asia Project, to focus our attention on the diverse and yet distinctively Asian voices of women. Kapila Vatsyayan urged us to explore the creativity of women as expressed through the word—poetry, fiction, drama. We responded to the invitation not realizing the many challenges that would come our way. At times we were diffident, almost hopeless, the paucity of material being the most obvious cause. It was a learning experience for us to know that despite the recent emphasis on women's empowerment there was no easily accessible source of obtaining suitable material for an anthology. Kapilaji kept up our enthusiasm and did not give up. The many discussions that we had with her will remain memorable. These extended from the age-old cultural dialogue between and amongst Asian countries as also discontinuties during not only the colonial period but also the post-colonial era. As we went along it became clear that women's voices from different parts of Asia extending over a very large geographical region could transcend local and immediate exigencies to seek, at times, perennial values. Women indeed have subversive and silent methods of asserting their place and much more.

The material presented in this book reflects the power of women's literature to manifest the trials and tribulations, the oppression and the freedom, the sensitivity and the strength that has survived tumultuous times in our age.

We express our sincere thanks to Dr Kapila Vatsyayan, Chairperson of the Asia Project, India International Centre (IIC), for her inspirational guidance of this project. We also thank Bela Butalia, Deputy Editor, IIC and Mr N. Ramachandran, Officer on Special Duty, IIC-Asia Project, for their constant help.

East Asia

China

One Centimetre

BI SHU-MIN

When Tao Ying rides on the bus alone, quite often she does not bother to buy a ticket.

Why should she? Without her, the bus would still be stopping at every stop, a driver and a conductor would still have to be employed, and the same amount of petrol used.

Clearly Tao Ying has to be astute. When the bus conductor looked like the responsible type, she would buy a ticket as soon as she got on board. But if he appeared to be casual and careless, she would not dream of paying, considering it a small punishment for him and a little saving for herself.

Tao Ying works as a cook in the canteen of a factory. She spends all day next to an open fire, baking screw-shaped wheat cakes with sesame butter.

Today she is with her son Xiao Ye. She follows him onto the bus. As the doors shut her jacket is caught, ballooning up like a tent behind her. She twists this way and that, finally wrenching herself free.

'Mama, tickets!' Xiao Ye says. Children are often more conscious of rituals than adults. Without a ticket in his hand, the ride doesn't count as a proper ride.

On the peeling paint of the door somebody has painted the shape of a pale finger. It points at a number: 1.10m.

Xiao Ye pushed through. His hair looks as fluffy as a bundle of straw—dry and without lustre. As a rule, Tao Ying is very careful with her purse, but she has never skimped on her child's diet. Nonetheless the goodness in his food refuses to advance beyond his hairline. As a result Xiao Ye is healthy and clever, but his hair is a mess.

Tao Ying tries to smooth it down, as if she is brushing away top soil to get to a firm foundation. She can feel the softness of her son's skull, rubbery and elastic to the touch. Apparently there is a gap on the top of everyone's head, where the two halves meet. If they don't meet properly, a person can end up with a permanently gaping mouth. Even when the hemispheres are a perfect match, it still takes a while for them to seal. This is the door to Life itself—if it remains open, the world outside will feel like water, flowing into the body through this slit. Every time Tao Ying happens upon this aperture on her son's head, she is overwhelmed by a sense of responsibility. It was she who brought this delicate creature into the world after all. Although she senses her own insignificance in the world, that her existence makes no difference to anyone else, she also realizes that to this little boy she is the centre of the universe and she must try to be the most perfect, flawless mother possible.

Between Xiao Ye's round head and the tip of the painted digit setting out the height requirement for a ticket rest the beautiful slender fingers of Tao Ying. Since she is in contact with oil all day, her nails are shiny, glistening like the smooth curved back of a sea shell.

'Xiao Ye, you are not quite tall enough, still one centimetre away,' she tells him softly. Tao Ying does not come from a privileged background, and has not read very many books. But she likes to be gentle and gracious, to set an example for her son and make a good impression. This elevates her sense of self-worth and makes her feel like an aristocrat.

'Mama! I'm tall enough, I'm tall enough!' Xiao Ye shouts at the top of his voice, stamping on the floor as if it were a tin drum. 'You told me the last time I could have a ticket the next time, this is the next time! You don't keep your word!' He looks up at his mother angrily.

Tao Ying looks down at her son. A ticket costs twenty cents. Twenty cents is not to be scoffed at. It can buy a cucumber, two tomatoes or, at a reduced price, three bunches of radishes or enough spinach to last four days. But Xiao Ye's face is raised up like a half-open blossom, waiting to receive his promise from the sun.

'Get in! Don't block the entrance! This is not a train, where you stand from Beijing to Bao Ding. We're almost at the next stop ...!' the conductor bellows.

Normally, an outburst like this would certainly have discouraged Tao Ying from buying a ticket. But today she says, 'Two tickets, please.'

The fierce conductor has beady eyes. 'This child is one centimetre short of requiring a ticket.'

Xiao Ye shrinks, not just one but several centimetres—the need for a ticket has all of a sudden become interwoven with the pride of a small child.

To be able to purchase self-esteem with twenty cents is something that can only happen in childhood and certainly no mother can resist an opportunity to make her son happy.

'I would like to buy two tickets,' she says politely.

Xiao Ye holds the two tickets close to his lips and blows, making a sound like a paper windmill.

They had entered through the central doors of the bus, but alight towards the front. Here another conductor is poised to examine their tickets. Tao Ying thinks that this man can't be very bright. What mother accompanied by a child would try to avoid paying the correct fare? However poor she would never have allowed herself to lose face in front of her own son.

She hands over the tickets nonchalantly. The conductor asks: 'Are you going to claim these back?' 'No.' In fact Tao Ying ought to have kept the tickets so that the next time there is a picnic or an outing at work, she could use her bicycle and then claim back the fare with the stubs. Both she and her husband are blue-collar workers, and any saving would have been a help. But Xiao Ye is a smart boy, and might well question her aloud, 'Mama, can we claim back tickets even when we are on a private outing?' In front of the child, she would never lie.

It is exhausting to follow rules dictated by parental guidebooks all the time, but Tao Ying is determined to be the ideal mother and create a perfect example for her son to look up to. She needs really to concentrate—living this way is not unlike carrying an audience with you wherever you go. But her actions are full of love and tenderness. For instance, whenever she eats a watermelon in front of Xiao Ye, she would take care not to bite too close to the rind even though she doesn't actually think there is much difference between the flesh and the skin. True, the sweetness gradually diminishes as you work your way through the red towards the green, but every part of the melon is equally refreshing. In any case the skin of a melon is supposed to have a beneficial cooling effect, and is often used as medicine.

One day, she came across her son eating a melon in the same manner she did. When Xiao Ye looked up, Tao Ying could see a white melon seed stuck to his forehead. She was furious: 'Who taught you to gnaw at a melon like that? Are you going to wash your face in it too?' Xiao Ye was terrified. The small hand holding the melon began to tremble, but the big round eyes remained defiant.

Children are the best imitators in the world. From then on Tao Ying realized that if she wanted her son to behave as if he were the product of a cultured home, then she must concentrate and never fail in her own example. This was very difficult, like 'shooting down aeroplanes with a small gun'—but with determination, she knew that nothing was impossible. With this clear objective in mind, Tao Ying found her life becoming more focused, more challenging.

Today she is taking Xiao Ye to visit a big temple. He has never seen the Buddha before. Tao Ying is not a believer and she does not intend to ask him to kowtow. That is superstition, she knows.

The tickets cost five dollars a piece—these days even temples are run like businesses. Tao Ting's ticket was a gift from Lao Chiang, who worked at the meat counter. The ticket was valid for a month, and today was the last day. Lao Chiang was one of those people who seemed to know everybody. Occasionally he would produce a battered coverless month-old magazine and say: 'Seen this before? This is called the Big Reference, not meant for the eyes of the common people.' Tao Ying had never seen anything like this before and wondered how such a small rag, smaller even than a regular newspaper, could be called a Big Reference. She asked Lao Chiang but he seemed confused. He said everybody called it that—perhaps if you were to take out the pages and laid them flat they would end up bigger than a normal newspaper. It seemed to make sense. Studying the publication written in large print, Tao Ying could see that it was full of speculation about the war in the Middle East. Foremost on everyone's mind seemed to be whether the export of dates from Iraq to China would continue as it did in the sixties during the famine. In any case, Tao Ying was full of admiration for Lao Chiang. In return for her indiscriminate respect, Lao Chiang decided to reward her with a ticket for the temple. 'Is there just one?' Tao asked, not without gratitude but with some uncertainty. 'Forget your husband, take your son and open his eyes! Children under 110 centimetres do not need a ticket. If you don't want to go, sell it at the door and you'll earn enough to buy a couple of watermelons!' Lao Chiang had always been a practical man.

Tao Ying decided to take the day off and go on an outing with Xiao Ye.

It is rare to find such a large patch of grass in the middle of the city. Even before they got there, there was something refreshing, something green in the air, as if they were approaching a valley, or a waterfall. Xiao Ye snatches the ticket from his mother's hand, puts it between his lips, and flies towards the gilded gates of the temple. A little animal rushing to quench his thirst!

Tao Ying suddenly feels a little sad. Is the mere attraction of a temple enough for Xiao Ye to abandon his mother? But almost immediately she banishes the thought—hasn't she brought her son here today to make him happy?

The guard at the gate is a young man dressed in a red top and black trousers. Tao Ying feels somehow that he ought to have been in yellow. This uniform makes him look somewhat like a waiter.

Xiao Ye knows exactly what he has to do. Moving amongst the crowd, he seems like a tiny drop of water in the current of a large river.

The young man takes the ticket from his mouth, plucking a leaf from a spring branch.

Tao Ying's gaze softly envelops her son, a strand of silk unwinding towards him, following his every gesture.

'Ticket.' The youth in red bars her way with one arm, his voice as pithy as if he is spitting out a date stone.

Tao Ying points at her son with infinite tenderness. She feels that everybody should see how lovely he is.

'I am asking for your ticket.' The red youth does not budge.

'Didn't the child just give it to you?' Tao Ying's voice is peaceful. This boy is too young, years away from being a father, she thinks. Tao

Ying is not working today and is in a really good mood. She is happy to be patient.

'That was his ticket, now I need to see yours.' The youth remains unmoved.

Tao Ying has to pause for a moment before it sinks in—there are two of them and they need a ticket each.

'I thought that children were exempt?' She is confused.

'Mama, hurry up!' Xiao Ye shouts to her from inside the doors.

'Mama is coming!' Tao Ying shouts back. A crowd is beginning to gather, so many fishes swarming towards a bright light.

Tao Ying starts to panic. She wants this fracas to end—her child is waiting for her.

'Who told you he doesn't need a ticket?' The guard tilts his head—the more onlookers the better.

'It says so on the back of the ticket.'

'Exactly what does it say?' This boy is obviously not a professional.

'It says that children under 110 centimetres do not have to pay.' Tao Ying is full of confidence. She moves to pick up one of the tickets from a box next to the guard and reads out what is printed on the back for all to hear.

'Stop right there!' The youth has turned nasty. Tao Ying realizes she should not have touched the box and quickly withdraws her hand.

'So you are familiar with the rules and regulations, are you?' Now the young man addresses her with the formal 'you'. Tao Ying detects the sarcasm in his tone but she simply nods.

'Well, your son is over 110 centimetres,' he says with certainty.

'No he isn't.' Tao Ying is still smiling.

Everybody begins to look at the mother with suspicion.

'He just ran past the mark. I saw it clearly.' The guard is equally firm, pointing at a red line on the wall which looks like an earthworm inching across the road after a rainstorm.

'Mama, why are you taking so long? I thought I had lost you!' Xiao Ye shouts to her affectionately. He runs towards his mother, as if she was one of his favourite toys.

The crowd titters. Good, they think, here is proof, the whole matter can be cleared up at once.

The youth is getting a little nervous. He is just doing his job. He is certain he is right. But this woman seems very confident, perhaps … that would be awful …

Tao Ying remains calm. In fact, she feels a little smug. Her son loves excitement. This is turning into something of an event so it is bound to delight him.

'Come over here,' the youth commands.

The crowd holds its breath.

Xiao Ye looks at his mother. Tao Ying gives him a little nod. He walks over to the guard graciously, coughs a little, adjusts his jacket. In front of the gaze of the crowd, Xiao Ye is every inch the hero as he approaches the earthworm.

Then—the crowd looks, and sees—the worm comes to Xiao Ye's ear.

How is this possible?

Tao Ying is by his side in two paces. The flat of her hand lands heavily on the little boy's head, making a sound as crisp as a ping-pong ball popping underfoot.

Xiao Ye stares at his mother. He is not crying. He is shocked by the pain. He has never been hit before.

The crowd draws its breath.

'Punishing a child is one thing, hitting him on the head is totally unacceptable!'

'What a way for a mother to behave! So what if you have to buy another ticket? This is a disgrace, hitting a child to cover up your own mistake!'

'She can't be his natural mother …'

Everybody has an opinion.

Tao Ying is feeling a little agitated now. She had not meant to hit Xiao Ye. She meant to smooth down his hair. But she realizes that even if Xiao Ye were bald at this instant, he would still be towering above the worm on the wall.

'Xiao Ye, don't stand on tip-toe!' Tao Ying's voice is severe.

'Mama, I'm not …' Xiao Ye begins to cry.

It's true. He isn't. The worm crawls somewhere next to his brow.

The guard stretches himself lazily. His vision is sharp; he has caught quite a few people who had tried to get through without paying. 'Go get a ticket!' he screams at Tao Ying. All pretence of courtesy has by now been eaten up by the worm.

'But my son is less than one metre ten!' Tao Ying insists even though she realizes she stands alone.

'Everyone who tries to escape paying always says the same thing. Do you think these people are going to believe you, or are they going to believe me? This is a universally accepted measurement. The International Standard Ruler is in Paris, made of pure platinum. Did you know that?'

Tao is flummoxed. All she knows is that to make a dress she needs two metres, eighty centimetres; she does not know where the International Ruler is kept. She is only astonished at the power of the Buddha which can make her son grow several centimetres within minutes!

'But we were on the bus just now and he wasn't as tall ...'

'No doubt when he was born he wasn't as tall either!' the youth sneers, chilling the air.

Standing in the middle of the jeering crowd, Tao Ying's face has turned as white as her ticket.

'Mama, what is happening?' Xiao Ye comes away from the earthworm to hold his mother's frozen hand with his own little warm one.

'It's nothing. Mama has forgotten to buy a ticket for you.' Tao Ying can barely speak.

'Forgotten? That's a nice way of putting it! Why don't you forget you have a son as well?' The youth will not forgive her calm confidence of a moment ago.

'What more do you want?' Tao Ying's temper rises. In front of her child, she must preserve her dignity.

'You have a nerve! This is not to do with what I want, clearly you must apologize! God knows how you managed to get hold of a complimentary ticket in the first place. To get in free is not enough, now you want to sneak in an extra person. Have you no shame? Don't think you can get away with this, go get yourself a valid ticket!' The youth is now leaning on the wall, facing the crowd as if he is pronouncing an edict from on high.

Tao Ying's hands are trembling like the strings on a *pei-pa*. What should she do? Should she argue with him? She is not afraid of a good fight but she doesn't want her child to be witness to such a scene. For the sake of Xiao Ye, she will swallow her pride.

'Mama is going to buy a ticket. You wait here, don't run off.' Tao Ying tries to smile. This outing is such a rare occasion, whatever happens she mustn't spoil the mood. She is determined to make everything all right.

'Mama, did you really not buy a ticket?' Xiao Ye looks at her, full of surprise and bewilderment. The expression on her child's face frightens her.

She cannot buy this ticket today! If she went ahead, she would never be able to explain herself to her son.

'Let's go!' She gives Xiao Ye a yank. Thankfully the child has strong bones, or his arm might have fallen off.

'Let's go and play in the park.' Tao Ying wants her son to be happy, but the little boy has fallen silent, sullen. Xiao Ye has suddenly grown up.

As they walk past an ice-cream seller, Xiao Ye says, 'Mama, give me money!'

Taking the money, Xiao Ye runs towards an old woman behind the stall and says to her: 'Please measure me!' It is only then that Tao Ying notices the old lady sitting next to a pair of scales for measuring weight and height.

The old woman extends with difficulty the measuring pole, pulling it out centimetre by centimetre.

She strains to make out the numbers: 'One metre eleven.'

Tao Ying begins to wonder if she has encountered a ghost or is her son beginning to resemble a shoot of bamboo, growing every time you look at him?

Something moist begins to glisten in Xiao Ye's eyes. Leaving his mother behind and without a backward glance, he starts to run away.

He trips. One moment he is in the air, taking flight like a bird, another and he has dropped to the ground with a heavy thud. Tao Ying rushes over to lend a hand but just as she is about to reach him, Xiao Ye has picked himself up and is off again. Tao Ying stops in her tracks. If she gives chase Xiao Ye will only keep falling. Watching her son's vanishing silhouette, her heart beings to break: Xiao Ye, aren't you going to look back at your mother?

Xiao Ye runs for a long time and eventually comes to a halt. He throws a quick glance backwards to find his mother, but the moment he can see her, he takes off once more …

Tao Ying finds the whole incident incomprehensible. She wanders back to the old woman and asks politely: 'Excuse me, these scales you have …'

'My scales are here to make you happy! Don't you want your son to grow tall? Every mother wants her sons to shoot up, but don't forget when he is tall, that means you'll be old! Mine are flattering scales …' the old woman explains kindly, but Tao Ying remains baffled.

'You see my scales are old and not very accurate and they make people seem lighter than they really are. I have also adjusted them to make them seem taller. These days it is fashionable to be long and lean—mine are fitness scales!' The old woman might be kind, but she is not without cunning.

So that is the reason! Xiao Ye should have heard this speech! But he is a long way away, and in any case would he have understood the convoluted logic?

Xiao Ye still looks suspicious, as if Mother has turned into a big bad wolf, ready to eat him up. Later when they are back at home, Tao Ying takes out her own tape measure and insists on measuring him again.

'I don't want to! Everybody says I am tall enough except you. It's because you don't want to buy me a ticket, don't think I don't know! If you measure me I am bound to get shorter again. I don't trust you! I don't trust you!'

The yellow tape in Tao Ying's hands has turned into a poisonous viper.

*

'Chef! Your cakes look as if they are wearing camouflage uniforms, all black and brown!' a customer queuing in front of her counter shouts out.

The cakes are ruined. They are full of burnt marks, and look like tiny terrapins.

Sorry, sorry, sorry.

Tao Ying feels very guilty. She is usually very conscientious in her work, but these couple of days she often finds herself distracted.

She must rescue the situation! At night, after Xiao Ye has gone to sleep, Tao Ying straightens his little legs so that he is lying as flat as a piece of newly shrunken fabric. Tao Ying then stretches her tape from the soles of his feet to the top of his head—one metre nine centimetres.

She decides to write a letter to the administrators at the temple.

She picks up her brush but suddenly realizes that this is harder than she thinks! Seeing her deep in thought with knitted brows, her husband says, 'So what do you imagine might happen even if you wrote to them?'

He is right, she doesn't know if anything will come of it. But in order to melt the ice in her son's eyes, she must do something.

At last the letter is done. There is a man in the factory nicknamed 'the Writer'. People say he has had some small articles published at the back of a news rag once. Tao Ying finds him and respectfully offers up her literary work.

'This sounds like an official communication. Not lively enough, not moving.' The Writer traces the letter with his nicotine-stained fingers.

Tao Ying doesn't know what an official communication is but she detects a tone of dissatisfaction in the scholar's voice. She looks at the lines he is pointing to, and nods in agreement.

'What you need to do is this. You must open with a strong and righteous claim, followed by a passage of stunning originality so that your work stands out and grabs the attention of the editor. This would make him pick it out of a large pile on his desk. It has to catch his eyes like a blinding light, an apple in a mound of potatoes. But most important of all, your letter must touch his heart. Have you heard of the saying, "Grieving soldiers always win"?'

Tao Ying keeps nodding.

The Writer is encouraged to continue: 'Let us look at the opening paragraph—it should go something like this: "The power of the Buddha is surely infinite! The foot of a five-year-old boy has scarcely touched the threshold of the temple and he has grown two centimetres; but alas, the power of the Buddha is finite after all—on his return home the boy shrinks back to his original size ..." I know this is not yet perfect, but have a think about it along these lines ...'

Tao Ying tries to memorize the words of the Writer, but she finds it hard to recall all of them. Back home she makes a few corrections as best she can, and sends out the letter.

✻

The Writer comes by her stall at lunch-time. Tao Ying's face is framed in a small window where she is collecting vouchers. She looks like a photograph, staring out at the camera with a sombre expression.

'Please wait a moment,' and she disappears behind the frame.

The Writer suspects the cakes are burnt again. Perhaps Tao Ying has gone to find a few which are less burnt than others, to thank him for pointing her in the right direction.

'This is for you, with extra sugar and sesame,' Tao Ying says shyly. This is the greatest gift a baker can offer a friend as a token of gratitude.

✻

Then comes the long wait.

Tao Ying looks through the newspapers every day, reading everything from cover to cover, including small classified advertisements for videos. In the meantime she would listen to the radio, imagining that one morning she will hear her own letter being read out by one of those announcers with a beautiful voice. Afterwards she would go down to the post office, in case the administrative department of the temple has replied to her letter, apologizing for their misdeed ...

She has imagined a hundred different scenarios, but not what actually happens.

The days have been like the white flour she works with, one very much like another. Xiao Ye appears to have recovered from the ordeal but Tao Ying firmly believes that he has not really forgotten.

Finally, one day, she hears a question, 'Which way is it to Comrade Tao's home?'

'I know, I'll take you.' Xiao Ye excitedly shows two elderly gentlemen in uniform through the front door. 'Mama, we have visitors!'

Tao Ying is doing the laundry, immersed in soap up to her armpits.

'We are from the administrative office at the temple. The local newspaper has forwarded your letter to us and we have come to ascertain the truth.'

Tao Ying is very nervous, and somewhat depressed, chiefly because her house is very messy, and she has not had the time to tidy up. If they think that she is prone to laziness they might not believe her.

'Xiao Ye, why don't you go out to play?' In Tao Ying's fantasies, Xiao Ye would be in the room to witness the revelation of the truth. Now that the moment has finally arrived, she feels uncomfortable having him there. She cannot predict what will happen. These are after all the people who employed the youth in red, so how reasonable can they be?

The younger of the two speaks. 'We have investigated the matter with the party concerned, and he insisted he was in the right. Don't tell the boy to leave, we want to measure him.'

Xiao Ye obeys and stands next to the wall. The white of the wall looks like a virgin canvas and Xiao Ye a painting filling up the space. He leans tightly against the wall as if the act of measuring his height has once again stirred up some terrifying memory in the recesses of his mind.

The men are very serious. First of all they draw a bold line across the wall from the top of Xiao Ye's head Then they take out a metallic tape and take the measurement from the line to the floor. The metal of the tape glistens like a flowing stream in sunlight.

Tao Ying regains her calm.

'What does it say?'

'One metre ten, just so,' the younger man answers.

'This is not just so. There was a delay of one month and nine days before you came. A month ago he wasn't this tall.'

The two officials look at each other. This is a statement they cannot refute.

They produce a five-dollar bill from a pocket. The note pokes out of an envelope. They have evidently come prepared. Before they left the temple, they must have checked the height of the earthworm, and realized it was not drawn accurately.

'The other day you and your son were unable to enter. This is a small token to redress the situation.' This time it is the elder of the two gentlemen who speaks. His demeanour is kind, so he must be the more senior of the two.

Tao Ying remains still. That day's happiness can never be bought again.

'If you don't want the money, here are two tickets. You and your son are welcome to visit the temple any time.' The younger man is even more polite.

This is a tempting proposition indeed, but Tao Ying shakes her head. To her, to her son, that place will always be associated with unhappy memories now.

'So, which would you prefer?' both men ask in unison.

In fact Tao Ying is asking herself the same question. She is gracious by nature—if the youth in red had come in person to apologize today, she would not have made him feel awkward.

So what is it that she wants?

She shoves Xiao Ye in front of the two elderly officials.

'Say Grandpa,' she tells him.

'Grandpa.' Xiao Ye sounds infinitely sweet.

'Dear Leaders, please take back the money, and the tickets. Kindly do not punish the guard on duty, he was only doing his job ...'

The two officials are puzzled.

Tao Ying nudges Xiao Ye closer: 'Gentlemen, would you be so kind as to explain to my son exactly what happened on that day. Please tell him that his mother has not done anything wrong ...'

Translated by Carolyn Choa

China

Melody in Dreams

ZONG PU

Murong Yuejun, a teacher of the cello at a music college, was wedded to her instrument. She and her cello were as one, and playing it she could express all her feelings. This day, however, she could not finish any piece. Putting the cello aside, she walked on to the balcony and gazed into the distance.

It was September 1975. In the setting sun a strand of her white hair gleamed. Although she was over fifty, her face was still attractive. She gazed at the end of the street, expecting a girl to appear, but no one came. This was the daughter of her close friend Liang Feng, whom she had nearly married. Although he had since died, she remained fond of his daughter.

At the outbreak of the Anti-Japanese War in 1937, Liang Feng and other youths had gone to Yan'an, the revolutionary base. Yuejun, however, who was a music student at Yanjing University in Beijing at the time, had been taken by her parents to the south. Then she had won a scholarship to study abroad and had not returned until after Liberation in 1949. After the death of her parents, she had immersed herself in teaching music.

Now it was growing dark. She went back into her room thinking.

In the first years after Liberation Liang Feng had worked abroad. In the sixties he had been recalled to China to do cultural exchange work. Yuejun had heard him speak at some meetings. She was impressed by his way of expounding the Party's policies and moved by his devotion to the Party. She even met his wife, a good comrade and kind mother.

Yuejun had met their daughter, but the girl had not left a deep impression on her, except on one unforgettable occasion. It was during the Cultural Revolution, when all sorts of bad characters emerged to slander celebrated artists and intellectuals. Yuejun, because she had studied abroad, was attacked. At a meeting, she and some others were lined up on a stage. Some famous musicians were pushed to the microphone to denounce themselves as reactionaries. Suddenly three or four youngsters beat and kicked a middle-aged man on to the stage shouting: 'Down with the revisionist monster Liang Feng!'

Stealing a glance at him, Yuejun was surprised to see her friend being forced to the microphone. Facing the crowd, he said: 'I'm Liang Feng, a Chinese Communist!'

No sooner had he said this when some thugs leapt on to the platform and punched him. Blood poured from his mouth. Then a girl's clear voice was heard shouting: 'Father! Father!'

There was an uproar as some protested against the beating, while others rushed to the girl and kicked her out of the hall. Though Yuejun's head was lowered she saw the whole scene, except for the girl's face. Whenever she thought of her, she felt a mixture of sadness and warmth.

Now she was expecting her.

There was a voice outside. Yuejun asked: 'Is that you, Pei?' A plump woman of Yuejun's age entered, a Party committee member in her department.

A bosom friend of Yuejun, she said: 'I just popped in to see if Liang Feng's daughter was coming to see you today.'

'She's supposed to, but she hasn't turned up yet.'

'Do you remember ...?' Pei looked out of the window.

'I haven't forgotten all those slanders.' Yuejun's mild glance rested on her. After each criticism meeting, Pei had whispered in her ear: 'Chin up! It's a test.' Or: 'Never mind. Don't let it upset you too much!' This had enormously encouraged Yuejun.

Pei had high blood pressure and was easily excited. Controlling herself she said: 'You must teach her well, Yuejun.'

'Of course. I want to, but could I supplement the material?'

'I think one should, but who has the authority? The bad people aren't only trying to destroy the good ones, but also our whole civilization and socialism.' Pei's voice quivered.

'But what can we do?' Yuejun muttered.

'Wait until ....' Pei slapped the arm of the armchair. After a while she said she was going to see her paralyzed husband in the hospital. Smiling bitterly, she left.

It was night as Yuejun gazed out of the window at the maple tree illuminated by neighbouring lights. Thinking of the girl, she supposed she wouldn't come that night. Then there was a knock at the door.

Before she could answer it, a girl came in saying loudly, 'Are you Aunt Yuejun? I had such trouble in finding your home, I must have asked about a dozen people the way. Your room's dark but I spotted your cello when I came in, so I guessed this must be the right place. I'm Liang Xia.'

Switching on the lights, Yuejun saw that Liang Xia was a pretty girl, with her hair cut short. She was wearing a cream-coloured jacket over a black woollen jersey, and deep grey trousers. With large eyes, slender eyebrows and rosy cheeks, she was smiling quizzically at Yuejun.

'So she's sizing me up too,' thought Yuejan, who shook hands with her, saying: 'I've been waiting for you ...'

*

Liang Xia was nineteen. She was ten years old in 1966 when the Cultural Revolution had begun and this marked a turning-point in her life. Until then she had been the pride of the parents, but her happiness had fled with the start of the Cultural Revolution. Since her father had been a leader of his office, one night some people broke into their home and dragged him away. Then her mother was separated from her. Liang Xia, bewildered, was alone at home, cooking meals to take to her parents. Her father liked eating noodles and flapjacks, while her mother liked sweet food. Sometimes, because Liang Xia hadn't cooked enough food, she herself went hungry in order to give her parents their meals. She did this until one day a man told her not to prepare any more for her father, since he had died days earlier.

After her parents were detained, some of their comrades invited Liang Xia to live with them, but certain people objected saying that she could only live with a relative. She had an aunt, her mother's sister, but she had refused to take Liang Xia, 'only allowing the girl to visit her and help her with various chores'. At that time Liang Xia was in the fourth grade at school. Because of her parents, she too was criticized from time to time.

In those unhappy days, Liang Xia often dreamed she was being weighed down by a heavy stone. Unable to remove it she would cry herself awake. But in time she became accustomed to the sneers, and hid the hatred in her heart. After her mother's release, her mother was sent to a cadre school to do manual labour and took her there. Then her mother was transferred to work in a small town in south China, where she met a cello teacher, who had been dismissed from his school. So that Liang Xia wouldn't idle away her time, her mother arranged for her to have cello lessons. Two months previously, her mother had died of illness. This was tragic because it was said there would soon be a meeting to clear her husband's name. Liang Xia came to Beijing and stayed with her aunt. She hoped that Yuejun could give her cello lessons. That was the reason for her visit.

'I'm sorry for being late, but I had to help my aunt with the washing up.' She glanced round the room in which Yuejun had lived for many years. Against the window was a marble-topped mahogany desk left to Yuejun by her parents. At one corner stood a piano against which leant a cello. In front of her bed was a folding screen painted with flowers and birds. Two armchairs flanked a stand, behind which was a lamp with an orange shade. The gentle light gave an atmosphere of tranquillity.

'It's nice and cosy here,' Liang Xia said as she followed Yuejun to the kitchen, where she took the thermos flask from her and poured herself a cup of tea. 'We were driven out of our home and had to leave everything,' she said matter-of-factly. 'When my parents were detained, I stayed in the attic. It seemed quite cosy at the time. But Mother was ill after her release and whenever she used the stairs I had to carry her on my back.'

Yuejun wondered how Liang Xia, with her delicate build, had managed that. Curious to know about her mother's illness, Yuejun nevertheless said nothing in case she opened old wounds.

But as if she had read her thoughts, Liang Xia continued: 'Mother had all sorts of complaints. I was like her doctor. I knew every medicine she took. In the end she died of pneumonia. I thought many times she would die, but she always survived. So I thought she'd recover that last time.' Her tone seemed detached. Yuejun, however, was very sad.

'How many years have you been playing the cello?' Yuejun looked at her cello. 'You love music, don't you?'

'No, I don't.' Her reply surprised Yuejun, who stared fascinated at her thick lashes and dark eyes. 'I have to learn something to get myself a job. I've been playing since I was fourteen, but I'm not interested in it. I really preferred working in the countryside, but since my mother was too ill to join me, I went with her.'

Yuejun was disappointed and wondered whom Liang Xia would follow now.

The girl added: 'My parents were always talking about you, so I feel as if I've known you for ages. Mother said you could help me to become a musician.' A flicker of hope came into her eyes veiling the indifference which seemed to say: 'Anyway, it doesn't matter if you refuse.'

'Why bother learning to play the cello if you don't like it?'

'To make a living of course,' Liang Xia giggled.

If she had heard such a reply ten years ago, Yuejun would have been insulted. Now nothing astonished her.

'Play me something,' she said after a pause.

When Liang Xia went to take the cello, she found a curtained-off recess behind which Yuejun stored her junk. Lifting the curtain, Liang Xia exclaimed: 'Goodness! Why do you store away all your things here, Auntie? One day I'll help you sort them out.' Then holding the cello she began to play.

She played the second movement of a concerto by Saint-Saëns. In spite of her poor technique, there was something moving in her playing which touched Yuejun. Although she failed to grasp the meaning of the music, she expressed her own feelings. She was making music.

'She has a good musical sense,' Yuejun thought.

Although she soon finished, the room was filled with the atmosphere she had created. Putting aside the cello, Liang Xia searched Yuejun's face.

'To have a feeling for the music is most important,' Yuejun said warmly. 'But you don't handle your bow correctly yet. Look, it should be like this,' and so saying she took the bow and gave the girl her first lesson.

*

After that, Liang Xia came once a week. When she wasn't studying, she'd chat or help Yuejun with something. She was bright and seemed to know a lot, though sometimes she was ignorant of the most common knowledge. For example, once a colleague was discussing some classical novels with Yuejun, when Liang Xia interrupted them saying she had read many of them. It seemed she had read whatever she could lay her hands on, but there were very large gaps in her education. She may have seemed self-centred, knowing how to take care of herself, because since the death of her parents no one had shown any concern for her. Sometimes, however, she was ready to help others.

One day Yuejun was learning to give injections. Liang Xia offered her arm because she said she wasn't afraid of pain. Then she added coolly: 'Trouble is, you're afraid because you haven't been beaten up enough!' She seemed to have seen through everything and scorned the glowing revolutionary jargon in the newspapers. She would say: 'All lies! Even Premier Zhou was slandered as a reactionary. Who's foolish enough to swallow that!' Her only belief was that Premier Zhou would triumph over those 'bastards'. Yuejun hoped the same.

When she referred to Jiang Qing, she called her a 'she-devil' who had created so many scandals and who still tried to fool the people. 'She praises a novel about vengeance, while she really intends to attack us. One day I'll take my revenge on her!' Her words puzzled Yuejun. She spoke freely, not caring about the situation. At times Yuejun was afraid lest she should get into trouble.

Pei, a frequent visitor, soon got to know Liang Xia well enough to make her drop her pose of flippancy and talk seriously.

One day Pei came to hear Liang Xia play. After listening to her she asked Yuejun, 'If you want to supplement your teaching material, why not use some Western eludes? You're too timid, I think.'

Bow in hand, Liang Xia protested: 'Of course she's timid, but what about you?'

'I never said I was bold,' Pei smiled, 'but we've each got a head on our shoulders, and we should use our brains to find ways and means.'

'My head's too heavy for me. I don't like it. If you want, Aunt Pei,

I'll give it to you. Then you'll be bold enough to make a revolution. Only don't get scared because you'll have to turn everything upside down.' She burst out laughing. 'Revolution sounds fine but they murdered my father under that name too!'

'No, that was counter-revolutionary,' Pei burst out. 'Stop playing the fool and remember what your mother said to you. Remember those who hounded your father to death. You must think seriously about your future.'

Liang Xia immediately became grave, bit her lip and stared at Pei. After a moment she lapsed into her usual flippancy and sneered: 'I don't give a fig for them! What about dinner? Let's go and make it. I'm quite good at cooking ...' She laughed.

That was how she had reacted.

Once when Yuejun asked about her future plans, she answered as briefly as before, adding with a movement of her eyebrows: 'I'll fool around until my aunt throws me out, but that won't be immediately. She knows that my father's name may be cleared and that she stands to gain.' Then she went to the recess and lifting the curtain, looked at it again.

Before long her aunt turned her out. It was on an early winter day, when Liang Xia should have arrived for her lesson. At sunset she still hadn't come. Yuejun wondered in concern what had happened to her.

Suddenly Liang Xia burst in, a bulky satchel over her shoulder and a string bag in her hand. With a face flushed with rage, she cried: 'Sorry to keep you waiting, but I've just had a hell of a row with my aunt.' Then putting down her bags in a corner, she sat down fanning herself with a handkerchief. Her eyes burned with resentment as she jeered and laughed: 'It's just ridiculous!'

'Don't laugh like that,' Yuejun said patting Liang Xia's shoulder. 'Tell me what happened.'

'My aunt said that my father's name can't be cleared because he was a reactionary and that he had killed himself to escape punishment. As for me, since I'm his daughter there's no future for me. My staying with her has caused her a lot of trouble. Since her husband is going to be made a deputy minister and their block of flats is for ministers, ordinary people like me shouldn't be living there. We're a security risk. What rot!'

Yuejun sympathized with her and wondered what she would do next.

'I'll stay with you, if I may? You aren't afraid?' she asked standing up.

Yuejun was silent. Of course she was afraid! To let Liang Xia stay with her could mean she too would be labelled as a counter-revolutionary. But how could she push her out? After all, she was Liang Feng's daughter.

Seeing Yuejun's hesitation, Liang Xia smiled with scorn. Then she noticed that she had reached a decision. Before Yuejun could say anything, Liang Xia walked over to the curtained recess and put her things by it. 'I've thought about it before. We can put a bed here.' As she spoke she began pulling out the junk. 'You sit over there, Auntie.' She sneezed. 'So much dust! I always said I'd help you spring-clean it one day. Now my words have come true!' She laughed delightedly.

Despite the dust she hummed a tune as she worked. Having finished cleaning, she arranged the things in two piles of boxes and cases, on which she placed some planks for a bed. Then she made it up with sheets and a quilt lent to her by Yuejun. With a board from the kitchen she made herself a desk. Among the junk she had found a tattered scroll on which was written a poem. This read:

Coming from your old home,
You should know what is happening there;
Leaning against the window,
Did you see the plums in blossom?

Holding it in her hands, Liang Xia softly read it twice.

'Who wrote it?' she asked. 'Both the poem and the calligraphy are good. Why don't you hang it up?'

'Wouldn't that be criticized?' Yuejun replied joking. 'It was only this year that I put my screen here. Honestly I'm afraid of courting trouble.'

'Well, I'm not.' Examining it, Liang Xia noticed the inscription: 'A poem by Wang Wei copied by Yuejun in G. city.' The girl exclaimed: 'So you wrote it! No wonder the calligraphy's so good.' Immediately she hung it above her bed. Stepping back she gazed at it and then, clapping her hands, asked: 'But where's G. city?'

'Geneva, in Switzerland.' Yuejun looked at the old writing with some emotion. 'I was there alone studying music and I felt very homesick. Once I listened to Dvorak's *New World Symphony* a dozen times non-stop. Whenever it reached the second movement I was deeply moved. So I wrote that poem on the scroll. What awful calligraphy!'

'There's patriotism in your words.' Liang Xia gave a bitter smile. 'Now even patriotism is getting criticized.'

'I didn't have any clear ideas.' Yuejun sat down at the table. 'But I truly missed China then. My ancestors and I had been born here. I was proud to be Chinese. That's why I appreciated that short poem. But if that is all wrong now, what's left?' Moodily she turned to the window: 'Of course I learned Western music, but only so that I could serve my country better.'

'Your country?' Liang Xia mocked. 'Today that means individualism, egotism and counter-revolutionary revisionism!' Then she laughed: 'Anyway you're all right as a musician. Isn't singing and acting coming into fashion?'

Yuejun didn't want to comment on her harsh words.

At last Liang Xia finished tidying up. 'My bed's rather like a raft, isn't it?' Going over to it she said: 'I'll stay on my raft. I'll be as quiet as a mouse in the day.' Having climbed on to her 'raft', she suddenly popped her head out of the curtain and quipped: 'Carefree on my raft, I don't mind whether the seasons come or go.' Then she was quiet.

'Now there's no need to act like that,' Yuejun laughed. Drawing back the curtain, she found that Liang Xia was lying back on her quilt, her eyes closed. On her rosy cheeks were streaks of dirt. 'Get up and wash your face, Liang Xia. We'll have a lesson. Since you'll be staying here for a while, you mustn't waste your time.'

On hearing her say 'for a while', Liang Xia smiled faintly and glanced sadly at her.

At half-past-eight that evening they had a lesson. Liang Xia played first. Her technique was improving. As Yuejun was correcting her, there was a knock at the door.

A youngster in a green uniform without any insignia entered. The expression on his regular-featured face was troubled. Seeing Liang

Xia sitting with the cello in her hands, he said to Yuejun: 'Excuse me, are you Aunt Yuejun? I'd like to have a word with her.' Then he smiled at Liang Xia.

Ignoring him, Liang Xia concentrated on her music, but after a while she explained: 'This is Mao Tou. A friend of my cousin. Let's continue our lesson.'

'Mao Tou? Is that a nickname?' asked Yuejun casually, wondering about their relationship.

'Actually I don't know his real name.' With this Liang Xia continued playing. Snubbed, the young man turned to Yuejun for help. She suggested, looking at Liang Xia, that they go for a walk in the fresh air. Then she went to her desk and switched on the lamp. Pouting, Liang Xia slouched out with her friend.

The next day at school, Yuejun told Pei about her decision. The latter was delighted. 'I agree with you. She should live in your home.' Some colleagues who sympathized with Liang Xia felt in this way she could have an opportunity to study, as she'd become an orphan and a loafer. 'But who'll be responsible for her?' Pei asked. Those who objected said: 'What if the police start making inquiries? And if Liang Xia does something illegal, Yuejun will be implicated.' Yuejun was worried, but decided that if the authorities insisted the girl should leave, then she must do so. Otherwise Liang Xia could stay as long as she liked.

Time passed, and Yuejun and Liang Xia got on well together. The latter was able, diligent and considerate. Always in high spirits, she reminded Yuejun of an elf from a dance by Grieg. But Liang Xia claimed to be a very down-to-earth sort of person. 'If you were me,' she argued, 'you'd be just as practical.'

The weather grew chilly and Yuejun bought Liang Xia some cloth, intending to have a jacket made at the tailor's. But Liang Xia took it and said she could make it herself. She went to Pei's home where there was a sewing-machine. On her return, she looked grave.

'What's the matter?' Yuejun asked.

'Oh, nothing!' Liang Xia fidgeted with the remnants of the cloth. 'Aunt Pei's husband's been paralysed for three years, and she has to go to the hospital every day to take care of him. Though she has high blood pressure, she still goes to her office and studies the works of

Marx and Lenin. She told me that in the Yan'an days, she wore straw sandals, yet every step she took seemed significant. Life was so full of hope. There she became friends with my parents.' After a moment her face brightened and she continued: 'Aunt Pei said my father helped to reclaim the wasteland and that my mother spun yarn. I'd like to live such a life, but now even playing my cello's illegal.' Scissors in hand, she shredded the cloth.

Her usual apathetic and scornful expression returned, her tender heart seemed to have hardened. As Yuejun stroked her silky black hair, there was a knock at the door. Two young men with high sheepskin hats and fashionable trousers entered. Seeing them, Liang Xia sprang forward and told them to get out, banging the door shut. Her friends annoyed Yuejun, who didn't know where Liang Xia picked them up. If she was at home, then Liang Xia would take them out, but while she was teaching or elsewhere, Yuejun was quite ignorant of what went on in her home. As most of them were boys, she once tentatively warned Liang Xia against falling in love too early.

Hearing this, Liang Xia burst out laughing. 'Don't worry, I shan't be such a fool! I don't respect those boys. When I marry, he'll be a high official!' She grinned pulling a face, as if in her eyes high officials were toys for amusement. Then affecting gravity, she added: 'Or perhaps I'll be a spinster like you. By the way, why didn't you marry, Aunt?'

'You tell me,' Yuejun countered trying to avoid the question.

'It isn't that you believe in being single, but that you've never met a man you loved.' She was sharp.

Since her arrival, Yuejun had been strict in making her practise various pieces every day. Though she did not assign any Western musical scores, Liang Xia often played some to amuse herself. One day when Yuejun returned, she overheard Liang Xia playing a plaintive melody by Massenet. It was so melancholy that she waited till Liang Xia had finished before entering.

Yuejun often wished that Liang Xia could attend a proper school, since she had real musical talent. But it all depended on when her father's name would be cleared. If that happened, then the girl would be in a better position to study.

Meanwhile Liang Xia led a seemingly carefree life. Apart from playing the cello and seeing friends, she often read some books on her 'raft'. One day Yuejun was shocked to find her reading a handwritten copy of an 'underground' book. 'Why are you reading that?' she asked.

'Why not?' Liang Xia retorted.

'The cover alone scares me.'

'You wouldn't even say boo to a goose!' Liang Xia giggled. 'When my parents were detained I was often criticized and beaten. Later I fought the boys back. They beat me and I punched them. I loved it!'

Not knowing what to say, Yuejun stared at her pretty, youthful face. Despite the merry, contemptuous expression, she sensed hidden apathy and misery.

'Since I'm older now, I've grown out of fighting. It bores me.' Then she tried to reassure Yuejun: 'Please don't worry, Auntie. But I can't play the cello all day long. I must read some books too. Since I can't find any good ones, I'm reading these, even though they're bad. It's like food. When there's nothing delicious, I eat anything. So there!' She glanced at the cabinet in which were locked some good books.

'You're wrong.' Yuejun tried to argue with her.

'I know.' Smiling she added: 'Now I just exist. If one day I can't go on like this, then I'll change my world outlook. That's how Mao Tou puts it.'

'You can read what he's read, I think.' Yuejun had found that Mao Tou was a thoughtful young man who had studied seriously some books on philosophy, literature and history. Although known as a 'scholar' in his factory, he refused to join any writing teams run by the authorities. His father was an old cadre, who had often shown concern for Liang Xia.

Yuejun's suggestion made Liang Xia smile again. After a moment, Yuejun opened the cabinet to let her choose whatever book she wanted. Happily Liang Xia looked through it until she suddenly murmured: 'My father had many books. However late he worked he never went to bed before he had read a little. What a pity I was so young! I ... I hate ....' Turning round she clutched hold of the cabinet, her eyes blazing. 'Oh Father! Father!' Her voice was as clear and pained as a few years before. 'I don't believe that my father, a Communist full of enthusiasm, committed suicide. They killed him, but insist that he killed himself.' She didn't choose a book, but stood there gazing wistfully at Yuejun. 'Do you think the day I long for will come? Mother told me I must live to see it.'

Yuejun couldn't bear to see her expression. Wanting Liang Xia to have a good cry, tears began pouring down her own face. Even if her father had killed himself, he would never have done so unless driven to it. He must have been in a terrible situation. She wanted to cry with Liang Xia hoping the girl's tears would wash away her cynicism. Instead Liang Xia rushed to her bed, leaving on the cabinet, two snicks from her nails.

It was 1976 and the Spring Festival was approaching. Despite the festival, everyone was grieving. Where was the spring? People were profoundly anxious about their future since the death of Premier Zhou. There was a dreadful abyss in their hearts, which could not be filled by their tears and thoughts.

Before she went to the cadre school in January to do some manual labour, Yuejun entrusted Liang Xia to Pei's care. When she heard the sad news of the premier's death, she felt desolate. Worried that something might happen to Liang Xia, she wrote to her asking how she was. After she had posted the letter, Yuejun was afraid lest Liang Xia reply in an incautious way, so she quickly sent a message telling her not to answer. However, her reply came. It said: 'I'm prepared to shoulder my responsibilities now.' Though cryptic, it signified that a storm was imminent.

On her return home, Yuejun found Liang Xia had changed. She seldom talked and never laughed in that old distressing way. She thought more about her responsibilities. Sometimes Yuejun told her to play her cello to find peace in the music, but thinking about Premier Zhou disturbed her playing. In the past three weeks she had suddenly matured. Her flippancy had gone. In her dark eyes was a clouded expression, since her thoughts seemed too heavy to convey. Some of her friends stopped coming, since they were just playmates. When asked by Yuejun where her friends were, Liang Xia blinked as if she had never known them.

She had got rid of those frivolous books, but she was not interested in serious literature either. To Yuejun's surprise, Liang Xia sometimes read works of Marx and Lenin. On the eve of the Spring Festival, Pei found her reading an article by Chairman Mao, a notebook by her side. Leafing through its pages, Pei was astonished to find a heading: 'Crimes perpetrated by Jiang Qing.' The charges listed were logical and cogent. Pei grasped Liang Xia's hand and said admiringly: 'I always thought you were a fine girl, Xia!'

Liang Xia smiled a genuine smile. 'I thought a long time about your advice. I shouldn't fritter away my life and youth. Especially at this time.'

Most of the notes had been made by Liang Xia and some by Mao Tou. As Yuejun read them, she felt they were telling the truth. But the truth meant trouble. She searched Pei's face wanting to know what to do.

Pei smiled at her. 'It's correct to expose them for what they are. These notes are what we've been wanting to say ourselves.'

Liang Xia told Yuejun: 'I know that's the way you feel too. But you are too timid, Auntie.'

Yuejun sighed: 'To whom could we speak?'

'We're only allowed to parrot the editorials,' Pei added.

Liang Xia was silent. Her smile faded into contempt and pessimism.

Yuejun anxiously looked at the girl, while Pei warned: 'It isn't just a question of daring to struggle. It's also knowing how and when to strike.'

After a quick supper in the dim light, Yuejun wanted to ask Liang Xia why she and Mao Tou had written these notes, but she didn't press her.

Suddenly there were three knocks at the door. Liang Xia immediately darted to open it and Mao Tou entered. Although he looked tense, he didn't forget his manners, greeting Yuejun before turning to Liang Xia. 'Let's go out,' he suggested.

'What's the matter?'

'Please sit down,' Yuejun urged. 'It's so cold outside. Don't go out. Tell us what's happened.'

Eyeing them both, he said: 'My father's been arrested!'

'What?' Yuejun was dismayed.

'On what charge?' Liang Xia asked.

'They can trump up anything,' he replied, trying to control his anger. Then he continued: 'A few days ago, my father told me they were concocting some charge against Premier Zhou. He said as long as he was alive he'd defend him and speak out. This morning your uncle told my father that they wanted him to attend a meeting. A neighbour reported that my father was bundled into his car. He wasn't even allowed to leave a note for the family.'

'I was luckier. I saw my father being dragged away,' Liang Xia murmured.

'When I went to their office to see my father, the man on duty told me coldly that he's to stand trial and wouldn't let me see him. Then he shoved me out of the door.'

Yuejun was outraged thinking how many families had been ruined by the 'gang'; how many young people had been deprived of their right to work and study or even lost their lives. They wouldn't even leave the premier alone. Their great hero had left nothing of himself after his death. Even his ashes had been scattered over the mountains and rivers. Now they intended to blacken his reputation.

Liang Xia trembled with rage. She suddenly laughed aloud. Yuejun took her hand which felt cold. 'Xia!' she exclaimed.

'Those monsters are about to tear off their masks!' Brushing Yuejun aside, she put one hand on the table and the other to her breast.

'Yes, I think they are going to show their true intentions soon,' said Mao Tou, looking coolly at Liang Xia. 'We must continue collecting our material. The day's coming when the 'gang' will be brought to trial and condemned.'

'If my father were alive today, he'd do as yours has done, I'm sure.'

Mao Tou paced the room and then said he was going to inform his friends about his father's arrest. He left after shaking hands with Yuejun and warning her to be careful.

At the door Liang Xia suddenly cried out: 'But you haven't had your supper yet!' Mao Tou shook his head and left. Yuejun knew that his mother had died of a heart attack after a struggle meeting. Now he had no parents to look after him.

*

Despite disasters afflicting society, time marched on. Tempered by grief, doubt and anxiety, the people came to see the truth.

On the eve of the Qing Ming Festival in April 1976, darkness enveloped Beijing's Tiananmen Square. But bright wreaths overlapped each other; the loyal hearts of the people challenged the sombre surroundings. Some wreaths were as high as a house, while others were very small. They stretched from the Martyrs' Monument to the avenue. It was like a great hall of mourning, unparalleled in history, made by the people for Premier Zhou. The pine trees, covered with white paper flowers of mourning, were like a bank of snow. Gaily decorated baskets hung from the lampposts. Balloons floated in the air with streamers inscribed with the words: 'Premier Zhou Is Immortal!' The crowds in the square were like a vast moving sea. They were silent, though all were indignant and at the end of their patience. The flames of truth in their hearts at last were about to blaze.

If the truth could be seen, Yuejun thought, it was in that square. The people were prepared to give their lives for it. She knew Liang Xia came every day to copy down poems and see the wreaths. Yuejun and Liang Xia were making their way to the monument in the middle of the square. They hung their basket on a pine tree. It contained pure white flowers entwined with silver paper, which glistened like their tears.

Liang Xia remembered pacing in the quiet square in January after the premier's death when she heard people weeping. A middle-aged woman had lurched towards the monument crying: 'Oh Premier, what shall we do in future? What? ...' Her cries were carried round the square and reverberated in Liang Xia's heart. Suddenly Yuejun felt Liang Xia shudder. Looking in the same direction, she saw a streamer by the monument which read: 'Even if the monsters spew out poisonous flames, the people will vanquish them!' Though the street lights were dim, these words seemed ablaze. This was the strength of the people! The people had begun to fight back!

Yuejun and Liang Xia walked among the crowds who were engrossed in copying poems. Some far away couldn't see clearly, so others who were nearer to the monument read them aloud. If some had no paper, others would tear out pages from their notebooks. People wrote leaning on others' backs. All the crowds shared one purpose and cherished a deep love for Premier Zhou.

Unexpectedly Mao Tou appeared. With a serious expression, he whispered something in Liang Xia's ear. She hurriedly pulled Yuejun away from the crowd.

On their way home, Yuejun was filled with grief and anxiety. She wasn't afraid for herself, but very worried about Liang Xia and Mao Tou, and all the other young people in the square who were reciting poems. On reaching home, she sat down at the desk in front of a photograph of Premier Zhou, taken when he was young. Yuejun wished she could talk to Pei who had given her this photograph, but she had been in hospital because of a heart attack since March. She had been working too hard.

Liang Xia was busy on her 'raft'. After a moment she emerged and poured herself a glass of water. She looked calm and happy, though pale. 'Would you like some water, Auntie?' she asked. There was no answer.

Then Yuejun said looking at her: 'I want to say something to you. I guess you're going to put up some posters. It's too dangerous!' She paused before adding: 'You're young. You must live to see the day .... You're the only survivor in your family.'

Not in the least disturbed, Liang Xia replied: 'I don't want to hide anything from you. But we must speak out and let those bastards know we are still living. As you know, I'm not afraid of anything.'

Yuejun said after a pause, tears streaming down her face: 'Then let me go! I'm old, but I can do it as well as you!'

'You?' Amazed, Liang Xia gazed at her kind, pleasant, tear-stained face. She too began to weep, though she tried to hold back her tears.

'Xia!' Yuejun hugged her tightly. Her tears dropped on the girl's hair, while Liang Xia's wet her breast.

Liang Xia soon dried her eyes. There was no time for a good cry. It was as if she heard the bugle call. Flames of love and hatred blazed in her heart, melting it. She had thought of telling Yuejun that she had already distributed some leaflets in the trolleys and parks. Some had expressed her views, while others contained only one sentence: 'Down with the gang, the cause of all disasters!' She was sure there wouldn't be any trouble, but still it was better not to involve Yuejun.

She decided to keep her in the dark and so she changed the subject: 'All right, I won't go out now. Where are you going, Auntie?'

'I'm serious, you little wretch!' Yuejun protested.

'So am I.' She wiped away her tears. 'You must rest. You're too excited.' With this, she went to make up Yuejun's bed and quietly slipped two sleeping pills into a glass of water. Handing it to her, she persuaded Yuejun to lie down.

Soon Yuejun felt very sleepy so she lay down, while Liang Xia paced the floor cheerfully. 'You should put on something more,' Yuejun advised, noticing Liang Xia was only wearing her woollen jersey. 'You must take care of yourself!' Then she wondered if she was really getting old, as she was feeling so tired.

Yuejun fell asleep and was unaware that Liang Xia had tidied up the room. Before leaving, she had fondled the cello and turned to gaze again and again at the screen behind which was Yuejun's bed. Finally she made up her mind and gingerly opening the door, went out ...

That night she didn't return. On the second and third nights she still hadn't come home.

One evening after her discharge from hospital, Pei came to visit Yuejun. It was already summer. Through the window the stars shone. The two women sat facing each other in silence. After a while, Yuejun took a notebook out of a drawer, saying: 'I found this yesterday. Xia made notes in it.'

Pei was startled when she flicked through the pages to read: 'I won't live under the same sky with the sworn enemy of my family and my country!' She read the sentence again and again before saying confidently: 'Don't be sad. I believe she'll come back one day.'

Yuejun nodded: 'I hope so. I know where Mao Tou is imprisoned. But I've no news about Xia.'

'We'll try to locate her.' The notebook was clenched tightly in Pei's hand.

Yuejun heaved a sigh: 'Recently I feel as if we've been playing a piece of music interminably but it may break off any moment now.'

'Don't worry. We'll end this symphony on a magnificent, triumphant note. By the way, in the past two months, an instruction came from our ministry to investigate the relationship between you and Liang Xia, but we refused to do it.'

Rising to her feet, Yuejun declared: 'Tell them Liang Xia's my daughter. I'll adopt her as my own daughter.' Her worn, sweet face brightened, and in her eyes shone determination.

Pei grasped her hand firmly.

That night Yuejun dreamed that she was playing her cello at a concert. The music from the cello was splendid and triumphant. In the audience a pair of dark eyes danced to the melody. They belonged to Liang Xia.

Then suddenly it was Liang Xia and not she who was playing on the stage. Her skilful playing was inspiring and encouraging. Happy tears poured down her cheeks. The stage lights shone on her white gauze and silver-threaded dress and on her glistening tears. The powerful music reverberated inside and outside the hall. She played what was in her heart and in the hearts of the people.

The dream of the people will be fulfilled. The reactionaries will be smashed. Historically this is inevitable.

Translated by Song Shouquan

Hong Kong

She's a Young Woman and So Am I

Wong Bikwan

I thought I could spend the rest of my life with Jihang.

Her name is Hui Jihang. When I met her for the first time, we were still college freshmen. Our paths first crossed when we were both taking 'The Art of Critical Thinking', a required course for all new students.

Among my peers, she was the only one I knew of who would wear a tightly fitting *qipao* dress and dainty embroidered slippers to class. What nerve! How fake! Yet how very eye-catching! I remember that pair of bright red, embroidered slippers. Her hair was trimmed evenly to just beneath the earlobes. Often, with her eyes cast downward and her head lowered, she would take notes, as if she were one of those exemplary students. However, she painted her nails peach-red. Only bad women would wear nail polish. The kind who would quietly flaunt their seductive wiles through such minutiae were especially bad. I didn't know that I might like a bad woman.

Not surprisingly, she was talked about everywhere. The boys in my class told me that her name was Hui Jihang, that she was a Chinese major, that she had graduated from the famous Sojit Public School, and that her family lived on Laamtong Street, an affluent neighbourhood. They would be talking about her in small groups in their dorms when we were in class studying Plato. I would girlishly laugh at them, but I began thinking of them with increasing contempt. They continued to talk about her, and among themselves called her 'Little Phoenix Goddess'.

Jihang consistently skipped class. Once I bumped into her at the train station. With her head bent down, she walked straight ahead, an obedient male student in tow.

The following year we met again in the 'Introduction to Sociology' class. The lecturer disliked roll call and therefore he wanted us to sit in the same seat throughout the semester, so he could tell at a glance who was absent. I grabbed the chance to sit down next to Jihang. I remember that day she was wearing a loosely fitting, white and dark mauve cotton *qipao*. The hair on her arms was very fine. In addition, she exuded a certain smell, a mixture of make-up, perfume, milk and ink. I called that odour the 'Phoenix Goddess Smell' ever after. Her hands were so smooth and cold that I felt like touching them. But I didn't, since she took no notice of my existence.

She had skipped class again. Only when we came to the Marxist notion of surplus value did she reappear. She asked to borrow my lecture notes. 'Even if I were to let you have them, they would be useless—only I can read these scrawls!' She lifted an eyebrow. 'Not necessarily.' Because I was lazy, I had written the notes in shorthand. My classmates all called them the 'telegraphic notes'. Hence nobody ever asked to borrow them. But she was copying them over just as rapidly as I had taken them down, and there was my 'secret code' translated into legible, orderly script—I suppose if one doesn't attend class for a month, one still needs a knack for something in order to pass. I like people who are clever and don't follow the rules, maybe that is the reason why I asked Jihang out.

I said, 'Let me take you out for coffee.' She said, 'Okay.' We also shared a telegraphic mode of talking.

We sat in the slanting sun without saying a word. I looked at her intently. She looked at me and said, 'I have seen you around. You are Yip Saisai. You practise the Shakuhachi flute all by yourself at night in the classroom. I have heard you play.' She was wearing several thin silver bracelets, which glistened and clinked as she moved. She said, 'I know that you lost a pink Maidenform bra last week, I read about it in the main hall of the dorm, on the events wall. It was yours, wasn't it?' She added, laughing, 'The whole dorm knows about it, even the guys do! How silly of you to lose a 32B Maidenform bra!' I said: 'No, 32A! I am thin you know!' I saw that her breasts were rather ample. 'I bet you are at least a 34B and after you get married, you will become a 38.' Jihang softly put her hand to her chest: 'Ayah, that's what I am afraid of as well.' Thus our rapport began somewhat unexpectedly over a Maidenform bra.

She suddenly started coming to class regularly and we would talk. 'The old instructor is such an old fogey, his flesh-coloured nylon socks are showing.' I asked her where she bought her *qipaos*. She said that that was a trade secret. I arranged for us to go see a film shown on campus, Lau Shing-hou's *The House of the Lute*. We laughed really hard. I dragged her to a showing of Eisenstein's October. We both fell asleep, and did not wake up until everyone had left. We then went out for a midnight snack. Jihang would sometimes wear jeans too, as on that day when she went for stir-fried mussels with me, but she always insisted on those embroidered slippers.

The second semester of our junior year, her roommate moved out of the dorm. Jihang did not tell the dorm matron, and I moved in with her. Actually, that was when it all really started between me and Jihang.

To tell the truth, I simply felt that Jihang was femininely seductive, clever in a petty sort of way, and even-tempered, yet I didn't really understand her conduct. That's probably where our relationship most resembled the love between men and women. Our respective initial attraction derived largely from the other's ability to show off her looks. Even though I was neither a beauty nor did I possess Jihang's allure, I knew very well how to subtly sell myself. I think Jihang liked my kind, it's a, ah well, understated, worldly, sort of charm. Not unlike her *qipao* and her embroidered slippers.

In our dorm room, we created our own 'smoke and flower alley', punning on the name for the traditional haunts of courtesans. We both smoked. She smoked Red Double Happiness, I smoked Menthol Dunhills, both irredeemably wild and wicked brands. We both liked Tom Waits. We would dance in our room, her body soft and pliant. We were both girls. On occasion I would translate some de Beauvoir, but after a while she did not seem up to snuff, and so I switched to Kristeva. Jihang liked to read Yi Shu, the popular romance novelist, to which I objected; thus she changed to Sagan, to which I objected again, so she read Angela Carter. We both gradually made progress. I got a scholarship. Jihang had applied for one as well, but did not get it. She lost out to me.

*

The day I received the scholarship, my picture appeared in the school newspaper. I remembered that once when I'd gone shopping with her, she had had her eye on a fire red cashmere sweater, but since it cost an extravagant sum, she could not bring herself to get it. I bought it for her now, planning to give it to her at dinnertime. However, she did not come back for dinner. I waited until it began to get dark. I was alone in the room and did not turn on the lights. It was already late autumn. Outside the window, the sea was alight with scattered fishing boats. I suddenly felt as though she were one of those proverbially heartless men. I had had boyfriends before, but never, once had I felt this anxious. Jihang had not made her bed that morning. Jihang was not wearing her embroidered slippers that day. Jihang's toothpaste was almost used up. I made a mental note to buy some for her. Jihang's Phoenix Goddess Smell filled the room. Her make-up and powder. Her tears. I motionlessly leaned against the side of the window. Two teardrops streamed quietly down my cheeks. Just two drops, then the tears dried up. Jihang, Jihang.

I woke up, ate some bread, suddenly finding that the bread had the stale smell of flour, a smell very similar to that of animal feed. I had been eating bread for more than ten years, and only now had I become aware of the smell and taste of bread. It was as if I had understood the truth about bread and could only feel a certain wistfulness. Wistfulness! What a commonplace thought! Yet at this moment I truly felt very wistful, mixed with a sense of seeing things afresh, as though for the first time. Ah, the feeling of tasting reality is difficult to describe.

An hour past midnight, as I stood by the window, I heard the sound of a car. Jihang alighted from a taxi. She was wearing a black skirt and top and black pumps. Poor woman! Even at this point I was still paying attention to what she was wearing. I realized I noticed her clothing and her smell much more than her character or her breeding—perhaps she did not have much character or breeding. I felt suddenly ashamed. How was I different then from those men? Just like the men, I set store by her looks, although I had never touched her. Perhaps because neither of us had wanted to broach the subject, we had neither done anything like kissing or caressing nor had we ever felt the need for it. Those so-called lesbian intimacies accompanied by moans and mutterings are merely a fantastic scenario men have imagined for the sake of feasting their eyes. Jihang and I had never done anything like that. I had never even said 'I love you' to her. However, at that moment I knew that I loved her very much, to the point of wanting to find out if she had any character or breeding.

I leaned against the window, my heart afire and beating hard. Jihang was coming! Jihang was coming!

The door opened slowly and she dropped onto the bed. Her whole face was flushed and her entire body exuded the sour smell of alcohol. Strangely enough, Jihang's face had been heavily made up, but now it was all smeared. I suddenly recalled the stale smell of bread. I remained silent, the words frozen on my lips.

She laughed, 'You must be happy today. I am very happy today.' Suddenly, a handful of coins came flying in my direction. 'Yip Saisai, I am merely an ordinary person.' I covered my face without speaking. The coins hit the back of my hands, causing a sharp pain. When Jihang tired of throwing coins, she leaned back against the bed. For a time, there was dead silence. The light hurt my eyes.

'Jihang.'

She didn't answer me. She had fallen asleep. I wiped her face with a washcloth, took off her clothes and her shoes, and kissed her feet.

I perfunctorily straightened the room, then left a note on her desk. 'Jihang, if one day we find ourselves drowning in a sea of people just living our lives in busy commonsense, that will have been because we did not try hard enough to live life to the fullest.' At the time, I had no ambitions, but Jihang did.

That same night, I went and knocked on the door of a guy. This guy had had a crush on me for a long time. His whole face was filled with impatient lust. Of course, I knew it would be like that. I had gone to his room on the spur of the moment. Quite possibly this was a way of taking revenge on myself and on Jihang and on this person, because I had no heart. And my body did not belong to me. The whole next day, I was very absent-minded. I had the guy rent a room for me off-campus. When he was gone, I didn't care. I continued to go to classes; in fact, contrary to my usual habits, I became more mindful of my schoolwork.

When I walked past the dorm, I would always look up. Was Jihang there? Was she combing her hair? Was she doing her homework? Was she reading a newspaper? Could she be thinking about me? Jihang had suddenly disappeared from my life. How calm I appeared, yet no one knew my heart's ups and downs. Jihang, Jihang.

One late autumn night, I was having dinner with the guy. The man's conversation was bland. I just kept drinking wine. At the end of the meal, my whole body turned red. Walking out into the evening chill, I vomited, my face soaked with tears. The man gave me his handkerchief and I held on to him tightly. At that moment, any man with a handkerchief would have been a good man. I could not help despising him a little less. Really, if at that moment I could have had some feeling for him and forever thence severed ties with Jihang, that would not have been a bad thing. The man drove a little Japanese car. As soon as he got into it, he grabbed hold of me and pressed his face against mine. I laughed, 'You could have been a good man, but since you are willing to kiss a woman who stinks of stale wine, I am beginning to strongly doubt your taste.' Visibly annoyed, he started the car to take me back to the flat. I said, 'Not so fast! I want to return to the dorm to get some things.'

It was three o'clock in the morning. Jihang had turned on the desk lamp, but did not appear to be in. I stood in the night, craning my neck as I looked up towards the window. There she was underneath the light! Jihang, I had never meant to take away your lustre, I am merely an ordinary girl who wants a simple emotional bond with another human being. Why won't the world grant me even that?

Suddenly, Jihang's shadow flitted past the window, and the light was turned off. In the space of that movement, had Jihang's hair grown? Was there anyone to cut her toenails? Anyone to paint her nails? After I'd left, who was there to button her dresses at the back? At night, who would come to see her or who would think of her? Who would know if she were happy or sad? Who would compete with her for that little bit of notoriety? Whom did she love and whom did she worry about?

I wanted to see her badly. Just one glance.

I rushed up the stairs. Jihang had locked the door, but I had a key. She was asleep, her chest moving up and down. Her breasts were as ample as they used to be. After a few weeks' separation, no tell-tale signs of being lovelorn: she had neither lost weight nor did she look haggard. I inspected her toenails—they were still well manicured and well painted, brilliantly red as usual. On her bed, there were a few more dolls. She was cuddling a stuffed toy rabbit, sleeping soundly like an infant. What a peaceful sight! The sun was still rising, night was still falling, and at three in the morning, there were still those who were sound asleep and those who were wide awake. Who was still typing away next door, busy with homework in search of success? My eyes suddenly overflowed with tears. My throat made a gurgling sound, as if someone were throttling me. Who was that? I was strangling myself as I thought to myself that tonight the stars were certain to fall like the rain. Jihang had betrayed my feelings for her.

My tears fell on Jihang's face. I had clutched my throat so tightly that my face was all red and I could breathe only with difficulty. Jihang suddenly awoke, and held tightly onto my hand, saying, 'Why do this?'

Jihang held me in her arms, and suffused in her Phoenix Goddess Smell, I quietly fell asleep. I vaguely heard the sound of a car's horn downstairs. So what? That man had already outlived his usefulness in my life, and from here on I would have nothing to do with him. For now, there was only Jihang.

Jihang held my face in her hands and said, 'You're so stupid.'

I didn't respond, wanting only to sleep. Tomorrow there would be sunshine.

After that, things with Jihang seemed a little better. When we studied until late at night, she would always boil a cup of ginseng tea for me. Jihang had always been too lazy to study hard. Why this sudden change of heart? I vaguely sensed that Jihang was different now, even her perfume, Opium, was a famous brand. I felt as though I was choking.

*

Jihang was going out again at night. At midnight, she always wore that large fire red sweater and black boots. She roamed like a leopard. There was always a bright blue sports car waiting for her downstairs. She always returned with flushed cheeks, bringing me warm, sweet rice balls that I could not swallow even if I felt like eating them. Once hardened, the rice balls were inedible. The next morning, faced with the hardened balls of glutinous rice, I was at a complete loss. Jihang was never there. We were now in our senior year; in all this time, she had only earned eleven credit hours.

Over Christmas break, I prepared to return to my family for one night. Jihang was packing, and I asked her how long she would be staying with her family. She shook her head, and said with a smile, 'I am going to Beijing.'

I silently stood there for a long time. We had been to Japan together, and had promised each other that next time it would be Beijing. That was last Christmas. I covered my face, saying, 'Jihang, Jihang, do you remember ...'

She pried open my hands, and looked me in the eye. 'I remember, but that was before. This time I have this chance. You too might have to make plans for your future. I don't have to live a commonplace life.' She kissed me on the forehead and left.

I collapsed into a chair, alone in the half-empty room. I thought I might as well sit there for the rest of my life. Then I lay down on the floor, and found that the carpet had gotten dirty. Jihang and I had looked for a whole afternoon in the upscale Central neighbourhood before finding and buying this carpet. She had insisted on an Iranian carpet, but I thought that was too unrealistic, and proposed that we get an Indian carpet instead. As a compromise, we settled on a Belgian carpet. We ate Dutch food while holding on to our new carpet. Jihang asked for a dozen oysters on the half shell. We spent all our money ... When did all that happen?

That Christmas, I spent every single, long day at the library feeling sickly and barely holding up. I leafed through a weekly magazine and came upon a big callow-faced fatso with a pair of flashy sunglasses. I flinched. I was struck by the sudden realization that the person standing next to him in all likelihood was Jihang. After closing the magazine, I went to the cafeteria as if nothing had happened. I found myself seated where Jihang and I had sat when we first met. A fit of nausea overcame me and I almost started to cry. I gritted my teeth and returned to the library. This time I finished my homework without a stray thought.

When Jihang returned, I was asleep with my head in my arms on the desk, and with the magazine opened to the page with Jihang's picture. I neither looked at Jihang nor did she move. She just sat there, smoking. Then she quoted the old adage describing a desperate situation, 'The general has not only lost his wife, but also his army.'

I went and made her a cup of hot green tea. She held tightly onto my hand, while I tenderly stroked her hair.

I did not press her further, and thereafter she never brought up the subject. Until now, I still don't know what exactly happened. She would no longer go out at night. Instead, she would stay in the dorm and assiduously practise all sorts of postures and expressions, holding her face this way and that, as though she were proud to look more and more sophisticated.

Graduation was drawing near. I too began to tone down what I considered my so-called understated, worldly charm. I was after all neither a society hostess nor a dance-hall girl, thus I could not make a living off my charm. I applied for graduate school, hoping to get a position in academia in the future. Frankly, in order to get a job as an intellectual one does not need much wisdom or courage; someone as useless as me will do just as well so long as one is suitably packaged. So I went ahead and immersed myself in the study of contemporary Western philosophy. It was the easiest subject, since neither the teacher nor myself understood any of it. When I finished my thesis, everybody could read it and feel smug. At least it was done. Everybody truly heaved a sigh of relief, as if a heavy load had been taken from us, and was very happy.

My relations with Jihang gradually cooled off. She was even more seductively beautiful than before. She would dress up to the nines even for the exams. I heard from my classmates that she was having an affair with a teacher. Then someone else told me that she had become a model for some fashion magazine. Why did all these people know more about Jihang than I? Jihang and I did not have many days left. I wanted to rent an apartment with her. She could continue her public career, while I would continue my studies. I wanted to raise a cat together with Jihang, and to own an Iranian handwoven carpet. Then, at midnight, Jihang and I could eat those warm, soft glutinous rice balls together. What I wanted from life was very simple.

As I was thinking about this, I bought a bouquet of flowers and returned to the dorms to spend some time with Jihang. The girls' dorm was very quiet in the afternoon.

On our doorknob hung a man's tie. With the bouquet of gerberas in hand, I stood outside the door, not knowing whether to stay or to leave. Jihang's was an old English habit, which indicated that we had male company in our room. How could this be possible? This was mine and Jihang's place! They might even be making love on my bed, which meant that I would have to wash the sheets. If that were the case, I would never be able to sleep in that bed again. I often think that men's semen is the messiest thing there is, even more disgusting than dishwashing liquid, snot, or phlegm. Jihang, how could you do this?

The dorm committee chair who lived just across the hall came back just then and asked me, 'What's the matter? Have you forgotten your keys? Do you want me to open the door for you?'

'No,' I said quickly, and got out my own key.

*

And they really were on my bed, Jihang and a man, their frenzied passion approaching a climax. I felt the gerberas in my hand trembling so hard they nearly dropped to the floor. I was afraid the petals would scatter all over. Jihang had her eyes half closed, as if she did not care at all, but the man had stopped moving, without having the sense to cover himself. The man had pockmarks all over his face and his hair was disheveled. He was about thirty or so. I looked at him, 'Mister, this is a girls' dorm, please put on your clothes.' Jihang glanced at him sideways and said, 'Don't listen to her.' I picked up the clothes from the floor and threw them at this pair, shouting, 'Get into your clothes! I refuse to speak to animals.'

The man quickly put on his clothes, while Jihang turned over and started to smoke. She let out a breath of smoke. She did not say anything. I picked up the condoms that were strewn all over the floor and said to him, 'Mister, here take these back, and please behave yourself.'

'… I'm sorry.' He hurriedly stuffed the condoms in the pocket of his pants while I opened the door for him. I said, 'Mister, my relations with Jihang are special, so please respect us and never again do what you did.' At first, his face was expressionless, then after a long pause, it registered panic. He hissed, 'You two! Perverts!'

I slapped his face and slammed the door shut behind him. Jihang glared at me, her eyes burning, her face flushed, and her cigarette about to singe her fingertips. She stared at me without moving the slightest. I leaned against the door, entirely still. What does time matter when all has been destroyed and nothing is left? Why bother keeping track of time? I don't know how long we held out like that, but her cigarette went out. A feeling of midwinter.

Night fell upon us, heavy and dark. Jihang suddenly laughed lightly, then two tears rolled down her face.

I said, 'Regardless of what has happened, we can still go on as before.'

She said, 'It's not the same. Really. You're too naive. In the future, you will be no match for me.'

I covered my face, 'I don't want to compete with you, why do you want to take advantage of everyone, everywhere?'

She said, 'He can help me get into a magazine or even become a famous actress like Isabella Rossellini. Can you help me do that?'

I said, 'Why should you want to take advantage of men? We are, after all, not prostitutes.'

She said, 'Have you never taken advantage of men? In this regard, it does not matter whether or not a woman is educated.'

I slowly sank into a chair. I thought of some of the men with whom I had had breakfast, dinner, a drink. I thought of that man who, just because he had a handkerchief when I was drunk, I had almost committed the rest of my life to.

Everybody had their weaknesses.

'I'm hungry.' Jihang got up. She was naked. She randomly grabbed some clothes and said to me, 'Excuse me, I have to go out.' I let her go, listening to her footsteps determinedly move off into the distance. The gerberas silently wilted in the dark. I closed my eyes, and I suddenly understood what was meant by 'external trappings of success'. From here on, all things would be 'external trappings'.

That night I went to sleep early, and woke up the next morning to find Jihang with her toy rabbit in her arms, sleeping soundly like a baby. I left a note saying that I would wait for her in the cafeteria for dinner that night, and went off to classes. I didn't think she would be there.

I sat near the sliding doors waiting for her. The wintry day was nearing its end, the dusk hanging heavy like death. Jihang walked over, her long hair half tied up, dressed in a sweater and pants, a scarf draped over her shoulders, and blue, precious stone earrings dangling in her ears. When she saw me, she smiled lightly, and I realized that she had grown into a woman. Even her smile was quite distinguished. She had not been a student in vain.

We put in our order for food and had some beer. Jihang had very little to eat but drank a lot, and before we had finished our meal, her cheeks had turned bright red. We talked about the sociology instructor. He had finally been persuaded by the school administration to accept early retirement. We felt victorious and drank to his early retirement. She said she had gotten a modelling contract. We both said that that was a fine thing. I told her I had finished writing a thesis proposal, had applied for a scholarship to go to England, and had already been interviewed. We were happy and kept laughing. Once outside, I was shaking from having had too much to drink. Jihang put her scarf around my shoulders. It was windy and I said, 'I'm cold,' and walked close against Jihang. She put her arm around me as we crossed the campus. The night was beautiful, the sky a deep dark blue. I said, 'Let us move somewhere like this after we graduate. You could go out and work, I will stay home and study.' She was silent for a moment, then said, 'I'm afraid you would not quietly stay at home.' I laughed, 'I would. Look at how thin I am, do I have what it takes not to stay at home?' She pressed her bosom once again, and said, 'Well then, I'm afraid I wouldn't be good and stay at home.' We were both quiet for a long time. Jihang suddenly hugged me tightly. I was shocked by the passion of her unexpected embrace. She let me go, then said, 'It's late, go to the library and get your stuff. I'm going back to the dorm.'

I waved my hand, turned, and left. She was waving at me, saying good-bye. I scolded her saying she was crazy, after all, this wasn't some final farewell like that of lovers parted by circumstance or death, and I left without turning my head.

When I returned to the dorm, I met the dorm committee chair in the lobby. She immediately pulled me aside and said, visibly relieved, 'The dorm matron is looking for you.' I said I had to put down my books and what was the hurry anyway. She said it was urgent and shoved and pushed me to go.

I waited on the sofa of the dorm matron's room. I was bored and browsed through a copy of the magazine *Breakthrough*. One reader asked, 'Mingsum, I am very frustrated, I don't know what to do, he has left me ...' The dorm matron had prepared a cup of hot oolong tea for me. She was from Taiwan, and her Cantonese had a thick nasal accent to it. I waited for her to speak with both of my hands clasped around the mug.

The television was on, with only muted pictures flickering past the screen. The dorm matron's face went bright and dark, blue and white. It was frightening. Amidst the play of light and shadows she held back for a while, then spoke slowly, emphasizing each word, 'I have received a letter reporting on the abnormal relationship between you and Jihang.'

The oolong tea was scalding and burned the tip of my tongue. I lifted my head to look at her, and without knowing why, I had a smile on my face.

'University students not only have to have knowledge, they must also have high moral standards ...'

'I don't think this is anything degraded. Many men and women behave in a much more degraded way than we do.' I looked straight into her eyes. She did not try to avoid my glance, but looked straight back at me.

'It is abnormal, what you two are doing; it obstructs the development of human civilization. The reason society is a whole and can remain an orderly system is entirely dependent upon natural human relationships ...' I no longer heard her clearly, I just picked up bits and pieces. I was no longer looking at her; instead, I began to flip through the pages of *Breakthrough*. Mingsum replies,

'Ling, that you should destroy another's relationship is not right, but the Almighty God will forgive you ...' I was so frightened I hurriedly put the magazine away. I stared absent-mindedly at the soundless images on the television screen. After a long time, I said very softly, 'Why impose your moral standards on us? We haven't harmed anyone.' I don't know if she heard; at the same time, my voice was so soft it seemed as if someone was whispering these words into my ears. I looked around in alarm, but there was no one beside me.

'Dorm matron.' I put down my teacup and said, 'As long as Jihang won't leave me, I will certainly not leave her.' Having said this, I abruptly got up and opened the door.

'But this afternoon she already promised that she would move out of the dorm. I in turn promised that I would not make this matter public. My asking you here is merely a formality.' Her words came from far away. As I stood at the door, I pushed the doorknob. My hand felt cold. 'Thank you,' I said. I did not make another sound as I softly shut the door and left.

I don't know how I made it back to my room. That staircase seemed simply endless. Was this perhaps Jacob's ladder leading all the way to heaven, which would ultimately lead to the truth? Every step was painful. It was as though my limbs had been ripped apart. Every single movement sent a searing pain through my eyes. I covered my eyes. Let it be. From here on out, I would go blind, unable to see the light of day.

The room was not locked. Someone was coming down the hall. I straightened my back, gritted my teeth, and slipped into the room. The good Jihang. In one afternoon, she had packed up everything and put everything back in order. The only things left were a pair of brand new, bright red embroidered slippers and a pink Maidenform bra on my bed. As I looked the bra over, I found that she had bought the wrong size—32B. I laughed, and said to myself: 'It's 32A, Jihang, 32A. I am skinny!'

After she left, I also moved out of the dorm and instead rented a dark and quiet little room near the campus. My life was especially dark and quiet. I became increasingly near-sighted but I kept wearing my old rimmed glasses, so I would stumble from the classroom to the library day in and day out. I began to only wear blue, purple and black. I quit smoking. I stuck to boiled water and vegetarian fare. When other people are heartbroken, they implore heaven and earth in their despair. I, on the other hand, found myself in a state so utterly calm that I could not imagine being any calmer. My heart was as placid and expansive as the landscape paintings from earlier periods, such as the Song and the Ming. At night, I would listen to the traditional, refined *kunqu* opera tunes, often retracing my own light and hurried footsteps, lonely as a shadow. I would hug myself and say, 'I still have this.' I would bite my lips and say, 'Don't cry! Don't complain!' I was hoping that I would become someone who would understand the reasons of things—everything had a reason. She too had her difficulties.

Later on, I saw her on the cover of a magazine. Her luscious lips. The smile. However, I did not open the magazine. She was merely one among many thousands of beautiful women, entirely different from the Jihang I had known. Afterwards, I saw her again at the commencement ceremony. With her gown flying, she smiled in the sunlight, looking at me from afar, her hand blocking the glare. I realized that she was too far away and I had no way of determining whether or not her smile had changed. I just stood there without moving, holding, embracing myself. Next to her stood a man. It seemed as though I had seen him before, and after a moment's thought, it turned out to be the guy I had seen in the magazine. Jihang had made her choice. She had left me because I was not good enough for her. But the Jihang I remember … we had never made distinctions between good and bad.

I remember her *qipao* and her embroidered slippers. I remember her self-contained confidence when she was copying from my notes. I remember her smile when she softly pressed her bosom with her hand. I remember her lazy demeanour when she used to lie in bed reading

Yi Shu. I remember the time I was cold and she gave me her scarf to warm me up, and the time when I was proud and she had thrown coins at me. When I was cold and distant, she had held my hand tightly and said, 'The general has lost his wife and his army.' I remember. I remember, I tied up her hair, cut her toenails, bought her a bouquet of gerberas. I remember I had once attempted to strangle myself; my eyes filled with tears. She had pulled away my hands and said, 'Why do this?'

Why do this. I thought I could spend the rest of my life with Jihang.

Translated by Naifei Ding

Hong Kong

My Cerebral Child

Agnes Lam

On the walls
of my cerebral womb,
you are knocking.
You scratch on my inner membrane
as I am about to sleep,
tickling me through my dreams,
wanting to be fed.
On the morning bus,
you want to chat.
Between classes,
you whine for patting.
You nudge me
when I do laundry,
chuckle to yourself
during dishes
and prattle incessantly
as the news reel …

Let me out,
You are thirty.

Child of my imagination,
what do you know
of the wombless world?

Tonight on live TV
the Challenger explodes

before schoolchildren's eyes
an earthquake in South America
leaves babies behind
muddied all over
with lava debris
from California
two kindergarten matrons
are charged with child abuse
and here in Singapore
we are talking
of Total Defence
midst streaming exams.

Child of my imagination,
what have I to offer you
beyond my uterine walls?

How should I reply
if you should ask
why we are eating
strawberries on vanilla
when infants in Ethiopia
are starved hollow
of bone marrow?
Should I offer you charity
and comfort in eternity
as an answer?
And would you then ask —
Why didn't you
let me remain
timeless from the start?

Child of my imagination,
would it be enough
for me to say

there in my womb

I have loved you,
I have hoped
you will make this world
more livable?

Or would you regret
and rather be fed,
clothed and loved
always in my imagination,
my cerebral home?

Tell me,
I am thirty.

Japan

Umbrella on a Moonlit Night

TSUBOI SAKAE

There were people who wondered whether our group wasn't some sort of gathering of women of leisure or ill repute, but this was far from the truth. We were housewives who, for some twenty years, had relied solely on our husbands' pocketbooks. Like tame dogs, we had, without even knowing it, lost what little rebelliousness we once had. We were, in short, faithful wives who took comfort in being ordinary mothers. That is the sort of women we all were. Our purpose, if you can call it that, was simply to get together and pass the time gossiping when our husbands weren't home.

It is only recently that we have adopted such fashionable terms as the English word 'group', but not out of vanity. Looking back—has it been that long?—well, anyway, we first got together during that period around the end of the war, a season our generation was forced to endure in place of life's springtime. Back then we thought nobody's lives could be harder than ours, and we complained freely among ourselves of how unfair and frustrating everything was.

Even after the war, when democracy was coming into vogue, we would still mope around with gloomy faces. As I recall, we were envious of the merry-looking gatherings that young single people had at book clubs, dance parties, and what not. I'm sure some people would say that it was too bad we just didn't go on out and have fun. But how could a woman do this when she had children, a mother-in-law, or even worse, a husband not yet back from the war? We had also taken a jaundiced view of women's liberation and democracy, as if these had somehow passed us by. Whenever two of us were together, we would talk about selling off our best kimonos to raise some money. If there were three of us, the discussion would turn to getting food from the countryside. Strange as it seems, I recall that though we tended to be melancholy, whenever four of us got together we would burst into laughter.

'Hey, look here, if we're not to be outdone by youngsters, shouldn't we start a club of our own? A club just for our enjoyment.' It was Mrs Ono, the only war widow in our group, who first proposed the idea to us.

'Of course! It could be our club that meets by the well. Every week, on Monday at noon, a weekly well-side gossip meeting!'

When Mrs Kurata, a mother of two, said this, everyone immediately burst out laughing. It just so happened that that day was a Monday, and Monday was usually the day we all got together. For us housewives with working husbands and children going to school, there was no time at which we felt so drawn together as Monday at noon. Usually we would all end up visiting one another's houses without even planning for it in advance. The easiest house for us to visit belonged to Murai Kaneko, who had been called by her nickname, Kăchan, since childhood. Only Kăchan's house had not suffered any direct war damage and was still the big, old home it had always been.

'If it's going to be a well-side club, then we'll have to meet at my place, right? The rest of you only have covered wells. None of you have open well-sides, do you?'

Kăchan said this because only her house still had in use an old well with a large drainboard. After being burned out of their own homes, both Mrs Kurata and Mrs Ono had had some bittersweet experiences by that well-side. Hearing that certain wild plants were edible, they would go pick them and wash them at the well. Then, after soaking some black rice, they would boil all this into a kind of porridge. They had, in fact, looked to Kăchan when they were seeking refuge. It was through Kăchan's efforts that they were able to rent rooms, and later to find inexpensive houses to buy. It was also Kăchan who assisted those of us who had been evacuated to the countryside to obtain land that, in retrospect, seemed ridiculously cheap.

We had all gone to the same girls' school, and the war forced us into the same neighbourhood. If we derived any benefit at all from the war, I guess it was this new friendship we developed.

'But calling it "The Well-Side Club"—isn't that expression a bit old-fashioned? I mean, I think it would be nice if we had something a little more … well, the kind of club where we seemed to dominate our husbands once in a while.'

Everyone cheered heartily when I said this. As it turned out, though, we lacked the ability to conclude a debate and ended up settling for a well-side club, one in which at least we wouldn't speak ill of others.

Our membership was made up of us four. All in our thirties, we felt a rivalry towards the younger women in the neighbourhood, who had formed the Young Cedar Club. Obviously, we were not satisfied with the name 'The Well-Side Club'. We would, after all, occasionally discuss politics and also read popular books.

'Since there are four of us, how about "The Four-Leaf Club"?'

When Mrs Kurata said this, the widowed Mrs Oho rejected it, complaining that it was too silly. 'We're not a bunch of schoolgirls. And a name like "Four-Leaf" would be laughed at by the Young Cedars. "The Well-Side Club" is still better.'

'Well, how about "The Monday Club"?' Kãchan suggested.

Mrs Ono folded her arms like a man and replied, 'Well now, are we all going to meet every single Monday? If we do that, I'll go broke. And besides, doesn't "The Monday Club" sound like a meeting for professors or politicians or businessmen? It just doesn't suit us very well. What do you think?'

At this point, I murmured as if to myself, 'A name like "The Social Club" is just too ordinary; I wonder if there's a word that means we share each other's joy and anger, pleasure and grief?'

'Huh? What? Joy and what?'

'I said joy and anger, pleasure and grief. We do share with one another the things we're happy about or sad about, don't we? Well, I was wondering if there's a word that means that.'

'Well then, what's wrong with "The Joy and Grief Club"? Let's go with that.'

From the very beginning, Mrs Ono had emerged quite naturally as our leader. Thinking back on it, this group of young women barely in their thirties was rather pathetic, but even so, our gatherings were certainly enjoyable. We all got together once a month. Being poor, each of us took turns at treating the others to a meal. True to our name, there were, in succession, times of joy and times of grief.

My story is jumping back and forth. But if I remember correctly, it was around the time of our club's third meeting that Mrs Ono became a widow. She received a letter from one of her husband's soldier-friends telling her of his death in the war. She brought it with her to our meeting and, without saying a word, laid it in front of us. For the longest time Mrs Ono didn't raise her head. I'll never forget that day's meeting, which happened to be at my house. I had made sweet dumplings with saccharin, but no one touched them. Instead, they each took some and went home.

For us, happiness meant getting hold of a few cups of polished rice; but we sure got angry when the clerks at the city hall were rude. From among these emotions of our everyday life, there was nothing which could begin to compare with the tremendous sorrow and anger caused by a person's death. And yet—shall we call it the power of human adaptability?—Mrs Ono seemed to recover quickly, which made us all feel very relieved. As if she had quite forgotten that only Mrs Ono was a widow, Mrs Kurata once remarked, 'Hey, do you know what? My husband has been secretly keeping money from me. Have you ever heard of such a thing? For a man, he sure is stingy.'

Encouraged by these comments, Kāchan quickly added, 'That's the way it is, all right. Used to be that hiding money was something only women did. They say that since the war men and women have equal rights in that department. As far as stashing away money is concerned though, a woman still has the upper hand, seeing how she's in charge of the household expenses. The stingier a husband gets, the more a wife will stash away for herself. That's only natural! And sometimes a wife is going to want to go see a good movie or something, isn't she? Even if a husband doesn't forbid her to go to a single movie, a lady might want to just pop out to a movie when her husband is gone, without having to get permission each time.'

No sooner had I thought that I'd go on to make a little speech against my husband than Mrs Ono commented with a smile, 'My husband this, my husband that! You'd think they were a terrible bother. Considering how lost you'd be without them, I wouldn't complain too much. What about me?'

Startled, I looked into Mrs Ono's face, but couldn't see into the depths behind her expression. Making full use of her sewing machine,

Mrs One has struggled all these years to support herself and her child. Yet, even now, she's the most cheerful of us four, and even looks the youngest. Whenever I notice these qualities in Mrs Ono, I suddenly wonder just what it is that makes women grow old.

Another housewife in the neighbourhood found out about our club and wanted to join in with us. She was envious of all the fun we seemed to be sharing. Once she happened to come by where we were meeting. After her unexpected visit, we discussed the problem.

'What should we do?'

'If we don't let her in, she'll think badly of us. We've got to tell her something ...'

'Ah! I've got it! What if we said it's a gathering of former schoolmates?'

'That's it! That's it!'

Without knowing it, we had shown what typically narrow-minded females we were. But this incident brought the four of us that much closer together.

'What do you think? Will "The Four-Leaf Club" really not do? "The Joy and Grief Club" is too complicated; little kids would never understand it. Besides, it's too gloomy,' Mrs Kurata remarked somewhat obstinately. She had been the first to suggest 'The Four-Leaf Club'. This time even Mrs Ono simply nodded in assent, 'Sure, that would be fine. "The Four-Leaf Club" or "The Group" or something like that. Let's set up a challenge to that Young Cedar Club and make ourselves young again.'

As a result of all this, the name 'The Joy and Grief Club' more or less disappeared. This doesn't mean that we always used the name 'The Four-Leaf Club'. Instead, we started calling ourselves simply 'The Group'. Compared to the Young Cedar Club, which made a great beginning but soon started to fizzle out, we flourished more and more as time went on. Even the boundaries of our adventuring slowly widened.

'Shouldn't we be a little rowdy sometimes? It's not right to leave all the drinking to our husbands. And we might learn a little something by playing pachinko at the game parlours.'

We were able to start talking like this mostly because we had gotten a little free time. Since rice was finally available at the distribution centre, a housewife could take a little more time to amuse herself. But we were, after all, housewives on fixed allowances. No matter how carefully one saved up pin money, there wasn't enough for a whole day's entertainment. In a family like mine, with no more than the income of a junior high school teacher, it was all one could do to save away, at most, ten yen a day. Even to hang onto five-yen coins or one-yen bills was an exacting task. Even so, never a month went by that, when payday arrived, that I didn't borrow some spending money for myself from the family budget. It was amazing that I could in this way save up five or six hundred, or sometimes even a thousand yen, without my husband ever knowing about it. This was my very own money to use without worrying about the other family members.

After we became the Four-Leaf Club, our monthly expenses rose drastically. No longer satisfied with just meeting at home, drinking tea, and nibbling at sweets, we started taking three to five hundred yen and going out to town. It wasn't enough anymore to meet only when our husbands and children were not at home. We would clear out of the house on a Sunday or holiday without apology and spend all day enjoying ourselves here and there. We had two approaches. One was to leave in the morning and not come back until it was time to start preparing dinner. The other was to leave at noon, eat dinner out, and even take time to sec a movie before returning home. On those days when we would be returning before dinner, we wouldn't give much thought to leaving our families. If we were going to be eating out, though, we'd have to worry about our children and husbands left behind at home. With that in mind, we'd start humouring them the day before. At such times, I was very grateful to my children.

'Mother, don't you worry about it; just go out and have fun! Take your time. It's only once a month, isn't it? If it's just a Sunday, we can take care of things at home.'

When my oldest boy, a high school senior, made that offer, my daughter—a year younger and not to be outdone—volunteered, 'That's right. I can take care of dinner. I'm great at making curry rice.'

Dinner on those nights was almost always curry rice. It was the only meal my daughter really knew how to make. My third child, a boy, was in the sixth grade. All of them acted as if they were full-fledged adults. In fact, it was my husband I always had to worry about. Whenever I had plans to go out, he would openly display a sullen, unhappy expression. 'Do I have a white shirt to wear tomorrow?'

'Yes, you do.'

'I had planned for everyone to clean the garden today, but never mind.'

'Well, let's postpone it then. All right?'

Whenever we had this kind of conversation, the children would all side against their father and come to my assistance.

'Daddy, you're mean. How can you say such nasty things when Mom's just about to go for her Four-Leaf Club meeting? You're feudal.'

My daughter had a habit of calling 'feudal' anything a male did—even her father or brother—that she felt was a little unreasonable. But it was surprising how much this word 'feudal' of hers actually contributed to the peaceful atmosphere of our home by making us think over just how feudal we were. It was a word which almost never crossed my lips but which the children used boldly. Such was the case on Mother's Day one May.

'It's unfair that there's a Mother's Day, but no Father's Day, don't you think?'

My husband had only been joking, but my daughter quickly turned on him.

'That's a lie! I don't think so at all! Having Mother's Day once a year isn't enough. Daddy, you have Father's Day every day. You're feudal!'

*

It was probably just my being old-fashioned, but I would get a kind of heavy, sinking feeling in my heart before our group was to get together. Sometimes I even thought of leaving the group. But when I attended the meeting after all, I was always happy I hadn't said anything to my husband. Still, I would quietly look around at the others' faces, wondering if they had had thoughts like mine.

For our meeting in July, we went out in Western clothes. I left the house wearing new canvas sandals and looking youthful for the first time in a very long while. Grinning at me, my oldest boy quipped,

'Hey, Mom, we're gonna have a present waiting for you when you get back. Oh my, it's all inside. Yes! Yes! Isn't that right, Jiro?'

As if enjoying a secret, the two boys looked at each other and laughed.

'Oh my, it's all inside', was the password my family used when referring to a secret matter. It had all started with my husband, who, when he was drunk, would sing a popular old song which began, 'I wanted that woman so bad I could die, good thing she finally became my wife.' There was a certain verse in it he would sing in a secretive tone of voice, 'Oh my, it's all inside. Yes, it's all inside.' My daughter and oldest boy found this line amusing and started using it themselves. It was the sort of song that even now I'd turn red all over if I heard it in front of others. At the time I was in fact very upset at my husband, thinking to myself, 'How could he, in front of our children?' But our children, of course, are from a new generation. With childlike innocence, they simply mimicked the verse they found pleasing. But children will drink from dirty water as well as clean and still not poison themselves. I guess we parents are out of date and there's nothing to worry about.

Our schedule for that day was to window-shop in the morning, see a fashion show, and then have a simple lunch of noodles. In the afternoon we were going to see an Italian movie, and for dinner we had decided that, even if we could only afford one à la carte item, we would go to a certain European restaurant. In the evening, we planned to relish the atmosphere along the Ginza, even trying a little pachinko, before returning home. We ended up heading for home without having set foot in a pachinko parlour, but this was the only activity we had to put off until our next meeting. We had put a five hundred-yen ceiling on our spending that day, and, as expected, had used it all up. It was an unusually extravagant meeting.

'Next time, let's set a strict spending policy,' Kāchan said. But Ono objected, saying, 'What do you mean? If anyone, I should be saying that. Don't you want to play sometimes as much as the men do, and spend everything you've got? But we can't go that far, so at least don't talk about running out of money! All your husbands got mid-year bonuses, didn't they?'

Mrs Ono pulled cut a lighter and lit up a cigarette, puffing out smoke like a real smoker. Mrs Ono had only recently started smoking, but she moved her hands as if she had been at it a long time.

'Hey, will you give me one too?'

Mrs Ono handed the whole pack over to Kãchan, who had stuck her hand out rather awkwardly to receive it. Looking me right in the face, Mrs Ono said, 'After Kãchan, Mrs Kurata will probably start. It'll be a while before you're smoking, huh?'

'That's not so!' I said. 'I'm the one who first suggested a club where we can dominate our husbands. I can at least smoke cigarettes. Give me one, give me one!'

'What?' Kãchan responded, 'Does smoking cigarettes and dominating one's husband have that much in common? That's crazy!'

At that, everyone burst out laughing, while I choked on my first puff and, with the tears streaming down, coughed violently. Right in the middle of the Ginza, flooded by neon lights, Mrs Ono gently patted my back and said, 'You idiot. You were trying to act like a widow or a lady hounded by her mother-in-law.'

'Now, that's crazy!' I said, still coughing and not willing to admit defeat. At the same time, though, for no particular reason I suddenly thought of my husband.

❋

Premonitions ... it's probably only old-fashioned women like us who speak of such things, but these premonitions are surprisingly accurate.

Even after getting on the train at Shinbashi, I felt terribly anxious about my family. It was a feeling of something depressing waiting for me. My anxiety must have shown in the look on my face. When we sat down together after changing to the Chũõ line at Tokyo Station, the first thing Kãchan asked me was, 'What's the matter? You're awfully quiet.'

'I'm a little tired.'

'I bet it's because we walked all eight blocks of the Ginza. But wasn't it interesting?'

'It was.'

Because I gave such an unenthusiastic answer, Kãchan quickly turned toward Mrs Kurata. I closed my eyes and silently began to think. I recalled how I left the house that day.

'... Highly inward. Yes, yes.'

'... It's bad luck if you tell anyone.'

It was 'our present for you' that my sons had jokingly sung about, and apparently they were even being 'on the inside' towards their father. I had guessed, from the fact that for some time they had been all on their own, saving up their allowances and then buying and collecting empty apple boxes, bamboo, and wire netting, that it was a henhouse they were making. As I tried to imagine where on earth they might have been building it, I became very uneasy. Had it been a day when my husband was at home the problem would have been simple, but I remembered that today, unfortunately, he had said he was going over to his friend's place to play Go.

'You know, all of a sudden I feel worried about my husband.'

Unable to stay silent, I disclosed this to Kãchan. She grinned and responded half-teasingly, 'That must be because it's getting late. It's the same for anyone. I've realized lately that at times like this it's better to take things in stride. If we start getting nervous about whether we've annoyed our families, we've lost, haven't we? But, when we go out on the town like this, don't you feel like you sort of understand what goes on in your husband's mind when he comes home from having his run? Doesn't he try to butter you up by bringing home a gift? And then doesn't that make you feel more like being hostile? Wouldn't you much rather he was honest and open? So, let's be honest and open.'

'Honest and open, just talking like that shows you're dishonest and sneaky. Let's go home with dignity.'

As Mrs Kurata said this, I thought to myself that she was also probably dishonest and sneaky.

At Asagaya we made the last bus going to Nakamura Bridge. Getting off at the second block of Saginomiya we parted with Mrs Ono, and the three of us headed in the same direction, turning left along the main road. As we walked along side by side, Mrs Kurata said in a dejected voice, 'Women are pathetic.'

'It's only because we say things like that that we become pathetic. Don't talk like that!'

Just as Kãchan was telling her off, we arrived at the corner where I had to part from the other two.

'Good night. Thanks a lot.'

I ran along a path that wound through the wide fields, taking short brisk steps at a pace far quicker than I could manage in the daytime. The lights were on in my house, and seeing it there underneath the starlit sky, I felt a sharp pang of nostalgia.

'I'm home!'

The instant I opened the front door my built-in radar sensed that something was wrong. 'I knew it,' I thought to myself. The children came out to greet me as I was untying my shoe laces. I had to force myself to sound cheerful.

'I had a delightful time today. Thank you.'

Looking over the children's faces, I handed my daughter a package of candy I had brought home as a gift.

'For us, today wasn't delightful at all. Daddy was totally unreasonable.' My daughter whined softly. 'Just now we were all complaining about him, weren't we?' She went on, turning to her elder brother.

From the gloomy look on her face it was obvious that she had a lot to complain about. 'What on earth's the matter? Don't you understand your Daddy's personality?' I scolded her.

'But it wasn't just his personality today. He was absolutely feudal. Tell her,' she said, looking over at my elder son.

'I can't even talk about it. He may be our father, but this is too much!'

My oldest boy was even starting to cry. Led by my children, I went into the boys' room, which was next to the front porch. One by one the three children told their story. As I thought, they had built a henhouse in the front yard. My daughter vented her indignation, saying, 'As soon as Daddy got home he got furious, and before we could say anything he kicked it with his foot. We'd worked hard on that henhouse, and he smashed it all apart. He broke up the poles. The wire is so tangled up it'll never be usable again.'

'You built it without permission, right? You never consulted with him. If you had handled it better, your father would never have done such a thing.'

'But we thought he'd be really happy,' my oldest son said. 'We could have eaten the eggs the hen laid, so we wouldn't have had to buy them. We were sure you'd both be really happy. Isn't that so?' he asked his sister.

Right down to my youngest boy, they all stood firm. As usual, it was my oldest son who, reconsidering things a little, was the calmest.

'But, Mom,' he said, 'even if it was wrong not to consult with Dad first, he didn't have to smash it up with no warning. We started the whole thing with completely good intentions. And just because Dad didn't like it, he smashed it all to pieces without even consulting with us a bit.'

'Now, you know your father's temper.'

'Well, then, just because he's the father, it's ok for him to lose his temper? That's why he's feudal.'

'But, anyway, leave everything to your mother. You mustn't oppose your father too much.'

'We're not giving in! Even if we act like we're trying to make up with him, our feelings won't change. From today on, we'll never feel the same way about him.'

'That's right! I don't see how you could have lived with that stubborn man for twenty years, Mommy. You've been so submissive—you act as if it's ok to just let him be so bossy. Mommy, you're as bad as he is.'

'I hate Dad.'

These condemnations were very noisy. My husband had never heard such talk. I was the one who made sure he never heard it.

My daughter had said, 'Mommy, you're as bad as he is!'—but I realized that 'Mommy' was even worse than he was.

'Well, what can we do? How about if your father apologizes? I'll say something to get him to apologize.'

'That's no good! Dad would never apologize,' my younger boy declared resolutely.

I responded with a laugh, 'Now, you don't know that for sure. All right, then, I'll get him to apologize. In exchange, you will all apologize for the bad things you've done.'

'We haven't done anything bad. Isn't that right?' he asked his sister.

'That's not so,' she answered. 'We dug up the moss Daddy was trying so hard to grow.'

My daughter was finally showing a more subdued attitude. However, she went on, 'But is moss all that important? I think eggs are better, right?'

'That's right,' her older brother agreed. 'Moss—it's a lousy hobby.'

I held my tongue and listened to all this. There was no reason why the children should comprehend the pleasure my husband got out of that garden moss, never forgetting to sprinkle it with water every day, and taking such good care of it. Indeed, it would have been unnatural if they had comprehended this even a little bit.

I let the children talk as much as they liked. After that, they were easy to deal with. I gave them candy and they quickly went off to sleep. Afterwards, their anger apparently having infected me, I had to control my temper while talking to my husband. 'Even though you're their father, this is too much. You may think they're only children, but they still understand everything that's happening.'

Completely indifferent, he remained silent. I thought his silence was a sign of penitence, but the next morning my husband left the house without saying anything, still unyielding.

Poor man!

I spent that whole day reflecting on my husband, from the time he was young until the present. Because of my outdated way of looking at things, I had never said this to anybody, but ours was a marriage of love. Even though there had been stormy times, it was with feelings of joy that we had had children and raised them. How could I keep silent when my husband was alienated from his children?

That night, without saying anything to the children, I left the house for the train station. It had been a long time since I had gone to meet my husband there. Even if it was raining, one could always rent an umbrella, so I almost never went out to meet him. When I was younger, I used to go boldly up by the ticket taker to wait for him, but this time I hid by a telephone pole near the front of the station and watched the passengers. My husband worked late on Mondays, so by this time the train wasn't very crowded, and I could pick out the passengers as they emerged one by one. I must have waited about fifteen minutes. My husband came out of the train car at the very front. Hs was holding an umbrella, and his shoulders were stooped in a posture so I could even imagine his facial expressions. He headed for the ticket taker face down. I don't know why, but while I watched him take one step after another I felt the blood rush to my head. Leaving the ticket taker, he stopped at a fruit stand, and, after having something wrapped up into a bundle, he finally headed in my direction. I don't know what he was thinking of, but as he neared the railway crossing, he opened up his umbrella. Having no way of knowing that I was secretly waiting for him, he walked calmly toward me. I let him pass on by me, while trying to keep myself from laughing. It wasn't raining. In fact, the moon was out. My husband seemed not to notice that. He also didn't notice me a few moments later when I came out and walked along behind him. After we turned into the big road leading toward our home, I even quickened my steps, but my husband—who was convinced that one carried an umbrella in order to use it—never once turned around. I followed quietly behind this strange figure holding an umbrella in the moonlit night.

Translated by Chris Heftel

Japan

The Tomoshibi

ARIYOSHI SAWAKO

It was almost incredible that a small, quiet bar like the Tomoshibi should exist in the Ginza. Although it was located on an alley branching off a back street of Higashi Ginza, a noisy place where bars stood side by side in a row, it was still part of the Ginza. To the right, there was a large coffee shop, and to the left there was a well-known men's clothing store. The three shops across the street—a restaurant, a coffee shop, and an accessories store—were famous, and so, this one corner overflowed, with a true Ginza-like atmosphere, almost as if it were on the main street itself.

However, the Tomoshibi was inconspicuous in all respects. It was only natural that it wasn't noticeable during the day, since the bar opened at five in the afternoon; but in any case, since the frontage was narrow—only about six feet wide—it was overwhelmed by the imposing appearance of the neighbouring stoics on both sides. It didn't seem likely that there would be such a bar in a place like this.

There was a small lantern placed outside, above the door, and on this 'The Tomoshibi' was written in quaint lettering. In the evening, even when it became both in name and in reality a *tomoshibi*, it did not shine very boldly.

When the night grew late and all the neighbours had closed shop, the street became silent. Even people looking for a place to drink would go right past it, not noticing that the street even had a bar.

The fact was, then, that the patrons of the Tomoshibi were an exceedingly limited group of regular customers. However, the Tomoshibi hadn't many of what one usually thinks of as 'regular customers', the type of people who gather together out of affection for the proprietress and barmaids.

There were few customers who came to the Tomoshibi every night; neither were there many stray customers who wandered in. Nevertheless, the bar was always filled to capacity, and although the popularity of the proprietress, who was called 'Mama-san', might have helped a little, the patrons and the barmaids all knew the exact reason why.

It is true that the bar was small. In a space of about ninety square feet, there was a cramped restroom, a large refrigerator, a tiny counter behind which Mama-san and one barmaid could stand, and just enough chairs and tables for the other barmaid to entertain customers. Even with only the three of them, when none of the customers had showed up yet, a dry wind did not blow in the bar. Thus anyone who casually entered the Tomoshibi alone would be enveloped by a warm atmosphere, and immediately feel at home.

Here, no one felt like chasing away the blues by noisily badmouthing their superiors while under the influence; nor were there any customers who told vulgar jokes to first get into a state of mind sufficiently disillusioned to bring on a quick drunk.

'Hello there!' Mama-san greeted a customer who hadn't come for several months. Speaking as if he had come the day before yesterday, the customer asked, 'It's been a while since I've seen the girl who used to work here—what's happened to her?'

'She got married,' Mama-san replied quietly.

'Hmm, got married, huh?' The customer spoke as if he were surprised and impressed, and he looked around the bar once again.

'I see .... I guess if she were from this bar, a barmaid could really get married decently.' As if he were quite convinced, he sipped his whiskey on-the-rocks and sighed.

Mama-san and a barmaid known as Shizu-chan, who were seated quietly on chairs away from the counter, exchanged furtive smiles.

The girl, Eiko, who had been helping Mama-san behind the counter, had committed suicide about three weeks ago.

Any girl who decides to come to work in a bar has her own complex reasons. And, while she works, her life usually becomes even more complicated. Although she had found employment in a quiet bar like this, Eiko probably suffered from more hardships than the average person. It had looked as if she was confiding everything to Mama-san, and had been seeking her advice. Yet there was probably something she had not been able to confide, and maybe that had become unbearable. One night, she took some pills and died. Since she was a quiet girl, perfectly suited for the Tomoshibi, there had not been anything out of the ordinary in her conduct, and even the worldly-wise Mama-san had not noticed anything.

Since it was a whole day before the suicide was discovered, nothing could be done. There was no will, and her humble one-room apartment was left neatly in order. There was a savings passbook left for her younger brother, her only blood relative, but it certainly did not contain an extraordinary sum of money. That a young, nameless barmaid had died one night was such a small happening that it wouldn't even be mentioned in an obscure corner of a newspaper.

That is why Mama-san did not want to do anything that would cast a shadow on the memories of the customers who remembered Eiko.

'Is that so? She got married? Hmmm ....' The customer, perhaps because the alcohol had begun to take its effect, re-articulated his initial surprise, but Mama-san only commented gently, 'Quite so, she got married.'

'What kind of guy was he? Was he a customer here?'

'There's no use in being jealous. It's already too late.' When Mama-san laughed in her sweet voice, the customer also gave a forced laugh, and at that point they ended the conversation.

'Another drink, please.'

'Coming! Coming! Isn't it cold today?'

Although there were peanuts and smoked squid on the narrow counter, with the second glass of whiskey Mama-san provided some fresh cucumber with a dash of lemon, free of charge. The customer picked up a slice with his fingers, and while eating with a crunching sound, asked, 'Did you choose all those paintings by yourself?' He was examining the inside of the bar again.

'Yes, but they're all reproductions!'

Several framed pictures, none of them any larger than fifteen square inches, were hung on the wall. Among these, two were Chagalls, one was a Miró, one was an oil painting by Takayama Uichi, and one was a woodblock print by Minami Keiko.

Those by Takayama and the Minami were originals, and those by

Chagall and Miró were lithographs, but Mama-san always said that they were replicas and didn't care to elaborate further.

Mama-san had bought them only because they were pictures that she had liked, and not because they were the works of famous artists. But if some customers didn't like the pictures, that was that, no matter what she said.

A picture in which lovers embraced on the roof of a small house in the moonlight. And a sweet, dream-like picture of a young girl singing, enveloped by a bird of fire. Next to the two Chagalls hung a surrealistic picture, with bright colours like a child's scribbles. It was the Miró. This was Mama-san's greatest pride, for she had thrown caution to the winds and bought it, although it was extremely expensive. Yet since the customers who came to the bar could barely appreciate the Chagalls, the Miró seemed even more incomprehensible to them.

However, when one looked at all of them, including the Takayama painting of greenery and butterflies, and the Minami woodblock print of autumn leaves and fish, even the Miró became part of a coherent whole which created a fairy tale-like, innocent, and happy atmosphere throughout the bar. Perhaps it was because of this atmosphere that customers were convinced that barmaids from this bar could become brides after all.

'Last night I had such a beautiful dream.'

All of a sudden, Shizu-chan started to speak. Since it was a small bar, whatever anyone said could be overheard by everyone else, so there was no need to turn their heads. The good thing about this bar was the fact that both Mama-san and Shizu-chan had beautiful voices. Some customers said flatly that it was better just to listen to their voices when they started to speak, rather than to look at their faces.

'What kind of dream?' Mama-san responded in a leisurely tone.

'In my dream, I met a boy whom I had been extremely fond of when I was small.'

'How incriminating!'

Because Shizu-chan had started to tell her story in such a passionate manner, one of the customers tried to tease her, but Mama-san waited patiently for her next words.

'This boy was the village headman's son. Since we were the children of tenant farmers, in spite of being in the same class at school, we didn't dare go near him. Even so, all the girls liked the young master. When he came close, I could hardly breathe!'

'It must have been your first love!'

'Yes, I guess it was. But it's been over ten years since I left the village. I've never had such a dream in all these years, so I wonder why I should have one now. Last night's dream just came out of the blue. It really surprised me!'

'Was the young master a child? Or had he grown up?'

'I'm not too sure. I'm not even sure whether I was a child or whether I was like I am now ...'

'Isn't that nice!'

'In any case, it was incredibly beautiful. There were birds of fire flying around us.'

The Chagall painting had apparently made its way into Shizu-chan's dream. Yet while she was talking, she seemed to enter a dreamy state of mind once again. Even after she had finished talking, she remained staring into space as if entranced.

'I'll go home after one more drink. I think I'll go to sleep early tonight and dream of my first love, too.'

Customers would be engulfed by the mood of the bar before they knew it. Shizu-chan was skilful at telling her life story in this fragmentary way, under the pretense of relating, for example, a story about her dreams. Since she differed from the many barmaids who allure customers by going over their sad life stories in great detail, from childhood to more recent hardships, there were quite a number of customers who came to the bar wanting to talk to her.

'And so, Shizu-chan, you haven't returned home ever since you came out to Tokyo?'

'No, even though my father and mother are there, and they've been asking me to come home soon.'

'Don't you like the countryside?'

'That's not the point. There are many reasons why I have to stay in Tokyo.'

'Is some man giving you a hard time, then?'

'No man would ever give me a hard time!'

Although she was replying seriously, it still sounded so funny that the customers would unexpectedly burst out laughing. It was probably because of Shizu-chan's natural virtue that nobody would think of teasing her by saying, 'Would you like me to give you a hard time?'

Only Mama-san knew that Shizu-chan's parents had died when she was still a child, and that she was having a rough time of it at her aunt's, into whose family she had been adopted. When Shizu-chan said her parents were awaiting her return, only Mama-san sensed the truth behind the lie.

In the back streets of the Ginza, drunken men would usually spend their time speaking loudly and amorously of women, and drunken women would speak similarly of men. Yet in this bar, even if conversations of that type did get started, they never lasted very long. Strangely enough, though, conversations about pet dogs or cats would continue on and on endlessly.

❋

There was a Siamese cat at the Tomoshibi. It was Mama-san's pet, and every day she carried it with her to work. It had a light gray, slender body, and its legs and the tip of its tail were dark sepia. Since it had a straight, shapely nose, Mama-san believed that it was a beautiful cat.

'Don't be ridiculous! Don't you know that the flatter a cat's nose is, the more attractive it's supposed to be?'

'Impossible! Cats or human beings, it's the same. The higher the nose is, the better.'

'You're wrong!'

'Well then, please look carefully. Use your aesthetic sense to judge this. Here ...'

Mama-san picked up her beloved cat and thrust it out in front of the customer's nose.

'I still think it's funny ...'

If the customer should persist in this manner, things would get serious. In high spirits, Mama-san would refill the glass of whiskey and say, 'Here, pull yourself together with this, and look carefully once again. Here Chika, Chika, make a nice face...'

One might wonder whether the customer or Mama-san would be the first to give in, but it was always the cat in question who, hating to stay still, got bored with trying to outstare the customer, yawned out loud, scratched Mama-san's hand, and jumped down. The area on top of the window above the heater was Chika's seat, and once she retreated there, she would not come out, no matter how one called or invited her.

'Mama-san, don't you like dogs?'

'I like them, but you can't keep a dog in a bar.'

'I really like dogs. Even when I get home late after drinking, I always wake up at seven in the morning, since I have to take Hachiro out for a walk.'

'Is his name Hachiro? How cute!'

'Is it an Akita?' Shizu-chan interrupted.

'How did you know?' the customer asked in surprise.

'Oh, it's just a lucky guess. I thought a name like Hachiro might be quite appropriate for an Akita.'

With this boost to his spirits, the customer drew out a billfold from the inside pocket of his suit and produced a photograph from it.

He was a customer who perfectly matched the proprietress and barmaids. The snapshot was of his dog.

'See, look, isn't he a handsome one?'

His eyes and mouth were certainly those of an Akita, but the line between the ears and the neck was rather questionable. Yet even so, Mama-san was charmed by the eyes and mouth and said, 'How adorable! He looks like a fine, lively dog.'

Her manner of praise was clever, but young Shizu-chan, who was peering over from the side, was too honest.

'Hmm, is this really an Akita?' she questioned in a loud voice.

'It's an Akita, all right. This dog's father, you know, has quite a pedigree.'

'What about the mother?'

'Well, you see,' he said regretfully, drinking up the remaining whiskey, 'it's a case of a woman of humble birth marrying into royalty.'

In other words, Hachiro was a mutt. However, if lineage were to be determined patrilineally, as in the imperial family, then without doubt he would be a descendent of the noble Akita breed.

Being quick with her wits, Mama-san said, 'They were quite gallant parents, weren't they?' and saved the customer from his predicament.

With this, the customer regained his balance. Ordering a double on-the-rocks, he began to speak in great detail of how Hachiro was such a fine dog that he didn't bring disgrace to his father's name.

Birds of a feather flock together, and that night as many as four dog-lovers had gathered there. Since each of them had to introduce the pedigree, name, personality and distinguishing features of his pet, the Tomoshibi didn't close until quite late.

'Since it's late, Shizu-chan, I'll take you home,' Mama-san said to Shizu-chan, who was waiting with her collar pulled up. Mama-san locked the door and stopped a taxi.

'Please take us first to Higashi Nakano, then Shibuya.' No matter how tiring a night she might have had, her manner of speaking was always kind.

As the car drove along through the night streets, Shizu-chan started to giggle about something she remembered.

'What is it?'

'Oh, I was just thinking of the dog contest we had.'

'Wasn't it funny—everyone thought his own was the best.'

'But they were all mongrels!'

'That's why we didn't get into a fight.'

Mama-san was smiling serenely, the pure bred Siamese cat fast asleep on her lap. It was a conceited cat with a picky appetite. None of the customers who boasted about their half-breed dogs dared to show their antipathy towards Chika, because she was protected by Mama-san's goodness.

'You know, Shizu-chan …'

'Yes?'

'If these late nights continue, we'll surely need a replacement for Eiko.'

'I think so too.'

'Unless we find someone who will take turns with you working late, you'll get too tired. Do you know of anyone who would be good?'

'Well, I don't have too many friends, so …'

After a while, Mama-san, looking out of the window, murmured, 'What a fool Eiko was to die!'

Almost ready to cry herself, Shizu-chan said hurriedly to the taxi driver. 'Oh, please stop here. That corner will be fine. Yes, right here.'

Although Mama-san had taken her home on several occasions in the past, Shizu-chan would always get off by the main road and avoid being taken by car to the front of her house. Since there must have been some reason, Mama-san didn't insist on accompanying her any farther. She would quietly see Shizu-chan off, turning around in the taxi which had started to move, and would watch her figure disappear into the darkness. Small dirty houses stood clustered, side by side.

⁕

'Position for barmaid. A young person, with or without experience. The Tomoshibi.'

Mama-san wrote this with a brush on a small piece of paper. For three days her routine was to put up the sign at night when leaving, and take it down before eight in the evening when the customers came. Three or four applicants came knocking at the door, despite the fact that it was such a tiny advertisement and for such an inconspicuous bar.

During the hours before her customers came, Mama-san held 'interviews' in the bar, and when there were customers, in the coffee shop next door.

One girl was so young she seemed like a firm plum still attached to a branch. It appeared that she had come to the accessories store across the street and read the advertisement by chance. Her family was apparently well off, and she had been casually thinking that she wanted to work. Mama-san shuddered at her naive boldness.

'When you discuss this matter with your parents, please make sure that you tell them I said this is not the sort of place you should be coming to.'

'Oh, then there's no use in discussing it with them. Am I unqualified?'

In the eyes that asked 'Am I unqualified?' shone fearless, youthful, as yet unblemished pride. Hoping that this child would be able to grow up just as she was, Mama-san gently smiled and nodded.

'Yes, you're unqualified.'

'Oh, shucks!'

Since she stuck her tongue out and left without seeming too

disappointed, Mama-san felt greatly relieved.

On another occasion, a sickly, tired woman came by.

'Why did you quit the other bar?'

'The proprietress scolded me too often. About not being lively and boisterous. She complained a lot, but how could I help it? After all, that's my nature!'

'That's true.'

'But I have my own good customers. That's why the proprietress didn't want to let me go, but I don't like working under someone I have personality conflicts with.'

Realizing quite clearly that she wouldn't get along with her either, Mama-san smiled and stood up.

'As you can see, our bar is rather small, isn't it? We don't need any more customers than we already have. If fate so ordains, I'll see you again.'

It seemed as if the many layers of grime from the woman's harsh daily life were smeared across her coarse skin. Wishing she had the confidence to try and wash away this person's unhappiness at the Tomoshibi, Mama-san was sad that she couldn't hire her.

However, even if Mama-san invited this person to come and work at the bar, sooner or later she would leave of her own accord.

Mama-san had always hired the type of barmaids who would stay only at the Tomoshibi.

*

'Good evening!' a voice called cheerfully.

A figure dressed in bright colours entered the door, and the bar became crowded at once. It was the madam of one of the five largest bars in the Ginza.

'My, I haven't seen you for such a long time!'

Mama-san, in her usual manner, invited her in warmly. Mama-san's smile never changed according to whom she was talking. Some ten years ago, Madam and Mama-san had worked in the same bar. They both became independent in the same Ginza area around the same time. However, Madam had been quite a businesswoman. Therefore, after moving from place to place, her bar and her name had become so noted that any person who dealt with the Ginza could not have failed to hear of them.

'This bar hasn't changed at all!'

'I guess it's been two years since you last came.'

'How I envy you! I suppose if you don't have to make alterations in the interior of your bar for two whole years, you don't have to spend much money. As for my place, since the customers are so demanding, we frequently have to change the wall hangings and the paintings ...'

It was probably because Madam had some good qualities that her constant complaining about her financial situation, as well as her total envy of this small bar were not intolerably offensive. Drinkers are very honest with themselves, so unless the proprietress is somewhat good natured, customers won't be attracted to the bar.

'I have something to talk with you about.' Madam said suddenly in a low voice, pulling Mama-san out to the coffee shop next door.

'Don't you have an opening at your place?'

'Well, I am looking for someone right now, but there aren't very many people who would come to work at a bar like ours.'

Madam took Mama-san's modesty seriously, and after firmly nodding, leaned forward.

'I know of a nice girl ... Will you take a look at her?'

'But isn't she one of the girls at your place?'

'That's true, but she won't last there. She's just too nice. I don't know what to do, because whenever a customer teases her even a little bit, she starts to cry. I tell her over and over again that unless you strike back when you're teased, you can't survive in the Ginza, but it is completely useless. The girls at my place are always being offered positions at rival bars whenever I'm not paying close attention, except for that one. She's fairly popular with the customers, but she still has an inferiority complex. Touch upon that complex and she gets depressed. I just haven't any idea what to do!'

'What kind of inferiority complex?' Mama-san attempted to pursue the matter further, but Madam waved her hands dramatically and ignored the question.

'Well, in any case I'll tell her to stop by and see you after work, so take a look at her. She's the perfect girl for your place. It would be easy for me to fire her, but she's such a nice girl that I don't have the heart to kick her out. Do it for me, all right?'

Madam pulled out a one-thousand yen bill and picked up the check from the table in one swift move. Having finished her business, she hastily paid for the coffee and left.

Forced to accept the proposition, Mama-san returned to the bar. She didn't feel so badly after she remembered that Madam always behaved in the same way.

Since the two bars belonged to such different categories, they were not in competition with each other, and even if Madam tried to pass on a second-hand article that was of no use at her place, Mama-san would not be offended. On the contrary, she rather enjoyed going over in her mind what Madam had said: 'She's such a nice girl that she can't work at my bar.' That she was such a nice girl, and that she was not even appropriate for the very best bar in the Giza district certainly pleased Mama-san.

Therefore, when the night grew late and Momoko appeared—quietly opening the door and inquiring, 'May I come in?'—Mama-san said almost by reflex, 'Oh, I've heard all about you. Everything's all set. Please start working here from five tomorrow evening.'

Shizu-chan seemed to take in Momoko's round face and lovely lips immediately, as well as the fact that her dark blue overcoat was very becoming.

Just before leaving for home, Shizu-chan asked nonchalantly, 'Is the person who came by a little while ago working with us from tomorrow?' But Mama-san, who was busy getting ready to close up and go home, answered without going into great detail, 'Yes, I'll introduce her to you tomorrow.'

Mama-san was rather noisily occupied in the restroom.

'Shizu-chan.'

'Yes?'

'It's quite late, so you can go home first.'

'Are you sure it's all right?'

Shizu-chan wondered what Mama-san could be up to, but anxious to head for home just as soon as she could, she left straight away.

The next day, having been delayed by collecting bills, Shizu-chan arrived at the bar a little later than usual and found Mama-san cleaning here and there inside the bar with the new girl.

'Good morning!'

'Oh, good morning! This is Shizu-chan, and this is Momoko-chan.'

Mama-san introduced them in an intimate manner, as if she were bringing together two of her children. Momoko bowed humbly, and Shizu-chan felt slightly embarrassed. Deep inside, she had received quite a shock.

Dimly aware of the fact that Madam, who was an old friend of Mama-san, had spoken to Mama-san about this matter, Shizu-chan had been worried about what kind of person was going to come. Yet unlike last night's impression of her, the minute she looked at Shizu-chan today, Shizu-chan was taken aback.

She's cross-eyed, Shizu-chan realized at once. To use a Japanese expression, her eyes were 'London-Paris'—her right eye was focused on London, while her left eye looked towards Paris. Furthermore, one of her eyes was a bit too close to the other. Besides these, there were no other faults in her appearance.

When Momoko went to the restroom, and there were still no customers, Shizu-chan found her chance to speak. 'Mama-san,' she began.

Mama-san, in a low, yet sharp voice, said firmly, 'Shizu-chan, the subject of her eyes is taboo.' Since Shizu-chan was also a nice girl, she accepted this immediately. Something deep within moved her to tears.

Perhaps because there was one more person in the bar than before, thus making it more lively, many customers turned up that night. The regular customers quickly took notice of Momoko. But since, unlike Eiko, she stood further behind the counter than Mama-san and was occupied with diligently opening and closing the refrigerator door, they couldn't talk to her very much.

Very few customers came to this bar simply for the barmaids, however, so no one was very dissatisfied with her behaviour. The Tomoshibi remained completely the same as it had been. The customers quietly tipped their drinks, and when once in a while they did say something, Mama-san would take up the conversation, with Shizu-chan in her carefree and easy-going manner joining in.

One customer did find something different from before. This man, who had been chugging his beer, returned from the restroom with a strange expression on his face and asked, 'What happened to the mirror?'

'Oh, someone broke it,' answered Mama-san.

'You must have had some rough customers!'

'We can get a new mirror, but it might be broken again. Besides, we really ought to be able to put up with the inconvenience.'

Probably only Shizu-chan noticed that Mama-san, upon realizing the source of Momoko's inferiority complex, had taken her in only after removing the mirror from the restroom.

'Anyway, our customers aren't the type that have to feel guilty when they look at their drunken faces in the mirror,' Mama-san said in her mellow voice.

'Right! That's right!'

This cheered the customers; there was no chance of them being put out by it. Although the type of customer who got drunk and became boisterous rarely came to the Tomoshibi, there were, among the regular customers, some young men who liked to sing quiet songs. However, once they started to get tipsy, they demanded that Mama-san and the girls sing too. Mama-san would say, 'No, I can't because I'm tone deaf,' and escape, refusing to sing under any circumstances. If one flattered Shizu-chan though, telling her that she was good, she would sing a number of songs in her melodious voice. Since she made every popular song come out like an elementary school tune, her specialty had become nursery songs. Everyone was impressed by her specialty. Her singing was popular probably because it was most appropriate for the atmosphere of the bar. She could certainly not have been called very talented.

'Mama-san, wasn't Eiko-chan pretty good, too? Wasn't she?' With his eyes half closed as if trying to remember, a customer asked, 'Didn't she go away to get married? Is she happy?'

'Yes, yes, she's very happy.'

Shizu-chan began to sing:

When she was fifteen Nanny got married
Letters from home
No longer came.

'In this present age, what do you think we lack the most and need the most?'

In one corner of the room there were customers discussing serious topics while drinking their whiskey.

'Hmmm, let's see ... how about dreams? As far as I'm concerned, right now that's what I lack the most and need the most.'

'Well, I agree, but I don't call them "dreams".'

'Then what are they?'

'Fairy tales.'

'Hmm, fairy tales. I guess you're right.'

While that conversation was going on, Shizu-chan was singing away in front of customers in another corner.

'Well, what do you think about being able to listen to nursery rhymes in a Ginza bar?'

'Now I'm beginning to understand why you said you wanted to come here.'

Sometimes a dreadfully tone-deaf person in high spirits would sing along with Shizu-chan.

After four or five days, Momoko was in a state of total astonishment. She wondered if this, too, could possibly be a bar.

Some types of people aren't affected by hardships; Momoko was the type who wasn't affected by past experiences. Even though this was the fourth time she had found herself employed in a bar, she possessed naive qualities which made it seem as if she had only worked in a bar for the first time yesterday. Shizu-chan began to act as if she were Momoko's elder sister all the time, and on occasions when Mama-san wasn't present, she would ask, 'Well, do you think you'll be able to handle working here?' and peer into Momoko's face.

'Yes, I look forward to coming to work. And also, it almost seems like this isn't a bar, but some other kind of place.'

'Well, if it's not a bar, what is it?'

'A kindergarten!'

Shizu-chan almost fell out of her chair, laughing. Before very long, Mama-san returned and Shizu-chan presented her with this masterpiece. Mama-san was reminded of the fact that the Chagalls and the Mini, all hanging on the wall, were also childlike. Even the small, low chair in the corner was appropriate for a kindergarten, she thought.

Around Christmas and at the end of the year, the Tomoshibi was not affected by irregular waves of customers. Just as there were never times when the bar was full and customers couldn't come in, so there was never a day when there were absolutely no customers. Momoko was most grateful for the fact that she wasn't compelled to wear a fancy kimono just because it was Christmas or New Year's.

Mama-san casually wore lovely, unobtrusive things, but she did not force her pleasure in clothes on other people.

'Happy New Year!'

'We value your patronage and hope to see you again this year.'

Early in the new year, one customer dashed in as soon as they opened the bar, crying, 'Happy New Year!' Mama-san politely repeated her New Year's greetings, and without waiting for any prompting from him, asked, 'Well?'

'They were born!'

'Well, that is an auspicious event indeed! How many of them?'

As usual, they were discussing dogs.

'Six ... I went out of my way to make sure that only purebreds got to her, but I failed again. Half of them are spotted. Even their faces are quite different from their mother's.'

'That's probably the after effects of a previous mate.'

'I've heard that's so ... once you've made a mistake, you can't breed purebreds.'

'But aren't the puppies cute?'

'Cute things are cute, even if they're mutts. There are too many of them, but I can't bring myself to give them away. My son also says that they're his children and loves them very much. It's a nice feeling.'

As they spoke, another person who shared their interest wandered in, and leaning forward, commented, 'Even though you may think they're mongrels, sometimes it happens that while you're rearing them, they become purebreds, just like one of their parents.'

'Isn't that a miracle!'

'A miracle, indeed. In my experience, this is where the owner's character plays a great part!'

'I see ...'

'Yes, it's really true. Was it in Aesop that the ugly duckling becomes a white swan?'

'Wasn't that Hans Christian Andersen?'

'Whichever! In any case, things like that happen.'

'So then, will you try to raise all six of them? A miracle might happen to at least one.'

For a while after that, miracles were the topic of conversation. After those customers had gone their merry ways, and before the next wave of customers arrived, Momoko said, 'Mama-san, miracles really do happen, don't they?' She started to speak very seriously.

When Shizu-chan asked, 'Have you ever seen one?' Momoko nodded in assent, saying, 'My eyes are getting better!'

Momoko continued in front of her two listeners who were holding their breath.

'From when I was small, I was always teased about my eyes. As I got older, it was even harder to bear, and I was always crying. Since I could make better money in a bar than at other jobs, I was able to help my family, but the customers always mentioned my eyes. It was really painful.'

Looking up suddenly, Momoko's eyes lost the correct balance between right and left, and one side inclined outwards.

'Ever since I came to this bar, nobody has commented on my eyes. In the beginning, I thought that you were purposely avoiding the subject. But even the customers didn't say anything. When I came to think of it, nobody seemed to even notice my eyes. On New Year's Day, I went to the mirror and was almost too scared to look—until then, I had always disliked large mirrors and had used a compact to do my make-up. Then, well, miraculously, my eyes were cured! I don't know why they got better, but I think that miracles do happen after all.'

Mama-san, who had been listening attentively to Momoko's story, said, 'Really? How wonderful!' She spoke with great feeling, placing her hand on Momoko's shoulder. Shizu-chan looked as if she were going to cry if she spoke, so she quickly turned her back to Momoko and said in a deliberately dry tone, 'How wonderful!'

To the two of them, it did not seem as if the miracle Momoko had spoken about had taken place, but if that was what Momoko believed, then a miracle had definitely occurred.

'Hello there!'

Once again familiar customers were coming through the door. 'Welcome! Happy New Year!' Momoko greeted them cheerfully.

Translated by Keiko Nakamura

Japan

The Silent Traders

TSUSHIMA YŪKO

There was a cat in the wood. Not such an odd thing, really: wildcats, pumas and lions all come from the same family and even a tabby shouldn't be out of place. But the sight was unsettling. What was the creature doing there? When I say 'wood', I'm talking about Rikugien, an Edo-period landscape garden in my neighbourhood. Perhaps 'wood' isn't quite the right word, but the old park's trees—relics of the past amid the city's modern buildings—are so overgrown that the pathways skirting its walls are dark and forbidding even by day. It does give the impression of a wood; there's no other word for it. And the cat, I should explain, didn't look wild. It was just a kitten, two or three months old, white with black patches. It didn't look at all ferocious—in fact it was a dear little thing. There was nothing to fear. And yet I was taken aback, and I tensed as the kitten bristled and glared in my direction.

The kitten was hiding in a thicket beside the pond, where my ten-year-old daughter was the first to spot it. By the time I'd made out the elusive shape and exclaimed 'Oh, you're right!' she was off calling at the top of her voice: 'There's another! And here's one over here!' My other child, a boy of five, was still hunting for the first kitten, and as his sister went on making one discovery after another, he stamped his feet and wailed 'Where? Where is it?' His sister beckoned him to bend down and showed him triumphantly where to find the first cat. Several passersby, hearing my daughter's shouts, had also been drawn into the search. There were many strollers in the park that Sunday evening. The cats were everywhere, each concealed in its own clump of bushes. Their eyes followed people's feet on the gravelled walk, and at the slightest move toward a hiding place the cat would scamper away. Looking down from an adult's height it was hard enough to detect them at all, let alone keep count, and this gave the impression of great numbers.

I could hear my younger child crying. He had disappeared while my back was turned. As I looked wildly around, my daughter pointed him out with a chuckle: 'See where he's got to!' There he was, huddled tearfully in the spot where the first kitten had been. He'd burst in eagerly, but succeeded only in driving away the kitten and trapping himself in the thicket.

'What do you think you're doing? It'll never let you catch it.' Squatting down, my daughter was calling through the bushes. 'Come on out, silly!'

His sister's tone of amusement was no help to the boy at all. He was terrified in his cobwebbed cage of low-hanging branches where no light penetrated.

'That's no use. You go in and fetch him out.' I gave her shoulder a push.

'He got himself in,' she grumbled, 'so why can't he get out?' All the same, she set about searching for an opening. Crouching, I watched the boy through the thick foliage and waited for her to reach him.

'How'd he ever get in there? He's really stuck,' she muttered as she circled the bushes uncertainly, but a moment later she'd broken through to him, forcing a way with both hands.

When they rejoined me, they had dead leaves and twigs snagged all over them.

After an attempt of her own to pick one up, my daughter understood that life in the park had made these tiny kittens quicker than ordinary strays and too wary to let anyone pet them. Explaining this to her brother, she looked to me for agreement. 'They were born here, weren't they? They belong here, don't they? Then I wonder if their mother's here too?'

The children scanned the surrounding trees once again.

'She may be,' I said, 'but she'd stay out of sight, wouldn't she? Only the kittens wander about in the open. Their mother's got more sense. I'll bet she's up that tree or some place like that where nobody can get at her. She's probably watching us right now.'

I cast an eye at the treetops as I spoke—and the thought of the unseen mother cat gave me an uncomfortable feeling. Whether these were alley cats that had moved into the park or discarded pets that had survived and bred, they could go on multiplying in the wood—which at night was empty of people—and be perfectly at home.

❋

It is exactly twenty-five years since my mother came to live near Rikugien with her three children, of which I was the youngest at ten. She told us the park's history, and not long after our arrival we went inside to see the garden. In spite of its being on our doorstep we quickly lost interest, however, since the grounds were surrounded by a six-foot brick wall with a single gate on the far side from our house. A Japanese garden was not much fun for children anyway, and we never went again as a family. I was reminded that we lived near a park, though, because of the many birds—the blue magpies, Eastern turtledoves, and tits—that I would see on the rooftops and in trees. And in summer I'd hear the singing of evening cicadas. To a city child like me, evening cicadas and blue magpies were a novelty.

I visited Rikugien with several classmates when we were about to leave elementary school, and someone hit on the idea of making a kind of time capsule. We'd leave it buried for ten years—or was it twenty? I've also forgotten what we wrote on the piece of paper that we stuffed into a small bottle and buried at the foot of a pine on the highest ground in the garden. I expect it's still there as I haven't heard of it since, and now whenever I'm in Rikugien, I keep an eye out for the landmark, but I'm only guessing. We were confident of knowing exactly where to look in years to come, and if I can remember that so clearly it's puzzling that I can't recognize the tree. I'm not about to dig any holes to check, however—not with my own children watching. The friends who left this sentimental reminder were soon to part, bound for different schools. Since then, of course, we've ceased to think of one another, and I'm not so sure now that the bottle episode ever happened.

The following February, my brother (who was close to my own age) died quite suddenly of pneumonia. Then in April my sister went to college and, not wanting to be left out, I pursued her new interests myself: I listened to jazz, went to movies, and was friendly towards college and high school students of the opposite sex. An older girl introduced me to a boy from senior high and we made up a foursome for an outing to the park—the only time I got all dressed up for Rikugien. I was no beauty, though, nor the popular type, and while the others were having fun, I stayed stiff and awkward, and was bored. I would have liked to be as genuinely impressed as they were, viewing the landscape garden for the first time, but I couldn't work up an interest after seeing the trees over the brick wall every day. By that time we'd been in the district for three years, and the name 'Rikugien' brought to mind not the tidy, sunlit lawns seen by visitors, but the dark tangles along the walls.

My desire for friends of the opposite sex was short lived. Boys couldn't provide what I wanted, and what boys wanted had nothing to do with me.

While I was in high school, one day our ancient spitz died. The house remained without a dog for a while, until Mother was finally prompted to replace him when my sister's marriage, soon after her graduation, left just the two of us in an unprotected home. She found someone who let her have a terrier puppy. She bought a brush and comb and began rearing the pup with the best of care, explaining that it came from a clever hunting breed. As it grew, however, it failed to display the expected intelligence and still behaved like a puppy after six months; and besides, it was timid. What it did have was energy as, yapping shrilly, it frisked about the house all day long. It may have been useless but it was a funny little fellow. Its presence made all the difference to me in my intense boredom at home. After my brother's death, my mother (a widow since I was a baby) passed her days as if at a wake. We saw each other only at mealtimes, and then we seldom spoke. In high school a fondness for the movies was about the worst I could have been accused of, but Mother had no patience with such frivolity and would snap angrily at me from time to time. 'I'm leaving home when I turn eighteen,' I'd retort. I meant it, too.

It was at that time that we had the very sociable dog. I suppose I'd spoiled it as a puppy, for now it was always wanting to be let in, and when I slid open the glass door it would bounce like a rubber ball right into my arms and lick my face ecstatically.

Mother, however, was dissatisfied. She'd had enough of the barking; it got on her nerves. Then came a day when the dog went missing. I thought it must have got out of the yard. Two or three days passed and it didn't return—it hadn't the wit to find the way home once it strayed. I wondered if I should contact the pound. Concern finally drove me to break our usual silence and ask Mother: 'About the dog . . .' 'Oh, the dog?' she replied. 'I threw it over the wall of Rikugien the other day.'

I was shocked—I'd never heard of disposing of a dog like that. I wasn't able to protest, though. I didn't rush out to comb the park, either. She could have had it destroyed, yet instead she'd taken it to the foot of the brick wall, lifted it in her arms, and heaved it over. It wasn't large, only about a foot long, and thus not too much of a handful even for Mother.

Finding itself tossed into the wood, the dog wouldn't have crept quietly into hiding. It must have raced through the area barking furiously, only to be caught at once by the caretaker. Would the next stop be the pound? But there seemed to me just a chance that it hadn't turned out that way. I could imagine the wood by daylight, more or less: there'd be a lot of birds and insects, and little else. The pond would be inhabited by a few carp, turtles and catfish. But what transformations took place at night? As I didn't dare stay beyond closing time to see for myself, I wondered if anyone could tell of a night spent in the park till the gates opened in the morning. There might be goings-on unfamiliar to those of day. Mightn't a dog entering that world live on, not as a dog but as something else?

I had to be thankful that the dog's fate left that much to the imagination.

From then on I turned my back on Rikugien more firmly than ever. I was afraid of the deep wood, so out of keeping with the city: it was the domain of the dog abandoned by my mother.

In due course I left home, a little later than I'd promised. After a good many more years I moved back to Mother's neighbourhood—back to the vicinity of the park—with a little daughter and a baby. Like my own mother, I was one who couldn't give my children the experience of a father. That remained the one thing I regretted. Living in a cramped apartment, I now appreciated the Rikugien wood for its greenery and open spaces. I began to take the children there occasionally. Several times, we too released pet turtles or goldfish in the pond. Many nearby families who'd run out of room for aquarium creatures in their overcrowded apartments would slip them into the pond to spend the rest of their lives at liberty.

Rocks rose from the water here and there, and each was studded with turtles sunning themselves. They couldn't have bred naturally in such numbers. They must have been the tiny turtles sold at fairground stalls and pet shops, grown up without a care in the world. More of them lined the water's edge at one's feet. No doubt there were other animals on the increase—goldfish, loaches, and the like. Multistoreyed apartment buildings were going up around the wood in quick succession, and more living things were brought down from their rooms each year. Cats were one animal I'd overlooked, though. If tipping out turtles was common practice, there was no reason why cats shouldn't be dumped here, and dogs too. No type of pet could be ruled out. But to become established in any numbers they'd have to escape the caretaker's notice and hold their own against the wood's other hardy inhabitants. Thus there'd be a limit to survivors: cats and reptiles, I'd say.

Once I knew about the cat population, I remembered the dog my mother had thrown away, and I also remembered my old fear of the wood. I couldn't help wondering how the cats got along from day to day.

Perhaps they relied on food left behind by visitors—but all of the park's trash baskets were fitted with mesh covers to keep out the crows, whose numbers were also growing. For all their nimbleness, even cats would have trouble picking out the scraps. Lizards and mice were edible enough. But on the other side of the wall lay the city and its garbage. After dark the cats would go out foraging on the streets.

Then, too, there was the row of apartment towers along one side of the wood, facing the main road. All had balconies that overlooked the park. The climb would be quick work for a cat, and if its favourite food were left outside a door it would soon come back regularly. Something told me there must be people who put out food: there'd be elderly tenants and women living alone. Even children. Children captivated by a secret friendship with a cat.

I don't find anything odd about such a relationship—perhaps because it occurs so often in fairy stories. But to make it worth their while the apartment children would have to receive something from the cat; otherwise they wouldn't keep it up. There are tales of mountain men and villagers who traded a year's haul of linden bark for a gallon and a half of rice in hard cakes. No villager could deal openly with the lone mountain men; so great was their fear of each other that, in fact, they avoided coming face to face. Yet when a bargain was struck, it could not have been done more skilfully. The trading was over in a flash, before either man had time to catch sight of the other or hear his voice. I think everyone wishes privately that bargains could be made like that. Though there would always be the fear of attack, or discovery by one's own side.

Supposing it were my own children: what could they be getting in return? They'd have no use for a year's stock of linden bark. Toys, then, or cakes. I'm sure they want all sorts of things, but not a means of support like linden bark. What, then? Something not readily available to them; something the cat has in abundance and to spare.

The children leave food on the balcony. And in return the cat provides them with a father. How's that for a bargain? Once a year, male cats procreate; in other words, they become fathers. They become fathers ad nauseam. But these fathers don't care how many children they have—they don't even notice that they are fathers. Yet the existence of offspring makes them so. Fathers who don't know their own children. Among humans, it seems there's an understanding that a man only becomes a father when he recognizes the child as his own; but that's a very narrow view. Why do we allow the male to divide children arbitrarily into two kinds, recognized and unrecognized? Wouldn't it be enough for the child to choose a father when necessary from among suitable males? If the children decide that the tom that climbs up to their balcony is their father, it shouldn't cause him any inconvenience. A father looks in on two of his children from the balcony every night. The two human children faithfully leave out food to make it so. He comes late, when they are fast asleep, and they never see him or hear his cries. It's enough that they know in the morning that he's been. In their dreams, the children are hugged to their cat-father's breast.

*

We'd seen the children's human father six months earlier, and together we'd gone to a transport museum they wanted to visit. This came about only after many appeals from me. If the man who was their father was alive and well on this earth, I wanted the children to know what he looked like. To me, the man was unforgettable: I was once preoccupied with him, obsessed with the desire to be where he was; nothing had changed when I tried having a child, and I'd had the second with him cursing me. To the children, however, especially the younger one, he was a mere shadow in a photograph that never moved or spoke. As the younger child turned three, then four, I couldn't help being aware of that fact. This was the same state that I'd known myself, for my own father had died. If he were dead it couldn't be helped. But as long as he was alive I wanted them to have a memory of their father as a living, breathing person whose eyes moved, whose mouth moved and spoke.

On the day, he was an hour late for our appointment. The long wait in a coffee shop had made the children tired and cross, but when they saw the man a shy silence came over them. 'Thanks for coming,' I said with a smile. I couldn't think what to say next. He asked 'Where to?' and stood to leave at once. He walked alone, while the children and I looked as though it was all the same to us whether he was there or not. On the train I still hadn't come up with anything to say. The children kept their distance from the man and stared nonchalantly out of the window. We got off the train like that, and again he walked ahead.

The transport museum had an actual bullet train car, steam locomotives, airplanes and giant panoramic layouts. I remembered enjoying a class trip there while at school myself. My children, too, dashed excitedly around the exhibits without a moment's pause for breath. It was: 'Next I want to have a go on that train,' 'Now I want to work that model.' They must have had a good two hours of fun. In the meantime we lost sight of the man. Wherever he'd been, he showed up again when we'd finished our tour and arrived back at the entrance. 'What'll we do?' he asked, and I suggested giving the children a drink and sitting down somewhere. He nodded and went ahead to look for a place near the museum. The children were clinging to me as before. He entered a coffee shop that had a cake counter and I followed with them. We sat down, the three of us facing the man. Neither child showed the slightest inclination to sit beside him. They had orange drinks.

I was becoming desperate for something to say. And weren't there one or two things he'd like to ask me? Such as how the children had been lately. But to bring that up, unasked, might imply that I wanted him to watch with me as they grew. I'd only been able to ask for this meeting because I'd finally stopped feeling that way. Now it seemed we couldn't even exchange such polite remarks as 'They've grown' or 'I'm glad they're well' without arousing needless suspicions. It wasn't supposed to be like this, I thought in confusion, unable to say a word about the children. He was indeed their father, but not a father who watched over them. As far as he was concerned the only children he had were the two borne by his wife. Agreeing to see mine was simply a favour on his part, for which I could only be grateful.

If we couldn't discuss the children, there was literally nothing left to say. We didn't have the kind of memories we could reminisce over; I wished I could forget the things we'd done as if it had all been a dream, for it was the pain that we remembered. Inquiring after his family would be no better. His work seemed the safest subject, yet if I didn't want to stay in touch I had to think twice about this, too.

The man and I listened absently as the children entertained themselves.

On the way out the man bought a cake which he handed to the older child, and then he was gone. The children appeared relieved, and with the cake to look forward to they were eager to get home. Neither had held the man's hand or spoken to him. I wanted to tell them that there was still time to run after him and touch some part of his body, but of course they wouldn't have done it.

I don't know when there will be another opportunity for the children to see the man. They may never meet him again, or they may have a chance two or three years from now. I do know that the man and I will probably never be completely indifferent to each other. He's still on my mind in some obscure way. Yet there's no point in confirming this feeling in words. Silence is essential. As long as we maintain silence, and thus avoid trespassing, we leave open the possibility of resuming negotiations at any time.

I believe the system of bartering used by the mountain men and the villagers was called 'silent trade'. I am coming to understand that there was nothing extraordinary in striking such a silent bargain for survival. People trying to survive—myself, my mother, and my children, for example—can take some comfort in living beside a wood. We tip various things in there and tell ourselves that we haven't thrown them away, we've set them free in another world, and then we picture the unknown woodland to ourselves and shudder with fear or sigh fondly. Meanwhile the creatures multiplying there gaze stealthily at the human world outside; at least I've yet to hear of anything attacking from the wood.

Some sort of silent trade is taking place between the two sides. Perhaps my children really have begun dealings with a cat who lives in the wood.

Translated by Geraldine Harcourt

Japan

Boxcar of Chrysanthemums

ENCHI FUMIKO

It must have been seven or eight years ago, since the highway wasn't as good as it is now, and travelling by car wasn't easy.

I was still staying in my summer house in Karuizawa even though it was mid-September. One day a women's group in the nearby town of Ueda asked me to give a talk. I've forgotten what kind of group they were, but I left my house in the late afternoon and spoke to the audience right after dinner, for less than an hour. If my memory is correct, it was a little after nine when I got on a train to go home.

It was too late for the express train that ran during the summer, but I heard there was a local that went as far as Karuizawa, and I decided to take it since I wanted very much to return home that night. There was no second class (in those days seats were divided into second and third class); the third-class cars were old and looked to be of pre-war vintage. There were only a few passengers.

Although I said, 'How nice, it's not crowded,' to the people who came to see me off, I realized after the train started to move how uncomfortable it is to ride on an old train that makes squeaky noises every time it sways, and that has dirty, frayed, green velveteen upholstery.

Well, even if this is a local I'll be in Karuizawa in two hours or so for sure, I said to myself as I turned to look out the window. The moon was nearly full and boldly silhouetted in dark blue lay the low mountains beyond the fields beside the tracks. The plants in the rice paddies were ripe, so of course I couldn't see the moon reflecting on the water in the fields. Plastic bird rattles here and there glittered strangely as they reflected the moonlight. The clear dark blue of the sky and the coolness of the evening air stealing into the deserted car made me realize keenly that I was in the mountain region of Shinshu, where fall comes early.

I was thinking that I wanted to get home quickly when the train shuddered to a stop at a small station. We had been moving for no more than ten minutes. I couldn't complain about the stop since the train wasn't an express, but it didn't start up for a long time even though no one was getting on or off. It finally moved but then stopped again at the next station, took its time and wouldn't start again, as it had done before.

The four or five passengers in my car were all middle-aged men who looked as though they could be farmers from the area. There was no one sitting near me, and I didn't feel like standing up to go and ask about the delay. I looked out the window and saw several freight cars attached to the rear of the car I was in. It seemed that the cars were being loaded with something.

I realized then that this was a freight train for transporting cargo to Karuizawa that also happened to carry a few passengers. If I had known this earlier, I would have taken the local express that left an hour before, even if I had had to rush to catch it. But it was too late for regrets; I told myself it would do no good to get off at an unfamiliar station late at night and resigned myself to the situation. The train would get me to Karuizawa sometime that night, no matter what; with that thought in mind, I felt calmer.

I took a paperback book from my bag and tried to read, but the squeaking noise of the car made it difficult to concentrate. I was tired, but I couldn't sleep because of the chilly air that crept up my legs and also because of my exasperation with a train that stopped so often.

When the train stopped for the fourth time at a fairly large station, I got off to ease my irritation. It would probably stop for ten minutes or so, and even if it started suddenly I thought I could easily jump on such a slow-moving train.

A few passengers got off. Some long packages wrapped in straw matting were piled up near one of the back cars, and the station attendants were loading them into the car as if they were in no big hurry. The packages were all about the same size, bulging at the centre like fish wrapped in reed mats, but the station attendants were lifting them carefully in both hands, as if they were handling something valuable, and loading them into the soot-covered car.

I was watching the scene and wondering what the packages were when I suddenly noticed a moist, plant-like smell floating in from somewhere. Then I heard a woman's voice ask hesitantly, 'Have you already loaded ours?'

I turned toward the voice. A middle-aged woman with her hair pulled into a bun was standing behind me. She wasn't alone; beside her was an old man with white hair and sunken cheeks. The moment I saw the pupils of his eyes with their strangely shifting gaze, and his slightly gaping mouth with its two long buck teeth and fine white froth at the corners, I was so startled that I stepped back a few paces.

'The Ichiges,' one of the station attendants said to another, motioning with his eyes, and then he turned to the old man. 'Yes, I loaded them. I put them in the best spot. They'll be in Tokyo tomorrow and will be the best flowers at the flower market,' he said, speaking to the man as if he were a child. The old man nodded with a dignified air.

'Oh, that's nice, isn't it? Now you don't have to worry. Well, let's go home and go to bed,' the woman said, also as if she were humouring a child, and patted the old man's shoulder, which looked as stiff as a scarecrow's.

The old man stood there and said nothing. Meanwhile the packages were being loaded one after another, and by then I realized that the fragrance in the air was coming from them.

'Oh, that one over there! Those are our mums!' the old man yelled suddenly, extending his arms as if he were swimming toward the package the station attendant was about to load on the train. The old man's little nose was twitching like a dog's. 'That smell ... It's the Shiratama mum.'

'Is it? Well, then, we'll ask them to let you smell them. The train's leaving soon, so you only smell once, all right?' the woman said and gave the station attendant a meaningful look. He put down the package the old man was trying to press his nose against and loaded another one first.

'That's enough now. You said good-bye to Shiratama, didn't you?' The woman spoke as if she were talking to a small child and put her arm around the stooping old man. She then took his hand and placed it gently on her lips. The old man let go of the package as if he were under a spell and stood up with his wife.

The door of the freight car finally closed, and the starting signal sounded. I got on the train in a hurry but didn't know quite what to make of the strange scene I had just witnessed. I couldn't believe that what I'd seen wasn't an illusion, like a scene from a movie.

'I feel sorry for them. Living on into old age like that.'

I turned around. A middle-aged man in a gray jacket was sitting across the aisle from me. His face was dark and wrinkled from the sun, but he didn't look unpleasant. I realized that he hadn't been on the train before we stopped at the last station.

'That man—is he mentally ill?' I asked, unable to suppress my curiosity.

'Not mentally ill, more like an idiot. I think the term they use nowadays is "mentally retarded".' The man spoke without using any dialect. 'The old man himself doesn't understand a thing, so he's okay, but I feel sorry for his wife. She's been married to that man for over twenty years now. If he'd been born into a poor family, marriage would have been out of the question, but simply because his family was wealthy, all kinds of cruel things happened.' Not only did the man speak without an accent, but his manner of speaking was smooth and pleasant. The name Ichige that the station attendant had mentioned turned my consciousness to some troublesome, submerged memory, but instead of mentioning this, I said, 'Were those chrysanthemums they were loading in that boxcar? That old man was smelling them, wasn't he?'

'Yes, those were the chrysanthemums they grow in their garden. Mums are the only thing the old man cares much about. When they send some off he comes with his wife to watch, whether it's late at night or early in the morning.'

'Then all of the packages are chrysanthemums?' 'That's right. Most of the flowers that go to Tokyo at this time of year are. Lots of farmers around here grow flowers, but they're all sold in Tokyo, so it's a big deal. Not only flowers, either. The people who work in the mountains around here collect tree roots, branches and other stuff, put prices on them and send them to Tokyo. Once they get them to the market they can sell them, I guess, because money is always sent back. Tokyo's a good customer that lets the landowners around here earn money that way.'

'I see. I was wondering why we were stopping so often to load things. It's a mistake for people to take this train,' I said, smiling.

'You're right. It takes a good three hours to get to Karuizawa on this train.'

'Oh, that's awful! No one told me that at Ueda when I got on.' 'I don't think the people around here know that there's a train running at this hour that carries mums. Well, you might as well just get used to it and consider it an elegant way to travel.'

My family would worry if I got to Karuizawa after midnight, but as the saying goes, there's nothing you can do once you're on board; even if no one had told me that I'd have to resign myself to the situation, I had no choice but to do so.

And so our conversation returned to the couple who grew chrysanthemums. The man across from me, whose name was Kurokawa, said he used to teach at an agricultural institute in Tokyo, but after he was evacuated to this region during the war he bought an orchard and settled down. He made extra income by collecting alpine plants, something he liked very much. He was taking this train because he had decided on an impulse to go to the town of Komoro and then climb Mt. Asama early the next morning.

❋

It was the year after the end of the war when Kurokawa learned about Ichige Masutoshi and Rie.

Luckily Kurokawa didn't have to leave the country to do his military service, so as soon as the war was over he went to a village where his family had been evacuated. The village wasn't far from where he was born, and since he had never been particularly fond of city life and had also been hit hard by the war, he decided to settle there. At first he taught at a middle school in a nearby town. It was quite a while later that he bought an orchard and began to grow grapes and apples for a livelihood.

Food was scarce for most people in those days. No one grew fruit or flowers; everyone was busy growing potatoes and corn on the plots of land that weren't suitable for rice paddies. Kurokawa's father was still alive and healthy then and worked hard with his wife and daughter-in-law to grow vegetables. After living there for a while, Kurokawa noticed a new Tokyo-style house on a fairly large piece of land not far from his house. On his way back from school he often saw a woman in her thirties busily working in the garden behind the house. She wore a kerchief over her head and work pants, but her fair, unburned complexion and fine features had a calm sadness that reminded him of classic Korean beauties.

'That house is built in a different style from the others around here. Was it built during the war?' Kurokawa asked his father one evening during supper.

'That one? That's the house Ichige from Tokyo built during the war.' His father, born and raised in that region, said this as if his son would know who Mr Ichige was even if he didn't explain.

'Who's Ichige?'

'Ichige? He's the owner of a big paper company in Tokyo. I heard that he went bankrupt after the war. His father was the famous Ichige Tokuichi.'

'Oh, I see.' Kurokawa finally remembered the name. 'But he's been dead for a long time, hasn't he?' Kurokawa had heard of Ichige Tokuichi of the Shinshu region, one of the success stories of the Meiji era.

'Right. Tokuichi was the father of Hanshiro, who was also known as a fine man. Hanshiro built the house, but his only son, Masatoshi, and his wife live there now.'

With this as a beginning, Kurokawa's father then continued: Masatoshi was Ichige's legitimate heir, but he had contracted meningitis as a child, and although he was not actually an idiot, he was capable of only a few simple words. When he reached adulthood, however, it was decided that he should have a wife. Rie, who had come from the city of Iida to work as one of the Ichige's servants, was chosen as the human sacrifice.

'That's ridiculous, like a feudal lord and his serf. There's something wrong with any woman who would go along with it, too,' Kurokawa snapped, but secretly he couldn't comprehend how the ladylike woman he saw when he passed the back of Ichige's house each morning and evening could be so lacking in expression and yet also give an impression of innocence and purity.

'That's what everyone says at first. When I heard the story, I despised the woman for agreeing to marry a man like that, no matter how much money was involved. But you know, after we came here that house was built nearby, and so I've seen a lot of Rie. She always showed up for volunteer work days and air raid drills, and ever since I was head of the volunteer guards I've known her well. Your dead mother and your wife Matsuko would agree that there's nothing wrong with Rie. She works harder than anyone else and doesn't put on the airs of a rich person. The catty local women used to sit around and drink tea and make fun of the Tokyo women who were evacuated here, but they stopped at Rie. They agreed that she took good care of that idiot husband of hers and only pitied her.

'It was like that for two or three years, and then before the war ended Hanshiro died of a stroke. His mother and son-in-law were careless and used up what money there was. They say only that house is left. In these times when there isn't much food, Rie has a hard time finding enough potatoes and flour to feed that glutton of a husband. She knits things for the farmers and sews clothes for their kids. You can't do that much for others if you're a fake and just trying to make a good impression. Sometimes I even wonder if she's a reincarnation of Kannon* ...'

Kurokawa's father spoke earnestly. He seemed to believe what he was saying. He was the kind of old-fashioned man who would want to believe that a person like Rie was a Kannon, or at least her reincarnation; at the war's end and in the years that followed he had seen whatever trappings human beings find to wrap themselves up in cruelly pulled off to reveal their naked, shameful parts.

Kurokawa certainly understood his father's feeling. He realized that he too wanted to purify his image of Rie and think of her as a reincarnated Kannon. Rie had lived up to the expectations of Kurokawa's father and had continued to be a devoted wife for more than ten years. She had converted most of Ichige's land into apple orchards and supported her husband and herself with this income.

---

* Kannon is the Buddhist Goddess of Mercy.

Growing chrysanthemums was partially for income but partially because Masatoshi enjoyed looking at flowers. Kurokawa said there didn't seem to be much money in it.

'It was two years ago, I think. Rie won some kind of prize. Hmm, what was it called? It was to commend her for having devoted herself to her mentally retarded husband for so many years; you might say for being the model of the faithful wife. In any case, it's a rare thing these days, and I think she deserved the praise.'

While I listened to Kurokawa's long story, the train kept stopping at every station, and it looked as though chrysanthemums wrapped in straw mats were being loaded into the freight cars.

Between Komoro and Oiwake the train picked up speed. The moon seemed to be high in the middle of the sky; I couldn't see it from the train window, but the rays of moonlight had become brighter, and they shone upon the scene along the tracks with the coppery glow of an old mirror. This copper colour changed to the smoky silver of mica when we reached a plateau and a mist settled onto the ground. After Kurokawa got off at Komoro, the only passengers left were a pair of men sitting near the far entrance to the car. Since it was late at night when we reached the high land, a chill that was enough to shrivel me crept up from the tips of my socks as I sat there and quickly permeated my lower body.

I didn't actually mind the chill, even though I shrugged my shoulders now and then and pressed my knees together tightly, shivering. I was too absorbed in adding some facts from my own memory to the story that Kurokawa had told me about Ichige Masatoshi and his wife.

When I heard the names Ichige Tokuichi and Hanshiro, I was reminded of the story I had almost forgotten about the retarded son of the Ichiges. I had barely stopped myself from saying to Kurokawa, 'Yes, of course, I've heard about him too.'

I happened to have heard about the marriage between Masatoshi and Rie just about the time it took place. It was a year or so after the outbreak of the China Incident, when the image of the red draft notice calling soldiers to the army burned like fire in young men's minds. I had a friend whose husband was a psychiatrist, and although he practised primarily in one of the private hospitals, he spent a few days a week at the Brain Research Institute of S Medical School. Interns and volunteer assistants who worked at this Institute often gathered at my friend Nagase's house to talk. I became acquainted with this group in the course of writing a play that dealt with a mental patient; I visited the hospital to ask the doctors questions about their experiences. One day when I met with three or four of these young doctors at Nagase's house, I noticed that Kashimura, who had always been with the group, was missing.

'Where is Dr Kashimura? Is he on duty tonight?' I asked. The young doctors looked at each other and laughed before saying things like, 'I guess you could call it "duty" ' or 'He sure is on duty,' or 'It's some duty.'

I thought he might have gone to see a lover, and so I kept quiet, but then Nagase interrupted and said, 'It's all right to tell her. It might be helpful to her.'

'It's not a very respectable story, though.'

'But a job's a job. Maybe she'll write a story about how we have to do this kind of work to support ourselves.'

One of them sat up straight and said, 'Kashimura is on night duty tonight at the home of one of the patients.'

'I see. Does the patient get violent?' I asked without hesitation, since such cases are common among psychiatric patients.

'Yes, you couldn't say he *doesn't* get violent, but it's a tricky point.' The young man who spoke, Tomoda, looked at another and said, 'How was it when you were there?'

'Nothing happened, fortunately. You always had bad luck, didn't you?'

Tomoda nodded. 'Yeah, my luck is bad. I'll probably die first if I go to war.'

'I don't agree. You got a chance to see things you can't usually see. A voyeur would even pay for the chance.'

'Idiot! Who said I'm a voyeur?'

'If everybody talked like that, no one would understand. I'll tell the true story in a scientific way without any interpretation,' Nagase said, and he then told me the story of Ichige Masatoshi's marriage. Of course he didn't mention the name, but I learned of it quite a while later.

When Masatoshi reached physical maturity, his father consulted with a professor of psychiatry because he was troubled about how to find a partner to meet his son's sexual needs.

'The best way would be to provide him with one woman who would be kind to him. You should disregard her family background and her appearance and find someone who would take care of him like a mother,' the professor told the father.

Masatoshi was particularly pitiful because his mother, Shino, had always disliked her retarded eldest child and had barely tolerated living in the same house with him. When she was young, Shino had been a hostess at Koyo-kan, a famous restaurant of the Meiji period, and had been popular among aristocrats and wealthy merchants because of her beauty.

Ichige Hanshiro had won her and made her his wife. For Shino the marriage meant an elevation in her own status, but her own background made her unyielding and vain, and she was determined not to be outdone by anyone. Her daughter was normal and married a man who was adopted into the family, but Shino was ashamed because she couldn't show off her only son in public. This shame turned into a hatred that she vented on Hanshiro.

Since Hanshiro had a sense of responsibility as a father, Masatoshi was raised at least to give the impression of being a son of the Ichige family. If the matter had been left to Shino's discretion, he probably would have been confined to one room and treated like a true moron.

When Masatoshi reached puberty he would sometimes become excited like a dog in heat and chase the maids and his sister. When Shino saw this happen, far from feeling sad, she would grow so livid that the veins would stand out at her temples.

'It's your responsibility! You let him wander around the house like an animal! Let's hurry and put him in a hospital. If we don't, all of our maids will leave us, I assure you,' she shrieked at her husband.

'You don't have to shout for me to understand. I have my own thoughts about this,' Hanshiro said calmly. Shino, who had given birth to Masatoshi, had no comprehension of the pain and unseverable strength of the parental bond Hanshiro felt in his very bones.

The next day Hanshiro went to see the psychiatry professor again and asked him to arrange for his son to be sterilized before he was married.

'I know a woman who might become my son's wife, but I can't imagine bringing the subject up with her whenever I think of the possibility of a child being born. Once the operation is finished, though, I think I can hope for a marriage. I feel sorry for the woman who'll be my son's wife, but from a father's viewpoint, I would at least like to give him the experience of living with a woman.'

The professor agreed to Hanshiro's request, and the operation for sterilizing Masatoshi was performed in the surgery department of the hospital where he worked. It was a very simple procedure and was guaranteed not to interfere with the performance of the sex act.

It was said that after this Hanshiro talked to Rie about marriage. No one knew how Rie had reacted, or how long it had taken her to accept the proposal, or what sort of conditions Hanshiro had promised. It was clear only that Rie was not promised a bright future. The young couple began their married life in a small house that was fixed up for them in a corner of the grounds. It was originally built as a retreat. Rie took care of Masatoshi by herself, without any help from the household maids.

On formal occasions like weddings and funerals, Hanshiro and his wife attended with their daughter and her husband—their adopted son and an executive at Hanshiro's company—and their second daughter, who was also married. Of course Masatoshi didn't go along and neither did Rie.

'When they were married, he gave Rie a lot of stock in the company,' one of Hanshiro's employees said, as if he had been there and seen this happen.

What I had heard at Nagase's house, that several young psychiatrists were hired to oversee the married relations of Masatoshi and Rie, was true; they were dispatched because it was assumed that there would be some times when Rie would be subjected to some violence. Hanshiro had heard from the psychiatrists that retarded men like his son sometimes perform the sexual act interminably, beyond a normal limit, since they are unable to control themselves, and that in some cases women had been killed as a result. To assure Rie's safety, Hanshiro had arranged for young doctors from S Medical School to take turns standing by every night in a room next to the couple's.

In teaching hospitals before the war, many young doctors worked for nearly nothing after receiving their degrees before they found a position somewhere. Of course not all of them had fathers who owned private clinics, so even if they were single it wasn't easy for them to support themselves unless they did some moonlighting.

The job at the Ichiges' was unusual even for psychiatrists, and the pay was much more than the average. There were many applicants. The professor chose several whom he felt could keep a secret; three of them were among the five or six young doctors who came to Nagase's.

'Rich people do such awful things. In fact, that woman was bought, but to have a doctor waiting on them like that … It's like some kind of show. Even if the father did want his son to enjoy sex, it's too big a sacrifice. Why didn't he have them castrate his son instead of sterilizing him? I think that father is perverted.' I spoke forcefully. I couldn't control my anger while listening to the story. Looking back on it now, I realize that at age thirty or so I knew little of life's unavoidable bitterness. I feel ashamed that I was so naive, but at that time I detested not only Hanshiro—though I didn't know his name then—but also Rie, the woman bought to be Masatoshi's wife, for her cowardice.

'Hey, don't get upset so fast. All of that made life a little easier for these guys,' Nagase said, trying to act the mediator.

'That's true,' I said, but I still felt revulsion, even toward Tomoda and Kashimura, who had worked for the Ichiges.

They say that when the wind blows, the cooper prospers; applying this logic, I could find no reason to criticize a man like Ichige Masatoshi, who had in fact helped the poor young doctors. Leftist ideology would probably explain this as the contradiction inherent in capitalistic society. Still, I simply could not feel comfortable with a situation where young, single doctors watched a young couple in bed from beginning to end, paying diligent attention until the two fell asleep. If one does not make a fool of himself when doing such things, then he is making a fool of his charges. The doctors were too young and well educated to see themselves as fools, and if they were making fun of someone else, it was of the woman who was the victim of this marriage. Obviously I didn't like their making fun of her or their seeing her as an object of erotic stimulation. At the same time that they were ridiculing her, they were acting like fools who couldn't see the spittle on their own faces. Someone had used the word 'voyeur', but I had thought at the time that there was a basic difference between a voyeur and someone who kept such a nightly vigil.

After that I heard nothing more about the Ichiges from the young doctors, but through Nagase I learned there were in fact times when what had once seemed an absurd possibility had come to pass; Rie had fainted once, and there was a big row when Kashimura went to take care of her. It turned out that Masatoshi had forced himself on Rie when she was menstruating, and as a result she had lost a great deal of blood.

The interns from S Hospital must have stood duty at the Ichiges' for about a year when they decided there was no longer any danger and so stopped going there. A few years later, in the spring after the outbreak of the Pacific War, Kashimura was drafted as a military doctor and left to go to the South Seas. At the party to see him off, he came to me with a sake cup in his hand.

'I've been wanting to talk with you, but it seems like time is running out. If I return safely I'll tell you. It's about the family where I did night duty,' he said.

'Oh yes, that family,' I said, nodding. It was better not to mention the Ichiges' name in a place where there were so many people.

'The wife—Rie, I mean—I fell in love with her. To tell the truth. I wanted to marry her and talked to her about it.' Kashimura spoke loudly, without concern for the people around him. Going to the battlefield seemed to have made him free from the petty restraints of normal times.

'Did you really?' I was intrigued and looked into Kashimura's eyes. I remembered that I had once secretly scorned the trio who had done that night duty for the Ichiges, including Kashimura. Now that I heard from Kashimura himself words that seemed to prove he had not been making a fool of either himself or Rie, I couldn't help reacting with a tense curiosity.

'What did she say?'

'She said no. She really loves her husband. But she said she was grateful for my having asked. She said it was more than she could have expected, after I had seen her in such unsightly circumstances. Masatoshi couldn't go on living, and probably wouldn't live for very long if she left, she said, and when she thought of this she felt sorry for him and couldn't possibly leave. Then she cried and cried. I thought there was nothing else I could do, and so I gave up,' he said. Kashimura's face was flushed with sake, and tears welled up in his bloodshot eyes.

'I got married after that and have children now, but I haven't forgotten her. For a while I thought I had to rescue her from that place, but now it seems natural that she stays with that husband,' he said.

'Why were you attracted to her in the first place?' I asked Kashimura impatiently, trying to make sense of a situation I could not comprehend in many ways.

'Well ...' After thinking for a moment, Kashimura said, 'I felt the same as I would if my mother were in an animal cage. It was like a bad dream.'

'Does she look like your mother?'

'No, not at all.' Kashimura shook his head vigorously.

'What are you two talking so seriously about?' said a colleague of Kashimura's, patting his shoulder. Seeing this as a chance to excuse himself, Kashimura stood up to leave. He didn't seem particularly interested in talking with me anymore.

I thought about my brief conversation with Kashimura more than once after I returned home that night, and I tried to imagine what this woman Rie, whom I had never met, looked like. His words about his mother being in a cage excited my imagination, but in truth I couldn't picture Rie herself.

She was the daughter of a quilt merchant in the city or Iida. Her father had not been very well off, and although she only finished grammar school, like many children in those days, she was smart, wrote neatly, learned to sew and knit after arriving at the Ichiges', and acquired the knowledge of a high school graduate. Nagase said he had not heard any rumours about her family receiving a large sum of money when she married.

I suspected that she might have had something physically wrong with her as a woman, but when I learned that Kashimura had proposed to her after doing that strange night-watch, I decided Rie must be normal.

It was extraordinary that a man who had witnessed a most private part of her life would ask her to divorce Masatoshi and marry him.

Kashimura was a quiet, scholarly type—tall, well-built and handsome. He was popular among the nurses and patients at the hospital, and I wondered how Rie felt when she was proposed to by a man who was beyond comparison with her husband. It puzzled me that she could calmly refuse such a proposal, since she was only twenty-four or twenty-five.

Four or five years after the end of the war, I learned from Tomoda, an old friend of Kashimura's, that Kashimura had died of malaria in the South Seas. Since my friends the Nagases had moved to the Kansai region after the destruction of the war, I heard almost nothing about that group of friends.

I myself went to Karuizawa to live after I lost my house in the bombings. A year after the end of the war when I returned to Tokyo, I became very ill, and for a year or two after having surgery I struggled to keep going during the hard times, even though I was still not completely well. In those days of rapid change after the war, I might have heard about the death of Ichige Hanshiro and the subsequent collapse of his family business, but it was not until I heard the news of Kashimura's death that I remembered Rie and her husband, whom I had forgotten; I thought at the time that I might write a story with Rie as the central character.

By then I had gained firsthand experience with the extreme situations of life, having gone through a war and a serious illness that had been a matter of life and death. I had lost the naivete that had made me feel indignant about Hanshiro for having married his retarded son to a girl like Rie, as if it were a privilege of the bourgeois class. Nevertheless, Rie still remained a mystery to me.

When I thought about the story I would write about Rie, I imagined Masatoshi as the young kleptomaniac owner of an old established shop. His wife, ashamed of her husband, had an abortion, but unable to get a divorce, she continued to live with him as the lady of the household. She then fell in love with a young employee and in the end poisoned her husband.

This was all my own fabrication, but since it had been Kashimura's death that prompted me to start writing it, the metamorphosis of the main female character into a malicious woman left a bad taste in my mouth, for this would surely have made Kashimura sad. Later I thought off and on of writing down just what Kashimura had told me that night, a more lucid account that would convince even me, but the limits of my own imagination simply did not include a woman like Rie. I felt that if I forced myself to write, the character of Rie would end up being like a listless, white cat. Meanwhile the months and days passed, and once again I almost forgot the name Ichige.

*

Only one or two other passengers, shrugging their shoulders as if they were cold, got off the train with me. The chrysanthemums were still shut in the freight cars, so their penetrating fragrance didn't reach the platform.

I didn't see a taxi in front of the station, so after I called home from a public phone and asked someone to meet me with a flashlight at the corner of a dark field, I started walking alone through the town.

The moon was at its zenith, and the night mist was hanging low under the cloudless sky, spreading its thin gauze net over the pine trees and the firs. I could see the swirling motion of the mist underneath the street lamps, where the light made a circle. As I walked along, treading on the dark shadows that seemed to permeate the street, my footsteps sounded clear and distinct. Between the stores with their faded shutters I could hear the thin, weak chirping of some insects. It felt like autumn in the mountains.

Now I recalled fondly that I had been riding on a freight train full of chrysanthemums. In those dark, soot-covered cars hundreds and thousands of beautiful flowers were sleeping, in different shades of white, yellow, red, and purple, and in different shapes. Their fragrance was sealed in the cars. Tomorrow they would be in the Tokyo flower market and sold to florists who would display them in front of their shops.

'She's a white chrysanthemum, that's what she is,' I said, and wondered the next moment to whom I was speaking. I realized immediately, however, that I was addressing the dead Kashimura. The words had come out so effortlessly that I felt vaguely moved.

That evening at O Station I had seen Rie with her husband for the first time, though only for a few minutes. Then by chance I had heard from Kurokawa about her recent life. Twenty years had passed since I had heard about Rie at Nagase's house. After that I had heard Kashimura's brief confession at his farewell party, and after the war I learned of his death. Did Rie know that he had died in the war? It didn't really matter now. I felt that Kashimura wouldn't mind if she was uninterested in his life and death.

Seeing Rie that night and hearing Kurokawa's story didn't add anything new to my image of her. Rie was the same as she had been; I was the skeptical one who hadn't believed she was like that.

Rie's devotion to Masatoshi had seemed absurd to me. I had no reason to say she was a fake, but I simply couldn't accept a way of thinking that was so different from my own. What I mean is that I couldn't accept what she did without imagining that some handicap was part of her devotion—she must have been jilted or raped or experienced something to make her unhappy. I even wondered if religion had motivated her, an inclination to follow an authority higher than that of human beings. That was why, when I had intended to write about Rie, I had explored the psychology of a woman who would kill her husband, and who was not at all like Rie. Even though Kashimura had said he had had no difficulty accepting Rie's refusal, I couldn't.

But now I was humbly reaching out to Rie. I wanted to accept the Rie who had lived with Masatoshi as she was and to disregard her background, any misfortunes she had had before her marriage, or any religious inclinations. I wanted to take her hand and say, 'I understand'.

Did this mean that I had grown old? Should I be grateful that I had reached an age when I could accept without explanation the fact that human beings have thoughts and behaviour that seem beyond rational comprehension? I felt a sense of joy in thinking of the flat features of Rie's melancholic, middle-aged face as being somehow like the short, dense petals of a modest white chrysanthemum.

Translated by Yukiko Tanaka & Elizabeth Hanson

Korea

Chinatown

Oh Jung Hee

Railroad tracks ran west through the heart of the city and ended abruptly near a flour mill at the north end of the harbour. When a coal train jerked to a stop there, the locomotive would recoil as if it were about to drop into the sea, sending coal dust trickling through chinks in the floors of the cars.

There was no lunch waiting for us at home during those winter days short as a deer's tail, so we would throw aside our book bags as soon as school was over and flock past the pier to the flour mill. The straw mats that covered the south yard of the mill were always strewn with wheat drying in the sun. If the custodian was away from the front gate, we would walk in, help ourselves to a handful of wheat, leave a footprint on the corner of the mat and be on our way. The wheat grains clicked against our teeth, and after the tough husks had steeped in our warm, sweet saliva, the kernels would emerge, sticking like glue everywhere inside our mouths. About the time they became good and chewy we would reach the railroad.

While we waited for the coal train we blew big bubbles with our wheat gum, set up rocks we had gathered from the roadbed and threw pebbles at them, or hunted for nails we had set on the rails the previous day to make magnets.

Eventually the train would appear and rattle to a stop with one last wheeze. We would scurry between the wheels, rake up the coal dust, and then hook our arms through the gaps in the doors and scoop out some of the egg-shaped briquettes. Usually, by the time the carters from the coal yard across the tracks had made their dusty appearance, we had filled our school-slipper pouches with coal—the bigger and faster children used cement bags. Then we would nestle the coal under our arms and hop over the low wire fence on the harbour side of the tracks.

We would push open the door to the snack bar on the pier and swarm to the table in the corner. Depending on the day's plunder, noodle soup, wonton, steamed buns filled with red bean jam, or some such thing would be brought to us. And sometimes the coal was exchanged for baked sweet potatoes, picture cards or candy. In any event, we knew that coal was like cash—something we could trade for anything around the pier—and so the children in our neighbourhood looked like black puppies throughout the year.

Some people called our neighbourhood Seashore Village, others called it Chinatown. The coal dust carried by the north wind all winter long covered the area like a shadow, and the sun hung faint in the blackened sky, looking more like the moon.

Grandmother used to scoop ash from our stove, apply it to a fistful of straw, and polish the washbasin to a sparkling sheen before doing Father's dress shirts. But even when the shirts were hung to dry deep inside the canopy away from the dusty wind, they had to be rinsed again and again and starched a second time before they could be worn.

'Damned coal dust! What a place to live!' Grandmother would say, clicking her tongue.

A certain reminiscence would invariably follow. I had heard it so often that I would take over for Grandmother: 'Let me tell you about the water from Kwangsŏk Spring. Now this was in the North before the war, you understand. When I used that water, the wash turned out so white it seemed almost blue! Even lye wouldn't get it that white.'

When we returned to school after winter vacation our homeroom teacher would take all the Chinatown children to the kitchen next to the night-duty room. There she would have us strip to the waist, assume a push-up position on the floor and take a merciless dousing with lukewarm water. Then she would check for coal dust behind our ears, on the backs of our necks, between our toes and under our fingernails. If she gave us an affectionate slap where the goose-flesh had erupted in the small of our backs, we had passed inspection. We would giggle as we slipped on our long-john tops flecked with dead skin.

Spring arrived, and with it the new school year. I was now a third-grader. My homeroom had classes only in the morning, and early one afternoon I was on my way home with Ch'i-ok. We had our arms around each other's shoulders, 'I'm going to be a hairdresser when I grow up,' Ch'i-ok said as we passed a beauty shop at a three-way intersection.

Her voice reminded me of yellow. It had been worm-medicine day at school, and our teacher had made us come to school on an empty stomach. I wasn't sure if it was hunger, the medicine or the swell of boiling Corsican weed, but everything seemed yellow—the sunlight, the faces of passersby, the blustery breeze that crept under my skirt and made it flutter.

Except for some makeshift stores, both sides of the street were virtually barren. Here and there the skeleton of a bombed-out building stood like a decayed tooth.

'Somebody said it was the biggest theatre in town,' Ch'i-ok whispered as she pointed out the one remaining wall of a building in ruins. Plastered in white, it resembled a movie screen or the curtain of a stage. But it too would soon be coming down. A row of labourers were taking aim at it with pickaxes, and in a moment the great white wall would roar to the ground.

Other labourers were removing the reusable bricks and reinforcing rods from a wall already demolished.

'The area was bombed to kingdom come.' Ch'i-ok said, mimicking the adults and repeating 'to kingdom come' over and over.

Diligent as ants, the residents had reclaimed the devastated areas and were rebuilding their houses. Pots of Corsican weed boiled on heaps of coal briquettes in stoves made from oil drums.

Ch'i-ok and I constantly stopped to spit big gobs of saliva.

'Feels like the worms took the medicine and went nuts.'

'Uh-uh, I think they're peeing.'

Whatever it was they were doing, it didn't make us any the less nauseated. The froth from the Corsican weed, the smoke from the coal, and the smell of plaster mixed with the seaweed smell of the Corsican weed were one big yellow whirl.

'I wonder why they use Corsican weed when they're building a house,' Ch'i-ok said. 'One whiff and I feel like my hair being pulled out.'

The arm looped around my shoulder dropped like a dead weight. I dawdled along, drinking in the smell of the Corsican weed. That yellow smell had been my introduction to this city, the very first understanding I shared with it.

❋

My family had moved there the previous spring from the country village where we had taken refuge during the recent war.

'If your father could only get a job,' Mother used to say while she was spraying her tidy stacks of tobacco leaves with mouthfuls of water. She would leave home at dawn, a sack chock-full of the leaves strapped to her back, and return looking half-dead two or three days later.

'I don't give up easily, but I've had it with this darn tobacco monopoly. Unless you have a license, you're always getting searched by the police. If your father could only get a job ...'

Father's job hunting consisted of looking up friends and classmates from the north who had immigrated to the south or had somehow managed to flee the war. Finally he got a job in the city selling kerosene.

The day the moving truck was to come, we ate breakfast at daybreak and then camped beside the road with our bundled quilts and our household goods tied up roughly with cord. Lunchtime came and the truck hadn't arrived. The endlessly repeated farewells with the neighbours were over.

Toward sundown, while we were plumped listlessly on the ground, fed up with playing hopscotch and land baron, Mother took us to one of the local noodle shops and bought us each a bowl of noodle soup. The two oldest boys and I had changed into clean clothes before going outside that morning, but by now our runny noses had left a shiny track down our sleeves and on the backs of our hands.

It was dark now, but Mother, sitting on the bundled quilts with our baby brother in her arms, kept glaring toward the approach to the bridge, waiting for the truck.

Long after sundown the headlights of the truck finally appeared near the bridge. 'It's here!' Mother shouted, and we children bounced up from our seats on the bundles. The truck briefly stopped. Mother rushed over, and the driver's assistant stuck his head out the window and shouted something to her over the roar of the engine. Mother returned and the truck left. My brothers and sisters and I looked at each other in bewilderment. The dark outlines towering above the high railing around the back of the truck were cattle. We could tell from the sharply bent horns and the soft, damp sound of their rumination, which flowed through the gloom.

'They'll be back after they unload the cattle. He arranged it that way because we pay half price if we use an empty truck going back to the garage,' Mother explained to Grandmother.

Grandmother nodded with a reluctant expression that seemed to say, 'I suppose you two know what you're doing.' We had never seen her disagree with Mother and Father.

A good two hours passed before the truck reappeared. After delivering the cattle to a slaughterhouse in a city ten miles away, the men had had to clean the muck from the truck bed.

Mother and the baby squeezed between the driver and his assistant after the rest of us and our baggage had been piled in the back. As the truck started out, we heard the faraway whistle of the midnight southbound train.

I stuck my head out from the bundles and watched our village recede into the night and blend with the hill behind it and its grove of scrub trees. They all undulated together, no larger than the palm of a hand, a darkness thicker than the sky. Finally they converged into a single dot that bounced up and down in counterpoint with the rear of the truck.

We crossed the township line and soon we were barrelling along a bumpy hillside road. Those of us in the back, stuck among the bundles like nits, kept bounding up in the air like wind-up dolls. It was as if the truck had lost its temper at the driver's rough handling. I could see Grandmother fighting to keep from crying out because of the jarring. With each bounce I felt certain we would fall headlong into the river below, so I squeezed my eyes shut and drew my four-year-old brother close.

Though it was spring, the night wind prickled our skin like the tip of a knife. It swept across the river, raked my scaling skin with its sharp nails, and gradually removed the smell of cow dung from the truck bed.

I suddenly recalled the soft, damp sound of the cattle chewing their cud in the darkness. 'Do you think all those cows are dead now?' I asked my big sister. But she kept her face buried between her raised knees and didn't answer. Surely the animals had been slaughtered, skinned, gutted and butchered by now.

The moon kept us company, and after a while my little brother shook his fist at it: 'Stupid moon, where you goin'?'

One or another of us always had to urinate, and so the truck stopped frequently. We would knock on the tiny window between the cab and the truck bed, and the driver's assistant would stick his head out the passenger window and shout, 'What do you want?'

'We have to go to the bathroom,' one of us would say.

With a wave of his hand the man would tell us to go where we were, but then Grandmother would raise a fuss, and the driver would reluctantly stop. The assistant would lift us down one by one and then bark at us to do our business all together. We shuddered in relief as we squatted at the side of the road. It took us a long time to empty our bladders.

Whenever the truck entered a different jurisdiction, which seemed to happen at every bend in the road, there was a checkpoint. A policeman in a military uniform would play his flashlight over the truck. Mother's tobacco peddling had left her with barely enough spunk to lean out of the window and yell. 'Help yourself, but all you're going to find are a few lousy bundles and some kids.'

All night long the truck hurtled across hills and streams and through sleeping towns, and after stopping once for gas, breaking down twice and going through a checkpoint at every turn in the road, we finally reached the city at daybreak. The streets seemed to perk up at the roar of the truck's old engine.

At the far end of the city we arrived at a neighbourhood that seemed to keep the sea barely at arm's length, and here we were lifted down from the truck along with our bundles. After chasing us all night the moon had long since lost its shine and was hanging flat like a disk in the western sky. The truck had stopped in front of a well-worn, two-storey wooden house. The first floor had sliding glass doors that opened onto the narrow street like those of a shop. 'Kerosene retailer' had been painted in red on the dusty glass.

This was the house where we would live. The blast of fresh cold air made my teeth chatter. I was supposed to be looking out for my little brother, so I put him on my back.

While the truck had rattled through the city we had craned our necks from among the bundles and gazed out in curiosity and expectation. The city was different from what I had dreamed of in our country village. When I thought of the rainbow-coloured soap bubbles that I liked to blow from the end of a homemade straw, or I imagined the Christmas trees from some strange land that I had dreamed of but never seen ...

Our street was lined on both sides with identical two-storey frame houses that had tiny balconies. The squeaky wheels of bicycles ridden by seafood vendors on their way to the wharf and the footsteps of people going to work at the flour mill filled the shabby, filthy street with a disordered vigour like that of chickens flapping their wings at dawn. The vendors and mill workers squeezed past the truck, which had planted itself in the middle of the street, avoided our carelessly discharged bundles and headed up the gentle hill that began at our house.

I was lost in confusion. Everything was different from the country village we had just left, but had we really moved? Was this really our new home? It had a dreamlike smell that filled the sky like an evening haze. It was like a once familiar dream now forgotten, leaving only its sensation. What was that smell?

Father shoved open the door of the kerosene shop and barked at the driver that he hadn't followed the terms of the agreement. The driver shook his fist at Father and pointed back and forth at the rest of us and our belongings. Curious and apprehensive, we could only gape at them.

You could see the bluish marks where the razor had scraped my neck between my gourd-bowl haircut and the yellow rayon quilted jacket that was losing its batting. A little nine year old whose skin was flaking all over, I looked around our future neighbourhood with a strangely uneasy feeling, my brother still riding on my back.

The neighbourhood had awakened at our noisy arrival, and heads with rumpled hair began poking out through windows and doors.

The dozen or so identical frame dwellings that lined each side of the street ended abruptly with our house. The houses that faced each other on the hill above also had two storeys but were much larger. Some were white, others were blue-gray like faded ink.

The houses on the hill were spaced apart, except for the first one, which practically touched our house. A broad wall enclosed the lot of that first house. The door and all the windows I could see were too small and tightly shuttered. I wondered if it was a warehouse—no one could have lived there.

With their steeply slanting roofs, and the pinched ridgelines that contrasted with their bulk, these Western-style houses looked strange and out of place to me. Perched on the hill that stood alone like a distant island amid the swarm of people on their way to the wharf, the houses had an air of cool contempt. They faced the sea, their orifices shut tight like shells, but they seemed somehow heroic even in their shabbiness, for they left you wondering how old they were and what their history might have been.

The truck started up but didn't leave. The driver hadn't been paid as much as he wanted, and for a moment he rested both arms on the steering wheel and shut his eyes as if he were about to enter a protracted battle.

'What's all this damn commotion so early in the morning? Are the Northerners invading again?'

A blunt, hard voice flew over our heads, ringing in my ears, and knocked out the menacing roar of the engine with a single stroke. Mother and then my brothers and sisters and I looked up to see a young woman on the balcony of the house across the street. Her legs were exposed to the thighs and an army jacket barely covered her shoulders. Her dyed hair swung back and forth across her back as she was about to go inside.

My big brother was running among the wheels of the truck. Father grabbed him by the scruff of the neck, hauled him out and rapped him on the head. Then he took a look at us standing in a bunch.

'Well, well, well,' he chuckled as if in amazement, 'we've got ourselves a platoon here.'

Sunlight began to break through the dawn clouds, but still the sleeping houses on the hill kept their shutters tightly closed. The bluish gloom in the sky, driven from here and there throughout the city, gathered ominously above the hill like clouds before a storm.

When the darkness had vanished, the smell I had first noticed began to trickle through the delicate rattan blinds of the night and then rose from everywhere in the streets like a deep breath at last exhaled.

All at once the smell dispelled my confusion and the neighbourhood seemed familiar and friendly. I finally understood the true nature of that smell: it was a languid happiness, an image coloured by our refugee life in the village we had left the previous night, the memory of my childhood.

Later that year, around the time the dandelions were blooming, I became chronically dizzy and nauseated and had to sit on the shoe ledge of our house, spitting foamy saliva while my little brother crawled about in the yard putting dirt in his mouth. It seemed Grandmother cooked Corsican weed all spring long. Whenever she forced a bowl of the broth upon me, I would drink it reluctantly, shaking my head in disgust, and then sink into a strange, languid stupor that felt like spring fever. The whole world was yellow, and regardless of the time, I would always ask Grandmother whether it was morning or evening.

'Are the worms stirring, you little stinker?' she would retort with a hearty laugh.

One day, while I sank into the familiar yellow stupor, as if I were walking into a forgotten dream, the two-storey houses on the hill suddenly swooped close; one of the shutters opened and the pale face of a young man appeared.

*

Mother became pregnant with her seventh child. Only fresh oysters and clams could soothe her queasy stomach, so every morning before school I would take an aluminum bowl and set off over the hill for the pier. I would dash by the firmly shut gates of the houses on the hill, sneaking glances at them out of curiosity and a vague anxiety, for these were the houses of the Chinese. When I had run a mere twenty steps down the other side of the hill, the Chinese district suddenly ended at a butcher shop and the pier unfolded before my eyes. I would stop to catch my breath and look back, and about that time the shutters of the shop would clatter open.

I went to this shop every week to buy half a pound of pork. Mother would place some money in my hand and send me on my way, always with the same warning: 'If he doesn't give you enough, ask him if it's because you're a child. And ask him to give you only lean meat, not fat.'

The butcher was an unmarried Chinese who had a growth the size of chestnut on his cheek. It looked as if someone had given him a terrific punch. Long hairs trailed from the growth, as if pulled by an unseen hand.

The first time I went to the shop. I found the man stropping his butcher knife.

'Are you only giving me this much because I'm a child?' I blurted. By standing on tiptoe I was just able to get my chin over the counter as I stuck out the money.

The man turned and looked at me, baffled.

Afraid he would cut the meat before I could finish saying what Mother had told me, I snapped, 'She told me to ask for lean.'

Stifling a laugh, the butcher quickly sliced the meat for me. 'Why only lean? I can give you some hair and skin too.'

Next to the butcher shop was a store that sold such things as pepper, brown sugar and Chinese tea in bulk. It was the only general store in Chinatown. The people from our neighbourhood occasionally went to the butcher shop for pork, but didn't shop at the general store. We had no use for dyes and firecrackers, and we didn't need decorative beads for our clothing and shoes.

The store's shutters were opened only on one side, and even on bright, sunny days the interior was dark and gloomy, as if enveloped in dust.

But in the evening the Chinese flocked there, creeping like dusk through interlocking alleys. The women had great thick lobes and wore silver earrings. They tottered on bound feet, baskets over their arms, and their heads bobbed, the tight buns looking like cow dung.

While the women shopped, the men sat in the chairs in front of the store and silently smoked their long bamboo pipes before creeping back home. Most of them were elderly.

We children parked ourselves in a row on the narrow, low curb, tapping our feet on the street and pointing at the men.

'They're smoking opium, the dirty addicts.' And in fact the smoke scattering from the pipes was unusually yellow.

Now and then the elderly men gave us a smile.

Our families lived right next to Chinatown, but we children were the only ones who were interested in the Chinese. The grown-ups referred to them indifferently as 'Chinks'.

Although we had no direct contact with the Chinese in the two-storey houses on the hill, they were the yeast of our infinite imagination and curiosity. Smugglers, opium addicts, coolies who squirrelled away gold inside every panel of their ragged quilted clothing, mounted bandits who swept over the frozen earth to the beat of their horses' hoofs, barbarians who sliced up the raw liver of a slaughtered enemy and ate it according to rank, outcaste butchers who made wonton out of human flesh, people whose turds had frozen upright on the northern Manchurian plain before they could even pull up their pants—this was how we thought of them. What was inside the tightly closed shutters of their houses? And what lay deep inside their minds, seldom expressed even after years of friendship? Was it gold? Opium? Suspicion?

*

'Let's do our homework here,' Ch'i-ok said when we arrived at her house. She looked up toward the quilt and the blanket stretched over the side of the second-floor balcony. This was a sign that Maggie was out. If she were in, she would have been in bed, beneath the blanket. I hesitated, glancing across the street at our house. Mother and Grandmother referred to Ch'i-ok's house as a whorehouse for the GIs. Our house was the only one in the neighbourhood that didn't rent out a room to a prostitute. These women threw open their doors to the street and thought nothing of letting the American soldiers give them a squeeze. Stained blankets and colourful underwear festooned with lace hung in the sun on the balconies, drying from the free-spirited activities of the previous night.

'Scum!' Grandmother would say, turning away from the sight. To her way of thinking, women's clothes, and especially their underwear, should be hung to dry inside the house.

Ch'i-ok's parents lived downstairs, and Maggie rented the big room upstairs with a darky GI. Ch'i-ok had to go through Maggie's room to get to her own, which was small and narrow like a closet. When I went to get Ch'i-ok for school in the morning I always encountered Maggie lying in bed with her hair dishevelled and the huge darky sitting hunched in front of the dresser trimming his moustache with a tiny pair of silvery scissors. Maggie would beckon me in with the slightest motion of her hand, but I always remained outside the half-open door to the room, peeking inside while I waited for Ch'i-ok. The thick flesh of the darky's chest looked like moulded rubber and his eyes were smoky. He always mumbled when he spoke, and he never smiled at me. What a gloomy man, I thought.

'Can't you call me from the street?' Ch'i-ok once asked. 'The darky doesn't like you going up there.'

But every morning I walked up the creaky stairs and called to Ch'i-ok while hovering outside Maggie's room.

'Maggie said she won't be back until tonight. So we can play on her bed,' Ch'i-ok cajoled me.

I thought for a moment: Mother had a bad case of morning sickness and was probably lying in the family room, looking vexed at everything. My older brother had likely gone outside to catch mole crickets. And I knew that as soon as I walked in, Grandmother would tell me to piggy-back my baby brother, who had just been weaned, and then shoo us out of the house.

And so I followed Ch'i-ok upstairs. Jennie, Maggie's daughter, was asleep on the bed, Curtains kept the sun out, making the room dim.

Ch'i-ok opened the storage cabinet, located a box of cookies, took two of them and carefully replaced the box. The cookies were sweet and smelled faintly like toothpaste.

'That's so pretty,' I said, pointing to a bottle of perfume on the dresser.

Ch'i-ok turned it upside down and pretended to gently spray her armpits with it. 'Made in America.' Again Ch'i-ok reached inside the cabinet and rustled around. This time she produced two candies.

'It tastes so good,' I said.

'Mmm, because it's made in America,' Ch'i-ok answered in the same blasé tone.

Jennie was now wide awake and watching us.

'Jennie, aren't you pretty? Now we have to do our homework, so why don't you go back to sleep for a little while?' Ch'i-ok spoke softly, brushing Jennie's eyelids down with her palm, and in an instant the little girl's eyes had closed tightly like those of a doll.

Everything in Maggie's room seemed marvellous. Ch'i-ok let me feel each of the things for just a moment, and every time I exclaimed joyfully as I caressed it. Then we replaced each item, leaving no sign that it had been touched.

'I have an idea.'

Ch'i-ok reached inside a cabinet at the head of the bed and took out a gourd-shaped bottle half full of a green liquid. After making a line with her fingernail on the side of the bottle to mark the level of the liquid, she opened the bottle, poured a small amount into the cap and handed it to me.

'Try it. It's sweet—tastes like menthol.' I quickly drank it and returned the cap to Ch'i-ok. She filled it and then gulped it clown. The level of the liquid was now about two fingers below the mark, so Ch'i-ok made up the difference with water, capped the bottle and returned it to the cabinet.

'Perfect! How was it? Tasty, huh?' The inside of my mouth was refreshingly warm, as if I had a mouthful of peppermint.

'Now don't tell anyone,' Ch'i-ok said as she removed a velvet box from among some clothes in one of the dresser drawers.

Everything in Maggie's room was a secret. The box contained a pearl necklace long enough to make three strands, a brooch adorned with garishly coloured glass beads, some earrings and other jewellery. Ch'i-ok tried on a necklace made of thick glass beads and studied herself in the mirror.

'I'm going to be a GI's whore when I grow up,' she said decisively. 'Maggie said she'll give me necklaces, shoes, clothing—everything.'

I felt as if I were dissolving and the tips of my fingers and toes had gone to sleep. I was short of breath and couldn't keep my eyes open. Was it the darkness of the room? I imagined that the peppermint was leaving a white trail every time I breathed out. I drew aside the curtain covering the door to the balcony. Seething yellow sunlight entered the room, illuminating the dusk and making the room look like a greenhouse. I touched my burning cheek to the doorknob and peered outside. Once again I saw the two-storey house in Chinatown with the open shutters and the face of the young man looking my way. A mysterious sadness, an ineffable pathos began undulating in my chest and then spread over me.

'What's the matter? Are you dizzy?' asked Ch'i-ok, who knew what the green liquid was and how it affected you. She snuggled up beside me against the door to the balcony.

I shook my head, unable to understand, much less explain the feeling I got from that face in the second-floor window, and at that instant the wooden shutter thumped shut and the young man disappeared.

The glass beads of Ch'i-ok's necklace clicked together, their colours dancing in the sunlight. Ch'i-ok took one of the beads in her lips. 'I'll be a GI's whore.'

I drew the curtain and lay down on the bed. Who could he be? I tried fretfully to revive my memories of a forgotten dream. I knew I had seen him the previous autumn at the barber's. I had had to sit on a plank placed across the chair because I was so short. I had instructed the barber as Mother had told me:

'Please make it short and layered on the sides and back, but leave the top long. I'm ugly enough already, so a gourd-bowl haircut won't do.'

But when the barber had finished, I looked in the mirror to find I still had a gourd bowl.

'Too late to complain now. I'll do better next time—promise.'

'I knew this would happen! Why can't you concentrate on cutting hair instead of gabbing with everybody?'

The barber jerked the plank away from under me. 'What a smart-alecky little girl. That's no way to talk. I'll bet that yap of yours was the first thing that came out when you were born,'

'Don't you worry about how I should talk. And I'll bet you're a hair chopper because you came out with scissors around your wrist.'

The other customers roared with laughter. I looked around with a triumphant air. The only ones who weren't laughing were the barber and a young man sitting in the corner with a bib around his neck. The young man was looking blankly at me in the mirror. He's Chinese, I suddenly thought. Although I had seen him only at an angle from across the street, never close up, his inscrutable gaze had given me that impression. I removed the towel around my neck and tossed it in front of the mirror. Then I stamped to the doorway, put my hands on my hips, and turned back: 'Until the day you die you'll be nothing but a hair chopper!' And then I ran home.

Father was constantly at work on our house, as if to compensate for the privations of our refugee life in the country village—the entire family crowded into a single rented room, and before that the many sleepless nights he had spent keeping the children warm in the arms under a bridge or inside a tent. He got rid of our tiny yard, adding a room and a veranda to the house in the way that girls who have just learned how to sew might add secret pockets to the inside of a book bag or the underside of their clothing. And so a maze-like hallway appeared in the house, long and narrow like an ant tunnel.

Along with the hallway there materialized a place where I could hide and no one would find me—the back room next to the toilet which was filled with old clothing, household stuff and other odds and ends. Once I ran inside the house, sneaked into this room and pressed my face against the narrow mouth of a jar hoping in vain that the sorrow sweeping over my bones like a strong current would empty into it.

Several times after that, usually when I was hunkered down in front of Father's shop waiting for the evening newspaper, I sensed that the young Chinese man had opened his window and was looking toward me.

'Jennie, time to get up. Jennie—your mom's here,' Ch'i-ok said in an affectedly sweet and gentle tone. Jennie opened her eyes and sat up. Ch'i-ok went downstairs and returned with a washbasin full of water. Jennie didn't cry even when the soapy water got in her eyes. We combed her hair, sprayed some perfume on her and changed her into some clothes we had found in the closet. Jennie's father was white and her mother Korean, and at the age of five she still hadn't begun to talk. She couldn't feed herself, much less put on her own clothes, and when she was fed, the food would trickle out the side of her mouth. Whenever the darky was there, Jennie would be moved to Ch'i-ok's room.

Grandmother occasionally saw Jennie on the balcony or outside the house. 'Whelp!' she would say, looking at the girl as if in amazement, her eyes filled with the hatred she reserved for fur-bearing animals. She frightened me whenever she stared at Jennie like that. Some time ago our house had become infested with rats, and so we had gotten a cat. The cat bore a litter of seven kittens in the back room, and Grandmother fed it seaweed soup to help it recover. Then she stared right into the cat's eyes and repeated several times, like a refrain, 'Kitty had some baby rats, seven baby rats.' That evening the cat ate all seven kittens, leaving only the heads. Then it yowled all night long, not bothering to clean its bloodstained mouth. As if she had been expecting this, Grandmother wrapped the seven tiny heads in newspaper and sent them down the sewer drain.

Mother used to tell me that Grandmother was so fastidious and cold because she had never had children of her own. She was actually Mother's stepmother. I had once overheard Mother whispering about Grandmother to an elderly woman who was a distant relative: 'They'd been married only three months when her husband had an affair with his sister-in-law—can you believe it? That's why they separated and she decided to come live with us.'

Jennie was like a doll to Ch'i-ok. Ch'i-ok could give her a bath and change her clothes every half hour, and never get a scolding from Maggie. To Ch'i-ok, Jennie was sometimes a baby, sometimes a sick little girl, sometimes an angel. I envied Ch'i-ok with all my heart, and it must have shown on my face.

'Don't you have a sister too?' Ch'i-ok asked me dubiously.

'She's my stepsister.'

'You mean that's not your real mother?'

'My stepmother,' I lied with a lump in my throat.

Tears gathered in her eyes. 'Well, well. Somehow I had a hunch. Don't tell anyone, but I have a stepmother too.'

There wasn't a soul in our neighbourhood who didn't know this.

I linked my little finger with Ch'i-ok's and we promised to keep each other's secret.

'So, does your mom spank you and tell you to get lost and drop dead?' I asked.

'Yeah, when no one's around.' Ch'i-ok lowered her pants and showed me her bruised thighs. 'I'm going to run away and be a GI's whore.'

How often I wished I really were a stepdaughter, so I could run away whenever I pleased.

Mother was still carrying baby number seven. None of us children in this poor district next to Chinatown believed that babies were brought to earth in the arms of an angel in the middle of the night. And they didn't emerge smiling brightly from their mother's belly button. Everyone knew a baby came out screaming from between the naked legs of a woman.

*

We were watching some GIs in T-shirts do target practice with knives on one of the tennis courts at the army base. The knives sliced through the air toward the concentric circles on the target. They had a piercing glint, like silver needles, a flash of light, a man's prematurely white hair. Whenever a knife whistled to the black spot dead in the centre of the target, the men howled like animals and we gulped in terror.

A white GI had been taking a step back every time he hit the centre of the target. He took aim once again, but as the knife was about to spring from his hand, he suddenly pivoted. The knife ripped through the air toward us. We flattened ourselves with a shriek in front of the wire fence surrounding the base. I felt a warm wetness between my legs. A moment later we lifted our pallid faces. The chuckling GI was pointing at something a short distance behind us. We turned and looked. A black cat lay rigid on its back with its legs in the air, the knife stuck in its chest. The cat was as big as a small dog. It was probably one of the strays that were always getting into the garbage cans on the base. Its pointed whiskers were still trembling as we crowded around it. Suddenly my big brother picked up the cat and ran off. The rest of us set out after him. My wet underpants chafed.

Brother stopped panting when we were out of sight of the Americans' barracks. Then he looked down at what he was holding. He shuddered and dropped the cat, which fell to the ground with a thud.

'How come you brought that thing?' one of the children demanded.

Thus challenged, my Little Napoleon of a brother pulled the knife from the cat's chest and wiped the blade on the grass. It was sharp and pointed like an awl. He folded the blade with a snap and put the knife in his pocket.

'Go get me a stick,' he said.

One of us snapped off a branch from a tree we had planted the previous spring on Arbor Day and returned with it.

Brother took off his belt and looped it around the cat's neck, then tied the end to the branch. We paraded down the street with the cat splayed out behind him. The cat's paws dragged along the ground, and its weight bent the branch on Brother's shoulder like a bow.

By the time we reached Chinatown the long summer day had begun to wane. As the sun slanted toward the horizon the cat's shadow seemed to grow interminably from its midsection.

The flour mill workers walked past us on their way down the hill, their hair frosted with flour, their empty lunchboxes rattling.

We walked toward the wharf, treading on each other's gigantic, frightening shadows and the shadow of the long, black carcass of the cat. And then I saw him again. The second-floor shutters were open, and he was watching our procession. I couldn't fathom his gaze, but I thought I saw sorrow, anger, and perhaps a subtle smile.

When we reached the wharf Brother put the branch down and removed the belt from the cat's neck. Spitting in disgust, he cinched the belt around the waist of his pants, which constantly threatened to fall down. Then he dropped the cat into a mass of garbage, empty bottles and rotting, white-bellied fish washing up against the bank.

As we often did when the sun was going down, we decided to go to the park. There we would usually lie on our stomachs on the endless expanse of steps and look up the hoop skins of the GIs' whores, exclaiming at the bare legs inside the bloated framework of whale tendon. Or we would loll on the grass and bellow one of the old standards that an aging prostitute might sing to herself;

When I look back. I see every step of my youth
stained with tears
When I look back at my regrettable past,
I hear the bells of Santz Maria.

But this time we walked up silently, one step at a time, toward the sky.

At the highest point in the park stood a bronze statue of the old general whose landing operation here just a few years before was already inscribed in legend. From this spot the entire city could be seen.

Boats and ships were moored at the pier, their flags fluttering like confetti. The jaws of a crane bit into their cargo again and again. At a distance from the pier floated something that looked like an islet or a huge old carp—probably a foreign freighter.

The bell from the Catholic church behind us kept tolling. It was the sound that had been tugging at us ever since—no, even before—we had thrown the cat into the water. Producing endless ripples at precise intervals, confined to a single tone, simplifying every desire and temperament into one basic harmony, the sound of the bell evoked in my mind the awesomeness of a peal of thunder heard on a summer evening upon being awakened from a dream, the mystery of train wheels rumbling through the deep of the night.

'A nun must have died,' said one of the others.

We all thought that a nun was dying peacefully whenever the bell tolled on and on like this.

Across the railroad tracks a black stream spewed from the smokestack of the flour mill, surging into the sky above the war-ravaged city like dust rising from a battlefield.

The intense bombardment from the warships during the landing operation would long be remembered in the history of warfare, the grown-ups liked to say. About the only structures to have remained intact were the old frame houses in our neighbourhood, which had been seized from the Japanese at the end of World War II and the two-storey houses on the hill in Chinatown.

The sunlight lingered in the western part of the city, but Chinatown was being saturated with darkness, as if the smoke were smothering it. Perhaps it was the dust carried by the north wind from the coal yard, settling there like ash.

Here at the highest point of the city we had a commanding view of Chinatown and the coloured blankets and lace underwear on the balconies of the sooty houses seized from the Japanese. These were the scenes, the underside, the mysterious smile of this city. Part of me would always be weighed down by these images. To me, Chinatown and my neighbourhood were the flooded stern of a listing ship about to sink.

Torches, lit too early in the evening, flared at the public playfield in the eastern part of the city. The flames swayed as if they were flickering remnants of the wind in the last traces of the sunlight. A crowd of people cried out, 'Czechoslovakia go home! Poland go home! Puppet regimes go home!' All summer long, one member from each household would report to the playfield as soon as the sun had vanished, and the throng would shout these slogans while stamping their feet. Grandmother would return from these rallies and groan all night long from the pain in her lower back.

One day at morning assembly our principal had explained why the people were protesting: Czechoslovakia and Poland, satellites of the Soviet Union, had forsworn their obligations as members of the neutral-nations peace-keeping force by digging for UN military secrets to pass on to the communist side.

If I buried my head between my knees, the outcry from the playfield would become a distant hum, like the sound made when I blew across the narrow mouth of an empty bottle. It was the sound of the earth groaning deep below the surface, a faint ripple foreshadowing a tidal wave, a lingering breeze licking the roofs of houses.

At home I found Mother retching beside the drain in the yard. For the first time I empathized with the brutish life that women must live. There was something pathetic and harrowing about Mother's retching, and this symptom of her pregnancy made me plead silently with her to produce no more brothers and sisters for me. I was afraid she would die if she gave birth again.

I couldn't get to sleep until the wee hours. My older sister had bound her emerging breasts with a waistband that Grandmother had torn from a skirt. The breasts were sensitive even to the touch of her sheet, so she tossed and turned, embracing them tightly and moaning. As I lay awake, I counted each time the night guards tapped their sticks together to signal their approach, and I tried to count the number of wheels of the freight trains that passed by. At daybreak I went to the wharf. The dead cat was neither to be seen among the garbage and rotting fish washing up against the bank, nor was it beneath an abandoned boat I spotted drifting a short distance offshore. Perhaps some children in a distant port were dragging its shapeless body around at the end of a pole.

Autumn drew near, but the bedbugs flourished as never before. When the sun shone full on the balcony, we would take the tatamis outside to dry and scour the wooden floors of our rooms for the eggs. Though our pajamas had elastic cuffs, the bedbugs would manage to crawl inside, making us itch and producing the smell of raw beans. The electricity stayed on until midnight, and so we usually went to sleep with the lights on because they kept the bugs away. But when the lights went out at twelve the bugs would swarm from the straw of the tatami or from cracks in the floor and launch their all-out attack.

One night, while I was half asleep and scratching away at the bugs, I was awakened by a thunk—it sounded like a block of wood being split. Before I knew it my older brother had thrown on his pants and was down the stairs like a bullet. The sudden hubbub from the street told me something had happened. My heart quickened, and I went out on the balcony. The electricity had been off for some time, and it was pitch dark outside, but I could make out the noisy crowd that had filled the street between our house and Ch'i-ok's. The neighbour's sliding glass doors scraped open, and people appeared on the balconies above, shouting for news. Among the hum of voices the word 'dead' came to my ears like a revelation. The word passed from mouth to mouth like a round. Some people reacted by shuddering in disgust, others poked their heads through the layers of onlookers. My chin trembled as I looked across the street and saw that the door to Maggie's room was open. The darky, dressed in an undershirt, looked down on the street from the balcony, his hands resting on the railing.

A moment later I heard the wail of a siren and saw an American army jeep. In an instant the crowd had separated. Maggie lay on the street, drenched in the brightness of the jeep's headlights. Her long, thick hair covered her face and was strewn every which way, like solar flares. 'He threw her into the street,' somebody said.

The darky was drunk. The MPs dressed him in his uniform, and as they loaded him into the jeep, his shirt unbuttoned, he chuckled.

The next day I found Ch'i-ok feeding water to Jennie, who had the hiccups. She patiently wiped the moisture that trickled from the corner of the little girl's mouth. But no amount of water would make the hiccups stop.

'They'll put her in an orphanage,' Ch'i-ok said. She sounded a bit sulky, as she had the day she told me that Maggie would go to America in the spring—the darky had decided to marry her.

Maggie had looked happy then. Once I had found her washing the darky's feet as he sat on high on her head, and as I stared at the clean nape of her neck she turned to me. Without make-up she seemed to have no eyebrows. She gently beckoned to me, saying, 'It's okay. Come on in.'

'Jennie went to the Catholic orphanage,' Ch'i-ok told me with a fierce scowl two days later. Her eyes were red and puffy. A younger sister of Maggie's had come to pack up the dead woman's belongings. Maggie's room remained empty for quite some time. But I didn't go up there to do homework or to play with Ch'i-ok anymore. Instead I called to her from the street on my way to school every morning.

I became more and more convinced that Mother wouldn't survive another birth, but her stomach continued to swell almost imperceptibly beneath her skirt. As it turned out, the one who failed was Grandmother, whose stinging hands and pungent, vicious curses had seemed to make her healthier by the day. One morning she collapsed while doing the laundry, and she never recovered. My baby brother, who had practically lived on her back, became my big sister's responsibility.

After Grandmother began needing a bedpan, Mother and Father agreed to move her to the countryside, where Grandfather lived.

'A stroke can last twenty years,' Mother whispered to Father. 'I can melt a rock.' And in a slightly louder voice. 'When you're old, there's only one place to be, and that's next to your husband, whether you love him or hate him.' Finally, in a loud tone, 'We'd better reserve a taxi for her.'

Grandmother became like a baby. As Ch'i-ok had done with Jennie, I would go into Grandmother's room when no one else was home and comb her hair, feed water to her, and sometimes gently feel to see if her diaper was wet.

The day Grandmother was to leave, Mother dressed her in clean clothes. 'She still has her figure because she never had children.'

Father went with Grandmother to the village where Grandfather lived with Grandmother's younger sister and their children. 'I don't feel right about it,' Father said falteringly when he returned. He sighed. 'I don't think they'll be happy with her. After all, she's an outcast. You know, it's amazing—I thought she wouldn't recognize anyone, but then she spread her jacket, took Father's hand, and placed it on her chest. She must have been so frustrated. Makes me wonder what it means to be man and wife.'

'There was a lifetime of bitterness inside that woman.' said Mother. 'But didn't I tell you? We did the right thing sending her there.'

Mother decided to open Grandmother's clothing chest. Grandmother had never let anyone else in the family touch it, and so we craned our necks to follow the movement of Mother's hands. One by one she removed the neatly folded articles of clothing piled inside and placed them on the floor. Out came Father's old long underwear, which Grandmother had hemmed for her own use, and the Japanese-style baggy pants that she had worn around the house. And there were clothes made from fabric woven in traditional ways, such as sheer silk and rough, thick, glossy silk. As Mother's outstretched hands continued to produce clothing that Grandmother had worn but once or twice in her life, I realized that she wouldn't be coming back, that the days she would wear such clothes were gone, and I felt as if a chill wind had swept through the depths of my heart. When had she worn such clothes? And for what special occasion had she saved them deep in the chest?

The last article of clothing was an otter vest. Mother then groped along the bottom of the chest and took out something small wrapped tightly in a handkerchief. With bated breath we fixed our eyes on Mother's nimble fingers.

With a quizzical expression Mother looked inside the handkerchief. A jade ring broken in two, a tarnished copper belt buckle that seemed about to crumble, a few nickel coins from the Japanese occupation, several buttons of various sizes that might once have been attached to clothing, some pieces of coloured thread—these and other things she found there.

'Really, Mother! Saving broken jade is like saving bits of pottery.' Clicking her tongue, Mother rewrapped the objects in the handkerchief and tossed them into the empty chest. She set aside the long underwear and other underclothing to use as rags, and moved the rest of the clothing to her own chest. The otter fur was of high quality, she said—she would use it as a muffler.

The next day I sneaked into Grandmother's chest and took out the bundled-up handkerchief. Then I went to the park and walked sixty-five paces, from the statue of the general to some trees—one step for each year Grandmother had lived. I found myself beside an alder—the fifth one into the grove—and I buried the bundle deep beneath it.

Towards the end of winter word arrived that Grandmother had died. It had been just the previous summer that she had left in the taxi. Mother, who was in her ninth month, did something uncharacteristic: she began crying while caressing Grandmother's clothing chest, now stuffed topsy-turvy with the children's threadbare clothing.

All evening I hid among the odds and ends in the back room, where no one could find me, and when everyone had gone to bed I went to the park. The sky was black, but I found the fifth alder tree without even having to take the sixty-five steps.

The damp handkerchief, buried for two seasons deep in the ground, stuck to my palm like rotten straw. I brushed the dirt off the pieces of the ring, the tarnished belt buckle and the coins and held them tenderly in my hand. They felt exactly the same as before. They were warm now, but the cold would soon return to them.

I returned the objects to their burial place beneath the tree. After I had tramped the dirt down and brushed off my hands, I started walking toward the statue, concentrating on taking even steps. At the count of sixty I was there. I began to wonder. Surely it had been sixty-five steps the previous summer. Did this mean I would reach the tree in fifty paces the following summer? And a year later or ten years later, would one giant step take me there?

Since it was still winter and late at night, I could climb up on the statue without any disapproving looks from others. And so I clawed my way onto the pedestal, then climbed onto the binoculars that the general held against his stomach. From there I looked down on the city sparsely dotted with lights. The outcries of the previous summer, swelling like dust from a battlefield, were gone. Now it was still. As I strained to listen to the sounds flowing gently in the darkness. I felt as if I were tapping an undiscovered vein of water in the deepest part of the earth.

The sea was a black plane. I drank in the wind that had been blowing all night from the East China Sea, and the seaweed smell it carried. I saw the oblong light framed by the open shutter of the two-storey house on the Chinatown hill, and imagined a pale face revealed there. I felt the soft breath of spring hiding in the chilly air.

Something was budding in my warm blood, something unbearably ticklish.

'Life is ...,' I murmured. But I couldn't find the right word. Could it be found, a single word for today and yesterday, with their jumble of indistinguishable, all too complicated colours, a word to embrace all the tomorrows?

Another spring arrived and I became a sixth-grader. My older brother was raising a puppy he had brought home one day. With Grandmother gone, the dog had the run of the house, pooping and shedding anywhere it pleased.

I had grown the better part of a foot in the past twelve months, and since the previous year I'd been carrying around my older sister's oxford-cloth school bag embroidered with roses.

All winter long my rat pack and I had sneaked coal from the freight trains, and as always we had run wild through the streets. Occasionally I had closeted myself in the back room at home to read popular romances and such.

One Saturday—the day we had no afternoon classes—I was on my way home from school. 'Tomorrow's worm medicine day, so be sure to skip breakfast,' our teacher had reminded us the day before.

'The worms won't take the medicine on a full belly.'

There was much less house rebuilding now, but Corsican weed was still being boiled and the smell still seemed to dye the air yellow.

In the simmering yellow sunlight I frequently stopped to spit. 'Feels like the worms are going nuts,' I muttered once again.

I saw Ch'i-ok mixing permanent-wave solution in a can in the beauty shop at the three-way intersection. Her father had lost a leg in a conveyor belt at the flour mill and had left the area with his wife the previous winter. Ch'i-ok had remained with the people who ran the beauty shop. Every day I passed by the place on my way to and from school and saw her through the glass door. She would be sweeping the hair on the floor while pulling down her small sweater, which was constantly riding up her back and revealing her bare waist.

I walked past the beauty shop. The yellow sunlight filling the street looked like thousands of feathers soaring up in the air. When was it? Shaking my head in irritation I tried to revive a distant, barely remembered dream. When was it? I continued toward home, and when I arrived I looked at the open window of the two-storey house on the hill. He was leaning part way out the window, beckoning me.

I started up the hill, drawn as if by a magnet, and he disappeared from the window. A moment later he heaved open the gate to the house and emerged. His yellow, flat-nosed face still wore that mysterious smile.

He offered me something wrapped in paper. When I accepted it, he turned and went inside. Through the open gate I could see the narrow, shaded front walk, the unexpected sight of a sunny yard, and the sunlight dancing and darting on the limpid skin of his feet with every step he took.

At home I went into the back room, locked the door, and opened the package. Inside was some bread dyed in three colours, which the Chinese ate on their holidays, and a thumb-size lantern decorated with a plastic dragon.

I hid these things in a cracked jar that no one used. Mother was in labour in my parents' room, but instead of looking in on her I went upstairs. I sneaked into a storage cabinet, as I did when playing hide and seek. It was midday, but not a ray of light entered. While listening to Mother scream that she wanted to die, I realized that the church bell had been tolling and I fell into a sleep that was like death itself.

When I awoke, Mother had pushed her eighth child into the world after a terrible labour. A sense of helplessness and despair came over me in the darkness of the cabinet, and I called out to her. Then I felt inside my underwear, and finally I understood the humid lever that had been closing about me like a spider web.

My first menstrual flow had begun.

Translated by Bruce Fulton & Ju-Chan Fulton

Korea

A Certain Beginning

KIM CHI-WON

Yun-ja floated on the blue swells, her face toward the dazzling sun. At first the water had chilled her, but now it felt agreeable, almost responding to her touch. Ripples slapped about her ears, and a breeze brushed the wet tip of her nose. Sailboats eased out of the corner of her eye and into the distance. She heard the drone of powerboats, the laughter of children, and the babble of English, Spanish and other tongues blending indistinguishably like faraway sounds in a dream. Her only reaction to all this was an occasional blink. She felt drugged by the sun.

Yun-ja straightened herself in the water and looked for Chong-il. There he was, sitting under the beach umbrella with his head tilted back, drinking something. From her distant vantage point, twenty-seven-year-old Chong-il looked as small as a Boy Scout. He reminded her of a houseboy she had seen in a photo of some American soldiers during the Korean War.

'Life begins all over after today,' Yun-ja thought. She had read in a women's magazine that it was natural for a woman who was alone after a divorce, even a long-awaited one, to be lonely, to feel she had failed, because in any society a happy marriage is considered a sign of a successful life. And so a divorced woman ought to make radical changes in her lifestyle. The magazine article had suggested getting out of the daily routine—sleeping as late as you want, eating what you want, throwing a party in the middle of the week, getting involved in new activities. 'My case is a bit different, but like the writer says, I've got to start over again. But how? How is my life going to be different?' Yun-ja hadn't the slightest idea how to start a completely new life. Even if she were to begin sleeping all day and staying up all night, what difference would it make if she hadn't changed inwardly? Without a real change the days ahead would be boring and just blend together, she thought. Day would drift into night; she would find herself hardly able to sleep and another empty day would dawn. And how tasteless the food eaten alone; how unbearable to hear only the sound of her own chewing. These thoughts hadn't occurred to her before. 'He won't be coming anymore starting tomorrow,' she thought. The approaching days began to look meaningless.

Several days earlier, Chong-il had brought some soybean sprouts and tofu to Yun-ja's apartment and had begun making soybean-paste soup. Yun-ja was sitting on the old sofa, knitting.

'Mrs Lee, how about a trip to the beach to celebrate our 'marriage'? A honeymoon, you know?'

Yun-ja laughed. She and Chong-il found nothing as funny as the word marriage. Chong-il also laughed, to show that his joke was innocent.

'Marriage' to Chong-il meant the permanent resident card he was obtaining. He and Yun-ja were already formally married, but it was the day he was to receive the green card he had been waiting for that Chong-il called his 'wedding day'.

Chong-il had paid Yun-ja fifteen hundred dollars to marry him so that he could apply for permanent residency in the US Until his marriage he had been pursued by the American immigration authorities for working without the proper visa.

'Americans talk about things like inflation, but they're still a superpower. Don't they have anything better to do than track down foreign students?' Chong-il had said the day he met Yun-ja. His eyes had been moist with tears.

Now, almost two months later, Chong-il had his permanent resident card and Yun-ja the fifteen hundred dollars. And today their relationship would come to an end.

Chong-il ambled down the beach toward the water, his smooth bronze skin gleaming in the sun. He shouted to Yun-ja and smiled, but she couldn't make out the words. Perhaps he was challenging her to a race, or asking how the water was.

Yun-ja had been delighted when Ki-yong's mother, who had been working with her at a clothing factory in Chinatown, sounded her out about a contract marriage with Chong-il. 'He came here on a student visa,' the woman had explained. 'My husband tells me his older brother makes a decent living in Seoul ... The boy's been told to leave the country, so his bags are packed and he's about to move to a different state ... It's been only seven months since he came to America ... Just his luck—other Korean students work here without getting caught ...'

'Why not?' Yun-ja had thought. If only she could get out of that sunless, roach-infested Manhattan basement apartment that she had been sharing with a young Chinese woman. And her lower back had become stiff as a board from too many hours of piecework at the sewing machine. All day long she was engulfed by Chinese speaking in strange tones and sewing machines whirring at full tilt. Yun-ja had trod the pedals of her sewing machine in the dusty air of the factory, the pieces of cloth she handled feeling unbearably heavy. Yes, life in America had not been easy for Yun-ja, and so she decided to give herself a vacation. With the fifteen hundred dollars from a contract marriage she could get a sunny room where she could open the window and look out on the street.

And now her wish had come true. She had gotten a studio apartment on the West Side, twenty minutes by foot from the end of a subway line, and received Chong-il as a 'customer', as Ki-yong's mother had put it.

After quitting her job Yun-ja stayed in bed in the morning, listening to the traffic on the street below. In the evening, Chong-il would return from his temporary accounting job. Yun-ja would greet him like a boardinghousc mistress, and they would share the meal she had prepared. Her day was divided between the time before he arrived and the time after.

Thankful for his meals, Chong-il would sometimes go grocery shopping and occasionally he would do the cooking, not wishing to feel obligated to Yun-ja.

Chong-il swam near. 'Going to stay in forever?' he joked. His lips had turned blue.

'Anything left to drink?' she asked.

'There's some Coke, and I got some water just now.'

Chong-il had bought everything for this outing—Korean-style grilled beef, some Korean delicacies, even paper napkins.

'Mrs Lee, this is a good place for clams—big ones too. A couple of them will fill you up—or so they say. Let's go dig a few. Then we can go home, steam them up and have them with rice. A simple meal, just right for a couple of tired bodies. What do you think?'

Instead of answering, Yun-ja watched Chong-il's head bobbing like a watermelon. 'So he's thinking about dropping by my place ... Will he leave at eleven-thirty again, on our last day? Well, he has to go there anyway to pick up his things.' While eating lunch, she had mentally rehearsed some possible farewells at her apartment: 'I guess you'll be busy with school again pretty soon,' or 'Are you moving into a dorm?'

Yun-ja was worried about giving Chong-il the impression that she was making a play for him. At times she had wanted to hand Chong-il a fresh towel or some lotion when he returned sopping wet from the shower down the hall, but she would end up simply ignoring him.

Yun-ja thought about the past two months. Each night after dinner at her apartment Chong-il would remain at the table and read a book or newspaper. At eleven-thirty he would leave to spend the night with a friend who lived two blocks away. Chong-il had been told by his lawyer that a person ordered out of the country who then got married and applied for a permanent resident card could expect to be investigated by the Immigration and Naturalization Service. And so he and Yun-ja had tried to look like a married couple. This meant that Chong-il had to be seen with Yun-ja. He would stay as late as he could at her apartment, and he kept a pair of pajamas, some old shoes and other belongings there.

Tick, tick, tick ... Yun-ja would sit knitting or listening to a record, while Chong-il read a book or wrote a letter. Pretending to be absorbed in whatever they were doing, both would keep stealing glances at their watches ... Tick, tick, tick ...

At eleven-thirty Chong-il would strap on his watch and get up. Jingling his keys, he would mumble 'Good night' or 'I'm going'. Yun-ja would remain where she was and pretend to be preoccupied until his lanky, boyish figure had disappeared out the door.

*

It hadn't always been that way. During the first few days after their marriage they would exchange news of Korea or talk about life in America—US immigration policy, the high prices, the unemployment, or whatever. And when Chong-il left, Yun-ja would see him to the door. The silent evenings had begun the night she had suggested they live together. That night Chong-il had brought some beer and they had sung some children's ditties, popular tunes and other songs they both knew. The people in the next apartment had pounded on the wall in protest. Chong-il and Yun-ja had lowered their voices, but only temporarily. It was while Chong-il was bringing tears of laughter to Yun-ja, as he sang and clowned around, that she had broached the subject: Why did Chong-il want to leave right at eleven-thirty every night only to sleep at a friend's apartment where he wasn't really welcome? He could just as easily curl up in a corner of her apartment at night and the two of them could live together like a big sister and her little brother—now wouldn't that be great? Immediately Chong-il's face had hardened and Yun-ja had realized her blunder. That was the last time Chong-il had brought beer to the apartment. The lengthy conversations had stopped and Chong-il no longer entertained Yun-ja with songs.

Yun-ja had begun to feel resentful as Chong-il rose and left like clockwork each night. 'Afraid I'm going to bite, you little stinker!' she would think, pouting at the sound of the key turning in the door. 'It's a tug of war. You want to keep on my good side, so you sneak looks at me to see how I'm feeling. You're scared I might call off the marriage. It's true, isn't it—if I said I didn't want to go through with it, what would you do? Where would you find another unmarried woman with a green card? Would you run off to another state? Fat chance!'

The evening following her ill-advised proposal to live together, Yun-ja had left her apartment around the time Chong-il was to arrive. She didn't want him to think she was sitting around the apartment waiting for him. She walked to a nearby playground that she had never visited before and watched a couple of Asian children playing with some other children. She wondered if being gone when Chong-il arrived would make things even more awkward between them. She wanted to return and tell him that her suggestion the previous evening had had no hidden meaning. Yun-ja had no desire to become emotionally involved with Chong-il. This was not so much because of their thirteen-year age difference (though Yun-ja still wasn't used to the idea that she was forty), but because Yun-ja had no illusions about marriage.

The man Yun-ja had married upon graduating from college had done well in business, and around the time of their divorce seven years later he had become a wealthy man, with a car and the finest house in Seoul's Hwagok neighbourhood.

'Let's get a divorce; you can have the house,' he had said one day.

Yun-ja was terribly shocked.

'But why? ... Is there another woman?'

'No, it's not that. I just don't think I'm cut out for marriage.'

In desperation Yun-ja had suggested a trial separation. But her husband had insisted on the divorce, and one day he left, taking only a toiletry kit and some clothes. Yun-ja had wept for days afterwards. She was convinced that another woman had come on the scene, and sometimes she secretly kept an eye on her husband's office on T'oegye Avenue to try to confirm this.

'Was there really no other woman?' she asked herself at the playground. 'Did he want the divorce because he was tired of living with me?' Their only baby had been placed in an incubator at birth, but the sickly child had died. Being a first-time mother had overwhelmed Yun-ja. 'Maybe he just got sick and tired of everything. Or maybe he just wanted to stop living with me and go somewhere away—that's how I felt toward him when he stayed out late. She had heard recently that he had remarried.

'Are you Korean?'

Yun-ja looked up to see a withered old Korean woman whose hair was drawn into a bun the size of a walnut. Yun-ja was delighted to see another Korean, though she couldn't help feeling conspicuous because of the older woman's traditional Korean clothing, which was made of a fine nylon gauze.

Before Yun-ja could answer, the woman plopped herself down and drew a crimson pack of cigarettes from the pocket of her bloomers.

'Care for one, Miss?'

'No thank you.'

The old woman lit a cigarette and began talking as if she were ripe for a quarrel: 'Ah me, this city isn't fit for people to live in. It's a place for animals, that's what. In Korea I had a nice warm room, with a laminated floor, but here no one takes their shoes off and the floors are all messy.'

'Can't you go back to Korea?'

'Are you kidding? Those darn sons of mine won't let me. I have to babysit their kids all day long. Whenever I see a plane I start crying—I tell you! To think that I flew over here on one of those damned things!'

The old woman's eyes were inflamed, as if she cried every day, and now fresh tears gathered. Yun-ja looked up and watched the plane they had spotted. It had taken off from the nearby airport and seemed to float just above them as it climbed into the sky. Its crimson and emerald green landing lights winked.

'I don't miss my hometown the way this grandmother does. And I don't feel like crying at the sight of that plane,' thought Yun-ja. Her homeland was the source of her shame. She had had to get away from it—there was no other way.

It was around seven when Yun-ja returned from the playground.

Chong-il opened the door. 'Did you go somewhere?' he asked politely, like a schoolboy addressing his teacher.

Yun-ja was relieved to have been spoken to first.

'I was talking with an elderly Korean woman.'

'The one who goes around in Korean clothes? Was she telling you how bad it is here in America?'

'You know her?'

'Oh, she's notorious—latches on to every Korean she sees.'

This ordinary beginning to the evening would eventually yield to a silent standoff, taut like the rope in a tug of war.

*

Chong-il's joking reference to 'marriage' the evening he had offered to take Yun-ja to the beach had come easily because his immigration papers had finally been processed. All he had to do was see his lawyer and sign them, and he would get his permanent resident card.

Though it was six o'clock, it was still bright as midday. It was a muggy August evening, and the small fan on the wall next to the window stuttered, as if it were panting in the heat of Yun-ja's top-floor apartment.

Realizing that Chong-il was only joking, Yun-ja stopped knitting. She got up and put a record on. The reedy sound of a man's mellow voice unwound from the cheap stereo:

Now that we're about to part
Take my hand once again …

Yun-ja abruptly turned off the stereo. 'Listening to songs makes me feel even hotter,' she said.

Several days later, after Chong-il had obtained his permanent resident card, he borrowed a car and took Yun-ja to the beach, as promised. Yun-ja had thought it a kind of token of his gratitude, 'Like the flowers or wine you give to the doctor who delivered your baby, or a memento you give to your teacher at graduation.'

*

They stayed late at the beach to avoid the Friday afternoon rush hour. As the day turned to evening, the breeze became chilly and the two of them stayed out of the water, sitting together on the cool sand. Whether it was because they were outside or because this was their last day together, Yun-ja somehow felt that the tug of war between them had eased. But the parting words a couple might have said to each other were missing: 'Give me a call or drop me a line and let me know how things are going.' Chong-il did most of the talking, and Yun-ja found his small talk refreshing. He told her about getting measles at age nine, practicing martial arts in college, and going around Seoul in the dog days of summer just to get a driver's license so he could work while going to school in America. And he talked about a book he'd read, entitled *Papillon.*

'If you have Papillon's will, the sky's the limit on what you can do in America. You've heard Koreans when they get together here. They're always talking about the Chinese. The first-generation Chinese saved a few pennies doing unskilled labour when the subways were built. The second generation opened up small laundries or noodle stands. Buying houses and educating the kids didn't happen until the third generation. Whenever I hear that, I realize that Koreans want to do everything in a hurry—I'm the same way. They sound like they want to accomplish in a couple of years what it took the Chinese three generations to do ... When I left Korea I told my friends and my big brother not to feel bad if I didn't write, because I might not be able to afford the postage. My brother bought me an expensive fountain pen and told me that if I went hungry in the States I should sell it and buy myself a meal. And then my older sister had a gold ring made for me. I put the damned thing on my finger, got myself decked out in a suit for the plane ride, and then on the way over I was so excited I couldn't eat a thing—not a thing. The stewardess was probably saying to herself, "Here's a guy who's never been on a plane before. That damned ring—I must have looked like a jerk!"'

Yun-ja related a few details about the elderly Korean woman she had met in the park. (Why did her thoughts return so often to this grandmother?) Then she told Chong-il a little about herself, realizing he had probably already learned through Ki-yong's mother that she was just another divorcee with no one to turn to.

The cool wind picked up as the sunlight faded, and they put their clothes on over their swimsuits. Chong-il's shirt was inside out, and Yun-ja could read the brand name on the neck tag.

'Your shirt's inside out.'

Chong-il roughly pulled the shirt off and put it on right side out. Her steady gaze seemed to annoy him.

The beach was deserted except for a few small groups and some young couples lying on the sand nearby, exchanging affections. Hundreds of sea gulls began to gather. The birds frightened Yun-ja. Their wings looked ragged, their sharp, ceaselessly moving eyes seemed treacherous. Yun-ja felt as if their pointed beaks were about to bore into her eyes, maybe even her heart. She folded the towel she had been sitting on and stood up.

'Let's get going.'

More gulls had alighted in the nearly empty parking lot, which stretched out as big as a football field.

'Want to get a closer look?' Chong-il asked as he started the car.

'They'll fly away.'

'Not if we go slow. God, there must be thousands of them.'

The car glided in a slow circle around the sea gulls. Just as Chong-il had said, the birds stayed where they were. Yun-ja watched them through the window, her fear now gone.

They pulled out onto the highway and the beach grew distant. A grand sunset flared up in the dark blue sky. The outline of distant hills and trees swung behind the car and gradually disappeared. Yun-ja noticed that Chong-il had turned on the headlights.

'You must be beat,' Chong-il said. 'Why don't you lean back and make yourself comfortable.'

Perhaps because he was silent for a time, Yun-ja somehow felt his firm, quiet manner in the smooth, steady motion of the car. She wondered what to do when they arrived at her apartment. Invite him in? Arrange to meet him somewhere the following day to give him his things? But the second idea would involve seeing him again ... The tide hadn't been low so they hadn't been able to dig clams ... 'I'll bet I've looked like a nobody to him, a woman who's hungry for love and money.' Yun-ja recalled something Chong-il had once told her: 'After I get my degree here, write a couple of books, and make a name for myself, I'd like to go back to Korea. Right now there are too many Ph.Ds over there. I know I wouldn't find a job if I went back with just a degree.'

'And for the rest of your life,' Yun-ja now thought, 'I'll be a cheap object for you to gossip about. You'll say, "I was helpless when they told me to leave the country—so I bought myself a wife who was practically old enough to be my mother. What a pain in the neck—especially when she came up with the idea of living together." And at some point in the future when you propose to your sweetheart, maybe you'll blabber something like "I have a confession to make—I've been married before ..." '

Chong-il drove on silently. His hand on the steering wheel was fine and delicate—a student's hand. Yun-ja felt like yanking that hand, biting it, anything to make him see things her way, to make him always speak respectfully of her in the future.

Chong-il felt Yun-ja's gaze and stole a glance at her. The small face that had been angled toward his was now looking straight ahead. 'She's no beauty—maybe it's that thin body of hers that makes her look kind of shrivelled up—but sometimes she's really pretty. Especially when it's hot. Then that honey-coloured skin of hers gets a nice shine to it and her eyelashes look even darker.' But Chong-il had rarely felt comfortable enough to examine Yun-ja's face.

'Mrs Lee, did you ever have any children?'

'One—it died.'

Chong-il lit a cigarette. Her toneless voice rang in his ears. 'She doesn't seem to have any feelings. No expression, no interest in others, it even sounds as if her baby's death means nothing to her. True—time has a way of easing the pain. I don't show any emotion either when I tell people that my father died when I was young and my mother passed away when I was in college. Probably it's the same with her. But her own baby? How can she say "It died" just like that?'

He had known from the beginning, through Ki-yong's mother, that Yun-ja was a single woman with no money. It had never occurred to him when he paid Ki-yong's mother the first instalment of the fifteen hundred dollars that a woman with such a common name as Yun-ja might have special qualities. What had he expected her to be like, this woman who was to become his wife in name only? Well, a woman who had led a hard life, but who would vaguely resemble Ki-yong's mother—short permed hair, a calf-length sack dress, white sandals—a woman in her forties who didn't look completely at ease in Western-style clothing. But the woman Ki-yong's father had taken him to meet at the bus stop was thin and petite with short, straight hair and a sleeveless dress. Her eyelids had a deep double fold, and her skin had a dusky sheen that reminded Chong-il of Southeast Asian women. She was holding a pair of sunglasses, and a large handbag hung from her long, slender arm.

As they walked the short distance to Ki-yong's mother's for dinner that first night, Chong-il had felt pity for this woman who didn't even come up to his shoulders. He had also felt guilty and ill at ease. But Yun-ja had spoken nonchalantly: 'So you're a student? Well, I just found an apartment yesterday. I'll be moving in three days from now. We can go over a little later and I'll show you around. It's really small—kitchen, bathroom, living room and bedroom all in one.' To Chong-il this breezy woman of forty or so acted like an eighteen-year-old girl. 'This woman's marrying me for money.' He felt regretful, as if he were buying an aging prostitute.

'Why don't you two forget about the business part of it and get married for real?' Ki-yong's mother had said at dinner. And when she sang a playful rendition of the wedding march, Chong-il had felt like crawling under the table. Yun-ja had merely laughed.

The traffic between the beach and the city was heavy, occasionally coming to a standstill. Among the procession of vehicles Yun-ja and Chong-il noticed cars towing boats, cars carrying bicycles, cars with tents and shovels strapped to the roof rack.

As Chong-il drove by shops that had closed for the day, he thought of all the time he had spent on the phone with his older brother in Korea, of all the hard-earned money he had managed to scrounge from him (did his sister-in-law know about that?)—all because of this permanent resident card. And now he couldn't even afford tuition for next semester. These thoughts depressed him. But then he bucked up: Now that he had his green card (his chest swelled at the idea), there was no reason he couldn't work. 'I'll take next semester off, put my nose to the grindstone, and by the following semester I'll have my tuition.' And now that he was a permanent resident, his tuition would be cut in half. He made some mental calculations: How much could he save by cutting his rent and food to the bone? 'But you can't cut down on food too much,' Chong-il reminded himself. There were students who had ended up sick and run down, who couldn't study or do other things as a result. 'This woman Yun-ja really has it easy—doesn't have to study. All she has to do is eat and sleep, day after day.' Chong-il felt it was disgraceful that a young, intelligent Korean such as himself was living unproductively in America, as if he had no responsibilities to his family or country. 'Why am I busting my butt to be here? Is the education really that wonderful?' In English class back in Korea he had vaguely dreamed of studying in America. Or rather he had liked the idea of hearing people say he had studied there. More shameful than this was the impulse he had to stay on in America. 'What about the other people from abroad who live in the States—do they feel guilty about their feelings for their country, too?' He had read diatribes about America's corrupt material civilization. But he couldn't figure out what was so corrupt about it, and that bothered him. He wanted to see just what a young Korean man could accomplish in the world, and he wanted to experience the anger of frustration rather than the calm of complacency. He wanted knowledge and recognition from others. But this woman Yun-ja didn't even seem to realize she was Korean.

The car pulled up on a street of six-story apartment buildings whose bricks were fading. Children were running and bicycling on the cement sidewalk; elderly couples strolled hand in hand, taking in the evening. Chong-il got out, unpacked the cooler and the towels, and loaded them on his shoulder. He and Yun-ja had the elevator to themselves. Yun-ja felt anxious and lonely, as if she had entered an unfamiliar neighbourhood at dusk. She braced herself against the side of the elevator as it accelerated and slowed. When she was young it seemed the world belonged to her, but as time went on these 'belongings' had disappeared; now she felt as if she had nothing. When it came time to part from someone, her heart ached as if she were separating from a lover. 'Am I so dependent on people that I drove my husband away? Nobody wants to be burdened with me, so they all leave—even my baby ... I wonder if that old woman at the playground went back to Korea. Maybe she's still smoking American cigarettes and bending the ear of every Korean she sees here. Maybe I'll end up like her when I'm old. Already my body feels like a dead weight because of my neuralgia—God forbid that I latch on to just anybody and start telling a sob story.'

Yun-ja unlocked the door to the apartment and turned on the light.

Today the small, perfectly square room looked cozy and intimate to them. They smelled the familiar odours, which had been intensified by the summer heat.

But Chong-il felt awkward when he saw that Yun-ja had packed his trunk and set it on the sofa. If only he could unpack it and return the belongings to their places.

'You must feel pretty sticky—why don't you take a shower?' Yun-ja said.

Chong-il returned from washing his salt-encrusted body to find

Yun-ja cleaning the sand from the doorway. She had changed into a familiar, well-worn yellow dress. The cooler had been emptied and cleaned, the towels put away. Yun-ja had shampooed, and comb marks were still visible in her wet hair. Chong-il tried to think of something to say, gave up, and tiptoed to the sofa to sit down. 'She's already washed her hair, changed, and started sweeping up,' he thought. As Yun-ja bustled about, she looked to Chong-il as if she had just blossomed.

'Shouldn't I offer him some dinner?' Yun-ja thought as she swept up the sand. 'He went to the trouble of borrowing a car and taking me out—the least I can do is give him a nice meal. And where would he eat if he left now? He'd probably fill up on junk food ... But if I offer to feed him, he might think I had something in mind. And when I've paid people for something, they never offered me dinner, did they?'

'How about some music?' Chong-il mumbled. He got up, walked stiffly to the stereo, and placed the needle on the record that happened to be on the turntable. The rhythm of a Flamenco guitar filled the room. Although Chong-il didn't pay much attention to the music Yun-ja played, it seemed that this was a new record. 'Why have I been afraid of this woman? You'd think she was a witch or something.'

'If that woman sinks her hooks into you, you've had it.' Chong-il had heard this from his roommate, Ki-yong's father and goodness knows how many others. 'Nothing happened again today?' the roommate would joke when Chong-il returned in the evening from Yun-ja's apartment. 'When it comes to you-know-what, nothing beats a middle-aged woman. I hope you're offering good service in return for those tasty meals you're getting.'

The shrill voices of the children and the noise of airplanes and traffic were drowned out by the guitar music. The odour of something rotten outside wafted in with the heat of the summer night.

Chong-il began to feel ashamed. Here he was about to run out on this woman he'd used in return for a measly sum of money—a woman whose life he had touched. He had visited this room for almost two months, and now he wished he could spend that time over again. 'Why didn't I try to make it more enjoyable?' he asked himself. He and Yun-ja had rarely listened to music, and when they had gone strolling in the nearby park after dinner he had felt uneasy, knowing that they did this only so that others would see the two of them together.

Yun-ja finished sweeping the sand up and sat down at the round dinner table. 'If you're hungry, why don't you help yourself to some leftovers from yesterday's dinner? There's some lettuce and soybean paste and a little rice too.'

Yun-ja's hair had dried, and a couple of strands of it drooped over her forehead. She looked pretty to Chong-il.

'And some marinated peppers,' she continued.

Chong-il's body stiffened. This offer of dinner was a signal that it was time for him to leave. He rose and fumbled for something appropriate to say about the past two months. The blood rushed to his head and his face burned. Finally he blurted out, 'What would you say if I ... proposed to you?' Then he flung open the door as if he were being chased out. In his haste to leave he sent one of Yun-ja's sandals flying from the doorway toward the gas range, Then the door slammed shut behind him.

Yun-ja sprang up from the table. 'What did he say?' Her body prickled, as if she were yielding to a long-suppressed urge to urinate. 'I don't believe in marriage,' she told herself. 'Not after what I went through.' She rushed to the door and looked through the peephole into the hall. She saw Chong-il jab futilely at the elevator button and then run toward the stairway.

'The boy proposed to me—I should be thankful,' Yun-ja thought. Like water reviving a dying tree, hot blood began to buzz through her sleepy veins. This long-forgotten sensation of warmth made her think that maybe their relationship had been pointing in this direction all along. 'It was fun prettying myself up the day I met him. And before that, didn't I expect some good times with him even though we weren't really married?'

Yun-ja turned and looked around the room. There was Chong-il's trunk on the sofa. 'But he'd end up leaving me too.' Suddenly she felt very vulnerable. Everything about her, starting with her age and the divorce, and then all the little imperfections—the wrinkled around the eyes, the occasional drooling in her sleep—reared up in her mind. 'But I'm not going to let my shortcomings get me down,' she reassured herself. 'It's time to take a stand.'

Translated by Bruce Fulton & Ju-Chan Fulton

Macau

The Lepers

MARIA ONDINA BRAGA

When the sun sank into the sea, the hill at the end of the island was a flaming torch. It was as if the world were going to end there, or perhaps begin, as if new forms, or else nothingness, were about to emerge decisively from the fiery mass of elements—clayish earth, sky and water set alight by the breath of the Spirit—and as if whatever time span were to begin there, it would do so with a perfect day in which nature had been cleansed.

A-Mou, whose face was marked by one or two of the red spots of a leper, went out every day to admire the sunset, trembling with anxiety and hope.

It was the hour when the other patients would retire to the corner of their bunks, either because the reflection of the sun in the sea burned their infected eyes, or merely because of some secret, inexplicable superstition.

A-Mou was young, and the disease, still in its initial stage, caused her no suffering. Indeed, all she had were the spots. The doctor had promised to cure her. She loved life, she liked to beautify herself with coloured dresses, flowers in her hair, varnish on her nails.

Late afternoon, hugging her beloved guinea pig, which slept at the foot of her bed like a cat, A-Mou would climb to the top of the hill, dreaming of a new, different and better tomorrow.

One could see the whole inland from up there: the marshy rice paddies down in the valleys, glimmering in the last rays of sunshine; the plantations of tea and of yam in terraces along the steep slopes; the black and yellow stones among the evergreen clumps of fir trees. And to gaze upon the island was, in some way, like contemplating the world, catching a glimpse of life beyond the leper colony. In the wide curve of sea, boats returned from the fishing grounds. Then, night descended upon the Earth. And A-Mou's romantic soul was filled with faith, with a feeling of warmth towards existence itself, with a happiness that brought tears to her eyes.

The others thought her strange: while they, like proper Chinese, enjoyed company, gossip, noise, especially as night fell, A-Mou liked to be alone. She didn't behave like a Chinese, they remarked. And if they asked her why she went out alone at that hour, she just smiled. She wouldn't say, nor would she know how to say it, that it was just because no one else went out, because something supernatural marked the moment, because it was dark when she returned, the first toads, the first field mice would venture out onto the path—and she would wait for them to start talking, just like in childhood stories, and the waves breaking among the caves in the cliff had the solemn sound of sacred music.

When she got back, A-Mou would find her companions crouching in the darkness of the yard, singing while combing their hair. Some asked her hushed questions about what she had seen in the darkness. They talked of spirits. The blind women, their eyes open and unmoving in the shadows, seemed like visionaries of unknown and mysterious horizons.

A-Mou sat among them, stroking her guinea pig in her lap and listening, transfixed, to the tales of ghosts and witches that the old women, without hands, noses or ears, recited in solemn tones.

That was how she learnt that love was a dangerous thing. In the old women's stories, love, passion, betrothals, were always subject to adverse fortune, curses, tragic outcomes.

A-Mou had never loved, nor did she quite know what it was.

She had fallen ill as a young girl, and as a young girl she had ended up there, ignorant of life: and she was growing bored. But every evening, she was touched by emotion. As if she were to be told she was cured on the following day: a farewell party in the leper colony, with kisses and presents.

Yet, as she thought of the day of her resurrection, sitting there in the yard among her companions, she wondered what she would do afterwards. She had no family. Her grandmother, with whom she had fled from somewhere near Canton, had died soon after she had been interned there. She was a sad little old woman, with a greenish-black velvet bonnet, who sat smoking opium for hours on end.

She remembered her grandmother's friends, who were also destitute: the elderly teacher, with his scrawny beard and learned words (she remembered poems he had taught her); the woman who sold snake oil by day, and at night spoke with the spirits of her ancestors.

Every morning, amid the clanging of saucepans in the kitchen, the sweetish smell of rice porridge in bowls in the refectory, dogs barking, A-Mou joyously greeted the sword of light that penetrated her alcove. In the mirror on her table, the blotches were still there on her cheekbones, sometimes pink, other times almost purple. But a new day beckoned. She had a lot to think about—plaiting her hair, seeing to her dress, waiting for the sun to go down.

Nor was she even aware of the arrival of the boy at the men's house, on the other side of the hill. The old women told how, one moonless night, he had crossed the river on a raft he had made himself. His condition wasn't serious. The doctor would put him right within a few months. He was a handsome boy.

A-Mou then began to imagine him as some sort of god, like the household deities at the entrance to the temple, brave, with birds on their shoulders, or like the evil spirit, who clutched a viper as if it were a sceptre—a god of terror as far as her grandmother was concerned, but whose beauty she, for her part, found seductive.

And so, without having tried to catch a glimpse of the new arrival, A-Mou found herself waiting for him all the time, and it was because of him that she took such care with her hair every day.

The boy, of course, would never come, for men were forbidden to invade the women's quarters, nor did she ever think of looking for him. But she thought of him in the morning, when she woke up, and during her evening walk, when she got dressed, and when she plaited her hair. She was convinced he had come especially to awaken her from the tedium of the passing hours.

Could it be that he knew of her existence? Surely, he must. Her grandmother used to say that threads of thought are stronger than those of a weaver. Thoughts could spin webs as long as imperial highways, capable of resisting typhoons, and crossing rivers and seas. She had thought so much about him that he knew all about her. And he had already committed himself to her.

Naturally, neither of them could expect anything lasting from each other. Once cured, if they happened to meet out there in the world of the healthy, they might pretend not to know one another. In the world of the healthy, nothing could be the same because they themselves would be different.

And she got to the point where she thought herself lucky for being ill, for their both being ill, for both rotting away there. What would become of him without her? What would become of her without him?

In the world of the healthy, they wouldn't need each other so much. Was that why God had sanctioned their illness ... and their exile? In their misfortune, people became more important. Take her grandmother: at the end of her life, she never lacked the *white powder* for her pipe. And what a funeral the old teacher had had! The rich old woman of eighty who sat out in the main yard—surrounded by maids, and with no legs from the knees downwards—in health, she was just the mistress of her house; in sickness, she had the entire hospital at her beck and call.

Yes, indeed, misfortune had its compensations. In the world of the healthy, they would both lose their individuality. And she would never be as sure as she was now. The tales the old women told were of jealousy and betrayal. In their case, such things could never happen. Stories of folk who were free. Freedom had its price. Although she might not be able to count on his constancy later, A-Mou could count on him completely now.

And she thought about the boy with devotion, like someone whose thoughts dwelt on household gods, like someone recklessly worshipping the spirit of evil.

Time rushed by. Evenings merged into night. The women no longer included the matter of the new leper in their gossip. And A-Mou waited.

It was on one of her twilight walks that the dream became reality. Suddenly, when the sun had already set, she noticed a shape by her side, a shape that addressed her, told her his name, wanted to know hers. It could only be him. None of the patients, male or female, ever came there at that hour, and the healthy were filled with fear at the very sight of the lepers' hill. In the darkness, A-Mou could only see his eyes. The sea echoed among the hollows in the rocks. He plucked a sprig of lemon verbena from a nearby bush, crushed its leaves between his fingers, and the perfume spread and took hold of the night.

After that, it was more or less always the same. He would come after sunset. There was the scent of lemon and the sigh of the sea. On moonlit nights they managed to see each other perfectly. He complimented her on her plaited hair. She, in her heart, compared him to the young gods in the temple. The meetings repeated themselves, always the same, but always unexpected: the hours doubled their time; their silence expressed more than their words; their gesture was freely given; their soul was released.

But the months given by the doctor to cure the boy went by quickly. Could it be that he no longer had any blotches on his body? She was incapable of asking him, and without even wanting to know it, A-Mou saw hers grow, day by day, in the mirror.

As the women chatted in the evening, they now directed more questions at her.

And A-Mou had less and less to say.

When it came down to it, what was there to say? The purple torches on her face spoke for themselves, just as the legs she no longer had, spoke for the grand old lady who sat in the inner yard, and for others, hands, noses and ears. All faithfully resigned to their misfortune.

But how good it was that he had come to her on one, three, thirty nights. And how good it was that she, during all those nights, had believed in the apparition.

She still went for her evening walk to the top of the hill, but she no longer did so in order to contemplate the blaze of sunset, or to dream of a better tomorrow. Nor did she do so because of a man. She did it for herself alone. Because she had to live, in spite of being marked by death. Because the doctor had never again mentioned the possibility of a cure, and she needed to know about the joys of love in order to be able one day, crouching in the yard, to tell of them to some innocent young girl who might be sent to the leper colony.

Translated by David Brookshaw

Sumatra

From Marsinah Accuses

RATNA SARUMPAET

A young activist who was murdered, presumably for demanding higher wages for her fellow workers, Marshall has decided, against the objections of her graveyard companions, to return to Earth. At a performance to be held in conjunction with the launching of a book about her, she intends to remind the audience that, although a number of years have passed since her murder, the case has yet to be solved. As the play opens, she can be seen on a platform in a cemetery, curled in a foetal position. Anxious about her decision to return to Earth, she moans softly.

If only, in this profound and spirit-filled silence, I could find true silence ...

If only, in this silence, I could shut out the moans of hunger, the frightening screams, and unending pain ...

If only, for a moment, I could feel that my body was still my own ...

In the background, the whispered sounds of people reading from the Koran can be heard. As the voices grow louder, Marsinah rises. She looks troubled and speaks as if partly moaning, partly complaining.

What would my father say about this—cruelly isolated, smothered by anger and hatred, suffocating in a shroud of fear, helpless to defend myself?

And then the voices that come again and again, like the pounding feet of a thousand jackals, coming to destroy my peace, following me even to this cemetery plot.

If death is a place of peace, then why am I surrounded by past struggles?

Why does the searing pain of old wounds still consume my heart?
Why do anger and disappointment still burn inside me?

A traditional Javanese song plays and seems to ease Marsinah's anxiety.

My grandmother, Nek Poeirah, taught me to be accepting, to be a child who yields ...

And the ability to yield became my strength, allowed me to smile at bitterness, no matter how strong—despite my family's poverty, despite not being able to go to school.

She taught me that to live requires determination, but what kind of determination do I have now? All that remains of me is my soul, and yet they continue to pursue me.

Poverty had a stranglehold on my family. Each morning and evening, I had to wander through the town, peddling my grandma's cakes for pennies.

I almost never played with children my own age.

I never experienced the happiness of childhood, but I accepted my lot because with the money I made I could rent books and read to my heart's content.

To want an education and a better life ...

Was that too much?

To have hopes and aspirations ...

Was that too much?

Then why did my aspirations reveal to me the true meaning of poverty?

Why did my hopes drag me to a knowledge of my inevitable impotence?

The sound of footsteps. Marsinah again becomes tense.

The last time I visited Nganjuk, my grandma tried to stop me from leaving ... How unlike her that was.

She spoke about a premonition she'd had.

I knew she was responding to my own anxiety, but I was in too much of a hurry to listen to her.

In the end, I left without telling her why the factory in Sidoarjo had taken on such importance for me.

Marsinah suddenly seems terribly sad.

But then, what could I say?

What did my old grandma know about freedom of speech or defending one's rights?

The only thing life had taught her was to be in the rice field before sunrise and to stay there till sundown, because food was needed to fill the stomachs of her three grandchildren.

Marsinah grows anxious. She hears voices from the past ringing in her ears.

You might think that what I'm doing doesn't make sense, that it's crazy. But I must go. With or without you, I must go.

Dead for five years now, I feel like I died in vain.

They're trying to cover up the causes of my death:

'Marsinah's murder is a strictly criminal affair, having nothing to do with workers' rights; the motive behind the crime, quite simply, was revenge.'

And they're writing books about me—a woman who in her lifetime rarely had enough money to even buy a book!

What more do they want from me?

They dig up my bones.

Twice with no results they've dug up my grave.

And this is what I hate the most: they think they can put one over on us again; they think everyone is stupid.

But that is merely proof that I—that we—are chosen people, chosen for a great plan. And now is the time for us: when we no longer exist. We cannot be killed because we are already dead.

Though they scream all they want, they will hear what we have to say. But will they beat us down? Is it possible for a soul to be beaten down?

Voices from the past are once more audible. They momentarily disturb Marsinah, but she recovers. She steps forward and juts out her chin in the direction of one of the voices.

These voices, they continue to follow me.

They try to harm me, but I will not be afraid and I will not stop. I will stand in their midst and I will face them down.

Yes, my executioners ...

The voices of people who tried so hard to end my life are mingling with those who are struggling to see justice done for me.

I'm certain they're out there now, among you, the audience, spying on my every move.

But I'm not afraid, and I will not stop.

I will face them—yes, you my executioners.

You who wanted so much to take my life—will face you down, all of you.

I will make them turn away from my stare, or bow their heads, or flee from their sins.

I will make them fear my coming: 'Marsinah is here to accuse you.'

A bloodied knife will appear before your eyes, long after you thought you had escaped justice.

As the voices fade, Marsinah grows sadder and more anxious. She throws herself onto the floor. She speaks as if to herself.

I see so many hands drenched with blood ...

I witnessed how greed was fed, how businessmen kept making profits, how the managers and powerful kept laughing over each drop of my sweat.

And I also saw how a small and unimportant worker like myself, when she got the nerve to open her mouth and demand a raise, could threaten them so much that they had to take her life.

And now look how the powerful make my death into a golden monument to humanity, using it to further justice, to improve the lives of workers.

Marsinah laughs bitterly.

Improving workers' lives—raising their salaries from 1,500 to 1,700 per day; from 1,700 to 1,900 per day.

And what do we need besides a glass of sweet tea in the morning, a bowl of soup in the afternoon, and maybe another one at night?

That's their idea of a happy worker, the very same person who is expected to give them all her strength and loyalty without complaint.

Oh, they know how to play with numbers, but have they ever wondered if these numbers allow workers to feel like human beings?

And they congratulate themselves on their columns and rows of numbers.

And that's what they call improving workers' lives?!

How could the death of a nobody like myself improve the lives of the workers when the nation is so sick?

Another chorus of voices from the past causes Marsinah to rise in anger. She screams at the voices.

I'm not afraid of you!

I'm not afraid!

I take responsibility for all that happened ...

My broken life, the fear forever haunting me—I accept it.

My agonizing death, my broken bones, the bloody pools that soaked your heels—I can accept all of that.

What did you expect me to call these people?

In that place where I scraped just for a spoon of rice, I was hounded and chased by your shouts and threats.

I was tortured, I was raped, and murdered cruelly.

That is how you killed me, how you took away my right to life.

So what do I call these kinds of people, this nation?

The voices from the past fade. Marsinah is anxious. She sits with her arms around her legs, rocking.

What am I doing now if not reopening old wounds?

Oh, God, it hurts ...

No! It hurts too much.

I can't do it. No!

To hell with this impotent struggle—now aimless and dirtied by special interests.

To hell with the threats repeated again and again.

To hell with all the potential victims standing at the edge of a great pit ready to swallow them up.

I am a soul, with unending tears, fraught with old burdens.

What am I to do?

No!

Marsinah straightens her body, raises her head, and addresses the now-silent voices.

Tell them I'm not coming!

Marsinah, the gentle one; the gentle and weak soul; the poor, helpless and ignorant woman …

No! She's not coming!

She's going to wait until Judgement Day arrives, so she can stand there as the principal witness.

The atmosphere suddenly changes. Light bathes the room. Surprised, Marsinah rises, turns and looks around her.

What is this glorious room?

And who are you who have gathered here?

Marsinah walks to the platform, puts on a sash, and turns to face the audience. She stares at one section in particular.

I am here now.

And you, all of you. I know who you really are: a generation that should be independent and carefree, but that is sitting here with mournful gazes.

Marsinah moves closer to the group.

In God's name, your existence hurts the most.

Your anger is my old anger.

Your hopes are my old hopes—ones too modest to sacrifice a life for.

One day, in the middle of a procession, I saw you looking angrily at the sky ...

You were foaming at the mouth.

You were screaming for change.

Each time I saw you screaming like that, I was full of fear.

I wanted to say, 'Don't!'

I am a victim of that kind of anger, and proof that none of us can avoid it; my death is a symbol of your death, a symbol of the death of a generation, of the death of all hope for change ...

Marsinah pauses as if reconsidering. She looks up and begins to speak again.

You might not understand what I'm going to say, but I understand it well: in death I made a backward journey, an exploration that opened my eyes to many things.

About the world into which I was born, the world that cruelly took away my life.

It is a sick place, where truth is something to be covered up, placed in a box, and buried deep out of sight.

In that kind of world I was silenced—not just with a shout, but with torture, rape, the vicious and secret plunder of my body.

And to make sure that I kept my mouth shut, they took away my soul.

So what must I say to you now?

I know you have the right to refuse to listen—the most basic right of every human being. But what lesson have you learned from my experience?

Marsinah takes a newspaper and looks through it.

You can't imagine how many truths I know—ones that you have the right to know as citizens of this country.

I'm sure you're not going to find such truths here, in the newspaper. I can't find any in here.

The news you read is only what you are allowed to read, not what you have the right to read.

That's because you only start making a fuss after the forest fires rage everywhere and begin to take victims; but I knew those things long before the first flame was ignited.

I know both who started the fire and why.

You get yourselves worked up reading about the fire.

You get angry and upset.

Newspapers, seminars, performances talk about the forest fires as if they were some kind of *force majeur,* God's will …

A fuss without power, without teeth.

She reads from the newspaper.

'Continued steps will be taken towards economic recovery …

'Don't turn me into a cult figure …

'But that doesn't mean I refuse to be made a cult figure …

'But think about it, deep in your hearts …'

Marsinah angrily throws down the paper, but then is suddenly struck by the meaning of her gesture.

Wait a moment!

Is there anyone from the intelligence service here? A high government official by chance?

Praise God in heaven you're here. I'd like you to make note of this.

The woman Marsinah does not actually want to make an accusation. It's only that she's surprised …

Who are the people who have time to think about economic recovery?

Who has time to think about such things when their stomachs are growling with hunger?

The people are being dragged down by the threat of hunger.

They are surprised to hear that hundreds have died from hunger in regions where others make money.

It is into such a world that you were born, a world where wolves are on the prowl, which is the very reason your ignorance and hunger must continue. A world where poverty is actually an important asset, because Poverty gives birth to a Hero who will be the eradicator of Hunger.

It is in such a world where you will be the next generation, where on your shoulders the future of a nation will be placed. At the same time, into your nostrils is steadily blown the dust that kills a healthy mind. A diseased generation ... An unfortunate generation ...

Marsinah looks away.

Frankly, facing you is the part I most fear.

What can I say to you?

My right arm is blue and stiff from being yanked by a security officer at the factory. He shoved his hand into my underwear to try to prove I had no need for menstrual leave.

For weeks Kuneng, an underaged worker, was paralyzed by fear after a security officer roughly caressed her adolescent breasts.

Security officers—people who are just as poor as we are, and suffer just as much, yet because they're men and they own billy clubs, they feel that gives them the right to join in mistreating us and to use us as punching bags.

But not Subiyanto—he was an exception.

When seeing how badly shaken the young girl was, he took her to a counsellor, borrowing money to do it.

For me, Subiyanto was a protector, yet he was accused of being one of my killers.

If a fly landed on his food, he wouldn't chase it away—that's Subiyanto.

Marsinah looks away, staring cynically into the distance.

I have watched the justice department become an institute of torture.

I have seen witnesses silenced, made to disappear.

I have seen false witnesses stand, broken and afraid, like puppets ... Which is what happened to Subiyanto, that kind-hearted man.

After he was stripped of his clothing, electric cables were attached to his genitals and he was forced to say that he had helped to murder me.

They made up lies, they slandered me.

They put on trial people who weren't even there when I died.

All of you know the testimony was false, the trial was engineered.

And I know that you finally succeeded in freeing Subiyanto from that insane legal trap.

But what about me?

How did my soul suddenly flee my body if somebody did not cause it?

What would you say about that?

That the law is silent in this case?

That the justice branch has no voice?

That at the bench, where justice is supposed to be upheld, there is an exchange of money, blood, and bullets?

In God's name, I can't imagine how, one day, you will be able to justify this to your children and grandchildren. The court is supposed to be the final recourse for people like us, the one and only place we can count on to protect us.

But what do we get?

Marsinah suddenly stops. Turning, she faces in another direction.

Just a minute. There's something interesting over there.

She takes a pair of binoculars from off a table to get a better look.

You, sir, you in the corner. Aren't you a Member of Parliament?

Oh … God forbid, you're from one of the opposing factions.

Hmm …

Kuneng …

Again that unfortunate girl reminds me of how terrible it is to be powerless.

For more than a year, she succeeded in delaying the demolition of Kampung Ijo, the area where her parents owned a small plot of land they had purchased with a loan—able to pay it back only in small instalments.

Back and forth Kuneng went to Parliament, convinced that her representative would defend her parents' interests and secure for them appropriate compensation.

One day, coming home from work, Kuneng was amazed to find Kampung Ijo had been flattened by a tractor.

And so she hanged herself … And until the moment of her death she never understood that games had been going on behind her back.

Since then, every time I see that big, glass-faced building in Jakarta, my heart seethes.

That building is the People's Building, we are told—where the people's rights are defended.

But what happened to Kuneng makes me unable to trust in anything coming out of that place.

Take the fate of us workers, for example. We're nothing to them. They don't even see us as members of society in need of justice.

I have witnessed people being stripped of their dignity.

I have seen people evicted from their homes—the women crying, their children in complete confusion.

I have seen rifle butts stealing lives and human dignity with complete abandon.

And from that grand-looking place nothing comes except silence.

And you, sir? What are you doing about it?

You're sitting here at a play about the death of a factory worker that resulted from your inability to defend her rights.

For God's sake …

I would really like to know whether your choice to be here is the result of …

Marsinah turns away from the man to speak to the audience.

Did you see what happened? Silence.

What did I tell you? A representative of the people should be for the people—not the other way around.

The sound of footsteps is heard. Marsinah realizes that she must finish. She retreats slowly. Suddenly the look en her face is one of darkness and anger.

A book was written about my death, and all of you are here showing your concern.

What concern?

If there's anyone here with the right to be concerned, it is I.

I am the unfortunate woman. I am Marsinah.

In God's name, I am forced to ask, 'What do you think you've actually done for me?'

Are those supposed to be laurels—those books and your other efforts to make me a hero?

I never dreamed of being a hero.

A new wave of anger washes over Marsinah.

My life was taken from me because I thought I had the right to say no, because I thought I had the right to hope; to have my own body and soul; to struggle for a bowl of rice so that I wouldn't starve; to struggle for a little extra pay so I could improve my education.

Beneath the threat of rifles, I saw my friends thrown out of their jobs and I defended them.

That's all I did ...

And because of it I was deemed to be a danger, and a candidate for death.

And do you know the saddest thing about all this?

That *you* let it happen, and accepted a lie in place of the truth. An insane truth that cannot be altered.

Tell me how much force it takes for an object to break through a woman's pelvic bone and rip into her uterine wall. Ask me the meaning of barbarism.

Voices from the past are once more heard. Marsinah panics. Her bitter experiences, the horrible attack on her cause her body to shake.

I remember clearly the fear that overwhelmed me when rough hands grabbed me from behind, covered my eyes with a cloth, and knotted it tightly.

I was pushed into a car that sped away in a direction I couldn't be sure of.

I don't remember any sound.

I don't know how far I was taken, but I do remember very well that when the car stopped, I was pushed outside, dumped onto the ground.

And then I was dragged until ... I don't know how far I was dragged, but I recall my body shaking violently from fear.

Then I heard a door open in front of me.

I don't know whether I hit my head against a wall, or if a billy club bashed my forehead.

I only know that I suddenly found myself lying on the floor, and that when I tried to get up, several pairs of heavy shoes stomped on me—crushing my shins, my stomach, my chest, my arms.

And the foul language and curses that were spat at me!

I can't count the number of times my body was picked up and thrown down, picked up and thrown down again—on the floor, against the edge of a table, onto a chair, until I had no strength left at all.

The barbarism had no end; when I couldn't even move the tips of my fingers, they really ran amuck, attacking me, pulverizing my body.

Marsinah stops. She stutters.

God! Stop this! I cried inside.

I moaned. I wailed.

I screamed as hard as I could, yet no sound came out.

My voice was stopped by the rag that was shoved in my mouth.

My mouth and my throat felt like they were being torn apart.

I struggled, tried to defend myself until … until I had nothing left.

My voice. My strength. Everything …

I let them devour me.

I let my bones be crushed, and …

Marsinah stops again. Her body shakes violently.

… and let an object—something large, sharp and hard, something I haven't the power to conjure an image of—split my pelvic bone.

Marsinah throws herself down, then moves by trying to crawl.

Why, dear God? Why me?

I wanted to cry, but I couldn't.

I was so broken, I couldn't even shed a tear.

The blood …

The blood was everywhere, black and dirtied, so very dirty …

It soaked my stomach, soaked the inner parts of my thighs, splattered the floor, the walls, the table, everything …

Those were the last moments when I could feel something, and it was something that hurt so much, something that terrified me so much …

The viciousness of it …

My God, no one deserves that.

I felt humiliated and defiled.

And I was alone, completely alone.

I tried to raise my body to look for …

To look for what?

What could I possibly find?

My grandmother, my sisters and brother?

My father?

Where were my friends?

And you … Where were you at that time?

Why, God, did You teach me about love, then allow them to terrify me, permit their greed to take from me everything I had a right to.

You gave me a womb.

You made a promise to me of miracles, but You let me be broken by fear and power.

Why?

Marsinah rises with difficulty. She appears as if she is going to faint.

I gathered all the strength that I could muster, then tried to make the confession of faith. But when I tried to open my mouth to call Your name … God … My mouth felt numb. I felt it wrong to pray. I felt unclean, so unclean.

And so I began to count: one, two, ten, one hundred, and so on.

I kept on counting: six thousand, seven thousand, ten thousand …

I wanted to forget my fear.

I wanted so much to rid myself of the loathing that consumed me, but I was not able to.

I was broken, I tried to rise.

Then I began to turn ...

Marsinah turns, slowly at first, then faster and faster.

I turned and I turned. I turned and turned and turned ...

Marsinah spins until she falls. The sound of a tambourine gets louder as a picture of the real Marsinah appears.

I celebrate my insanity from the suffering I could not bear.
I dance in a festival of sin and outrage.
I burn a coal in my chest.
I let the smoke waft from my pores.
Fire flows through my veins. The fire of breath is in my lungs.
My entire body is charred and burned by my hatred of injustice.

A vertical shaft of light suddenly shines on Marsinah's body. She thrusts out her arms and grabs at the earth around her. In the background a person recites a Koranic prayer: 'Yaa Arhamar Raahimin, ir hamna ...' *(Oh, God, the Most Loving ...)*

This land that once gave me hope and life is now united with my blood, with my flesh and bones. And now I am one with the land and the dust.

Marsinah crawls towards the platform. She speaks now in a clear voice.

I'll go. I must go now.

The light on Marsinah dissolves, then illuminates a screen where the picture of Marsinah is projected.

My God, there was nothing strange about what happened to me. Nothing odd about a fate that has befallen millions of people like me.

We are all children of this land.

A corrupt land, a people for whom power is everything, a nation where the exercise of power justifies anything.

In the background someone recites 'Yaa Arhamar Raahimin, ir hamna …'

To all of you I leave this reminder: *you* allowed my life to be taken from me.

Don't let my death be for nothing.

If you find my killers now, it means nothing to me at all.

But I beg you, find them for my friends' sake!

Lead my friends away from unclean hands.

Save them from those rapacious people who in their arrogance think this country is theirs alone.

Remember this …

Save them and you will save this country you love.

The light slowly fades.

Translated by John H. McGlynn

Taiwan

Flower Season

LI-ANG

It was a minor incident that occurred during the days of my now lost radiant youth.

I was quite young then, a period that should have witnessed the flowering of my youth; but all I possessed were a few translations of novels I'd bought in some bookstore and a prince on a white horse who existed only in my dreams.

Such a simple affair, one that now seems so trite. It was a December day just before Christmas, on perhaps the sunniest morning of the month, when the cold, dry sky was washed clean by the beautiful, sparkling rays of the sun. After getting out of bed, I hung around the back yard, deeply moved by the way the morning sunbeams brought new life to the sleepy garden.

The slowly rising winter sun now shone over the entire garden. It was time to go to school, but the thought of sitting in a boring classroom in my present mood was a fearful prospect, and seemed a waste of time. Why not give myself a holiday? Father and Mother had already left for the factory, so no one would know whether or not I went to school.

I hung around the garden awhile longer as the sun climbed in the sky behind me, gently caressing my back through a thin sweater. I began to turn around ever so slowly, ever so gingerly. As my imagination took over, I expected to see a pair of beautiful black eyes amid the trees or among the flowers scrutinizing me. They should have a mournful gaze with just a hint of derision. I spun around, but the black eyes were nowhere in sight.

Just sitting there under the sun was so boring I went inside and got a picture book, which I flipped through casually. All the people resembled flecks of dust whirling back and forth under the sun's rays. On the last page a prince and princess stood beneath a tall Christmas tree holding hands and smiling. The caption read:

> Tiny bells rang as the tree rustled in the wind:
> The Prince and Princess sought eternal happiness
> During Christmastime.

Ah, Christmas! I muttered, tears welling up in my eyes. I might not be able to celebrate Christmas as they were doing, but I could have my very own Christmas tree, to decorate with little golden bells.

So I went to the marketplace, where I wandered among throngs of shoppers and stepped over fruits and vegetables laid out on the ground until I found a florist shop tucked away in a corner.

I want to buy a tree, about two or three feet tall.

What kind of tree?

Any kind's all right, as long as it has lots of leaves.

I see.

A large woman suddenly grabbed hold of the florist and said something to him excitedly, then darted back in among the crowd of shoppers. All I could see of her were two sinewy legs that looked like the coiling dragons on temple pillars; but before long even they were swallowed up by thc sea of legs—fat, thin, long, and short.

I just stood there. Everything that had happened so far today, from this morning when I decided not to go to school, up till now, struck me as funny. Playing hooky, the prince and the princess, the strange departure of the florist, the flowers all around me, the clamour of people beyond the flowers—everything seemed unreal and laughable, as though everything were being thrown into incredible disorder by some mischievous spirit.

The florist returned, pushing a bicycle ahead of him.

Get on, he said roughly.

Where are we going? I asked.

To get a tree.

Oh, what a strange florist.

Won't someone steal your flowers while you're gone?

No. There was a note of impatience in his voice.

I straddled the bicycle behind him. Okay, I said.

He started off slowly, steadily, as if the person sitting behind him were his daughter of something, not some customer. I smiled at the people on the street teasingly; if people who knew me could see me now their mouths would drop open in amazement, their gold-capped teeth glinting in the sunlight. I kept smiling, but after the bicycle had made its way through the crowds of people, my smile was no longer a natural one. I hadn't seen a single familiar face, no one who would have made a fuss over spotting me like this; my smile was soon erased by feelings of disappointment.

The bike sailed along the level asphalt road heading out to the suburbs. As I raised my head, the cold December air brushed past my cheeks and blew my hair straight back. What a marvelous pose I struck, I thought; that pair of beautiful black eyes is probably off in the distance staring at me. I drifted into a fantasy about those black eyes.

Where's your garden? There weren't many people on the road now; they were replaced by man-high stalks of sugarcane on both sides. I'd returned to the here-and-now and asked this question with a tinge of anxiety.

Up ahead a ways, the florist answered.

Are we nearly there?

Pretty soon.

His calm voice didn't comfort me much, for the desolate scene around me made me think of what I might be getting myself into. He'd stop the bicycle and turn around, a sinister smile on his face, then grab me and drag me into the dense sugarcane field, where he'd rip off my clothes with his sunburned, slightly mud-caked hands and caress my unsoiled, virgin body. A feeling of disgust welled up inside me; I shifted my position on the bicycle, as though that were all I had to do to avoid such a calamity.

What should I do, I asked myself, to keep from becoming a sacrificial victim? I was so young, and a girl in the bloom of youth should not be made to wither.

A farmer with a pole over his shoulder, a basket on each end, approached from the opposite direction. My first impulse was to jump off and run to my farmer-saviour. For a moment I didn't even consider the injuries I might sustain by jumping off the bike. But then the thought of the pain made me hesitate for an instant, and in that brief moment the bicycle sped up, leaving the farmer far behind us. There goes that plan.

I decided to stay put and see what happened. If the florist tried to do what I feared, I could still run away. As one of the fastest runners in my school, I was sure I could beat a doddering old man in a footrace.

I sat there calmly and dreamt up a happy scenario: the florist was unable to run another step, while I was as fleet of foot as ever, turning my head back with a broad smile as I ran, like a forest nymph teasing her admirer. I tried to imagine the look on the florist's face at that moment: it would, I thought, be a contorted look of frustrated desire.

How much farther? I asked petulantly.

Not much, he said, turning back slightly with a comforting grin on his face.

As he turned his sunburned face toward me, the silhouette of a sharply hooked nose and thin, protruding lips under sunken cheeks came into view. He had a high, arched brow deeply creased by wrinkles and sunken eyes that seemed to reflect the rays of the sun under eyebrows that were still black. No evidence of desire on that face, only the dark, stern mien of an old man for whom sexual desire was a thing of the past. I was disappointed.

The bicycle suddenly lurched, and when the florist turned back to look at me, I could tell he'd run into something. I jumped down sprightly.

I'll have to be more careful, he mumbled. He bent over to straighten the handlebars, which had been knocked out of alignment. I stood to the side, experiencing a return of my playful mood of a moment before. The humour of the situation struck me: here I was, with a strange man in a place I seldom ever went, watching him fix his bicycle, and I was reminded of a pair of lovers on a private excursion in a French movie.

I nearly said, let's just forget it. I want to go home. But all I did was walk around in circles on the road, possibly because the placid look on the florist's face was reassuring.

Get back on, he said as he remounted the now-repaired bicycle.

I climbed on behind him. Okay, I said.

Now that my anxieties had lessened, my imagination took over again. Maybe the florist was an educated man, after all, I was thinking (his brow gave me the impression of a man of learning). Maybe he had had the misfortune of being burdened with a wife of little virtue who had run off with another man, thus forcing him to make a living as a florist. I was now being taken to his garden, where delicate flowers flourished, and in the centre of which stood a small white house with ivy-covered walls and a tiny chimney that emitted ethereal wisps of smoke at eventide.

In order to substantiate my imaginings, I cocked my head to look at the man sitting in front of me, but what I could see of his straight back told me nothing.

Next I thought that maybe he was just what he appeared to be—a florist, possibly a pervert. There is a vast difference between appearance and actions. Someone once told me the story of a respected old man who had violated a grade-school girl.

The bicycle stopped with a screeching of the brakes. Having not yet completely lowered my guard, I jumped to the ground, prepared to run away if need be; I knew I had to put myself at an advantage from the beginning if I was to avoid getting swallowed up in the sea of sugarcane stalks all around me.

The florist got off the bicycle and turned slowly toward me. Here it comes, I thought, so I retreated a step. My legs were shaking and I wasn't sure I'd be able to run when the time came. Yet even then a strange sensation of excited curiosity came over me: a race was about to begin. and not the everyday, meaningless type, but one with a clear purpose. This wasn't the sort of emptiness one experiences while waiting for the only theatre in town to begin running a new movie.

We have to take this path, the florist said as he walked the bicycle up to a narrow, nearly hidden pathway.

I could feel the slow, heavy beating of my heart as I followed him: I was dragging my feet, feeling empty inside.

The path narrowed even more as we went along, and we had to part the sugarcane stalks that bent inward from both sides. Dry yellow leaves hung on the plump, ripe, reddish-brown sugarcane stalks and made whispering sounds with each gust of wind. There was a sense of evil created by the dimly visible reddish-brown sugarcane stalks and the signs of withered death in a field so dense that the sun's rays could not penetrate it. Reminded of the face on an icon at the monastery, I shuddered.

The fatalistic resignation created by a sense of forlornness was suddenly replaced by new fears. The florist and I were separated by five or six paces, a distance I imagined to be sufficient to bolt when the need arose. The sugarcane field and my fear of the florist brought a rush of memories of all the strange stories I'd ever read. At one point it got so bad that the florist, who was still walking several stops ahead of me, seemed transformed into a reddish-brown rabbit.

I tried with all my might to clear my mind of these strange illusions, but was not very successful. Only when we'd emerged from the sugarcane field and begun climbing a small hill was I able to finally rid myself of that horrid reddish-brown colour—complete with hair and blood.

The earth beneath my feet was so soft and shifting that I slipped as I proceeded ahead laboriously. The sun's rays scorched my face and the steamy heat made the footing on the small hill so difficult I felt completely helpless. There was nothing anywhere I could hold on to for support—no trees or plants, not a single green object. The sky was a clear blue—not a hint of a cloud—and the winds had stilled completely, Behind me was the sugarcane field, a mixture of withering yellow and reddish-brown, but there was nothing around me now but gray sandy earth. I longed for a helping hand—whose it didn't matter, as long as it could aid me in extricating myself from the trap I'd fallen into. But the sight of the florist ahead of me laboriously pushing his bicycle along kept me from calling out.

I finally made it to the top of the hill just as a blast of cold wind brushed against my sweating face, the cold bringing with it increased fears. Seeing the florist far up ahead, I sat down to rest. At that moment, to my surprise, I discovered I could catch an occasional glimpse of my school building through the trees swaying in the wind in front of me. I looked at my watch—nearly ten o'clock, so everyone was still in second period. Today that would be Chinese literature; I tried to imagine the soft voice of the newly married teacher as she explained the lesson. It was so funny, I thought, how a woman turns into a marshmallow as soon as she gets married, and how she is forever trying to make a show of the unbearable new sweetness that has entered her life.

Down we go, the florist said as he got to his feet.

I stood up and promptly slid forward on the shifting sand, nearly falling down in the process: I remedied the situation by running and hopping clown the hillside.

We really shouldn't have taken this path, although it's faster and saves us from having to go the long way round, the florist mumbled as he straightened up the bicycle.

Get on, he said.

As soon as I was seated, we headed off again. There were no longer any sugarcane fields around us: now we were surrounded by paddy fields. The water-bamboo shoots had already been harvested, so all that remained in the watery fields were a few dried stalks here and there. These dried stalks were familiar to me, and if my guess was correct, this road would take us straight to school. The schoolhouse would come into view as soon as we rounded the little Earth God temple.

The other girls were still in class: if I were in class. I'd probably be estimating how much my Chinese literature teacher's belly had swelled and trying to figure out if she was pregnant when she got married. The word pregnant lingered in my mind for a moment: what if that happened to me? What would I do then? Would I fret all day long, or commit suicide, like the fallen heroines in storybooks? Have an abortion? No, not that, I thought, shaking my head. I was a fast runner; besides, we weren't far from school.

The sight of the school pond brought a new fear: how would I explain what I was doing if I ran into one of the teachers at the school gate? Yet even that could work to my advantage, since at least I'd be extricated from the game I'd gotten myself into, and which was now completely beyond my control.

But there wasn't a soul at the main gate of the school, and I was filled with strangely mixed feelings of discomfort and joy. Before I had time to decide what to do next, we'd left the school gate far behind.

How much farther? I asked wearily after we'd continued for a while up the road.

It's right up ahead, there at the bend, the florist answered in the same calm voice.

We were approaching a cemetery. The cluster of gravesites reminded me of a grove of heavily laden fruit trees. The sun's rays glinting brightly off the tombstones hurt my eyes. Why hadn't I considered this? Maybe after he finished with me he was going to kill me and dump my body in this neglected cemetery, where I'd go unnoticed. I felt a chill and shifted my position as if to ready myself to jump down.

It's right up ahead, beyond the bend in the road, the florist said, seemingly sensing my feelings of disquietude.

We made the turn, and as the cemetery receded into the distance behind me to the right, I felt better. The florist dismounted and pushed open a bamboo gate.

Here we are. Come in and have a look.

The garden wasn't very large. In it were planted several rows of plants and shrubs, the names of which I didn't know, except for a few anaemic-looking chrysanthemum bushes blooming here and there. The sight nearly made me cry, for on the way over I'd entertained hopes of seeing a garden resplendent with all kinds of beautiful flowers, even though it was already winter and Christmas was approaching.

The florist pointed out several small trees to me, but they were too puny for any decorative use. I looked around, but found nothing I liked.

I have some more over there. Why not take a look?

All right, I said, falling in behind him as he walked over to another, even smaller, garden. From there I could see scattered gravesites off in the distance; it was a bad omen. It was then I noticed that this particular garden was completely enclosed; all around me was a barrier of thorny bushes resembling prickly-pear plants, the only break in the enclosure being the small gate through which we'd entered a moment earlier. I took a quick glance all around to find some avenue of escape. At last I spotted a hoe leaning up against a corner of the wall. Pretending to be interested in a tree planted there, I walked over slowly and tentatively.

These over here aren't bad, the florist said, falling in behind me.

Wanting to leave the place as quickly as possible. I pointed to one of the small trees at random; the florist bent over and began to dig it up. I backed up to a spot where I could easily reach out and grab the hoe. I stood there, feelings of fear and playfulness surging over me again. I could imagine scenes of the impending struggle.

The florist suddenly straightened up: I took a firm hold on the handle of the hoe, drawing it nearer to me; but the florist, unaware of my actions, merely stretched momentarily, then bent down again. The hoe slipped from my grasp and fell into a bush behind me, making a muffled sound.

That does it, he said. He wrapped the uprooted tree for me and walked out through the garden gate. I followed.

Passing through the small bamboo gate. I emerged onto the main road. After taking a few steps, I turned a corner, from where I could see the gravesites again. Holding firmly onto the scrawny tree, I broke into a run, not stopping until I'd put the cemetery far behind me. I was breathless.

And that's all there was to the incident: nothing, nothing at all, had happened. But had I hoped for something to happen? I wasn't sure. Realizing I had a long walk ahead of me, I held on to the little tree and started off, listlessly dragging my feet towards home.

Translated by Howard Goldblatt

Tibet

An Old Nun Tells Her Story

GEYANG

The month I was born, my mother dreamed that there was a gold Buddha as long as her arm inside our stove. As she carefully lifted it out, the Buddha's head fell off. Several days later, I was born. My father had wanted a boy. My mother told me that if I'd been a boy, I wouldn't have lived because, as her dream showed, it wasn't her fate to have a boy. Except for my father, everyone in the family was happy about my arrival, especially my sister. Before I was born, she was lonesome. My five brothers, by my father's other wife, spurned her company. The afternoon Mother was giving birth to me, my sister was in the Sutra room, praying for a girl. When, years later, she told me this, I was quite moved.

My father was an able merchant. By the time I was born, he owned a silk-goods shop, a tea and porcelain shop, and an estate in Toelung that he had bought from an impoverished aristocrat. However, the estate was not completely ours: we still had to pay annual rent to the Kashag government. There were thick groves of willows on the banks of a little brook gurgling past the back of the house, and a garden that overflowed with the scent of roses. But we stayed on the estate only for short periods, every now and then. It was only after I was grown that I realized the soil on the estate was so poor, and its irrigation system so inadequate, that the harvest sometimes wasn't enough to cover our rent.

Father was of pure Khampa ancestry. When he was fourteen, he left the tiny temple where he'd been a lama and came to Lhasa to seek his fortune. He had realized that the powerful ambition surging within him would be a kind of desecration in the monastery. The wealth and influence he acquired proved the wisdom of his decision.

Father had two wives, so I had two mothers. They lived peaceably, like sisters, and together bore my father five sons and two daughters.

Old Mother was a devout Buddhist. She passed the greatest part of her day in our Sutra room. As far back as I can remember, she ate vegetarian food—rarely having her meals with the rest of us—and sometimes she fasted. Despite this, she was fat; so I think whether one is fat or thin is probably fated by heaven. She wasn't my natural mother, but it was from her that I received most of my childhood education, just as my brothers and sister did.

Without any doubt, my natural mother was a beauty. She was fond of dressing up and gave herself a fresh, new look every day. It was she who managed all the affairs in our home, and under her direction, everything in the household was kept orderly and neat as a pin. She liked to sing and play the *dramnyen* and knew all the street singers' popular songs. The trouble was that she was so busy she never had time for us children, who needed her care and attention.

My only companion was my older sister. I always gave in to her whims, and she always discovered fascinating things for us to see and do.

The year I was five, Father and my eldest brother set out on a long business journey. They were gone almost two years. When they finally returned home, I thought: Why are these strangers hugging and kissing us? I didn't dare approach them.

Barely three years older than I, my sister had the opposite reaction. She threw her arms around Father the moment he entered the room. I found this strange because she'd told me that she hated him so much she hoped he'd never come back. Pretence isn't always a bad thing; on the contrary, sometimes it makes us lovable.

When I was eight, my natural mother told me I would be taken to a convent in Gyantse to become a nun. She dressed me in a reddish-brown skirt and robe and told me I looked lovely in them. I stood a long time looking at myself in the mirror, worrying that I wouldn't be beautiful after my hair was cut off. As I look back now, I realize how ridiculously vain I was. Fortunately, reddish-brown becomes me.

Who decided to send me away to be a nun—my father or my mother? I hadn't the understanding to consider the matter then. I only hoped the place I was going to would be as beautiful as our manor. So, bewildered and confused, I left my family and home.

It was a fine temple: the solemn, magnificent Sutra hall; the glistening snow-white stupa; the great, heavy gate painted with elaborate designs; the narrow, stone stairway up the hillside; the green trees; the bright, many-coloured flowers, the little birds whose names I didn't know. I couldn't help immediately falling in love with it. It was so much more wonderful than I had imagined.

There were seventy or eighty nuns. When I looked at their placid faces, I hadn't the least doubt that I would become one of them. We were so tiny, so insignificant. We could only kneel before our Master, the incomparable Lord Buddha, and pray—not only for liberation from our misdeeds, but also for the liberation of all sentient beings.

Convent life was austere, but once I had grown accustomed to it, it didn't seem so. It was monotonous, but once I accepted it, it no longer seemed monotonous.

The convent had a dozen yaks and a few dozen sheep. Winters, the nuns took turns tending these animals in the fields. Summers, the temple turned the animals over to herdsmen who took them to distant mountain pastures. All this followed an ancient unwritten practice: when summer comes, the herdsmen pack up their tents and take the animals up to the mountains to graze, leaving the lowland grass to grow for the herds in winter.

The winter pasture was quite a distance from our little temple. More often than not, we were completely exhausted by the time we reached it. Still, I liked being sent there, liked the boundless grasslands, lying on the grass and looking up at the sky, and the feeling I got watching the smoke rise into the heavens as the tea brewed over the fire. Sometimes the nomad herdsmen teased us with brazen jokes so that we blushed until our ears turned red.

We went to the pasture in pairs. I was usually paired with Nechung, who was four years older than I. From the time she was little, she had neither father nor mother and was brought up by her brother and his wife, and so she knew how to do many things I didn't, but she was understanding and sympathetic and didn't mind my mistakes. She was not beautiful, but in my eyes she was lovable. The year she turned fourteen, a young herdsman fell in love with her and was always thinking up ways to get near her.

One beautiful sunny afternoon, Nechung and I built a fire, made our tea, ate the *tsampa* we'd brought with us, and then lay down on the grass. A light breeze was blowing, and the sun was so dazzling that we couldn't keep our eyes open. Gradually, we fell asleep.

I'm not sure how much time had passed. A cry awoke me. The young herdsman was clutching Nechung in his arms and kissing her. Presently, he stood up and walked off a few steps. He'd put his arms around her before to tease her. I felt it was all silly, lay down again, closed my eyes, and fell asleep. When I woke up, Nechung was sitting at my side with a blank stare on her face. She looked at me. Something in her expression made me uneasy.

'He made me sleep with him,' she said calmly. 'He was so strong I couldn't stop him.'

I knew she was upset, but I didn't know what to do for her. We went back to our temple, returned the livestock to their pens, filled the water jars, ate our supper, chanted the Sutras, and went to bed. I woke up in the middle of the night and heard Nechung crying. We sat with our arms around each other until dawn, terrified.

Looking after the livestock was no longer something beautiful for us now. The moment we set foot on the pasture, fear was at our side. Fortunately, the weather turned warm early that year: the herdsmen soon took the herds off to the mountains, and we no longer had to look after the livestock.

I was only ten at the time, too young to understand what had happened to Nechung. I couldn't comprehend her anguish, and she was afraid to express it; neither could I console her. I realize now that she didn't expect a ten-year-old girl to help her solve her problem. She just needed me at her side.

Before this happened, she had been a happy girl, though no one ever came to visit her. Her faith told her that everything that happened to her was determined by her actions in her previous life, so she wasn't worried about this life. She believed that if she just tried hard, her next life would be one of good fortune. And so she chanted more Sutras than other nuns, worked harder, and bore the misunderstandings and burdens that others created for her. But with this calamity, her purpose in life was snatched away: she believed she had defiled herself in the eyes of Lord Buddha.

Worst of all, she was pregnant. We realized this months later, when her stomach was so swollen it was impossible to hide. If we hadn't been so naive, perhaps we might have realized it earlier and thought of something to do about it—perhaps ... But until our teacher explained it to her, we were paralyzed by anxiety and didn't know that inside her slender body a tiny life was stirring.

She told her teacher everything. But it wasn't a story that everyone could believe. Probably everyone but I doubted her story to some degree. I was disgusted with the nuns around me, but I realize now that I ought not to have blamed them. Anyone with common sense would have had some misgiving.

One morning our teacher came to tell Nechung that the abbess would permit her to have the baby in the convent, but Nechung would have to leave after that. She was devastated. She told me that she didn't want to go on living. To leave the temple, she thought, was to forsake all hope for a good life in her next reincarnation.

In the convent barn, among the piles of hay, Nechung gave birth to a sturdy, healthy boy. The sight of the baby dissolved the nuns' misgivings and moved the abbess's heart to compassion: if Nechung and her child were to leave the temple now, how would they survive? The abbess said she would allow Nechung to remain a year.

And so she should have enjoyed a year of peace and security, during which her wounded soul might have healed. But this was not to be.

Another nun got pregnant, and the abbess's rage fell like lightning on Nechung. The abbess felt that the second nun had gotten pregnant because she hadn't punished Nechung severely enough. Our convent's reputation for purity and upright conduct had been blackened. The abbess announced that both Nechung and the other nun were to leave in ten days—never to return.

For two days Nechung spoke to no one. There was no resentment in her eyes, no blame. She accepted her expulsion as her fate. She gave no thought to how she would live after she left the temple, or where her path in the world might lead. She was waiting for death.

When punishment for someone else's misdeed crushes us, may we put an end to our life? May we ignore the teaching that, by choosing to die, we terminate the cycle of our reincarnations and suffer in hell for eternity?

It was my turn to take out the herds. Out of breath and panting, I reached the pasture with my new companion, a girl of infectious merry spirits. Our laughter attracted a crowd of other children watching their livestock. Someone began singing, and we danced around in a circle until we were worn out. I lay down on the grass.

Suddenly, my thoughts returned to Nechung. When I got back that evening, would I find her dead by her own hand? The boy who'd violated her was nearby, cheerfully drinking his tea. An irresistible impulse brought me to my feet.

His eyes shifted nervously as I stood before him. I discovered that I was frightened too. How should I begin talking? He had made love a pretext for doing what he wanted and had no idea of the suffering he'd caused. I wanted to chastise him, curse him, beat him, stab him, kill him. I didn't dare. I couldn't even scold him.

Stammering, I blurted out everything—what I should have told him and what I shouldn't have—as if I was just telling a touching little story. When the story was finished, I had nothing more to say.

There was an awkward silence. He sat silently, and I walked away.

Had I run all this way just to tell him he had a son?

When I got back to the temple, I was relieved to find Nechung still alive. She rushed up to me and said, 'He's here.'

'Who?'

'The boy who …'

'What for?'

'I don't know.'

'Where?'

'With our teacher.'

Like criminals awaiting sentence, we mutely sat side by side, gripping each other by the hand as if we would never see each other again once we let go. Nechung clutched her baby to her breast. Presently, the sound of approaching steps jolted us out of our daze. Then he was standing there before us. 'I confessed everything to your teacher,' he said. 'If the abbess won't let you stay, there's a place for you in my tent.' He looked at the baby, reached out, stroked it, and said, 'A child without a father …'

The abbess changed her mind about Nechung staying at the convent, but now Nechung insisted on leaving—with the man she'd feared and hated. 'It isn't my fate to serve Lord Buddha in this life,' she declared. 'Heaven sent that man for me to take care of. I'll keep in my heart everything I've learned here in the temple.'

I was so young I didn't understand what it meant to part with someone. I thought she'd remain in the pasture lands nearby, but though I later searched and searched, I never found her. She and her man had disappeared forever.

My only good friend was gone. I grew lonely again. Luckily, people from home came to visit me. They brought alms for the temple, as well as things that I needed.

Sometimes I left the convent in the company of other nuns to go begging in distant cities. Often we'd stop several days in towns along the way, and so I saw something of the varied, colourful life of the world. But it did not make me want to change where I was.

When Old Mother died, the family sent a servant to bring me back home. As I again stood at the gate of the courtyard where I was born, my heart grew anxious. How much had changed in four years? How much had I forgotten?

The face of my own mother seemed strange to me. Watching me from my mother's side, dressed in violet satin *pume* and matching yellow *puyod,* was my sister. Could this beauty be the girl I'd slept with in the same bed when I was little? Her skin was so fair, so lovely! Suddenly I thought of my own face. How long had it been since I'd looked in a mirror? Did I look like her? I must look like her—we had the same mother! But maybe I didn't—maybe I didn't look like her at all ... As my imagination was running away with me, my father walked into the room as solemn and majestic as ever. He was genial, even smiled at me, but I was still afraid of him.

Several of my brothers were there, but I couldn't tell them apart. Only my second brother, who was lame, told me which one he was.

I must have been a stranger in their eyes as well.

Though Old Mother had already died when I arrived, she is the only distinct person in my recollection of that time. She had visited me once a year at the convent. The donations she had brought made me proud. Her words, her tone, the expression on her face had given me such courage.

The whole house was grief stricken. Father had lost a good wife.

My mother had lost a friend and sister. My brothers and sisters had lost a compassionate mother. The servants had lost a benevolent mistress. She had treated everybody kindly, done whatever she could to help people, and never caused trouble for anyone. She considered everyone's mistakes forgivable. A person like her was sure to be reborn into a beautiful next life and to enter the way of future reincarnations in peace. If we were grief stricken merely because we would not see her again and benefit from her kindness, wasn't there some selfishness in our sorrow?

I stayed on at home for four months, gradually becoming reacquainted with my family. They were especially attentive to me; still, I spent most of my time in the Sutra room.

I didn't know what I would have felt in a truly rich house, but the luxury of our home shocked me. I recalled our little temple, where we considered radishes a treat, where we had our tea with just a tiny lump of yak butter or nothing at all, where we never thought of cake or candy. We worked so hard, got up with the stars still hanging in the sky and recited so many Sutras. Yet it all made sense. Watching the life of my family after Old Mother died helped me to understand how impossible it is to set out on the path that leads to self-liberation and peace without deep faith and prayer in our hearts.

My sister turned sixteen that year. Beauty is always something good—her loveliness delighted me. My brothers were frequently away from home, absorbed in their own affairs. I never bothered to discover what they did. My mother was still the same: elegant and graceful. The daily round of life in the house went on beneath her watchful eye, as before. She had two more helpers now: my two new sisters-in-law. My sister took no trouble to conceal her strife with them.

A merchant friend of my father gave him a piece of beautiful white Russian cloth. To this day, I can't say what kind of material it was. Its texture, its sheen, its pattern—everything about it mesmerized my sister and my two sisters-in-law, but it was only big enough to make two skirts. I knew that dividing this piece of cloth would create a problem. Without the least hesitation, my father gave it to my two sisters-in-law, and my sister was heartbroken for an entire week.

Finally, I returned to the remote little temple, where there were always tribulations but nothing of the sort to make me think there was anything wrong with convent life.

I next returned home three years later. What a difference between one person's death and another's! Till then I had naively associated death with the elderly. My sister's death hurled me into depression.

If only she had lived, she would have been a bride and then a mistress of an aristocratic home. She would have borne beautiful children, devoted her life to her husband, and become a radiant star in society. Her fatal illness had snatched away a vibrant, lovely girl with such magnificent hopes ... Death was truly omnipotent.

My companion was gone, and our home seemed alien to me.

My sister's death aged my mother. The first wrinkles appeared on her face. She was my mother, but we had never been close, never confided in one another. Still, I loved her, and her anguish troubled me.

I'd been home half a year, and still there was no sign of any preparations to send me back to the convent. Early one morning, when I was chanting my Sutras, my mother came to me carrying a light blue robe and matching skirt and a pair of black leather shoes. She told me to put them on.

'Why?' I asked, surprised.

'Your father wants you to wear these. Guests are coming.'

She looked over my hair and seemed quite satisfied. Though it was only an inch long, it had a natural curl and probably didn't look too unattractive.

She left. Bewildered, silent, I changed my clothes. In the past when guests had come for dinner, nobody had called me to join them. I ate alone in the Sutra room. I thought solitude was the lot of a nun. After I changed into the new clothes, I felt ashamed. I didn't return to the Sutra room. To sit on the cushion dressed like that, reciting my Sutras, would somehow be improper.

When Mother came to call me, she had recaptured the radiance she'd lost after my sister's death. There was only one guest, a man thirty or forty years old, not very tall or robust, a very ordinary-looking person. As I sat at the table and started to eat, I found myself doing such ridiculous things that I regretted having come. I dropped my food in my lap. My spoon rang against my bowl. The noise I made as I began to eat my soup was so loud that I couldn't bear to take another mouthful. It had been so long since I'd eaten in the company of other people! My hands were shaking. I must have blushed to the roots of my hair. For the first time in my life, I felt like an ugly little buffoon.

I was weak with the realization that I was embarrassing my father and mother. Thank heaven, dinner finally ended. Alone again in the Sutra room, I realized that the life I'd led in the convent had been so remote from anything my family had experienced that I could probably never be like them again.

Another month went by, and still there was no sign of preparations to send me back. My mother now insisted that I begin wearing bright, colourful clothes and taught me how to match the colours. She made me put on showy rings and bracelets. Was this how she thought a nun should dress? She gave me jars of fragrant facial creams, a box of face powder, and a make-up kit and taught me how to use them. In the convent, we just rubbed our faces with a bit of yak butter and never gave it a thought. I would sit like a variety storekeeper's daughter, perplexed by this dazzling display of glittering objects.

When Mother went out to play mahjong with her friends, she insisted I accompany her, and along the way, she would explain how to walk, smile, eat, and talk in public. She taught me how to use a phonograph. She even wanted me to learn to sing. Everything she said made me feel uneasy. I began to have a premonition.

I had always been a good daughter and believed it would be wrong to defy my parents. At the same time, I gradually began to understand my position in the family and in society. I sat and reckoned to myself—it had been a whole year since I'd left the convent.

'Mama, I think I should go back.'

'You don't like it here at home?'

'No, no. But my teacher won't like it if I stay here longer.'

'If your teacher says it's all right, will you stay?'

'I'm a nun. I should live in the convent.'

'No, you're not. You've left the convent. We arranged it all for you six months ago. You don't belong to the convent anymore. You're our only daughter now, you belong here at home, and your father and I have decided to arrange a much better life for you.' Mother gave me a little hug. 'We know you probably haven't gotten used to it yet, but you will in a while. Remember, from now on you're not a nun, you're the young lady of our family. We're not aristocrats, but we don't lack for money, and the day will come when you'll become a true noblewoman.'

To become a noblewoman was probably my mother's greatest dream, but such a notion had never entered my head. Her words startled me.

Half a year later, I was married. My husband was the man who had come to our house for dinner—the only man outside our family with whom I'd eaten at the same table. Though his family was far from prosperous, he had pure aristocratic blood. By my marriage to him, I'd become a true noblewoman, and my mother rejoiced.

My father had originally picked him out for my sister. If she had lived, she would have made him a fine wife. Her beauty, warmth and charm would have assured his happiness. Stupid and clumsy as I was, I made up my mind to please him. I had to do this for my sister.

And so another phase of my life began. I was nineteen, he thirty-nine. Our life was uneventful, even dull. Time passed, we had four children, and I discovered the joys of being a mother. I had learned many things at the convent, and I realized that I was a knowledgeable mother. Of this I was proud.

He never shouted at me or hit me—unlike in my own family, where my father had struck my mother brutally. And he was a good father. I still recall the tears that came to his eyes when our son fell down the stairs.

His father had died when he was young and his mother had gone blind, so his only sister, who was older than he, had left her convent and come home to manage the household. She had never married. I was terribly frightened of her. Through the disgust and contempt in her eyes, I came to know the arrogance and prejudice of aristocrats. To her I was just a little beggar-devil; and she took every opportunity to create trouble for me.

The family took its meals in a dark red room. I could see in the walnut table and elaborately carved chairs the luxury of bygone days. Although the family's financial circumstances were nothing like in the past, their lifestyle had barely changed. My husband's sister obviously believed I was not worthy of sharing this lifestyle. Her hostile, overbearing glare so spoiled my appetite that I always left the table half hungry. My husband simply thought I couldn't eat any more. As a nun, I had learned to make an effort to look on the good side of things; I had my sister-in-law to thank for my slender figure.

In my new home, I undertook many things that I'd never attempted before, and discovered that I learned quickly. The convent had taught me that life takes hard work. Gradually, I became accustomed to my sister-in-law's slights and provocations. I did my best to ignore them, and when I had to cry, I went off to cry alone. From the first I gave in to her. After a time I found that her troublemaking left me unmoved, and I wasted fewer tears, until I eventually became indifferent to it all.

I assumed she could never like me, never cease trying to provoke me, but one day she started being nicer. I didn't know what to make of it, but in fact it made me happy. As we began to get to know and understand each other, I discovered that she was really a most sincere person, a woman who expressed all of her feelings and held nothing back. If she hated you, she hated you to the marrow of your bones; if she liked you, you never needed to keep up your guard. My arrival had caused turbulence in their family; as it subsided, everything became quiet again.

My husband had two younger brothers. One had left the family and become a monk. The other lived at home. He and his wife were mild, gentle people who never bothered anyone. Ten years after I joined the family, he fell ill of some disease that baffled the physicians, and he died. Their uncle asked my husband to take his brother's widow as his second wife, for the sake of stability in the family.

I didn't mind. Hadn't my own father had two wives? My sister-in-law was a good woman, and my husband a good man. Why shouldn't two good people come together?

But my husband refused.

He said to me, 'I don't see any need for it. She's still part of the family. I can fulfill my responsibility to my brother by taking care of his widow and children. Besides, you and I have a good life together. Why should someone come between us?'

In the ten years of our marriage, my husband had treated me well;

he'd looked after my health, but he'd never revealed anything of a man's feeling for his wife. I had always thought his concern for me was nothing more than a father's for a daughter. But the emotion I saw in his eyes now could only be love!

To accept the love of a man nearing fifty and try to love him in return ... Although it might have been called late love, there was nothing late, nothing incomplete about it. For the first time, I knew the incomparable joy of being a woman, a wife. Ten years I had remained aloof. I thought that as long as I looked after him and bore his children, I would be fulfilling my duty. Deep in my heart, I had always thought of him as my sister's husband. It took me ten years to begin to understand him, to let him into my soul. What a difference when a man and woman rely on each other ... how much the heart can accomplish!

Our children were growing up now, and several years later, his sister-in-law remarried and left the household. Then his sister died, and I had to manage the household finances and oversee our expenses. When I realized our situation, I persuaded my husband to sell our unprofitable manor in far-off Kham, dismissed some of our servants, and cut our expenses. Things were easier for a time, but after a few years we were again short of money.

My husband had little understanding of financial matters, and his health had begun to deteriorate. If I'd explained our situation to him, he never would have stopped blaming himself, so I kept my lips sealed. My one consolation was that our eldest son was now a grown man, and my chief support.

Now I faced the greatest calamity of my life: my husband was ill, and the family's finances were collapsing. I had nothing but prayer to keep me from despair. One evening my husband died ... at dusk, in my arms. Fortunately, by then I had become indifferent to death.

He was gone; I remained. I called my children together and told them that from then on we had to be tough, learn to bear hardships, live by our skills. They hardly grasped the full significance of what I told them. We had no choice but to sell our home, and now, aside from our aristocratic blood and noble name, we had nothing. When, half a year later, my children found themselves penniless, trudging along the streets of Lhasa, my one hope was that they might keep their courage.

I'd brought them into this world. They were the tender spot in my heart. When they came in the door dejected over some opportunity lost through their own mistake or stolen because someone had cheated them, I tried to bolster their self-confidence by reminding them of past successes. I hoped they wouldn't dwell on defeat. I witnessed their vulnerability, their frustration, their suffering, and their toil ... Most often, hard work leads to defeat, of course, but I saw that they had begun to understand how to face defeat. Reversals and disappointments, bumps and bruises are unavoidable out in the world. From what I endured in those days, I learned that the most beautiful thing in life is not splendour and luxury, or wealth and rank, or occupying a position of power wherever you go, but the self-assurance that comes from having overcome obstacles, step by step, through your own perseverance.

It is a beautiful thing to raise children. So many things you do not experience directly, you experience through your children. Children represent hope for the future. But what do old people represent? My braids are silver-white, but I still have hope.

My children were busy with their own affairs, and at last my spirit was free to find itself a home. I'm a common, ordinary person, and like most old people, I've chosen an ordinary way to spend my remaining years. I left my family and became a nun again. I've returned to the little convent where I lived as a girl. At sixty, I've shaved my head and put on a reddish-brown robe again.

Many of my convent sisters of bygone years are still alive. We tell each other the stories of our lives, and everything we've suffered becomes something beautiful. We discuss our hopes for the future, after this life is over. The pasture where I tended livestock as a child is as vast as before, the sky as blue. The white stupa, the red walls, the green leaves ... Nothing has changed. And I realize now that the tumultuous life of a human being is no more than a passing flash of light against the timelessness of nature.

Translation by Herbert J. Batt

Tibet

Journal of the Grassland

YANGTSO KYI

I

'Now if you wanna talk about the old days ... Our yak-hair tent back then was cured with smoke! We had a huge iron pot—soot-black we used it so much! Hmmph. And who was that, you ask? That was *my* family ... Wa Tar's family in Logor. I'm the son of an outstanding man! The hide of an excellent yak! Who else but *me*, Norbum, was raised reining in wild horses, leading wild yaks by the nose, seizing the chests of charging tigers, and grabbing the horns of rampaging yaks?! Hmmph. And why do I mention this? ... ' By this time, Akhu Norbum's eyes were bloodshot, and his strength having waned, he could no longer hold himself steady. A long strand of drool wound its way to the ashes below.

'Ano! ...' called Norbum's younger brother, Tsewang, who was seated across from him and was now quite concerned. He tried to quiet Norbum. 'Ano, now you're drunk!'

Akhu Norbum simply ranted all the louder. 'I'm *not* drunk! Ever since the world began, people have had to pay for brides and the mother's milk that nourished them. Especially these days—now that Party policy has improved ... Besides, this daughter of mine is our firstborn, the first pup of the litter. We need *something* to tell our relatives, no? Something to show up our enemies, right?'

Akhu Tsewang looked uncomfortable. He repeated, 'Ano, you're drunk.'

But the guests who had been asked by their relatives to arrange this marriage hastened nervously to defer. 'Of course! You're absolutely right.' Showering Akhu Norbum with such remarks, they adorned with ornamental laurels the worthy points he'd just made.

2

It was nearly midday. Ama Dzomkyi was seated in the doorway of the tent she shared with Akhu Tsewang, sunning herself, as she did every day. One end of the wide sash at her waist was draped over her head to shield her from the sun's bright rays. Under her *chuba* of navy-blue wool, she wore a tattered, white silk shirt. Where its collar button was left unfastened, one could see the string of her amulet pouch and a soiled, red silk cord blessed for her protection. Ruddied by sun and oil, her face was flushed and happy. While her fingers kneaded the time-worn prayer beads, Ama Dzomkyi peered out lazily towards the grassland. Her glance fell upon the young woman who was spreading out wet dung to dry in Akhu Norbum's yard. It was her niece, Drolkar. Ama Dzomkyi continued to recite under her breath, concluding, 'I dedicate any merit accumulated now and always to the Buddhahood of sentient beings who have all once been my mother.'

With these words, she turned around slowly toward her husband, Tsewang, who was busy arranging the cloth that covered the *thangka* painting of Sakyamuni Buddha. 'Why give that girl to a family who lives so far away? It will be difficult for us to visit each other even once.'

'Who? Oh. Drolkar?'

'It's not like there aren't other families. What about giving her to Uncle Sonam Tsering's family? Our nephew is practically a young thoroughbred. He's from a good family. And in terms of property, while they might look flashy on the outside, down deep they're as rich as dark earth. Or you could give her to Yangbum Jyal's family. They're respectable—and rich too! That's for sure. Why give her to some farmer?' She sat with her head turned away in disapproval, but Akhu Tsewang's attention was wholly fixed on covering the *thangka* and he didn't respond.

Ama Dzomkyi drew the wrinkles of her brow into a single furrow and placed around her neck the prayer beads she'd been holding. '*Nama!* How about making some tea? We've missed teatime again.' She stretched her legs out, then folded them back to the other side and continued, 'It's too cheap, sending her to some old farmer. If you're going to buy, then buy right. If you're going to sell, then sell right.'

Akhu Tsewang stopped what he was doing and glanced down at her. 'Hold your tongue! You're a woman. What would *you* know about it?'

Ama Dzomkyi snorted in disgust. 'Ho ho, ya! Oh, my! If it wasn't me, then *who* let golden light into your starving valley? *Who* allowed greasy pools of fat to form on your deprived family's meals? We know perfectly well how your family used to live! I took care of *everything* for our eight children and managed to find three daughters-in-law. Was all *this* the fault of my ignorance and the virtue of your knowledge?'

'You?! ... My background, this business about Drolkar ... What's it to you? Why not chant some *mani* instead, and that will be your virtue!'

Ama Dzomkyi yanked the sash from her head, infuriated. 'I am the very blood of your flesh, the stuff of which your bones are made! Do you think I want to bring your family down?! Don't I have any right to discuss Drolkar's business? Pfft! That old farmer is a donkey racing against horses, a goat trying to outdo sheep. Is he not?'

'What difference is there between farmers and nomads except a few fields and yaks? If you'll recall ... our families were also farmers once. It's just that they left Rebgong Gartse. Now be quiet. Hush.'

'Ya! And if I don't, so what?! I've a mouth on me. Fruit hangs on a tree! Don't I even have the right to speak these days?!'

'Aarrgh, women!' As Akhu Tsewang's anger flared, his tone grew harsher. 'Have you gone mad?!'

'Your face just looks stonier the older you get! If you can't agree to my having a happy life here with our son and daughter-in-law, *you'll* be the one to suffer. Even if the sky ripped open with your anger and the dragon up there fell to earth and died ... *I would speak!* I'd be *happy* even.'

Akhu Tsewang was incensed. With a rage from somewhere deep inside, he grabbed the poker off the hearth and rushed towards Ama Dzomkyi.

Ya, ya. That's it. I'll end my writing here for now. Anything further surely wouldn't bode well for this old couple.

3

And whose tent have we here? Oh. It belongs to Akhu Norbum's older sister. So sad. I first heard a bit about this woman's story some time ago, but it's too long to tell here now. Anyway, her karma isn't good. She was married four times and had three young boys, like tiger cubs. But it was all as if a magician had performed some sleight of hand. She alone remains after so many have died, abandoned like the adobe stove of a deserted nomad camp. It's truly difficult to take one's life when, even after several attempts, the Lord Death won't come.

Again today, when Ama Huamo had performed all the chores a nomad woman must, she looked up at the ray of sun streaming in through the opening in her tent and said to herself, 'Oh, it's time for the midday meal.' She fanned the fire in her stove, coughing as she blew.

One can tell by the dusty look of her dress, by the dried dung and milk stains on her padded clothes, that this is what she always wears. It's as if her dingy hair, bared shoulder, and many rows of wrinkles are meant to serve as fearsome warnings to folks that such is the twisted path of time. Just look. Who knows how many cups and such have been washed with those grime-eaten ends of her sash?

'*Ayi!* This meat is for you from Uncle Ano's family!' Akhu Tsewang's young son arrived with a share of freshly cut meat for his aunt.

'Oh, honey, you didn't need to bring that, I don't eat *nyinsha* [meat of an animal killed the same day]. Besides, today I'm on a fast.' After a long sigh, she added, 'I'm preparing the midday meal right now.'

But what can a young boy know of an old woman's sigh? He placed the cuts of meat inside the tent and skipped off. Ama Huamo called out after him, 'Lhakho! Tell Ache Drolkar that I need some help softening a sheepskin!'

A moment passed. Suddenly a sob rose and caught in her throat. Perhaps it was Drolkar's situation that came to mind. 'Now my niece will have to go. How can that beast even think about giving his daughter away to some farmer? It's like they say: old people are powerless. Am I invisible to him? As if I haven't had experience with in-laws! Marrying her off without any choice! She may be a devoted daughter, but it will certainly crush her. It's never easy holding one's own under a mother-in-law's thumb. Had she agreed to it herself—farmers or not—it wouldn't matter *where* she went; she could stand any amount of her mother-in-law's ill will. Honestly! Are those two folks half crazy? If they weren't planning to find a *mogwa* [a husband who lives in the home of his in-laws] for their only daughter, why did they send their two sons off to be monks? Oh my goodness! Now look, ignorant old woman that I am—reaping the bad *karma* of unmindful speech. It's a blessing from Kunchog Sum that I have so many nephews who are monks, right? But once they've given their daughter away, my sister-in-law will have to suffer what I did. And now they don't have any sons to get a daughter-in-law. Uh, oh. The tea has boiled over.' She hastily removed the kettle from the stove, burning her hands as she set it on the ground.

Akhu Norbum's old dog is barking and rattling his chain. A visitor must have arrived. But I am drawn to look back at Ama Huamo. 'Pity,' I think. 'Not until the day she dies will this old woman's lonely conversations cease.'

4

Oh. The visitor is Akhu Norbum's younger brother, who was offered to a couple many years ago to be raised as their foster son in Dragmar Village. Really, it's just like the old saying: 'Mistaking animals provokes a fight, but mistaking people—laughter.' Just look. Akhu Norbum and his younger brother resemble each other in every feature: the strong but slightly stooped frame, the aquiline nose, broad forehead, jaunty chin, and long thick beard—even the way their lips twist to the right when they laugh. Nevertheless, one can be sure who's older and who's younger by the amount of white hair they have, the depth of their wrinkles, and their temperaments.

Looking exhausted, the younger brother took off his felt hat and laid it on the ground. He wiped his face several times and huffed. 'Ah, la la la! It's so far! I rode that blessed horse non-stop.'

Akhu Norbum inhaled from his pipe and asked, 'How was your family's party? We couldn't go. The two of us were just leaving for Lhasa at the time ... How old is your daughter-in-law anyway?'

'The party wasn't bad. She's sixteen.'

'Good, good. It's good if there's someone who can take on the busy work.'

Akhu Norbum's wife sat in the doorway stirring the *chura* that she'd laid out to dry. 'It's hard to find such a daughter-in-law these days. Druglha Jyal gave that girl's family fifteen hundred *yuan,* a horse, seventy bottles of *chang,* and forty sets of clothes just to get her as a daughter-in-law. And then later, he still had to take more clothes, turquoise, coral, and what not for the girl herself. I heard that her father was saying that if the wager for the hand of Drugmo [heroine of the Gesar epic] was a horse race, then wealth could certainly win *his* daughter. He said that unless he got enough turquoise and coral to measure by the kilo and a beaver skin at least two handspans wide, then it would be meaningless to say he'd acquired any real wealth, and one might as well say, 'Drugmo was a nobody.' A family like ours—really!—we could never match that, even if we emptied our grazing yard out front. The Druglha Jyal family has relatives everywhere, enough wealth to fill the sky. Pride like that can't lose.' She tossed a piece of dried cheese in her mouth and chewed on it while she shuffled inside and took her seat next to Akhu Norbum. 'Now let's have tea. Never mind breakfast. I haven't had time to set this bum down since dawn.'

Truly. Clearing dung from the yard, spinning and weaving—for women of the grassland, such endless work is fusing their flesh to their skin and distilling their bones. Yet, far from being bored, they feel these chores should be done in high spirits. See for yourself. Akhu Norbum's wife, Ama Drolma, is now sixty, but still she … Oh, it's too sad to talk about just now.

'Uncle, have some tea.'

'Ya, such a sweet girl.' Akhu Norbum's younger brother took the cup and set it on the ground. He glanced again at Drolkar and addressed his brother, 'I came here today because of this business with your daughter. Ano, what kind of man are you?! We came from the same womb. Couldn't you have at least discussed it with me?'

Ama Drolma, who had never approved of the marriage, aired her frustration. 'You're absolutely right! I can't even talk to him about this business! …'

The younger brother continued, 'Our family is well known. We've always been highly regarded. If you don't uphold our honourable name and our father's estate, who will? Even if you can't decorate our good father's bones with gold, don't scatter his white hair to the bitter winds! I trust that a meat-eating hawk like our father didn't sire a shit-eating crow. You haven't consulted our uncles or said a word to our guardian aunts. Think about it! This is bound to start some serious quarrels.'

'Whether I ask them or not, whether they agree to it or not, I *have* to give her to that family.' Akhu Norbum puffed on his pipe as he made this pronouncement. 'In the first place, the boy's father and I are sworn brothers. In the second place, we went to Lhasa together. And third, I have a lama's prophecy.'

'A prophecy? Which lama's prophecy?'

Akhu Norbum took a large sip of tea and then tapped his horn-bone pipe against the bottom of his shoe. Once he'd cleared the ashes, he coughed and said, 'It's not your fault you don't understand. This business started forty years ago. Drolkar, could you please get some *chang* for your father?'

I make this offering to the lamas, the yidam, *and Kunchog Sum.*
I make this offering to the noble dakini *protectors.*
I make this offering to the eight families of god,
the nagas, and the six spirit families.

For a few moments, Akhu Norbum's tent was filled with the aroma of *chang* and the murmur of his chanting. 'Of course, only an old couple like us knows about this stuff. Again, it's like that old saying: 'No one has faith when the lama's present, but when your faith is there, the lama isn't.' He was *so* compassionate—my lama—but now he's already passed away.' He gulped down some *chang* and stared at his younger brother. 'Ya, I forget. How old were you when they sent you to live there?'

His brother replied, 'I must have been about eight.'

'Ya, that's right. That's right. It was four years after you left. Our father—bless him—he took me to Lhasa, on foot. Gompo Kyab, who's county governor now, and Kalbha—do you know him, Director of the cultural bureau? We all travelled to Lhasa together. It took us a full year—there and back. Can you imagine? We certainly were something in the old days, huh?' A proud smile came over his face. He swallowed some more *chang* and continued, 'I was eighteen at the time. So proud of myself—my long hair all braided and wrapped around my head. Of course, we *did* have to carry a sack and beg for food. Heh, heh. Kalzang's father—you probably don't know him ... *Om mani padme hum.* That was when he and five other old people drowned—swept away looking for a place to cross the Drichu. Of course, with such a pure goal they must be in a higher realm now. Several of the people we met on the way we already knew. One of these was this friend to whom I'm bound by oath. I don't know why, but we felt really close to each other. On the way back, we met a famous lama from Kham and told him about our friendship. The lama said, 'You two are connected by good karma. It is really rare to have a son in the male tiger year and a daughter in the female dragon year, but ... ha, ha, ha.' The way he laughed is still clear in my mind. Based on what the lama said, we made a pledge then, but never entirely believed that anything like this would actually happen. We met again, because of our karma, shortly after the Cultural Revolution. Only then did we discover that everything the lama had predicted had come true—his son, my daughter, even their birth years and signs. But the lama was killed many years ago in a struggle during the Cultural Revolution. I've never met a Buddhist like him. He knew exactly what would happen.' Whether Akhu Norbum lost himself in reminiscences about his pilgrimage or had come to the end of his story—I don't know. But it goes without saying that he sat sipping his *chang* for some time.

As she wiped the tears from her eyes, Ama Drolma turned to her brother-in-law and asked. 'Now what to do? Never mind how different farming is compared to a nomad's life—we won't be able to see her even when we're on our deathbed.'

'I won't give her away. No, I just won't do it. This niece means as much to me as the moustache on my face or the hair on my body. Don't I have any rights in this?'

Kunchog Sum! This younger brother is emphatic too! Perhaps alcohol, which fortifies tongues and emboldens hearts, caused a quarrel to explode between these two brothers—like the sparks that fly when metal strikes metal. But, after all, what significance do farts have if everyone's asleep? What meaning is there in chang-*laced speech?*

5

While they were milking together, Ama Drolma took the opportunity to say, 'Drolkar, I heard that Akhu Hualo's family has just returned and set up camp again this year on the back slope of the mountain. I'm sure their son Wema Dorje will visit you tonight, but it would be good if you kept this marriage matter to yourself for a while. Otherwise …'

Even as her mother spoke, tears began to fall like a string of pearls from Drolkar's eyes, onto her turquoise and coral necklace—only to sink into her heart again. The sight pierced Ama Drolma's own heart with a thorn of anguish, since she herself had endured much and had few happy tales to tell. Wiping tears from her own eyes with the back of her milk-caked hands, she continued, 'It's like they say: "A woman—tressed and to be wed—should leave her father behind, however good his name, for her husband ahead, however poor his name." What is there to do but go?'

Ama Drolma spoke more or less decisively, but when she saw the broken hope in Drolkar's eyes and the tears she shed and heard the sound of her daughter's listless milking, the mother's heart was suddenly gripped with fear. She thought of the saying 'The fox smoked out of its lair escapes only to sacrifice its life.' Might her daughter look for a way to take her own life if her mental suffering grew too painful? Ama Drolma quickly added in a softer voice, 'Honey, don't cry. Look, it's not your father's fault. And even though all of this is the fate given to you by Kunchog Sum, we still have to discuss it with the elders. It's possible that you won't even be given away.'

Drolkar. Where did Drolkar go? Oh, she's finished milking the *drimo,* Blaze. Now she's milking Chestnut. Though from her size the *tulma* looked young, her horns had grown sharp and held a certain strength, a boundless, untamed spirit. Her body, strong and fleshy, evoked autumn's abundance. From time to time, the *tulma* would toss her horns with displeasure, switch her tail sadly, or even give some warning kicks. Nevertheless, Drolkar had laid her head upon the *tulma's* haunch, crying softly with frustration—perhaps she was listening to her mother. She wanted to tell this *tulma* with silent, gentle words all the stories she had strung on the ribbon of her mind—stories of women who had come from other plains, stories of the countless brides who had left this grassland home. But—bang! The *tulma* unleashed a frustrated kick straight at the small milk bucket. She turned towards her calf and lowed, then ran off, leaving milky hoof prints. As Drolkar watched the retreating *tulma,* she was overwhelmed with intense anger. Gradually, the sense rose in her that this anger had several causes. At the same time, she felt admiration for the *tulma's* youthful courage to resist. But with a deep sigh and eyes that had turned again into pools of sorrow, she stared at the milk for a long time—watching it seep into the grass. Then she slowly wiped up some milk with her hand and smeared it respectfully across her forehead.

Usually, Ama Drolma would let out an endless string of curses if even a cup of milk were lost. But today she needed to be absolutely patient.

Akhu Norbum's yard was gradually suspended in particles of darkness. Mother and daughter remained, breathing in the air, each sitting with her own recollections and tears. There was nothing left to say. And yet still there sounded in the dark the endless milking of the grassland—*sshh, sshh, sshh, sshh* ...

Translated by Lauran R. Hartley

South-East Asia

Cambodia

The Dinner Guests

PUTSATA REANG

Every year, when my family finds reason to gather—for a holiday, birthday, graduation, and sometimes just because—when the coconut curry is cooked and smoke swirls heaven-bound from burning incense, the ghosts come home to feed.

Before any guests are allowed to eat, my mother prepares a tray of food, her best dishes—sticky rice, glass noodles fried with banana buds, steamed pork buns—and my father lights a handful of incense sticks. Setting these on an altar, we pray to the spirits of our dead relatives and invite them to the feast. These spirits are the ghosts of my grandfather, Khan Reang, a rice farmer; my uncle, Sao Kim Yan, a math professor; my aunt, Koh Kenor, a housewife who was married to a businessman, and so many others who died during the war in our homeland. They are the restless ones who cross oceans and continents to find my family, now safe and comfortable in America. They are the ones who did not make it while they were living.

Whether by luck or by fate, the rest of my family made it. When war tore through Cambodia in 1975, we got on a boat that carried us to freedom. A boat that brought us to America, far from the burning villages and the thunder of bombs breaking earth, but not far enough to escape a past that returns each year to haunt us.

I was too young to remember that time twenty-eight years ago when my family was forced to leave our country, and our lives changed instantly and forever.

On 17 April 1975, the Communist Khmer Rouge invaded Phnom Penh, forcing those they didn't kill to walk for days to concentration camps. In remote corners of the country, those who survived were forced to live in work camps as part of leader Pol Pot's design to create a classless, utilitarian society of peasant farmers.

That April day, my mother was at home in our village, Riem, taking care of her four children: my sister Sinaro, who was then eight; my brother, Sophea, then five; my sister Chanira, then two; and myself, the youngest, almost a year old. We were living in Kompong Som Province, in Cambodia's southern seaport, because my father worked as an accountant in the Cambodian navy. This job provided my father with a good salary, but only later, when the war erupted, did we realize its true worth.

My mother was listening to her short-wave radio when the news came crackling through the speaker: the Cambodian government had been toppled, and the regime of the Khmer Rouge, an insurgent guerrilla group made up of peasant fighters, had taken over.

The villagers immediately began evacuating. My father, who was down at the docks, rushed home to round up my family and relatives. He took us three or four at a time by motorbike to the port. There, one of three naval evacuation ships was waiting to take government personnel and their families to safety.

My father took my family to the boat first, then returned to Riem to gather others: my grandfather, my aunt and uncle, several cousins. Meanwhile, my mother huddled with her four children on the ship, flinching with each pop! pop! pop! of gunfire in the distance. She watched in horror as other people tried to claw their way onto the boat, only to be plucked off like crabs by crew hands worried the ship would become overloaded and sink.

Three hundred people made it onto the sitting-room-only boat. My family, allowed to board only because my father worked for the Cambodian navy, was among the lucky ones.

For three weeks, the ship drifted at sea, stopping in Thailand and Malaysia only to be shooed away by port officials who refused to accept refugees. During that time, my mother kept her children close to protect them from the waves crashing over the ship. She wondered where we were going and worried about the relatives she had left behind. She had eight siblings whom she feared had died in the bombings. But she soon realized she had a more immediate concern: the small baby lying in her sarong—her youngest child—was dying.

That baby—was me!

I was dehydrated and sick. My eyes had rolled back into my head, and my chest had stopped rising and falling. At one point, my mother couldn't bear to hold my listless body and handed me to an aunt.

'You small like a mango,' my mother would tell me years later, recounting the story. 'You not drink milk, you not cry, you look like a dead.'

The captain of the ship thought so, too. He threatened to throw me overboard, fearing a corpse would infect the other refugees crowded on the ship.

My mother wailed and clutched me tighter. She could not bear to lose another child. Seven years before I was born, she had my father bury their second daughter, Kombaleen.

She begged the captain of the ship not to take me. Even if I was already dead, my mother insisted, she and my father needed to bury me in the earth. She worried that my baby spirit would never rest in peace if I was tossed unceremoniously into the water.

The captain persisted, but my mother refused to give me up. Reluctantly, he finally agreed to let me stay on board until we stopped for food and fuel at the US naval base at Subic Bay in the Philippines.

'I have a hope, just a little, you not dead,' my mother would tell me years later, looking into the distance as if trying to hold on to that moment twenty-eight years ago.

When we reached land, my parents rushed me to a hospital, where nurses inserted an IV into my arm. After several hours, my mother placed a leaf in my hand, and my tiny fingers twitched. I was still alive.

Staying in the hospital, I was treated for dehydration and measles. At night, my mother slept on the floor beside the baby crib, keeping vigil over her fragile child.

Three long weeks later, news blasted over the naval-base loudspeaker. We would be sent to America. I was still sick, but we had to leave immediately. My mother once again wrapped me in a sarong, and we boarded a plane to start our new lives.

My immediate family and several relatives settled in Corvallis, Oregon, a small farming community about eighty miles south of

Portland. A local Presbyterian church sponsored us and helped my parents find work and the two-bedroom apartment where all fifteen of us lived. My father washed dishes at a local restaurant and took night classes to get a certificate in accounting, and my mother worked two jobs: as a janitor at the Oregon State University health centre and a cook at the campus dormitories. My siblings went to school, where they fell in love with pizza and French fries, and my cousin and I rode tight circles on Hot Wheels at our daycare centre.

My family quickly became absorbed in their new lives, and I grew up protected from stories of the war. For the most part, my parents never spoke of our past. There seemed to be a door shut tight and locked. No trespassing.

Only recently, as more relatives who survived the war have immigrated and settled in Oregon near my parents, have the stories started to emerge.

At family gatherings a heavy silence surrounds my parents when we talk of Cambodia. When pressed, my aunts will tell their stories of survival as my mother prepares our holiday meals, our summer picnic food, and the funeral feasts for my grandmother and grandfather, who recently passed away here in America.

There is always a tray for them: the first sweet tastes of curry and rice.

Here is my Aunt Vuthy, whose husband was beaten to death with a shovel by Khmer Rouge soldiers for stealing a potato for his hungry wife. Here is my Aunt Nang, a schoolteacher, who was sent to a torture prison after her husband, a military official, was shot to death. Her two boys, aching with hunger, ate crab shells and chicken bones tossed in the dirt by Khmer Rouge soldiers. Here is my Grandpa Khan, my father's father, a Chinese rice farmer, who died of starvation; the single cup of watery rice soup rationed out to everyone was not enough. Here are aunts who were tied to trees and beaten to death, and cousins who were worked to death in the rice paddies. These are the stories of the ghosts we pray for. This dinner is for all of them.

Come feast. Here is the food my mother prepared; we have plenty. Here is my bed, which I have made for this occasion. Come rest with us. Come rest within us.

Cambodia

My Sister

Mey Son Sotheary

It was already 7 pm. We'd been strolling happily along the boulevards of Phnom Penh, my younger sister Mourn and I, oblivious to time. Nightlife in the big city especially intrigued me. Modern cars were parked around big restaurants frequented by fashionably dressed customers. We were overwhelmed by it all.

I must confess that I'm from the countryside. My village is in Prey Veng province. When my parents were alive, my dad worked for the provincial office of cultural affairs and my mother was a respected seamstress. Due to their efforts, we three children had an easy life. When my elder sister finished high school, a relative took her to continue her studies in Phnom Penh.

In Prey Veng, my younger sister Mourn and I had just finished junior high school when our parents died. We would have to quit school without their financial support. Fortunately, Elder Sister insisted on our education and gave us money for school whenever she came to visit. Personally, I was delighted with the chance to continue my studies.

Elder Sister often told us about her Phnom Penh job working for a foreign investment firm. With such a good job she could finance our high-school education, so I felt motivated and never neglected my schoolwork. My dream was to graduate from high school, then to continue my education at any university in Phnom Penh. Finally, I passed the entrance exam for the Literature Faculty at the Royal University of Phnom Penh and Mourn passed the exam for the Faculty of Law, thus fulfilling her own dream.

We moved to our aunt and uncle's home in Phnom Penh to prepare for the new school year at the university. Elder Sister explained why she couldn't live there. She was very busy with company business, working long hours on site, so she stayed in company housing. After all, she explained, our relative's house wasn't near her company. If she stayed with us, she would waste a lot of time commuting.

Elder Sister only came to visit us on the weekends. I remember how the three of us were so happy then. She'd become a big city girl, the way she talked and acted. What I completely adored about her was the financial support. She made our lives so easy.

*

It was still exciting to stroll along the streets of Phnom Penh at night. One evening, Mourn and I were out fairly late when I remembered I'd better take her back home. I worried about our aunt, who probably would be waiting up for us. I called to my younger sister, and we walked toward my motorcycle parked nearby. It was a gift from Elder Sister so we would have some transportation to school. Just as I approached it, I noticed a group of bargirls across the street. Wearing heavy make-up, those ladies of the night were arriving and departing on motorbike-taxis in front of a bar, gaily laughing and teasing each other. I turned to look at Mourn. She was frowning at those girls.

I said, 'Mourn. Don't look at them!'

She glanced away. Later, on the motorcycle, she asked: 'San! Why are there so many girls like that in Phnom Penh?'

I knew that Mourn wanted to talk about those prostitutes.

'It's the city. You'd better ignore it. It's like that in the city ... '

Mourn was silent. When we arrived home, I went to bed exhausted yet obsessed with the image of those bargirls. It's right, what Mourn said, that kind of girl creates a bad impression, one that slowly destroys Cambodian values and tradition. I don't understand them, I thought. What I do know is that kind of business is a big mistake for Cambodian girls. Even if they say it's for survival, that kind of work is still completely wrong. They could clean floors, or wash noodle dishes, or sell vegetables. They could survive that way too. But that's my idea; those girls don't think like me. Anyway, I'd better forget it and get some sleep. I need my energy to study so I won't disappoint Elder Sister, who is working so hard to support me.

*

A whole year passed before I found out about it.

By then I'd grown used to city life. I'd been studying foreign languages at a private school where I did well. This encouraged me to study even harder in anticipation that after graduation I could work for a foreign company. That would enable me to help Elder Sister financially. She still provided everything, so I never worried about the money required for my education, and my academic performance continued to improve.

Soon my fluency in several foreign languages enabled me to get a job in radio broadcasting. I translated foreign news and received quite a good salary for it. I was very happy and satisfied with this job although it meant I wouldn't finish my university studies. This job gave me hope that I would be able to support myself in the future. Now I could use part of my salary to help my older sister Keo pay for our younger sister's education.

It was the last night of the month when I found out. We had just been paid. Some of my friends and I went to a party at a restaurant. We had a grand time there until about 9 pm, when we decided to go home. I walked along with one of my friends who had become quite drunk.

I chided him, 'Hey, come on! All of us are fine except you!'

While my friends were getting their vehicles, I walked him over to mine. My drunken friend murmured, 'Hey, San, look at that girl! She's really neat! Too bad she's already in somebody else's car. I'd pay anything for her!'

I was really disgusted with his nonsense, such inconsiderate talk about those ladies of the night. I laughed uncomfortably and looked at the girl he'd admired as she got into a car across the street. I chided him again.

'Such a guy, aren't you! Whenever you get drunk, you say anything. Let me take you home.'

My friend kept mumbling, 'San! She's so beautiful. Wow!'

I was really bored with him now. Since I had to steady him as he walked ahead, I just glanced surreptitiously at the bargirl. I was stunned when she turned her face toward me. Why did she look like my sister?

I immediately dropped my friend and rushed across the street through a path of oncoming vehicles. When I got there, I noticed she had turned to look at me in astonishment. I was shocked, feeling I'd received a death sentence. It was my sister, definitely my sister. I stood silently under her sad gaze. Then I saw two men pulling her hand so she'd get into their car. They drove off leaving me standing there alone. I couldn't even cry.

I went back home in grief. I felt both betrayed and terribly insulted. My aunt was watching TV in the living room when I arrived. I didn't speak to her but went directly to my room. I passed Mourn's room where she was writing something. This distressed me even more and then I noticed she was wearing the necklace Elder Sister had just given her last week. I was pondering whether to tell Mourn what I'd seen when she noticed me and stopped writing.

'San! Why so late? Did you have dinner yet?'

I tried to remain calm. The truth would devastate her. I entered my room, slammed the door and took off my shirt, throwing it on the bed. I just wanted to take a shower and to forget everything I'd previously seen. But that horrible scene appeared every time I closed my eyes. Why *my* sister? Why had she chosen such a stupid path? Turning, I noticed the computer she'd purchased for my studies. I knocked it off the desk in a rage. It broke with a loud crash on the floor. I was obsessed with the scene of my sister being pulled into some car. I kicked the computer hard so it rolled across the tile floor.

My uncle, aunt and sister opened the door to my room. They looked at me with amazement. I sat down on the bed, tears streaming down my face like I was a little child. Mourn noticed and approached me.

'San! What's the matter with you? What's wrong, San?' she asked in a choked voice.

I wanted to answer but didn't know what to say. Crying, I shook my head childishly. This was the worst moment of my entire life. I felt so hurt. I didn't understand how my sister could let herself be so degraded like that.

Having spent a sleepless night, the next morning I went to the living room exhausted. Gloomily, I sat, down on the sofa, picked up the newspaper, and started to read. Then Mourn appeared.

'Aren't you going to work?'

'No,' I murmured.

Next I heard Mourn's happy voice as the front door opened.

'Keo! Don't you work today?'

I knew my elder sister would come. I suddenly blew up when I heard her quietly say: 'Mourn, here's some food. Eat, then go to school!'

I got up from the sofa and saw the food from Elder Sister in Mourn's hand. I rushed to grab it, then hurled the snacks on the floor, shouting: 'Stop bringing that filthy stuff!'

Mourn looked at me incredulously. I glanced at Elder Sister's disheartened face as she stood in the doorway. She pushed the door closed, not wanting anyone outside the house to hear.

'Look at you!' I said. 'How cheap you are. What a role model for our younger sister!' I was suffering and out of control. Right or wrong had no meaning. I just had to scold her. But suddenly Mourn cut me short.

'San! Don't do that to Keo.'

I looked at Mourn and angrily told her to shut up: 'From now you don't take anything from her, understand! If you need something, tell me. Stop using her indecent money. You hear me?'

I saw her hesitate. My elder sister looked down and started to gather the snacks scattered around the floor. Mourn sat down to help her. I pulled her hand shouting, 'Go to school, now!'

Mourn jerked free of my grasp and angrily started to walk out while loudly shouting: 'Don't be so unreasonable! What about your rudeness to Keo?'

Frowning, I retorted: 'So go ahead. Ask her what kind of work she does.'

Mourn answered bravely, 'Whatever she does, she's still our sister. You've no right to despise her!'

I was so mad. I turned and pointed at Elder Sister, who was still gathering the scattered food.

'Say it; say it now! Tell her what you've been doing. Are you good enough to be our sister?'

Mourn furiously yelled at me: 'San! Be careful. If you keep this up, I'll tell aunt and uncle when they get home from work. Don't be so unreasonable!'

I was still angry. Then Elder Sister slowly stood up and carefully articulated each word: 'All right. I'll tell you if you want me to.'

I turned away when I heard her sobbing.

'I am an indecent bargirl. Not only that, I sell my body. I have sex with anyone who pays me well.'

Before Keo had finished speaking, Mourn was leaning dejectedly against the wall, her eyes wide with astonishment. I knew this would be devastating.

Elder Sister continued speaking: 'I know how much this hurts you. But both of you should realize I'm the one who hurts the most. Brother works for a famous company and younger sister studies law with a bright future ahead of her. But I understand. From now on don't regard me as your sister. Even if by chance we meet along the road somewhere, let's pretend not to know each other. Okay? I'll just discard these snacks. From now on, I won't dare buy anything for you since I've lost the right to be your sister.'

I was looking at the plastic bag full of snacks my elder sister had just thrown into the trash. She turned and left. I forced back my tears since I didn't want to cry while Mourn was sobbing.

❋

Night arrived. I was sitting at a bar angrily drinking beer when a prostitute approached me. I told her to sit down, then gave her ten dollars. Seeing her delighted smile, I decided to ask some questions.

'Can I ask you something?'

She laughed and answered: 'I'm sitting here for you to ask, darling. For ten dollars you can ask a lot.'

I was clueless about her values. Feeling awful, I asked her: 'Why do you do this kind of work?'

She laughed cynically while waving the ten-dollar bill. I understood so I asked the next question.

'For money, huh? Is this the only way you can get money? With so many decent jobs available, why not find one?'

She blushed and then forced a smile.

'I'm not educated; I have no skills. What can I do? Even if I found another job, the most I could make is thirty or forty dollars a month.'

I felt irritated and thought of Keo. I asked her again: 'Why do you need so much money? It's true you'll earn just a small salary with an unskilled job, but it's enough for one person to survive.'

Now she seemed angry and answered rudely: 'Right. I can survive, just me by myself. What about you? Do you survive just for yourself and that's it? I have brothers and sisters, and they have to go to school. How can I pay for their education? You just want them to be illiterate and then get a job like me? Young man, why don't you just go back home and ask all your sisters if there is a woman happy being a bargirl.'

I was appalled at her demeanour as she switching from calling me 'darling' to 'young man'. Now I felt embarrassed.

That night my uncle and aunt were waiting up for me when I arrived home. My uncle spoke as soon as I entered the house.

'It's so late. Where have you been?'

I answered with the usual response: 'My friends invited me to a party.'

He spoke louder. 'You're an adult now, uh? You work, get a salary, and spend it on dancing and drinking almost every night. I'm becoming increasingly annoyed with you.'

I remained silent. Actually, I couldn't comprehend the reason for uncle's anger. Then my aunt spoke.

'I heard that you scolded Elder Sister Keo. Is that right?'

When she reminded me about Keo, I glanced down at the floor and said nothing. Then my aunt, approaching me with fiery eyes, said: 'Are you an animal or a human being? You have a job and a good salary. You dare to bum around and then despise your sister, uh?'

I answered her without admitting anything: 'Aunt, do you know what Keo does in public?'

She replied, eyes filled with tears: 'I know! But just think. Don't you realize whom she prostitutes herself for? Is she some goddess with magical powers to conjure money for you to spend frivolously? Could you and Mourn have financed your university education alone? Could you have acquired the money to procure the necessary training needed for your great broadcasting job without her doing this? I don't think so.'

I finally realized what Keo had done for Mourn and me. The depth of her sacrifice shocked me, but I was still stubbornly insistent.

'You already knew about this? Our family used to have a good reputation. Everyone loved us, got along with us. Why didn't you stop her? Don't you know Mourn and I don't want her doing this for us? Don't you realize how much we suffer from this shame?'

She continued loudly: 'You suffer! Don't I suffer? Doesn't Keo suffer? I couldn't get the money you needed for school. But your sister ... she wanted you to study so you could have a great future. Do I have the right to stop her? You are her brother and sister. She does this for you, and then you say she's wrong. Please ask the bargirls around town if they have any problems. Do you think they are carefree? Did you ever hear Keo grumbling about her problems when she gave you money to spend heedlessly?'

Irritated, I walked to my room and slammed the door. I noticed the broken computer lying in the corner. I slowly sat down next to it, touching it gently, then felt some incipient emotion. In sorrow I remembered the day she had purchased this computer for me. She had brought it over with a beautiful smile and asked if it made me happy. I didn't realize what she'd had to do to buy it. Why did I get so angry yesterday and break it?

Actually, my aunt is right. Whatever Keo did was for us. She didn't do anything wrong. I was the brute who dared to scold her.

I remembered the bag of snacks she had brought for us yesterday as she had done for many years. I pondered why, only yesterday, I demanded she throw them in the trash, and then I decided to find her.

I know self-forgiveness will be difficult. I just feel compelled to find her, to let her know she's a great person regardless of that profession. She is still noble, I still respect her. One day I hope to find Keo, to beg forgiveness for my cruelty. If I don't succeed, I may blame myself forever.

Translated by Tomoko Okada, Vuth Reth & Teri Shaffer Yamada

Cambodia

Caged Bird Will Fly

POLLIE BITH-MELANDER

People say that rivers flow only in one direction, but in Cambodia, whether the Mekong flows into the Great Lake of the Tonle Sap or to the ocean depends on the season. During the rainy season, the water flows into the Tonle Sap, filling the lake as it rises and expands across the plain; during the dry season, the water reverses direction, draining the lake back into the sea.

Kunty stood alone in her family's small house, which had been built along a tributary of the Tonle Sap. She did not want to leave, not yet, so she packed her bag slowly as she gazed through the window at the river a few feet away. In the water, close to the bank, was the wooden pole that her father used to tie up his boat. It had been there for as long as she could remember. Her father was a fisherman and had taught her to read the seasons by watching the water rise and fall in relation to that pole. She had once spent an entire day braiding strips of cloth from an old shirt into a long thin rope her father tied to the pole to mark the water's level. Kunty knew that when the water rose above the rope, her father would soon return.

Today, she would be gone by the time he came home. It was easier to leave this way, while her father was away fishing and her mother was at the market. As Kunty packed the last of her belongings into her only bag, she wondered what would become of the pole when she was no longer around to keep it painted and retie the rope. Would her father get lost when he returned from one of his long fishing trips? Kunty had worked with her father to make the pole more visible to him in the heavy rains. Together they had painted it in two colours: green and blue. Through the years, while parts of the house were removed or added, the wooden pole had remained intact. It was the only thing about their house that had never changed.

She looked around the house one last time, zipped the bag, and placed it near the door. Still unwilling to leave, she went outside to sit on a plank that jutted out over the water. As a child, she used to sit there and watch the river flow past. 'Be careful, daughter, you might fall off,' her father would say when he saw her dangling her feet above the current. Kunty would smile at his concern.

'Father,' she would say, 'Kunty could swim to the pole and hold on to it until you came and saved her. Father, you would rescue Kunty, wouldn't you?'

She wished her father could rescue her now, but she knew that she would have to face her fate alone. How she wished she could turn back time to when she was a girl playing in the rain. She wanted to run along the levees in the rice fields when the rice was just ready for transplanting, still green and fragile. She wanted to climb a *sdaov* tree and pick the young leaves and flowers for her mother to cook, and gather lotus blossoms to sell to tourists who travelled the road to Siem Reap. She wanted to collect snails and shrimps from the river and cook them for her father to eat. More than anything else, she wanted to watch her own children doing such things as they grew up beside the river.

*

Kunty thought back to the first time she had left her home. If she had known that her decisions would lead her to this moment, she would have rejected the marriage proposal. She remembered clearly the day a man had passed her house in a boat, watching her from a distance. She had been sitting on the edge of this same plank, dipping a bucket into the water, and hadn't thought anything of it. But that night, she dreamed that her body was a white feather floating on the wind. When she woke up, she felt light headed, dizzy and weightless. She had tried to tell her father about the dream, but he hadn't had time. And then the matchmaker had come. Her father couldn't refuse the offer of money and gifts.

She had been married less than a year when her daughter was

born; the second year, she had a son. Her family's house on the river became too crowded, so she, her husband, and her children moved to her husband's village and into the house of her in-laws. That was the first time she had ever left home.

Soon after their move, her husband quit fishing and started working in the central part of the province as a motorcycle taxi driver, in order to make more money. The job took him away for weeks and sometimes for months at a time. One day, he came home sooner than expected. His face was drained of life. His eyes used to be alert and bright as stars; now they were like the dull eyes of the dead fish her father had brought home from his trips to the lake. Her husband was sick with severe diarrhoea all night and into the next morning.

Kunty begged her husband to see a doctor in the village. When he returned home that afternoon, he sat in the front yard in silence. His mouth drooped at the edges and his lips sagged open. He didn't say a word to her.

'Dear,' Kunty finally said, 'what did the doctor say?'

'It's nothing,' he said. 'We will be ok. Please take good care of the children when I am gone.'

'Why are you talking that way? What's the matter?' She was on the verge of tears and could hardly breathe. She felt as if someone had driven a stake into her chest. 'What did the doctor say?'

'Nothing,' he repeated, barely loud enough for her to hear. 'I'll try to go back to work soon.' Then he got up and left her standing in the front yard alone.

After that day, he hardly spoke to her or anyone.

A week later, in the darkness before dawn, he drove away from the village. He did not return for a year. When he reappeared, he was wearing only a dirty pair of torn pants. Large blisters covered his left arm. He was so thin that it seemed the only thing left of his body was the skin attached to his bones. His emaciated form reminded her of a picture of a skeletal Buddha in the state of nirvana; she had seen it on an Aids poster outside of a restaurant. At the time, she had thought the disease was caused by starvation.

Her husband was at home for six months. One night, he cried until no more sound escaped his lips. Kunty thought he had finally fallen asleep. But the next morning, he was dead.

In their grief, the parents of Kunty's husband blamed her for their son's sickness and his death. They threw her out of their house but kept her children and forbade her to see them. Kunty had no choice but to move back to her childhood home.

'The city killed him,' the people in Kunty's village said. That's what her parents said too. But something had changed in the way people looked at her.

One afternoon, a stranger from the city came to her family's home, claiming that her husband owed him money. When he learned her husband was dead, the man turned on Kunty. 'I have no money,' Kunty pleaded. She explained that all her husband's money, along with her own meagre savings, had been used to pay for his medical treatment and his funeral. 'Please.' Then, in front of her father and mother, the man said, 'He had Aids. You should get yourself tested to know for sure whether or not you were infected by him.' She watched her mother's expression change from shock to anger. Kunty's father looked like all the blood had drained from his face. He began blinking his eyes rapidly, as if he were trying to hold back tears. He turned away and covered his face with the cotton *krama* he wore around his neck.

The man stormed out of the house to the dirt road and began yelling so that all the neighbours could hear, 'She has Aids!' He whirled around and pointed to her parents' house. 'The woman who lives in this house has Aids!'

At that moment, Kunty knew that, for the sake of her parents, especially her father, she would have to leave. Her mother had rushed outside to drive the man away. But her father held everything inside. The truth was that, if she hadn't loved her father so much, she wouldn't have cared what the neighbours thought; like her mother, she would have defied them. Kunty had always been rebellious. But she had grown up wanting to be like her father. She preferred going fishing with him to staying home with her mother. Before she married, she had thought only of fishing with her father in the Tonle Sap, watching the river overflow its banks while they glided over the flooded rice fields.

✻

As Kunty silently said goodbye to the river, tears welled up in her eyes. Her sadness came not only from leaving the home she grew up in, but also from her fear that she would never see her children again, not in this lifetime, or in this physical form. She turned and walked back inside. 'Someday,' she whispered to the empty room. 'Someday when I can fly, I will come back.'

She picked up her bag and closed the door behind her.

✻

Kunty followed the dirt road in front of her house until she had reached National Highway Number 6, which connected Siem Reap to Phnom Penh. As a little girl she had watched travellers on motorcycles pass by on this road, raising clouds of red dust. It had never occurred to her that one day she would be one of those travellers. She watched several motorcycle taxis pass, then flagged one down.

'How much to the city?' she asked.

'Where are you going?'

'I have an aunt who lives on Penh Chet Boulevard.' The driver smiled when he heard the name of the street. It wasn't really her aunt that Kunty was going to see, but rather a woman she had once met in the village, who had promised her work if she ever wanted to live in the city. Even then Kunty had suspected what kind of work it was. Work in the city for a woman like her, with no skills, connections or education, could only mean one thing.

'Five thousand *riels,*' the motorcycle driver said.

Kunty didn't flinch. She tried to keep her face smooth. 'I'm afraid I only have twenty-five hundred *riels,*' she countered, staring him straight in the eyes. 'Don't waste my time,' the driver said. 'You need a ride to the city and you only have twenty-five hundred *riels*?'

'Please,' Kunty said. 'I have more, but if I give you five thousand then I won't have anything when I get to the city. And suppose I can't find my aunt?' In fact, Kunty was telling the truth. Her parents had given her nearly all their savings and had borrowed money from their neighbours.

'All right,' the driver said, his eyes narrowing. 'Four thousand *riels.* And maybe your "aunt" will pitch in the rest when we get to the city.'

Kunty felt a sense of dread as she got on the back seat of his motorcycle. She watched the passing rice fields and sugar palms for the last time. The wind stung her face, and she closed her eyes against the dust, holding the end of the *krama* over her mouth. She thought of her children as each kilometre took her further away from them. Would her in-laws comfort her son when the thunder frightened him? Would they remember to sing her daughter her favorite lullaby? Would her children even remember her?

She didn't speak to the driver until they reached the outskirts of the city. 'Why are we turning here?' she asked. Even though she had never been to Phnom Penh, Kunty had heard Penh Chet Boulevard described by the villagers. The huts they passed along the dirt road seemed to fit the description, but nothing else did. It was still daylight. She saw several girls in front of a small hut eating with chopsticks instead of spoons, the way that Cambodians do. A man in an olive green uniform sat beside them. The girls had light skin and wore their hair short. She assumed they came from Viet Nam. The motorcycle slowed as they passed over some railroad tracks. A sign read POLICE STATION. Nearby was another sign that read WOMEN'S ROOM. She wondered what the sign meant.

When they reached the end of the dirt road, the man parked the motorcycle on the corner next to a small hut, opposite an auto-repair shop. Kunty quickly jumped off the back seat. 'Don't go anywhere,' the man warned. Then he laughed in a way that made Kunty anxious. 'Don't worry,' he said. 'I'm just going to see my auntie who lives here.'

'Don't be long. I need to get to Penh Chet Boulevard before nightfall,' she called out after him, but he had already entered the hut. Bright purple curtains covered the two windows. Above the narrow door hung a sign: WE'RE WAITING. The driver returned shortly with an older woman who wore a bright floral sarong and a red t-shirt. Beneath her thin shirt, her breasts dangled loosely, nipples pointed in opposite directions. She wore red lipstick and a pair of red platform shoes that made her bounce up and down as she walked.

'Let me see her face,' the woman said without a trace of politeness. 'She'll do, but I can't pay much for that. She's too short and too skinny. She looks like she's had kids.' The woman walked around Kunty, staring her up and down as if assessing livestock. 'Eighty dollars,' she said. 'That's it.'

'One hundred,' the driver countered.

'All right. Ninety,' said the woman. 'Come with me.' As the driver followed the woman inside the hut, Kunty heard her say, 'She's not going to run.'

Kunty just wanted to get out of there and to Penh Chet Boulevard before dark. She had to find the woman she'd met in her village who had promised her a job.

When they returned, the woman yanked Kunty's hair and dragged her into the front guest room. She pushed her into a chair opposite a dirty love seat and ordered her to sit. Kunty was so stunned she didn't have time to react when she saw the man drive away down the dirt road and disappear from sight.

'Rule number one: bargain with the men.'

As she spoke, the woman paced back and forth, stopping once in a while to stare at Kunty like a mother scolding a child for doing something wrong.

'Rule number two: you take the money from them before letting them in. Do you understand?'

Kunty was staring out the front door.

'Don't think about it,' the woman said. 'You owe me ninety dollars. And until you work it off, you belong to this hut.'

'How do I owe you money, ma'am?' Kunty asked.

'Don't be stupid,' said the woman. 'From now on, you will address me as "Mother". Understand?'

'Yes, Mother,' Kunty said. 'What have I done, Mother?' She asked the question again as she set her bag down on the dirty wooden floor. She stared through the holes and cracks to the ground below. She saw used condoms and a small empty box that read Number One. She wondered what kind of men came to this little hut. The idea of having to serve them had not yet sunk in. She had the sensation that she was still on her way to somewhere else. She could not believe that her journey had ended there.

Where am I? she thought to herself as she got up and followed Mother to the back of the hut. Although it looked small from the front, the hut was long and narrow inside. As Kunty stepped from the guest room into the corridor, she saw three small rooms on each side with purple curtains instead of doors. The rooms were lit up with bright red lights and each had a small bed, barely large enough to fit one person. At the end of the corridor was a kitchen with a two-burner stove placed on top of a small table by the window. Behind the kitchen were six other small rooms—the girls' living quarters—each decorated in a different colour.

Mother pointed to the last of the small bedrooms. 'This is your room: Room Number Six.' Mother explained this was her sleeping room, while the front room was for men who came for a short service: payment was rendered, no name asked, and there was no need for politeness. If they paid more, they could spend the night with her in the sleeping room.

As she stepped out the door, Mother turned to add, 'Listen, rule number three: don't try to run because you will not like the consequences.'

'Yes, Mother,' Kunty said.

'You're an easy girl,' Mother said. 'Just follow Mother's rules and you'll be fine.'

*

'I thought we agreed on five thousand *riels*' Kunty said to the man after he had finished.

'You did, but I didn't,' he said. 'You're dark and not even pretty.' He threw two thousand five hundred *riels* on the table and walked out.

It wasn't just the pain that made her first day difficult. She hadn't yet been able to adjust her mind to accept her new vocation. As she was trying to figure out how to tell Mother about the fee, a hand smacked her hard across the face. She grabbed the metal stool at the bed's edge to keep from falling.

'What did I say?' Mother asked when Kunty looked up to see who had slapped her.

'Take the money before I let him in?' Kunty whispered. She sat on the bed and looked down at the floor. Her face stung and she wondered if it would bruise.

'Why didn't you follow my rule?'

'I'm sorry, Mother,' Kunty said. 'I thought he was—' She stopped; there was no use in trying to explain.

'Since it's your first time, I'll spare you the pain.' Mother looked straight at Kunty. At the door, she turned to add, 'Oh, by the way, you owe me an extra two thousand five hundred *riels*. It will be added to your tab.'

*

After a month of working, Kunty was used to the routine at the hut. Monday nights, only a few regulars came in, and so the six young women in the hut could talk to one another. They would close the door that separated the working rooms up front from the sleeping rooms in the back.

'So, Room Number Three,' Kunty asked, trying to join the conversation, 'how did you manage to steal the ten thousand *riels* from the man?' They called each other by their room numbers, instead of older sister or younger sister as they might have if they had been family. Kunty had told Room Number Three her real name, but she only used it when the two of them were alone. None of them talked about their lives before they had come here, and none ever spoke of children or parents.

'Well, Room Number Six,' Room Number Three said, bursting out laughing, so that Kunty could see the dimple on her left cheek. 'Oh honey, boom, boom!'

'That easy, huh?' Room Number Two teased.

'Really,' said Room Number Five. 'How? Honestly, we're desperate here for a little extra cash.'

'Well, you talk to them,' Room Number Three explained. 'But not too much, just enough to get their attention away from their wallets and then you take just a little.'

'Why not all?' Kunty asked.

'If you steal just a little, they won't notice that the money is missing. Try it sometime.'

Kunty was grateful for the way Room Number Three answered her questions without making fun of her inexperience. And she liked these moments in the back room, where the girls would gather away from Mother and the guard whenever they had the opportunity.

'You know,' Room Number Three said, 'I have a lover.'

'Yeah?' said Room Number Two. 'How much did he give you when you let him in?' They all laughed.

'Enough to buy new red lipstick,' Room Number Three said when the giggling subsided. 'He said he would come back to see me next week if he could send his wife away to the province.'

'Are you sure you want to get involved with a married man?' Kunty asked shyly.

'They're all married!' said Room Number Two, bursting into laughter.

'Well,' Room Number Three continued, 'he gave me more money than he was supposed to. Maybe I can save that money to pay my debts to Mother, if I can keep him long enough.'

*

One night, several months after Kunty had arrived, she started feeling sick. Constant pain and diarrhoea were normal for her, but this was different. She hardly spoke to the other Room Numbers that night because of the headache: it felt like someone was hitting the back of her skull with a hammer over and over. The pain was so intense she vomited.

On the third day, she called out from her front room, 'Room Number Three!' No one responded. 'Room Number Three!' She tried again, yelling louder this time, 'Help me, please!'

Exhausted, Kunty stopped calling out and gave in to the pain in her head. She passed out. As in the dream she had long ago, before the matchmaker had come, she imagined herself being lifted up and being carried away. 'Oh Father!' she cried out. 'Kunty misses you so much!'

She thought she heard a faraway voice faintly calling her, but she didn't want to leave the dream of her father. She wanted only to drift in the sensation of her body carried away by him. But the voice grew louder. 'Please, Father,' she pleaded. 'Take me away now. It's too loud and I can't stand it anymore. Father, please.'

'Kunty!'

Painfully, she opened her eyes and saw faces staring down at her. She recognized Room Number Three. Sitting next to her was a lady in a long white uniform.

'Are you ok?' Room Number Three asked.

'What happened?' Kunty murmured.

'You fell and lost consciousness, so we carried you here. This is Sister Cecelia.'

'Where am I?' Kunty asked weakly. She tried to raise herself, but Room Number Three gently pushed her back down.

'This is the Women's Room,' Sister Cecelia said. She looked almost Cambodian—short with dark skin—but she spoke with an accent. 'This place is for women who work along this dirt road, to come and talk about whatever problems they have.' It wasn't really a room, just a thatched roof with no walls and a wooden floor.

'What's wrong with my head?' Kunty tried to smile at Sister Cecelia as she reached out with her hand to touch the nun. 'Please, tell me.'

Sister Cecelia held Kunty's hand and returned her smile. 'You might have a secondary infection, a type of meningitis.' Kunty looked confused. 'You might have fungus in your brain. It causes serious pain. The pain will come and go.'

'How do I get rid of it?'

'It's not easy. You will have to move to another place where we can help you recover.'

'Where, Sister? I have no money and I still owe Mother ninety dollars and two thousand five hundred *riels*.'

'You need no money there,' Sister Cecelia said. She explained that she had come to Cambodia from the Philippines to work with the Charity, a religious organization that provided help for Aids patients. 'I just need to know if you have any family.'

'They are dead to me now,' Kunty said. 'Maybe someday I will ask for something from them, but not now.' She thought of asking Sister

Cecelia to arrange for her to see her children.

'We can admit you only if you show that you have no one to support you or care for you.'

'Look at me, Sister. Do you suppose if I had anyone to care for me that I would be working here?' She pointed down the dirt road. 'I lived an honest life until last year. I don't ask for your forgiveness because of my work. And I don't ask for your sympathy.'

'Please forgive me,' Sister Cecelia said. 'When you're ready to talk, I would like to listen.'

*

It felt strange to Kunty to be taken to the Charity. Sitting in a car for the first time in her life, Kunty wanted to vomit. Sister Cecelia sat next to her, explaining something about the Charity, but Kunty felt too sick to pay attention to what she was saying.

When they arrived, the first thing Kunty noticed as she stepped from the car were pink lotus blossoms in two ponds. She watched the petals bend in the wind as she followed Sister Cecelia down a dirt path that led between the ponds and to the high fence surrounding the Charity. The fence was so tall that only the roof of a building was visible from the road.

Sister Cecelia led her past several buildings and down a pathway lined with shrubs and flowers. The white wild daisy reminded her of the life she had led before she had married. She wanted to be that daisy so that she could dance on the wind and grow wild and be left alone. But instead she felt heavy and surrounded by her past.

The Charity's dormitory was the cleanest building Kunty had ever seen. It was sterile and new, and the garden in front was unusually healthy, even greener than the other gardens she had passed. Sister Cecelia took Kunty to a room with a dozen beds in it. Everything was white: ceiling, beds, windows, walls, even the small table placed in the far corner. The only other colours in the room were the yellows, greens and oranges in a basket filled with jackfruit, mangoes, papayas and a few sweet potatoes.

Sister Cecelia handed Kunty a bag of clothes, towels and a plastic box with small compartments for medicine. She explained that the ward was divided into two sections, one side for men and one for women, separated by the nurse's room. Each side had a row of toilets and showers. During the day, men and women could socialize in each other's rooms, but after dark they had to return to their own rooms. 'Please, don't worry about anything. When your mind is happy, your body is healthy. Rest now.'

That afternoon, Sister Cecelia introduced Kunty to the others in the ward. They were sitting in chairs in a circle. The one Kunty later remembered best was a woman in her early twenties. Her arms and legs were unbelievably thin, and her eyes were deeply sunken. She had crooked teeth and long pointy nails that she had painted bright red. She wore a pair of loose floral pants with a tight purple top. She whispered to Kunty that she had been out dancing all night and had not yet changed out of her party clothes. Kunty wondered how the woman had snuck out of the ward. In a way, Kunty admired her for living her life as if she wasn't sick. Some day, she would ask the woman how she could do it, how she could have the energy to sneak out on a date with a man, how she could go on living as if she were not sick at all.

A week later, Kunty was awakened before dawn by someone crying. It was faint but so distinct she recognized it right away. It was like the sound of a child who had wept all day long, so the only sound that came from her throat was a suffocating hiss. It was the sound of her husband's crying just before he had died.

Kunty could not lie in the dark and listen, so she bathed, dressed and walked outside. In the early morning light, the air was still cool. The yard was lined with papaya trees planted in three rows. In the front row, most of the plants were barely knee high and the soil around them had been disturbed from recent tending. The second row was taller, with trees just starting to bear fruit. The back row had the oldest plants; some were so old they were dying. She stared at the tallest tree in the back row. More lush than the others, it was the healthiest of all the papaya plants in the yard.

'You like that one, huh?'

She turned to see a man whose face seemed too large for his

shrunken body. 'I planted that one myself.' He smiled at her, and she gave a small smile back.

'Who planted the others?'

'Different people who lived here ... ' He stared at the rice field beyond the wall, barely visible from where they were standing. 'Well, this first row was planted by people who still live in this ward, except for one who left to go home yesterday.' As he began to walk in between the trees, Kunty followed him. 'Some of those who planted the second row are still here as well, but others have gone away. This back row was planted by the people who went to live in another world. Well, most of them.' He stopped at the tallest plant, the one she had admired. 'This one is mine. You know why it's the healthiest plant here? Because I'm still here to take care of it.' He exhaled and looked down at his own fingers.

The nun was walking toward them from the back door. 'I see you met Chivit.'

'Yes,' Kunty said. 'He was just telling me about the papaya trees.'

'Chivit has been here a long time.'

'He has a pretty name. Do you know what it means?' she asked teasingly because she knew the nun was still learning the Khmer language. Sister Cecelia shook her head. Kunty was surprised that Sister Cecelia, who knew so many medical terms, didn't know the meaning of this word. 'Life,' Kunty told her.

❋

Kunty lived at the Charity for three months. The patients came and went, and she kept to herself. The woman who used to sneak out of the ward at night had died. Chivit was still alive, and he had helped her plant a papaya tree in the front row. The morning after planting it, she found Sister Cecelia in the garden.

'You said that when I am ready—' Kunty began. She felt nervous and didn't know whether it was the right time to bring this up. 'I remember you said at the Women's Room that when I was ready to talk, you would listen.'

'Yes, I remember,' Sister Cecelia said. 'Do you want to talk about your family?'

'No. Not about my family. It's about me.' She sat down beside Sister Cecelia on the bench but didn't look at her. 'First, I want you to promise me that if you ever meet my two children, you will tell them that I am sorry I was not a good mother to them.'

'I promise,' Sister Cecelia said.

Kunty paused. Her eyes studied the daisies near her feet as they swayed in the wind. They were the same kind she'd noticed the first day she had walked along this pathway.

'There was a short period in my life when I did things that I now wish I hadn't done,' Kunty finally said. 'It was during the time when my husband left me, before he came back sick.' Kunty spoke slowly, staring at the ground with her hands folded. 'I thought I would never see him again. I had no way to support my children. After several months, I secretly remarried. I told my parents-in-law the man was my cousin, and he moved into the house, in his own room. They didn't say anything because he helped support us all. But after a while, he started staying away on weekends, and then he left, like my first husband. I thought he was cheating on me. Actually, he was already married to someone else.' Kunty turned her face away from Sister Cecelia so that she would not see that she was crying. 'I have kept this secret even from my parents.'

Kunty was silent for a long time. She folded and unfolded her hands in her lap. Sister Cecelia remained quiet next to her. 'I didn't think my first husband would ever come back. But eventually he did come back and he was very sick.'

Kunty couldn't say what she had wanted to ask next. She wanted to ask the nun if she could have caught this disease from her second husband rather than from her first—if it was her adultery that had caused her illness. All this time, she had wondered if it had been her fault.

'I've made a mistake,' Kunty finally said. 'I thought I wanted to talk, but it doesn't matter now. You see, I have already lost everything that is important to me.' Kunty rose from the bench and looked straight at Sister Cecelia. 'I just wanted to let you know that I love my children. All my life I tried to do my best to provide for them.'

✻

Kunty didn't want to eat anymore. The food had no taste to her, and she wondered why the Charity had hired such a terrible cook. But the food was not the only problem. She could no longer control the functions of her body. She seldom got out of bed.

One morning, she woke up from an unusually good night's sleep and felt slightly better. She decided to take a walk in the garden. She saw a peacock feather floating just above the lawn. On the feather's tip was a black spot surrounded by three colours: red, green and blue. The colours reminded her of the pole back home that her father tied his boat to. She stared at the spot until she felt she could see beyond its shape, until it became an eye staring back at her. She picked the feather up off the grass and went back into the building.

She walked to her bed and pulled a blue shirt and a pair of green pants out of her bag. She put them on, then climbed into bed and under the white sheets. She had no energy left. The only sound she could hear was that of her own breathing. She closed her eyes.

'We need serum,' she heard someone say. The voice seemed very distant. 'Please hurry. We don't have time.'

The harder Kunty tried to listen, the fainter the voice became. Behind her closed eyes, she saw the peacock feather floating just above her head. It flew near her face, then moved away. Each time she was able to fix her eyes on it, the feather suddenly moved a little farther away. She felt light and dizzy.

'Come here,' she said, amazed by the power of her own voice, how strongly it resonated in her ears. She couldn't remember the last time she had heard herself speak with such force. She opened her mouth again, took a deep breath, and yelled, 'Come here!' Her voice echoed off the white walls. She could feel the peacock feather brush against her nose and move away again.

'What are you trying to tell me?' The feather flew close to her cheek for a brief second and then flew off again. 'Oh, now I see,' she said. At first she didn't think that the air would support her, not even as weightless as she felt. But the feather lifted her up from below and took off with great speed. 'I can fly!' she yelled as she willed the feather to turn left, turn right, then up and down, and around in circles. In a corner of her vision, she saw a dark bird swoop past her, and she felt even lighter than before.

*

'Mother,' Kunty's father said, 'come and look at this hawk.'

'It arrived early this morning,' Kunty's mother replied. 'It hasn't left the pole. We have had no death in the family. I don't understand why it has to stop here.'

'Maybe it needs water,' he said, but he knew that the black hawk could only signify a returned spirit. When someone dies, such a bird guides the spirit to its desired destination.

The bird did not move as Kunty's father approached the edge of the platform. He stared straight into the hawk's eyes. Profound sadness overcame him. He used the *krama* from his neck to wipe his tears, chanting Buddhist precepts to himself. When he had dried his eyes, he looked up. The hawk hadn't moved.

'Please, drink some water,' he said. The hawk shifted its footing on the top of the pole, and then Kunty's father added, too softly for his wife to hear, 'Be careful, or you might fall off.'

The bird continued to watch him. He turned away, looking down at the wooden planks. Through the spaces between the boards, he could see the current of the river flowing toward the Great Lake of Tonle Sap.

Indonesia

The Purification of Sita

LEILA S. CHUDORI

Night broke on her so suddenly. Flung into the darkness surrounding her, she scanned the scene, wide eyed, stunned and anxious. And so night did finally arrive, though hardly, she thought bitterly, with the nobility befitting a warrior. Indeed, the proper way for night to fall is gently, in a feminine sort of way, gradually replacing the twilight, which merely mediates between day and night. And because of its gentleness, the creatures of the world would be able to feel the nuances of freshness that the change of day should bring. But because the night vented such fury, she faltered, unsure how to react. For the first few moments she was held captive by the mugginess which had presented itself uninvited. The air felt so close, so uncomfortable, she thought as she tried to suck back into herself the beads of sweat even then beginning to dampen her clothes.

Agitated, she took a deep breath. The power that was evident in the long letter from her fiancé seemed to pursue her; the chase had left her completely winded. She couldn't imagine how she might react if he were there with her now.

Amidst the unrelenting and restless heat of an unfriendly Peterborough summer, she could hardly interpret the arrival of his letter as a joyous occasion.

Four frozen years, she mused as her mind suddenly filled with the image of knee-deep Canadian snow. For four years she had to steel herself, had to guard her defenses ...

Beads of sweat, a continuous flow, moistened her temples and brows. He, her fiancé, would be unable to fathom how she had managed to maintain her good health and her sanity through the onslaught of sixteen changes in seasons. He would not understand. He won't believe it! He'll refuse to pull back his blinders when judging me, she thought, stung by paranoia.

Her entire body grappled with the stifling heat. God, it's hot, she thought, as she wrestled with the flames that were about to consume her.

She got herself a glass of cold water. Through one gulp and then another she panned the world outside her window. Even though the sun was still round in the sky, the thought of the darkness that lay ahead made her skin crawl. She seemed oblivious to the screams of the neighbour's children as they played in the water outside. She heard a different sound, a loving but authoritative voice. Then she beheld the image of Vishnu, the Great King, in one of his reincarnations …

'My dear wife … I know you have no reason to doubt my love for you. We have been separated by a vast and raging sea, one so vast that a legion of faithful soldiers was needed to build a bridge to reunite us … But you know, my darling, even without that bridge, the fact remains that you have spent time in this evil, foreign kingdom … '

The Great King loved his wife … However, after she had been abducted by the ten-headed giant, he spoke no more of his undying devotion to her. Instead, he questioned her as to what had taken place during the long period she was held captive in that alien land. And as his concern about her fidelity grew, her obstinacy in answering his questions perturbed him all the more.

It was so hot. The woman sighed irritably, replaying in her mind the scene that only moments before had chilled her to the marrow. They were husband and wife, yet they still did not trust each other!

She ran to the shower and frantically, turned the cold water tap on full blast. And there she stood, eyes closed, completely motionless, beneath a flood of water pouring over her body. She emerged from the bathroom a few minutes later, her sopping clothes clinging to her body.

Looking out the window she smiled at the sight of the neighbour's children playing naked in the water. Their stark white flesh glistened in the sunlight. Yelling and screaming, they took turns splashing each other until their mother shouted for them to stop. What? She was surprised. It was not yet dark after all …

*

'Will you sleep with me?' A slight tremble heightened the intimacy of the man's voice.

Strangely enough, contrary to the way one might have presumed she would react, the man's overture left her indifferent. She walked to the door, opened it and stood there smiling disparagingly.

'Are you asking me to leave?"

'Well, there's nothing more to be said,' she replied calmly.

'So this is what they mean when they rave about the chastity of Asian women?'

The woman shook her head. 'I like you, really, I do. But I'm not going to sleep with you.'

'Why?'

'Why? Because I'm not going to sleep with a man who is not my husband … How many times do I have to tell you that?'

'Even though we love each other? Even though we've been seeing each other for nearly two years?'

The woman opened the door wider. The man just stood there, miserable, shaking his head.

'Good night,' she said, kissing his cheek.

*

God, she moaned as she leaned against the door. It was so incredibly muggy! And those insidious flames keep coming back to torture me, she wailed to herself. She pictured the giant approaching the beautiful goddess. Was he, the ten-headed beast, really so evil? Was he, the creature portrayed in the ancient Hindu epic, really so horrible? In what manner had he approached the goddess whom he abducted? Had he been aggressive or had he been gentle? If he really was as cruel as all that, would it not have been a simple matter for him to subdue the goddess? Yet, in the end, she had proved her purity, had she not?

The woman was seized by paranoia. Although her lover, if that is what he could be called, had never so much as laid a finger on her, she still felt that she had entered the realm of the ten-headed giant. God, she thought, suppose that out of the blue my fiancé were to show up at my door and find me with him. What would happen? She let her imagination run wild ... Her fiancé would kill him; that's the first thing he'd do. And after that, assuming the worst of her, he would launch into a series of accusations ... Just like the reincarnation of the Great King Vishnu, he too would scatter pearls of wisdom about undying love and affection. Comparing love to the endless sea, the open sky and so on and so forth, and so forth and so on. But then, like a saint from some hallowed land—her fiancé did, in fact, have a strong religious background—he would say to her: 'Even so, my love, given my position and my prestige as a man held in esteem by the religious community, it is only natural that I ask you about your faithfulness, your purity and your self-restraint. In the permissive West, where physical relations are as easy to come by as cabbage at the market, it is not without justification that I ask you about the four years that we have been apart ... '

The words would roll from his tongue as swiftly as water courses through a broken dam. And his accusations, thinly veiled as innocent questions, would flow with equal speed, drowning her in her inability to maintain her defence. Her defence? Must she prepare some kind of testimony? Or submit proof that, even though she and the Canadian man had become close friends, he had never touched so much as a hair on her head? Wouldn't the truth of their relationship provide its own defence? But would her fiancé be perceptive enough to sense the truth and to realize her commitment to him? ... But even the Great King Vishnu had demanded that his wife immolate herself in the sea of fire to prove that the ten-headed monster had never touched her.

She felt herself consumed by the flames. The clock struck three times. The other occupants of the building must have melted into oblivion. The morning was so quiet and still. She could take it no longer and ran into the bathroom once again to let the flood of water pour over her. Fully clothed, she drenched her entire body till her clothes clung to her. Behind her eyelids, the image of her fiancé alternated with that of the Great King. 'Darling, for the sake of the community, for the sake of my reputation as a man, for the sake of … '

❋

'Pardon me, but were you the one taking the shower last night?' the old woman whose flat shared a wall with her bathroom inquired.

The younger woman nodded slowly. 'I was hot. I'm sorry. I hope I didn't disturb you '

'Oh, no, not at all. I was just wondering … Um, what's happening with your fiancé? Isn't he planning to visit?'

The young woman steadied herself against the hallway wall and drew in a deep breath.

'You look pale, dear,' the old woman ventured. 'Are you all right?'

She shook her head vigorously, 'I'm fine, really. He's supposed to arrive this evening. I guess I'm just excited, that's all … ' she said, hastily slipping behind the door.

Outside the door, the old woman chuckled and shook her head. 'Young ladies always get so nervous when their prince is about to come … '

And indeed, inside her room, the young woman was anxious. Darkness crashed down on her once more, leaving her utterly bewildered. Night had fallen impulsively and arbitrarily overthrew her day. 'I can't take another minute of this heat!' she screamed as she ran towards the bathroom and the refuge of the rushing water.

She stood there for hours, and hours …

❋

'You look so pale and worn out,' her fiancé observed, embracing her tightly. 'Didn't you sleep last night?'

The woman shook her head weakly. 'I just feel so hot … '

'But your body feels cold. And look at your fingers—they're all wrinkled! Do you have a fever?'

She shook her head and quickly changed the subject. 'Would you like some tea or coffee?'

'That can wait. Let's sit down. I want to feast my eyes on you …

' Her fiancé's eyes studied her from head to toe. 'I guess we have a lot of gaps to fill in for these last four years,' he added, gently taking her two hands in his.

Her hands suddenly felt frozen. So, she thought bleakly, the trial is about to commence.

'Four years away from each other probably isn't the most ideal way for future newlyweds to live,' he began. 'We've both had obstacles to deal with, I'm sure, like hills and valleys on a road. But the important thing is to ascertain how low the valleys were and how high the hills have been ... '

A sweet and diplomatic beginning, the woman thought to herself as she fixed her gaze on her fiancé's face, which seemed ever so much to resemble that of the reincarnation of the Great King Vishnu.

'We both have had ample occasion to run into—and to search for ways around—hazards along the way. Now we have to fill in and smooth over some of the potholes. We have to deal with the realities of the last four years, head-on and honestly ... What's wrong? Aren't you going to say anything?'

'Well I don't know about the hills and valleys that I've had to pass, but ... '

'Don't say it, please. I know, you're too good for me. I know that you are pure. It's me ... I'm the one who can't match your loyalty ... ' Her fiancé paused. His eyes were glassy as he caressed her cheek. 'What I mean is that we have to deal with the barriers that have come between us by expressing ourselves honestly ... '

The woman frowned.

'I'm sure you had no problem in conquering all the hills and valleys during our time apart. But you are a woman and women seem to be more capable of exercising self-control. In a typhoon a woman somehow manages to stay dry. Even after climbing the highest mountain, a woman somehow manages to remain strong.'

The woman sat, spellbound.

'But I'm a man ... and you know what they say: that the die has been cast and men are damned to be less adept than women in coping with the hills, which are not really so high, and those valleys, which are not really as low as they seem. When it comes to dealing with temptations of the flesh, men for some reason don't seem willing to be rational or to keep a level head. We've been spoiled by what is accepted as the man's prerogative. Society grants us complete freedom to give free rein to our desires, without need of having to feel treachery or shame. Maybe I'm a fool but I'm one of those rare men who do feel deceitful and contemptible. I feel so small knowing that you have remained true. I don't know what came over me when I was away from you these last four years. I'll never be able to forgive myself ... '

The woman focused on the movement of her fiancé's lips. Yet in his eyes lurked the image of King Vishnu beside Queen Sita as she prepared to purify herself in the sea of flames. She suddenly remembered that the queen had never been given the opportunity to question her husband. Supposing that she had asked, 'During the time that we were separated, my husband, were you tempted to involve yourself with another woman ... ?' But, no, that sort of question was not raised. And never would be allowed to be raised. How strange ...

And now the evening, stooped low, crawled slowly and politely forward.

Translated by Claire Siverson

Malaysia

Dance of the Bees

NORAINI MD. YUSOF

The building overwhelmed her. Tilting her head back, she gazed at the tip of a looming tower where a metallic 't' pierced the blue sky. Another huge one, the biggest one she had ever seen, was engraved on the wall. She wondered who had carved it into the stone. What she feared most was the man hanging on it. His arms and shoulders were stretched tight across the bar, forming a human 't' over the cold, concrete one. There at the top of the front door, with blood running down his face, arms and legs, he looked like he was crying; only they were not tears but rivulets of blood. What seemed like nails pinned him up, and the skin on his torso strained under his weight. Through the wide-gaping mouth of the front door, she saw a huge hall with seats facing the altar like wooden rows of teeth. There was another of those huge 't's on the wall behind the altar. She wanted to cry when she saw the same man hanging there; only now, he seemed even bigger from the distance. Sal was so scared, she felt like crying aloud. She couldn't restrain a sob from escaping her lips.

'Remember what I told you, Sal? Now, don't cry.'

'Yes ... yes, Father. I speak English. Thank you, hello, my name is Salmah. What is yours? Please, Teacher, may I go out? I do what others do. Do what Teacher tell us, and wait for you,' she recited, sniffing.

'Good girl. I'll see you later. You won't cry, will you?'

'No ... no, Father.'

'Good. Now, kiss me good-bye.'

The little girl obliged. Her father's words were the only familiar sounds to her ears. She put her plump arms around her father's neck and gave a tight hug. He was crouched opposite her; and as he held her close, he was not eager to let go. Like a little mongoose squirming in the coils of a snake, she was already wriggling to escape his clutch. A final squeeze, and he let the child go. As he stood, he realized how towering the church spire was behind her. Other parents, who were registering their children in the kindergarten, filled the front yard of the church grounds. Many began to enter the chapel. Voices hummed like bees in search of the molten cores of flowers; when one bee caught a whiff of a sweet scent, the message was passed to the next; and a few seconds later, bees converged on the spot and buzzed an excited dance. This group of people danced to a similar tune, coming together and separating at intervals as they greeted each other. Heads nodded, hands touched, hugs and smiles were exchanged as friends met friends. Only the father and his child stood slightly apart from the rest. A little hand crept into his when he smiled a warm welcome to the approaching figure.

'Mrs Wong, it's a pleasure meeting you again,' he greeted in Malay.

'It's always my pleasure to meet you, Encik Supyan. How are you?' Mrs Wong responded.

'Good, good, and I wish you that too.'

'Thank you. And who is this sweet little girl? Hello, what's your name?' The last question was posed in English.

'Sal, *jawablah*. Go on, answer your teacher.'

'Hello, my name is Salmah, and what is yours?'

'Oh, how sweet. She speaks very well. Hello, I'm Mrs Wong, your teacher. Who taught you English? Your father? This is really good, Encik Supyan. You must be really proud of her.'

'I'm afraid that's about all she knows. I taught her two weeks ago, after I received the letter confirming her attendance here. I'm not so good myself.'

'No, no, it's great.'

'She's going to need some time to get used to this place. I just hope she won't have many problems fitting in.'

'That's what we're here for, to ease her into the school system. I'll look out for her. Don't worry, I'm sure she'll be fine.'

'Thank you, Mrs Wong. You're very kind. I'm sorry, but I have to go now. I only got an hour off from the school to do the registration here.'

'I understand that you must have classes today. Leave Salmah with us. She'll make friends in a couple of days. Good day, Encik Supyan.'

'Good day. Bye, Sal. Listen to your teacher. *Jangan nakul,* behave.'

Thus began Sal's first day at kindergarten. She watched her father's retreating back, but was too nervous to cry. She wanted to run after him. Mrs Wong looked down at her, smiled and took hold of her arm. She started to speak. Sal stared in fascination at the moving red lips.

'Sal, don't cry. Your father will be back soon in the afternoon. Meanwhile I'm here and we'll make friends. Don't be shy, come, let's go meet the rest. Come on, sweetheart.' She tugged at the little hand.

Sal started crying when she saw that she was being pulled toward the door and the man. The wide mouth swallowed her into its cavernous depths. It was dark and hollow inside, like moist and musty sweet breath. She was pulled closer to him, that man who was hanging and bleeding at the back of the throat. Other people were already seated on rows of teeth, with children sitting gingerly on the wooden edges. The hum of murmuring voices vibrated in the huge room. Mrs Wong slid into the front seat, pulling Sal after her, and they sat and waited. Sal squirmed beneath the bleeding man's stare. Her fear dried her tears.

A woman in a black robe approached the altar and started speaking. Another person, also robed, but this one male and in white, joined her and faced the crowd. The woman sat down beside Sal. The man talked for a long time, and when he stopped, music came suddenly from an organ behind him. Sal was surprised when the whole crowd, as if on secret cue, rose and started singing from a small black book. She saw one on the bench beside her. The song vibrated through the whole room, causing the hair on Sal's arms to rise in reaction. She wished she were home. When she closed her eyes tightly, the choral voices and piano music reverberated in her brain.

'Are you very sure?'

'To tell you the truth, no. But, there is truth in what has been said. Sending the children to English schools will provide them with more opportunities in the future. That means Sal will have to go to an all-girls school and not be with the boys.'

Supyan looked at his wife. They sat facing each other on the prayer mat. She was still in her *telekong,* the all-white robe donned by the women for prayers. Every part of her was covered, except for her face and hands. It was evening and they had just finished praying together, the whole family. The children had gone off to watch TV after kissing their parents' hands, which they did after every prayer time. He studied the face before him and sensed troubled thoughts.

'I don't like it. She'll be alone. At least the boys have each other. Imagine the problems she has to face alone.'

Niah was distressed. She remembered her own first day of school; she had cried when her parents left her in class. And she was among the familiar faces of the children in her village.

'I know, I know. But English schools are either all boys or all girls. The two years at kindergarten will help them adjust. Even then, when Sal goes there, the boys will already be in school. I know what you mean, but we can't send the boys and not Sal. How will we explain to them later if they ask?'

'I don't know. Are we doing the right thing? A church runs the kindergarten. A school run by nuns and priests! What will the neighbours say?' Niah asked quietly.

'Why care? We do this for the children. If they follow the neighbourhood children to the nearby school, what will they become? At best, if they do well, they will get to enter the Teacher Training College. Like me. If not, they end up working the land. Like my father, and yours too. Look at Haji Salleh. He sent Abdullah to the English school in town, and look at Abdullah now. He's in England with a scholarship, and when he comes back, he'll be an Assistant District Officer. And that is just the beginning for him. We went to school together, Niah. I got better results, but my father could not pay for an English education. Why worry about what the neighbours will say? It's the children's future. They'll win scholarships, study overseas. Don't you want that for them?'

*

Supyan knew his arguments were sound. Yet he wondered why, somehow sometimes, the same arguments could not convince him. When he talked to the other teachers at school, it seemed easy. It was just a choice of pedagogy for the children. It was not like he was planning their conversion to Christianity. The only way for the children to have an English education was for them to attend missionary schools. Now, more Malay parents were doing this. But Supyan knew that it was his being a Malay language teacher that was the issue here. Some of his Malay colleagues were already calling him a traitor. They said he should have shown more loyalty to their cause; theirs was to fight for the dignity of their mother tongue, this newly accepted national language for this newborn nation. Yet, they claimed he was now joining the long queue of many Malay parents who craved an English education for their children. The queue of parents who wanted children who could speak English, who could work alongside the English, who could dress like them, wearing shirts, ties, black blazers (even under the sweltering equatorial sun) and matching pants and shoes. The women wore dresses, short and flared, barely covering their kneecaps, and matching high-heeled pumps. They talked like the English, but their skin belied the fact. Supyan knew he was taking a risk in allowing that educational system to mould his children. But the opportunities that he knew would come along with it tugged at his heart.

❋

In the evenings after *maghrib,* the fourth daily prayer, Supyan sat in front of the three children: Kamal, Khalil and Salmah. A Qur'an, splayed across the small crossed-plank stand, was in front of each one. Their shrill, singsong voices chanted the Arabic verses. Little palms cupped against small ears helped to improve the tone of their voices, as cleaned turkey feathers clutched in warm fists flitted across the pages. Once in a while Sal fumbled, and Supyan corrected her pronunciation. The two boys barely needed help. The children had started their Quranic lessons early, at the age of four. At six now, Sal was already twenty pages into the holy book, while the boys were about to end their first round of reading. Niah and Supyan had argued about the lessons. She had wanted them to have daily lessons with Haji Mail, the *imam* at the small mosque near the house.

The neighbourhood children thronged the small building where the villagers performed their prayers together every evening; and a few minutes later, the cherubim choir beckoned the coming of night.

The sound droned on for a couple of hours until lanterns illuminated the darkness. Insects, finding the lights irresistible, killed themselves, dropping on the heads below. Once in a while, a sharp crack interrupted the choral song. Voices momentarily stopped in midair, while one deep voice snapped rebuke; then the choir resumed in volume and energy. Haji Mail had just caned a slow learner, which was the reason why Supyan had decided to teach his own children. He had survived the old man's quick arm and temper as a young boy; thus he could not bear the thought of the cane slicing the soft skin of his children's palms.

His decision angered the neighbours. They accused Supyan of humiliating Haji Mail and of rejecting tradition. Haji Mail had taught all the children in Kampung Pokok Mangga to read the Qur'an, and his father before him. What Supyan was doing was just not right. When Supyan started his children's prayer lessons, the neighbours buzzed with anger. Niah cried but Supyan was adamant. It soothed his heart to see the boys in their miniature sarongs and Sal's little form enveloped in a *telekung,* miming his every action on the prayer mat. He cherished every *amin* they chorused after his own.

❋

'Dear Lord, bless this food we are about to have. Amin.'

A chorus of young voices echoed, 'Amin … ' Heads were bowed, eyes clenched tight and fingers clasped in prayers at the table. Sandwiches were piled on the plate in front of them; tea steamed from little colourful cups. Each table sat eight little children dressed in pink organdy shirts or dresses. Sister Claire smiled. She turned when she heard a commotion from a table in one corner of the hall.

'That's wrong!'

Sal just stared at him.

'You hold your hand this way.' He waved his entwined fingers in her face.

Sal looked down at her hands, palms cupped in prayers, just as her father had taught her at home. She shook her head and pulled her hands away from the boy's prying fingers.

'Like this!' Another fist jabbed her face.

Sal turned away.

'Sister Claire, she did it wrong!' the boy cried to the black-robed woman. Sister Claire approached the table. She recognized the new girl Mrs Wong had told her about. She looked at the bristling boy next to her.

'Richard Tan, why aren't you eating?'

'Sister, she didn't want me to show her the right way to pray,' he announced, a little frown etched into his forehead.

'Salmah, go on. You may eat.' She gestured towards Sal. Turning she continued, 'Richard, it's all right. Salmah prays differently from us. She doesn't have to follow your way. Now, go on and have your meal before it's too late. Lessons will start again in a few minutes.' She walked around the other tables, stopping once in a while to talk to some children.

'Why you different?' A probing pair of eyes questioned.

'No.' Sal stammered back, not knowing what to say. She could not understand all his words, but she instinctively knew they had something to do with the way she had said blessings. She grasped at the unfamiliar word. 'Different? What different?'

'You do this; we do this.' The boy acted out his words. 'Different.'

Sal nodded. She now began to understand the looks thrown in her direction, the different way the teachers talked to her as compared to the other students. She was still having problems with the language, and she thought that was why they had looked at and talked to her differently. She studied the boy sitting beside her: his needle-black hair cropped close to the skin of his head; eyes, charcoal black, peered from flat lids, slanted at an angle toward his temple; a flat nose and a huge grin spread across his round face.

After two weeks at the kindergarten, she began to grasp new words, expanding her once very limited vocabulary. The teachers helped by speaking very slowly to her, allowing her to hear each syllable and on many occasions prompting her to repeat them. Words were also acted out in class. The little children hooted in glee to see the antics of their teachers. While not really comprehending every word, Sal was able to grasp the message by combining the words with the action. She, too, smiled in class but was still too intimidated by the others to participate. The other children could already speak the language.

Many of them were Chinese, and some were Indian and expatriate children, who jumped and skipped and chattered in breathless English. Sal stood apart from them during game hour, craving to join in the chanting games, but her silent tongue was a barrier.

'What's your name? Me, Richard.' Mr Right beside her asked.

'Sal,' came a shy response.

'Is it short for Sally?'

A shake of the head.

'It's okay. I call you Sally. You want to eat?'

A sandwich, squeezed in a grubby hand, was shoved into her face. Sal accepted the friendly offer gratefully. She smiled at Richard, her heart going out to this first friend. If a change in name would win her one, she would accept any.

'Sally' and Richard were inseparable after that day. His little shoulders swelled as he took on the responsibility of being her spokesperson, advisor and guide. With his hand tightly clutching hers, he dragged her into the little games played during the breaks. Richard was a self-appointed leader, bullying the other children into letting Sal play. He vehemently refused to join any game unless Sal did too. Sal was pressured into mimicking every action in the game, memorizing every sound in the little songs, and her heart burst when one day other hands started to clutch at hers too. She looked forward to these sessions. From marching in giggling lines to the London Bridge and being caught in its falling arms to trekking round mountains, Sal never stopped being amazed at the wealth of games to play. Besides her classmates, she found new friends in funny characters like Judy, Miss Muffet, Little Jack and Humpty Dumpty. She treasured all of them, but Richard was her favourite. After all the games and songs were played and chanted, the two of them sat together in one corner away from the rest and giggled. And when she reached home, tales of these adventures were recounted to her parents.

One day during lunch hour, Sister Claire asked the usual question. 'And who would like to say prayers before we eat today?'

Little arms waved to volunteer.

Richard stood and said aloud, 'Sally.'

Sal's heart stopped. All eyes swerved to hers.

Sister Claire smiled, 'Sal? Yes, would you like to say the prayers?'

A bony elbow poked her waist repeatedly. A few other voices chirped up, 'Sally ... Sally ... '

'Children, hush ... Sal?'

Another nudge and a hiss. Sal nodded, her heart beating too fast. Sister Claire gave her a smile. She sat upright and cupped her palms. A quick look at Richard's consternation made her change to clasp her hands together on the table. She could not breathe. Richard nodded, his face flushed red. Her voice trembled, 'Dear Lord, please bless the food that we're about to have. Amin.'

A chorus repeated, 'Amin.'

Another smile from Sister Claire, 'That was very good, Sal.'

Richard grinned. He crowed. Sounds of eating in the hall drowned Sal's heartbeats.

*

Supyan watched Sal's progress with pride. He saw her stumbled reading quickly improve to a more confident pace. She read aloud more, often now at home. The two boys sometimes helped to correct her pronunciation. Supyan had even caught her going through their school books and reading their story-books from the library. She had adapted very well to the kindergarten, better than he had expected. He bought more story-books for her. She became an avid reader, preferring to read rather than play with the boys in the evening. Her sixth birthday was approaching fast and he looked forward to giving her the present she had been begging him for.

'Happy birthday, *sayang*. Kiss me.' Supyan hugged the little girl.

He got a little peck and with a quick wriggle she was out of his arms.

'Present?' Present?' Sal jumped up and down.

With a laugh, Supyan handed her the package that was wrapped in multicoloured hearts. Frantic fingers tore at the paper and revealed a doll, upright in a box with a plastic window on the front. Her limbs were pink and plump, her dress dark blue and laced at the collar. She had black wavy hair that was sculptured onto her plastic head. The smile on her lips was plastered in a frozen friendless gesture. Sal's lips wobbled in disappointment.

'I don't want. This is not Sally.'

'Eh, why Sal? You said you wanted a doll. Isn't this pretty?' Supyan answered her in Malay.

'No!'

'Why?'

'No hair. Sally must have hair.'

'No, no, she has got hair. This is her hair. It's just stuck to her head, see?'

'No, I want hair. Real pretty hair, gold colour. Real curls. Not this ... this ugly black head!' The offending doll was hurled. Tears accompanied the action. Feet stamped in anger.

Supyan frowned. Niah bit her lips. The boys chuckled, grabbed the doll, pulled off the plastic head and started kicking it around the room.

'Sally ... Sally ... ' Khalil chanted. The head was kicked.

'Sally has black hair. Ugly head! Black hair! Sal has ugly hair!' Kamal kicked back. Laughed.

'Sal wants gold hair,' Khalil howled. Another kick.

The plastic head bounced on the floor and hit Sal's head. She screamed.

*

One morning all the children were huddled and made to line up in pairs facing the chapel. There was talk about a celebration and a feast. This was the first time since her initial experience that Sal found herself looking at the hanged man again. She had always avoided going near the chapel, pulling back whenever Richard moved towards it. She had never told anyone about her fears; she did not even talk about it at home. For the past months she had managed to avoid looking at him. There were pictures of him that she sometimes saw in the books the teachers used, but she would always look away or just close her eyes. By now she knew his name: Jesus. Even his name mentioned aloud caused the hair on her neck to rise. Goose pimples rose like little mountains on her arms and legs. Now, she felt the same panic coming again.

'Richard, I don't want to go in.' Sal tugged at the hand in hers.

'Don't be silly. This is Easter, we sing songs.'

'No.' Sal hung back. Obstinate.

'Sally, quick!'

Hands pulled her arm in the direction of the chapel door. Jesus looked down at them sadly. Sal started to whimper and desperately tugged her hand back. Other hands pushed her from the back. The door yawned open; Jesus was still crying blood. His cuts were still not healed and the blood still red. The eternal pained sadness on his face remained. Sal began crying.

'Sister, look at Sally,' Richard called out.

Some teachers approached the little commotion in the line. Other children crowded around and Sal cried louder. Richard made another attempt to push her forward. Sal refused to budge; her sobs caused her little chest to heave and a warm trickle of urine flowed down her leg. The children gasped in shock. Mrs Wong quickly pulled Sal away from Richard and hurried her to the classroom across the grounds. Sister Claire got the children to line up again and the procession continued into the chapel amidst an excited buzz. Richard hung back, but after some urging from Sister Claire, he walked in with a long face.

'Sal, talk to me, dear.'

Sal burrowed her head in her lap; she was still crying hard. She was shivering in the hot room, and Mrs Wong fanned the child with a book taken from a nearby table. Sal pulled away from the kind gesture.

'Dear, tell me.'

The truth was Sal feared her own answer. Many things terrified her: the dim solemnity of the chapel, the hanged man's silent pain, Richard's high expectations of her, rejection from the other children, the shame of not comprehending the teachers and making mistakes in class, the confusion of being different and the pain of wanting to belong. She shook her head, unsure of Mrs Wong's reaction to her fears. She clamped her mouth shut, dried her tears, and remained silent the rest of the day. The teachers discussed the matter and decided upon the best solution: to inform En. Supyan of the incident and let him talk to his daughter to find the root of the matter. Hence, he was made aware of the situation when he came to pick Sal up. Sal realized her father knew when she saw Mrs Wong whispering to him and the concerned looks he threw in her direction. She resented the fact that they were talking about it in front of her. The trip home was stony quiet and the whisperings continued with her mother.

Everything else that happened after that was a blur. That night, the boys were solemn. Her father prayed and recited a longer blessing than usual. Sal's hands shook when she chorused her silent amin. A sob choked her. Every few minutes, eyes turned to her. She refused to look at them and her lips remained clamped until bedtime.

*

She broke into cold sweat. She dreaded opening her eyes, knowing that he was still hanging onto the 't'-bar. She could hear his agonized breathing—the heaving chest inhaled deeply until the chest cavity was filled to capacity and then exhaled with a hissing sound as the air passed through his narrow nostrils. She could hear the stretch of his muscles pulled tight by the bar. She could hear little droplets of blood seeping through the tiny pores on his skin; and when they clotted into a bigger drop, the blood-tear rolled down his face, engulfing the little hairs for one second and then leaving them behind, drenched and neglected. Bees, she knew not from where, buzzed a busy dance around her head. She felt sharp stings on her arms and legs. A slow moan started deep in his chest and crept slowly up his throat and escaped from his lips. The pained sound grasped at her, ripped her lips apart, and forced its way into her heart. Strong fingers of sound clenched the muscular walls of her heart, constricting her breath, and squeezing out the last particles of air. Pain shot through her body, droplets of blood seeped from the stings, and another moan started deep inside, only this time from her. She clawed at her chest, choking back the moan. Pray, pray for help, ease all the pain. She cupped her palms together, praying; droplets of blood dripped into the clammy cup. More and more drops. The small cup spilled and blood overflowed. She screamed.

Myanmar

An Umbrella

MA SANDAR

Ko Yay Geh was dozing off, leaning against the wall. He had a short cheroot that had gone out and was being lightly held in the corner of his lips. Every time Ma Sein Mya saw him like this, she got a feeling of uneasiness in her mind. Then she remembered the words her mother often used to say: 'A woman who has no husband to lean on is like a person walking in the rain without an umbrella. There is no one to shield her from the rain and wind.'

Even though she married him out of love and by her own choice, Ma Sein Mya was not quite satisfied with her husband, Ko Yay Geh. It is true that he gave her all of his small salary without keeping even one *pya* to himself. However, she became very irritated when she could not hold on to it, for the money diminished gradually until there was nothing left. By the middle of the month, Ma Sein Mya repeated the following words twice a day: 'Since we have a bunch of kids, it's not enough to depend only on your salary, Ko Yay Geh. We need to plan for some extra income.'

To this, the snoozing Ko Yay Geh agreed by straining to open his eyes and saying, 'Um ... of course! You plan that. Plan. Plan.' Then he tried to close his half-open eyes.

'I'm asking you to do it because I don't know how to. I'm asking you!' Ma Sein Mya curtly retorted. Ko Yay Geh's eyes became a little wider and he sighed unobtrusively.

'Okay. In that case I will have to do it.'

'How are you going to plan it?'

'Oh! Do I have to do it right away?'

'All you have to do is to say it. What's so difficult? Say it. Say it now!'

'Oh! Do you think it is easy to say it? If I'm that good why am I working as a clerk? I'd be working as a director general or a managing director.'

Ma Sein Mya gave Ko Yay Geh a big dirty look. She muttered. She banged things around. At that moment, bad luck fell upon the eldest and the middle sons, who happened to be messing around in front of their mother and got a good spanking from her.

Ko Yay Geh heaved a big sigh. He took the short cheroot out of his mouth. Then he put it back. He reached for the matches and lit it again. He ignored everything as if he did not see or hear any of it. He puffed on his short cheroot until there was a lot of smoke. About ten minutes later he leaned back on the wall again. He puffed on the cheroot absent-mindedly. After ten more minutes he narrowed his eyes and dozed off again.

'Whenever I talk to him it always ends like this. You don't know how fed up I am.' Ma Sein Mya poured her heart out to her elder sister Daw Sein Kyi, whose husband, Ko Yu Swan, was part Chinese.

Even though he had the same habit of sitting and leaning against the wall like Ko Yay Geh in the evenings, Daw Sein Kyi's husband did not doze off. He constantly used his abacus. It seemed like he was always calculating in his small head which commodity he should sell, which commodity he should be buying at a reduced price, and which commodity he should be storing. He was someone who could contrive to increase his monthly income in accordance with the ever-rising prices of food and commodities. That is why even though there were five children in both of the families, Daw Sein Kyi's family was able to have elegant meals with the good white Nga Kyweh rice, meat and fish curries with enough oil.

Ma Sein Mya, on the other hand, was rather fed up with life. She told her sister, 'We never make ends meet each month. We have to borrow, or pawn, and it's always a vicious circle.'

Even if Indra,* king of the gods, showed up in his headdress and said, 'Ask for anything you desire,' it was unlikely that she would even make a wish to reach Nirvana within a few days. It was more likely that her prayer would be: 'Dear Lord, may my husband Ko Yay Geh be a good provider like my sister Daw Sein Kyi's husband.' However, it did not seem that the magic emerald slab in the world of the thirty-three gods hardened to remind Indra that a good person was in trouble. The king of the gods did not show up. And so, while Ko Yu Swan was diligently using his abacus, Ko Yay Geh kept snoozing.

'Ko Yay Geh is a good man.' Even though her sister had never responded to Ma Sein Mya's complaints before, this time she defended Ko Yay Geh. Her daughter brought them a plate of *lahpet thouq*, pickled tea-leaf salad. 'He doesn't drink, gamble, and have affairs,' continued her sister while pushing the salad plate toward Ma Sein Mya. 'When you become husband and wife, loyalty is more important than financial matters, Sein Mya. How can you have a happy marriage if you can't trust each other?'

Ma Sein Mya gave her sister a quick glance. She immediately noticed a gloomy pair of eyes full of hurt. 'What's wrong sister? Is Ko Yu Swan ... '

'Yes, your brother Ko Yu Swan has a mistress,' said her sister curtly, turning her head away from Ma Sein Mya. 'The girl is young. She's also beautiful. About the same age as your elder niece Mi Tu.'

'Wow! His own .daughter's age!' muttered Ma Sein Mya in shock. She thought that Ko Yu Swan was only devoted to doing business. She never thought he would be interested in seeking other pleasures.

'As for me, I'm over forty, close to fifty. I'm fat. My stomach is bulging. My waist is thick. There's no way I can compete with a young mistress in good shape, Ma Sein Mya.'

'Oh God! ... Oh God!' Looking at her sister's protruding stomach, Ma Sein Mya secretly called out to God. Even though it was not as bad as her sister's, her stomach was also protruding. Her abdomen was thick; the waist was also thick. She noticed that her stomach and

---

* It is believed that Indra sits on an emerald slab that is soft like velvet. Whenever a good person is in trouble, the slab becomes hard as a reminder for Indra to assist that person.

waist were in a straight line. She remembered how once in a while Ko Yay Geh jokingly called her 'Miss Turtle Waist' or 'Miss Frog's Butt' instead of her real name 'Ma Sein Mya'.

Besides, it had been a long time since she wore a shapely bodice. And so, not only was her body below the waist ugly, it was certain that her body above the waist was not a pretty sight either. As for her face, even before she got married it was only mediocre. Now without powder and lipstick …

'Oh God! … Oh God! I wonder if Ko Yay Geh also would like to have a mistress if he could afford it.' This unhappy thought came to Ma Sein Mya while she put a spoonful of pickled tea-leaf salad into her mouth in a delirium.

'Has it been long since you found out?'

'Uh huh. About two months, I think.' Ma Sein Kyi wiped her tears. 'Of course he tries to cover it up. Since he looked suspicious to me, I followed him without his knowledge. I found them right away.'

'What did you do then?'

'Me?' Elder Sister Sein Kyi clenched her teeth tightly. Then as if to swallow something, she gulped labouriously and gave Ma Sein Mya a weak smile.

'I left that place quietly so that he wouldn't know.'

'Oh no!'

'Think about it. What would he do if he knows that I know? He would move forward boldly since it's no use hiding from me anymore. From supporting her secretly, he'll support her openly. I have five children. I'm just sitting and eating what he earns. I have no skills … If we divorce, how will I get an income? Since there's no divorce yet, I think it's better to pretend that I don't know anything about it.'

This time Ma Sein Mya really admired her sister. But she also felt a deep sorrow for her. It was certain that if Ko Yay Geh behaved this way her reaction would not be the same as that of her sister.

'You are angry with Ko Yay Geh for not earning enough money. He can't find a lot of money, but everything he earns goes into your hand. Shouldn't you be satisfied with that?'

'Should I be satisfied?' Ma Sein Mya asked herself and became very sad. How could she be satisfied with a head of the household who was always sitting and dozing off whenever there was free time—in a poor household like theirs.

'You know Ma Shu Kyi, don't you? Ko Yu Swan's sister.'

'Yeah. I know.'

Ma Sein Mya recalled that Ma Shu Kyi was fair skinned, slender and very pretty before she was married. She got married to an officer who worked in a department that brought in a lot of extra income. Ma Sein Mya heard that they lived quite elegantly and had saved quite a bit of money.

'Her husband is very nice if he doesn't drink. But as soon as some alcohol gets into his body, he picks fights with her. He'll try to find any old reason to scold and beat her.'

'Oh, really?'

'When he's sober, of course he'll say, "Ko Ko made a mistake." Of course he will pacify her. But this Ko Ko keeps making mistakes again and again. So poor Ma Shu Kyi is always in tears ... She came yesterday. One cheek was swollen. Ko Yu Swan was so angry that he was even saying, "Why don't you divorce this animal?" and so on and so forth.'

'Yes, of course. Divorce him.'

'But they've already got two children. Will it be easy to divorce him? And in our culture, a widow might get respect from people. As for a divorcee, even the neighbours don't respect her,' said Elder Sister Sein Kyi reflectively. Her lifeless eyes looked grim and dark. The colours were dim and faded. 'Nowadays I meditate at night when I'm free.'

'You do?' Ma Sein Mya knew that even though her sister had a tender heart, she was not a very religious person.

'Earlier of course, I thought of all kinds of things—whether I should cut my hair, or perm it, take an aerobic dance class, or go on a diet to become slender. But whatever I do, a person over forty is over forty. I'll never be pretty again like a twenty year old. When I realized all this, I gave up. Now I read prayer books. Meditate. I'll only try to have peace of mind this way.'

Ma Sein Mya heaved a deep sigh. She thought: 'Why are there so many unpleasant marriages in this world? If there is money, there is no loyalty. When there is money and loyalty, there is no compassion. For those marriages with compassion, money is lacking. Since basic needs are not met, people become short-tempered and have fights.'

'This is depressing. I'd better go home.' Ma Sein Mya got up and readjusted her long Burmese skirt. She saw a reflection of a not-so-pleasant-looking body with a loose bodice, a protruding stomach, and a thick waist in the cupboard mirror.

'Hmmm. It's worse because there are no pretty new clothes to decorate this body and turn it into a bearable sight,' thought Ma Sein Mya bitterly while looking at the reflection in the mirror with a frown.

'Hey, are you leaving already?'

'Yeah. I haven't prepared dinner yet.'

'Here. Here. Take some snacks for the kids.' *Ama* Sein Kyi gave her a packet of biscuits and twenty-five *kyat.* 'It's so cloudy and dark. Did you bring an umbrella with you?'

'Yes, I did. Here it is.' Ma Sein Mya reached for her big umbrella which was full of holes and patches and put it under her arm. The black colour of the umbrella had faded due to its old age. You wouldn't need an umbrella this big for a little drizzle. Her sister gazed at the umbrella under Ma Sein Mya's arm for a while and gave a forced laugh.

'Ma Sein Mya, do you remember what Mother used to say often?'

'What?'

'That a woman without a husband is like someone walking in the rain without an umbrella.'

'If only Mother were here I would like to tell her that I'm using an umbrella; but if that umbrella is a ragged one, I still get soaking wet from the raindrops that keep dripping.'

This time both of them looked at each other and laughed heartily. Then *Ama* Sein Kyi said quite loudly, 'The good folding umbrellas and the ones with steel handles are not reliable either. When there's strong wind and rain they turn inside out.'

*

On the way home it rained heavily. So, Ma Sein Mya had to use her old umbrella. Since it was a locally made cloth umbrella, it did not turn inside out like the folding ones.

'It should be enough that it does not turn inside out. Tolerate the leakage. Tolerate it,' said Ma Sein Mya to herself.

The rain got to her from the side. It also beat her from the front.

On top of that, the umbrella cloth could not keep the rain from dripping on her. By the time Ma Sein Mya got home, her whole body was soaking wet. Also the biscuits in the plastic bag that *Ama* Sein Kyi gave were moist and soggy.

'*Ama* Sein Mya, were you caught in the rain?' asked Than Than Khin from next door. Her little face, full of *thanakha* powder with thick circles on her two cheeks, lit up the gloomy room like a little light-bulb. 'The rain is really heavy. It never rains but pours. I'm lucky that I didn't go out today.'

(Than Than Khin owned a treadle sewing machine. She was a seamstress. However, since the blouses she made were not so shapely, there were not many customers. Every afternoon, she dressed up and went out. Even though she said she did some buying and selling, Ma Sein Mya did not know for sure what she sold and what she bought. Ma Kyawt from the front house gossiped: 'How much income will she get from sewing? Will it be enough for the mother and daughter to eat? You don't know what she is up to going out in the afternoons.' Sometimes young mischief makers from the neighbourhood sang out from the dark some lyrics from a well-known romantic song: 'Ma Than Khin. Oh, Than Khin. I'd only like to see you beautiful like a flower. I'm also concerned that like a little flower you will wither away. I'm concerned.'* And they giggled.)

'I did take my umbrella along, but I still got wet.'

'Hmmm. When the rain gets really heavy, how can you remain dry with an umbrella of this size?'

'Oh, it's also because the umbrella is ragged. It would have been better had I walked in the rain without it.'

Ma Sein Mya handed the biscuit packet to her middle son with her left hand and with her right hand forcefully threw the umbrella down on the floor of the front room. She was irritated with the ragged old umbrella as well as with Than Than Khin, who was smelling sweet and looking beautiful.

'Daughter, bring me a kimono from my cupboard. I'm going to use it as a bathing garment,' she yelled out sarcastically while gathering

---

* In polite Burmese society it is frequently considered embarrassing for a young, unmarried girl to have a tête-à-tête with a bachelor.

the lower end of her long Burmese skirt and squeezing out the water from it. The older son, however, not realizing that it was only a sarcastic remark, muttered with surprise, 'You have a kimono? Do you?' With wide eyes he looked at the faded Chinese print garment that the middle daughter brought to her mother.

'You stupid ass,' swore Ma Sein Mya in her mind at her son while changing. She picked up the wet skirt that fell near her feet and squeezed out the water. Even though she had not glanced at Than Than Khin, she could hear her whisper: 'When the rain is really heavy you get wet no matter what kind of umbrella you are using, *ama*. At least this one makes you look dignified.'

Translated by Than Than Win

Philippines

Caravan of the Waterbearers

(Mitzvah with Grace)

MARJORIE EVASCO

We will not forget the evil eye
of the storm they raised,
gutting the ground we defended.
We have been trained
to look away too often
when man's flesh, muscle, bone
knifed woman, to protect
the child's eye from the dust
of the lord's sin against
our kind, pretending
our tears are daughters of the wind
blowing across no-woman's land.

We have had to seek the centre
of the storm in the land we claim
is ours, too. Faces keening towards
the full force of winds
once blinding us, we see
the blur of broken earth,
blasted wastes, damned seas.

Our vision clears in our weeping.

We have joined the trek
of desert women, humped over
from carrying our own oases

in the clay pots of our lives,
gathering broken shards we find
in memory of those who went
ahead of us, alone.

When we seize the water source,
our ranks will complete the circle
we used to mark around our tents,
making homes, villages, temples,
schools, our healing places.
And we will bear witness
for our daughters and sons,
telling them true stories
of the caravan.

Philippines

Ochre Tones

Marjorie Evasco

The benediction in the air—
A lizard, translucent and newly broken
From its shell, kisses the earth
At sundown, repeating the ritual dance
Of marsh and cloud dragons.

My best friend, Grace, says baby lizards
Are messengers, presaging heat or rain.
She believes in omens: earth calling
The littlest creatures to drink
The first mists of evening.

Who is to say it is instinct, merely,
Or moisture-need, that makes us
Crawl or bend our lizard lips
Unto the ground? Dusk cools our fevers
And there is joy in this surrender.

Even now, the tips of bamboo leaves
Hold water gems. In the early evening air
I remember Grace and somewhere,
An old gecko clicks its rhythmic
Yes   yes   yes.

Singapore

Sunny-side Up

TAN MEI CHING

Wednesday was the day the Ramons ran out of eggs, so when Mrs Ramon got up Mr Ramon had already left the house. He knew that on Wednesdays he wouldn't get his breakfast eggs (cooked with Mrs Ramon's homemade pickle sauce) until nine o'clock, when Mrs Ramon came back from the wet market, so he took himself off for a cup of coffee first. They had coffee in the house, of course, the instant kind that didn't taste too bad with lots of condensed milk, but he wanted conversation.

Mrs Ramon pottered around the kitchen fixing a cup of black coffee (she didn't like condensed milk) and read the first part of the newspaper. 'Look at that,' she said to herself. 'A grandmother climbing up Mt. Fuji every year.' She read the story thoroughly, and then sat back, forgetting her usual search and cutting of special offer coupons.

Buzz! She jumped. What was that? It was a strange and urgent buzz. Mrs Ramon was sure no insect ever made that kind of buzz. There it was again! She pounced, as only a small, plump woman could pounce, on the refrigerator. When she opened its door, the yellow light blinked lethargically at her. 'Oh dear, what's happening?' she asked. She closed the door and opened it again. The light blinked once, twice. Mrs Ramon cocked her ear and listened. There were no untoward sounds.

When Mrs Ramon finally sat down to her newspaper again and raised her eyes to the clock, she muttered, 'Oh dear.' She put her hand on her chest to quiet the flutters. Mr Ramon wasn't too exacting a man, but there were some things he was absolutely set about, and one of them was his breakfast eggs, cooked in her special sauce.

Mrs Ramon hurried. She wasn't good at hurrying because she was fifty-five and plump and had small feet, but she understood the importance of the eggs. There's nothing she and her husband liked better than fresh eggs sunny-side up in pickle sauce, with undercooked, gooey, golden yolks that oozed out in their mouths. That was one of the three things that she and Mr Ramon shared. The second was the flat and the third was their daughter, Cindy.

So Mrs Ramon made good time and trotted off to the market with her red shopping basket. Halfway to the market, she saw Mr Lee, who was almost always the last one to the market on Wednesdays. This time, Mrs Ramon was even later than Mr Lee. She quickened her footsteps as much as her short legs would allow, and reached the first stall ready with her purse. 'Oh,' she said, staring in dismay. Normally, when the eggs came in, they were stacked three to four cartons high all over the counter. Mrs Ramon has never seen the counter-top because of that. She saw it now.

'Late, Mrs Ramon,' said Joseph, popping up from behind the counter.

'Any more left?' Mrs Ramon asked. 'I was going to come earlier, but our refrigerator was a bit funny.'

'All sold!' Joseph said, scratching his arm. He always scratched his arm when he was sorry.

'Oh dear, what's Mr Ramon going to do without his breakfast eggs?' Mrs Ramon frowned. Could she buy some from the coffee-shop? She's never done that, but then, Mr Ramon has never been in danger of going without his breakfast eggs before. She started to walk away.

'Wait,' Joseph said, holding up an egg carton that looked like it had been stepped on.

Mrs Ramon shook her head. 'They're all broken. I don't want broken eggs.'

Joseph used his fingers to clear away egg white and yolks and bits of eggshell, and came up with something smooth and brown. 'Still good,' he said, turning it around in his hand. 'Have you seen such a big egg before?'

Mrs Ramon had indeed never seen such a big egg before. It was the size of an orange. 'Are you sure it came from a chicken?' she asked.

'The box says so,' Joseph said. And because he had only that one egg for Mrs Ramon who had been his faithful customer for ten years, he gave it to her for free. Mrs Ramon wrapped the enormous egg in newspaper and wedged it carefully in a corner of her basket. Then she bought carrots, onions, potatoes, celery, and chicken drumsticks to make stew. After some thought, she brought strawberries rather than the usual oranges.

Mr Ramon hadn't returned when Mrs Ramon reached home. Sometimes, when his coffee-shop friends had more to say about their singing birds or aquariums or soccer matches, he would stay a little longer and have toast with *kaya.* Mrs Ramon knew that when he got back home, he would say, 'Eggs, please.' That was the only thing Mr Ramon ever said to her in the mornings. This time Mrs Ramon could answer, 'I'll show you an Egg.' Mrs Ramon unpacked her groceries with greater enthusiasm than usual. She placed the enormous egg in the middle of the table, surrounding it with two dishcloths. Then she made her second cup of coffee and sat down to stare at the egg. What was really in that egg? Was it an egg in the first place? 'You need a chicken as big as a pig to lay that egg,' she said.

After some minutes, Mrs Ramon got down on her knees and hunted for her baking scale that had been retired to the dark corners of the kitchen cabinet a few years ago. She weighed the egg. It was almost 120 grams, equivalent to the weight of three eggs. 'Hm,' she said. She switched on a strong light and tried to see what was inside the egg, but the shell was extraordinarily thick and she couldn't see a thing. With a spoon, she gave the shell an experimental tap, just to hear if it sounded like an ordinary egg. Toc! Toc! Toc! She couldn't be sure, but it did sound very solid, as if the insides were frozen. She tried again, this time harder. Toc! Toc! She tried again, harder still. Then she heard it, something strange, like a high whine, and a small dot appeared on the smooth brown shell. The dot lengthened and became a tiny squiggly line. The squiggly line lengthened and spilt into two, then three, then four. Like the fissures of an earthquake, the eggshell cracked.

Mrs Ramon, who didn't like to do things in a hurry, could be very fast if she chose. In one second, she grabbed a bowl and held the egg over it. Just in time too. The shell cracked open and the insides gushed out, as if they were glad to be released from their absolute cell. Then

Mrs Ramon stared, because this egg, instead of having one yolk like all ordinary eggs, had two yolks, two perfectly golden-yellow globules, nestled in translucent white.

'Well!' Mrs Ramon exclaimed. This egg must be one in a thousand, no, one in a million. It was special all right.

In a moment, Mrs Ramon was no longer Mrs Ramon, ordinary housewife. She was now Owner of the Extraordinary Egg. She would be on the news—why, it was only last week she read about the peapod that grew inside another peapod. Mr Ramon would say to his friends with the fine singing birds and expensive tropical fish, 'Look at my wife's egg.' Instead of going out for morning coffee, his friends would come over to have theirs and Mrs Ramon would sit with them and have a cup too. Neighbours would come to their little three-room flat to look at the wonderful egg. She would tell the story of her discovery at least ten times.

There she stopped. She remembered she didn't actually pay for the egg. It was a gift from Joseph the egg-seller. Would he want it back after he found out it was an Extraordinary Egg? The more she thought about it, the more it worried her. In the end, Mrs Ramon picked up her little beaded purse and stuck on her soft blue shoes and proceeded to the market.

Joseph was nowhere to be seen. Mrs Ramon walked around the market, peering into the coffee-shops. She finally found Joseph sitting with one leg up on the stool and the other tapping to a melody only he could hear. Mrs Ramon marched up to him and placed a dollar on the table beside his chipped plate of toast.

'What's this?' Joseph was rightly surprised. Mrs Ramon never, ever, went to the market twice in a week, much less twice in a day.

'It's for the egg,' Mrs Ramon explained.

'I gave it to you for free,' Joseph said.

'I don't want it for free. I want to buy it,' Mrs Ramon said.

'One dollar is too much.' Joseph dug into his pocket and gave Mrs Ramon fifty cents. 'Is that okay? I have no more coins.'

Mrs Ramon nodded. She wasn't concerned about coins. She just wanted to make sure the egg was hers.

On the way home, she thought about what she would wear if she was interviewed, or, gasp! appeared on TV. She realized she hadn't gone shopping in four years. All her clothes, and she didn't have many, were quite worn. Could she remember how to make a dress? She used to make dresses for herself and her Cindy. When Cindy grew up and started buying off-the-rack clothes that came in fancy shapes and material, Mrs Ramon stopped making clothes. Cindy liked her simple tank tops though. How long was it since she made a tank top for Cindy? How was Cindy doing at the bank?

Mrs Ramon stopped outside the door of her flat, her brain buzzing. So many things to do. She could be tomorrow's news and she would have to live up to it. Why, she hadn't planned so far ahead in a long time. Mrs Ramon felt flutters in her chest again, but this time she didn't put up a hand to stop them. Instead she smiled, opened the door and went in.

Mr Ramon was home, sitting at the dining table with the newspaper. 'Where did you go?' he asked, his mouth full of food. He had been quite surprised by her absence. He'd thought that he had timed his return home right, just before the sizzling eggs slid onto the plate on the table.

'Come and see something wonderful,' Mrs Ramon said, going to the refrigerator for a certain bowl.

'The refrigerator stopped,' Mr Ramon said. 'Luckily we didn't have much in it.' He swallowed. 'There were some eggs though.'

Mrs Ramon's hand hovered over the refrigerator door.

'Two eggs actually,' Mr Ramon continued. 'I fried them up. Kept you one if you want it.'

Mrs Ramon opened the refrigerator. The bowl was gone. The egg was gone. It was halfway through Mr Ramon's digestive system by now. She couldn't help it; she covered her face with her hands.

'What's wrong?' Mr Ramon asked. 'We can buy a new fridge, maybe a smaller one since we don't cook much.'

'The egg …' Mr Ramon moaned. She kept her face in her hands.

'I kept one for you,' Mr Ramon said, a trifle alarmed—Mrs Ramon seemed so unlike herself.

'It was one egg,' Mrs Ramon said through her fingers.

'One egg? No, there were two yolks,' Mr Ramon said.

'Yes! One egg, two yolks! I was going to call the newspaper.' Mrs Ramon finally looked up, her face quite tragic.

'One egg, two yolks!' Mr Ramon was relieved. He'd thought Mrs Ramon was ill. 'That's a funny thing, eh? And I ate it. Half of it.'

Mrs Ramon was still too pale for her normal self. Mr Ramon straightened up and put down his newspapers. 'I didn't know,' he said.

Mrs Ramon looked at him. His eyes were wide open and the corners of his mouth were turned down. 'I know you didn't,' Mrs Ramon said. Her legs were a bit wobbly, but she managed to walk to a chair and sit down. 'It was a one-in-a-million egg.'

'Yeah,' Mr Ramon agreed. He shook his head. 'How does one egg get two yolks? Never seen anything like that before.'

Mrs Ramon went to the cupboard and took out what looked like a small brown ball. 'Look at the eggshell.'

'That's a big eggshell,' Mr Ramon exclaimed. 'It's as big as an orange!'

'That's just what I thought!' Mrs Ramon said.

'Wait till Huat and the others see it,' Mr Ramon said, holding up the eggshell against the window. 'You remember Huat? You saw him once. He always wears a purple silk shirt.' He turned the eggshell around carefully. 'The shell is so thick!'

Seeing her husband's eyes crinkle against the light, Mrs Ramon thought, 'What nice eyes he has.' Suddenly, she said, 'I'm going to make you a shirt.'

'You are?' Mr Ramon lowered his arm.

Mrs Ramon nodded.

'Not purple?' Mr Ramon said.

'Light brown, I think.' Mrs Ramon smiled.

Mr Ramon smiled.

They sat side by side, examining the eggshell, and Mrs Ramon ate her share of the Extraordinary Egg with some pickle sauce.

Singapore

Journal Week

HENG SIOK TIAN

[I]

I crammed
into hand-me-down shoes
learning to stride graceful
with big flat feet,
taking light dainty steps
with bones crushed by foot-binding.

[II]

I wrecked my teenaged nights
with angst familiar to all,
blinded myself with opaque colours
and snapped
like a burst balloon.

I took to
wallpapering my room
with brochures,
conspired with clouds,
floated to lands untravelled
to wink at unreal man
in the arms of a surreal paradise.

[III]

I wanted to be
clearly unlike mother
who accepted rice and water,

I would trudge on
making up my own croissants on a horizon.

[IV]

Along the way on ghost roads
I drove alone to reservoirs,
watched dragonflies in early dew.

[V]

Images flooded my mornings and nights:
my bedspread is a bloodshed of broken palette,
my room is an oyster howling in an ocean,
my limbs are chilled in champagne bottles,
my body an oversized doll with feet hanging upside down,
my mind a wheel cycling without geometry
my emotions are dried-up tubes of colour wound up in
decrepit shapes.
My images and me:
we stalk each mother

[VI]

I decide:
not to live
in a fairy-tale castle
awaiting rescue,
witness the unsung tragedies of
heroines, maids, beaten wives,
see myself in my sisters
equally born
of sinful apples.

[VII]

All this while
I am deaf to whispering hymns
of passing night clouds.

Singapore

Medusa: Stone Poems

QIAN XI TENG

There are things you've heard about me.
A lot of heroes
creep here with over-polished shields.

When you arrive it will feel like a museum
as you walk among the statues
and perhaps find a face you remember having
settle like ashes over your own.

I lied. There are no heroes here.
Only stone men. Their eyes are
marbled like graveyard angels.

What they don't tell you is that my face
only turns your skin to stone.
Brains and tongues
remain in the body like red fruit.
Ripe then rotten.

It happens to everyone anyway, doesn't it—
This reliance on one hardened posture?
Glass fangs, lidless eyes
watching you.

What a thing it is to be free.
Now rest your hand against my hair.
Feel the tails flickering under my skull
at the places you touch.
Look at my smile. Surprise me if you dare.

Thailand

The Defiance of a Flower

CHIRANAN PITPREECHA

Woman has two hands
That hold tight to the substance of life;
Her ply of ligaments is meant of heavy task,
Not for the craving of flimsy silk and damask.

Woman has two feet
To climb the ladder of aspiration,
To strive and stand together,
Not to lean on others.

Woman has eyes
To search for new life
And look far and wide into the world
Not to lure or seduce men.

Woman has a heart
That glows unchangingly,
Amassing all the strength
Because she is complete and human.

Woman has life
That erases errors with reasons.
The value of a free person
Is not to feed the lust of others.
Flowers have sharp thorns,
Not just to blossom and await admirers;
But to bloom and embrace
The fertility of the land.

Translated by Sudchit Bhinyoying

Vietnam

Thuong

Phan Thi Vang Anh

When Miss Thuong first arrived, Mr Hao was outside gardening. Out of breath, she dropped her suitcase in the yard, unbuttoned her collar, and blew inside her blouse to cool herself off.

Hao was so flustered that he threw down his spade near the bed of roses, wiped his hands on his trousers, and muttered, 'Oh dear me—very good, very good. Come in, come in!'

Even though the difference in their ages was great, they were good friends. He hadn't seen her for about three years, and except for being a little heavier, she hadn't changed a bit. The corners of her eyes were sharp as knives, her mouth wide, and her lips a deep red. She had long legs and strode on them as gracefully as a leopard.

Hao asked her why she had come to his remote town. She smiled.

'Oh, I felt sad and decided I needed to take a trip. As for why this town, well, it was actually at the suggestion of a friend. She said that if I was feeling sad, I should go far away. And this place has both mountains and sea. And when I was on the bus, I suddenly remembered an old acquaintance I had here. Luckily, I'd written down the address in my book.'

Hao had been busy brewing *nhan tran* tea, but on hearing those words, the heightened sense of anticipation he'd felt since she arrived died. He knew his disappointment was his own fault, though. He kept up an animated facade, and they both chattered enthusiastically. Thuong had her own style of telling stories. Each new piece of information was followed by a few sharp commentaries, all sarcastic. But her remarks were not meant to be malicious—unlike those of his wife, now dead, who used to make jibes during festive occasions and the Tet holiday that were always a source of discomfort for him.

Thuong liked to smile, and when she did, her eyes sparkled like water in a spring, often startling people. Suddenly, she stopped in the middle of a sentence, turned around, and asked with whom he was staying. He pretended to smile sadly.

'Nobody.'

It was true; he lived alone in this house, which his children had repaired for him the previous year. When he had requested that they paint all of his blinds green, they had called him trendy. Now, for the first time in his life, he had a guest room, though he had yet to have a guest. He asked Thuong if she would mind staying in his house. She laughed and said her reputation wouldn't suffer; she had been running around for some time and was no longer a naive girl.

This statement stirred up some hope in Hao, and his enthusiasm quickly returned. He took a small desk fan from the cupboard—the same fan that would leap like a toad onto his bed in the morning, after it had been on all night. He gave Thuong a pink, Thai-made fan and saved the defective one for himself. Then he mopped the guest room and unrolled a floral mat on the bed.

Finished, he stood back to take in the whole picture, his eyes wide as a child's.

'Anything missing?' he asked Thuong.

She was all smiles.

'It's just fine, Uncle. First rate.'

Thuong stayed away from the house all day. When she returned, she washed her clothes and sang melodious Russian songs. She looked absent-minded, like a person being rocked gently back and forth in an ox-drawn cart. The pace of life in this place had awakened in her a strange feeling of purity. She would go into the garden, knife in hand, and return with a few nameless flowers and sheaves of withered grass, just enough to fill a vase and make Hao blush at this reminder of how countrified and monotonous his life was.

And she cooked. Mostly simple food, but when she had more time, she'd rustle up sophisticated dishes.

On one holiday, Hao's grandson, Lam, a student who lived in the city, came for a visit during his summer break. Stretched out on the hammock, he said spontaneously, 'If only I had a braised duck!' Thuong didn't say a word, but smiled to herself.

That evening, the two men feasted on braised duck washed down with apricot wine. Picking the lotus seeds from the duck's belly, Lam asked, 'Does Thuong run a restaurant?' He waited for her to come home so that he could congratulate her. But she didn't come back. Finally, at ten, Hao urged him to go home so that his parents wouldn't worry.

The road was steep and long, but Hao was insistent that the young man—the only member of his family who had made it to university—leave and get his sleep. Seeing him to the garden gate and feigning indifference, Hao said, 'It's certain she will not be back tonight.'

Lam smiled. 'The lady seems to be untamed.'

He started his motorbike. Hao watched its red rear light zigzag down the hill and disappear into the darkness.

Two days later, when Lam came back, his grandfather was ill. Lam found him sitting in the middle of the house, wrapped in a red blanket as if he were about to hold a séance. He spoke through a stuffed-up nose.

'Is that you, Lam? I'm going to have a steam bath.'

Then he sneezed repeatedly.

Thuong emerged from the kitchen, her eyes shining, her complexion ruddy. She smiled. 'Be careful—I don't want you to stick your foot into this pot of water. Go in first, and I'll bring it in after you.'

Lam, who had stretched out his legs on the divan and was reading a newspaper, hurriedly lowered his feet, greeted her, and then returned to his reading. All of a sudden, something prompted him to look up. Thuong was bending over, stretching her long arms down to pick up the pot of steaming water. Silhouetted through her thin clothes, her body looked as beautiful and pure as an ancient statue, though she had a look of resignation on her face. Lam jumped up. 'Let me take that for you,' he said. And then he asked himself. *Why do I suddenly feel so noble and manly?*

Thuong handed him two pieces of cloth, her gesture confident rather than shy. Lam searched for something to say.

'Where did you get the leaves for the steam bath?'

'From the garden,' Thuong said softly, walking behind him.

Lam pictured her carrying the basket, her hair unkempt, pictured her hands picking the leaves.

'I feel ill also,' he said. 'Do you think I need a steam bath?'

Three days elapsed, but Thuong hadn't returned. Hao had ventured into her room and found that everything was just as she'd left it before saying she was going to the market to buy a few things. He lay on the cot, and then he sat on the divan. He skimmed through the newspapers, but didn't take in a thing.

Late in the morning, as he was napping, he heard the noise of motorbikes at the gate. He didn't rise. He was angry with her. She was so impulsive. At times she was hardworking and considerate, a kind-hearted housewife; at other times, she could behave like a whore. Now some people had come for her, probably the artists she'd been looking for.

'Daddy! Daddy!' His daughter's piercing voice sounded like a policewoman's—even more authoritative than usual.

He heard Lam's voice also: 'Hao, my parents are here.'

Lam walked in, went into the kitchen, stayed there for a while, and then came out, saying nothing.

Ngoc, Hao's daughter, asked solemnly, 'Are you all right now?' She glanced surreptitiously at her husband, as if signalling him to do something they had planned. 'We'll stay for lunch with Daddy, right?'

The noises Ngoc made from the kitchen—the meat being cut, the water being poured over vegetables—would not allow Hao to forget Thuong.

She would often wear a sleeveless dress of thin, printed cotton and would sing, the sun shining on her, as she drew water from the well. In the evening, she stretched out her legs on the floor and cooked dinner by the fire. Whenever he pictured this scene, it was as if the two of them were lost in a deep cavern, out of earshot of all other human voices. Only the sound of a falling coconut frond could bring him back to reality …

Nobody, including Lam, mentioned Thuong.

Only two days before, he and Lam had laughed together. His grandson had stayed with him until midnight and at the gate had asked, 'Thuong often goes for walks, doesn't she?'

Now, it wasn't until the round tray had been placed on the table that Ngoc asked with a smile, 'Daddy, where is Thuong?'

'How should I know?' Hao replied.

Ngoc concentrated on sorting the chopsticks into pairs. 'Then when will she leave?'

'I don't know.'

His son-in-law put down the newspaper and said proprietarily, 'Let's eat.'

They all sat at the table. But the atmosphere was heavy and not at all like the other days when his children would come to visit. 'We want to say something, Daddy,' Ngoc began, but she was interrupted by the sudden appearance of Thuong in the doorway.

She looked even more beautiful and careless than usual. With her quiet, leopard's grace, she made a slight bow.

'Good morning, everyone.'

Hao pointed. 'This is my daughter, and my son-in-law. And this is Thuong.'

Thuong smiled again, looking at Phuong, the son-in-law. 'Yes. How do you do?'

'Will you join us for lunch?' Hao asked.

Thuong shook her head. 'No, thank you. All of you, please go ahead; I've eaten already.'

She passed behind the table, her handbag brushing gently against Phuong's chair. Phuong thought: *She hasn't changed.*

Hao felt relieved. His anger vanished.

He heard the sound of water being drawn from the well. 'Have a rest before you take a bath,' he called to Thuong, starting to rise out of his chair. 'You don't want to catch a cold.'

'I'll go!' Lam said quickly, then jumped up.

He went into the kitchen, opened a jar, and extracted a few hot chillies. When he got out to the well, he saw that Thuong was shampooing her long, black hair, revealing the nape of her snow-white neck. He completely forgot what he'd wanted to say, blushed, and went back into the house.

Hao slept. The old man's mouth opened and closed as he breathed in and out. Ngoc lay curled on the divan like a homeless person on a sidewalk. Looking at her, Phuong was suddenly struck by the thought that his wife was terribly ugly and looking more and more like her mother. And she was too talkative and told the same, bland jokes. And just like her mother, she went on and on, day after day, year after year, as monotonous as a clock.

Phuong rose and walked ever to the closed door of the inner room, lingering there. Perhaps Thuong was sleeping, her black hair spread all over the pillow. He remembered the way she would lie, peacefully, as if in a meadow, breathing so lightly. Sometimes, at night, he would shake her gently, to see if she was still alive. Those days were so distant now. But she seemed exactly the same. He knew she was easy; he knew he was a man who didn't mind taking advantage of her Western ways. He'd thought their relationship was a good one. But it turned out he was just another of her distractions. The way she had left had offended him. She had been completely indifferent, as if he were a whore whom she was fed up with and was simply abandoning. The only thing that had comforted him that day was the knowledge that he had deceived her; to the very last minute, she had thought he was unmarried. He had been lying. But then again, he wondered if knowing his marital status would have had any real effect on that woman, that tramp.

All these thoughts passed through Phuong's head as he stood by her door. He raised his hand to knock, but at that moment the door opened and she came out. She gave him a wry smile. 'Well, well, aren't you bold? But you'd better get out of here quickly—your wife is up already.'

Instinctively, Phuong spun around. Then, feeling ridiculous, he turned to her and frowned. 'What are you doing here?'

Thuong stood in the doorway, her arms akimbo, her hair tangled. 'You can be sure that it wasn't to look for you.'

Ngoc could be heard coughing.

'I'm sorry to have lied to you,' Phuong said hastily. 'At the time, my wife and I—'

Thuong waved his words away, 'It doesn't matter to me—what difference does it make?' Then, as if by impulse, she burst out laughing. Taken aback, Phuong raised his hand as if he was going to cover her mouth. Instead, he spun around and walked quickly into the garden, kicking dead coconuts out of his path as he went.

The commotion woke the whole house. Lam, who had been picking berries from some wild bushes in the back, rushed in to see what the laughter was all about. At the kitchen door, he caught sight of Thuong putting her hair up in a bun, her eyes shining. She waved to him and said, 'If someone asks, just say I was laughing with you.' Lam nodded. At that moment, his mother walked in, a concerned expression on her face. 'I'm sorry,' Thuong said softly, lowering her head.

'It's my fault,' Lam interjected, 'I was joking.'

'Get in!' Nigoc shouted at him, and short mother and tall son went back into the main room of the house.

That afternoon, Thuong left, carrying the same large suitcase and wearing the same clothes as on the day she'd arrived. Hao looked older. He insisted to her that this was his house and that she could stay as long as she wanted and that Ngoc had no right …

Thuong smiled. 'I'm just leaving because it's been a long trip—nothing more, Uncle.'

'Let me see her as far as the bus station,' said Lam. He insisted on strapping the suitcase to the front of his motorbike so that he could be closer to her. He started the bike, and off they went. Below was the vast, indifferent sea. Thuong gazed at the nape of young Lam's neck. How many years had it been since she'd last been stirred this way? She felt she was about to embark on another adventure, another game of hide and seek. After some hesitation, some struggle with herself, she said, 'You know, I don't want to go straight home. Take me to the Hong Hoa Hotel. Tomorrow afternoon, if you have some time, meet me and take me to the beach.'

'What time?' Lam said.

When he arrived the next day exactly at five o'clock, the people at the hotel told him she had just left. First she had given them a letter, they said, but then she had taken it back. If he went after her quickly enough, they said, he might still be able to catch her.

Translated by Nam Son & Wayne Karlin

Vietnam

Woman Wearing B!ack

LAM THI MY DA

A woman walks down the road
Spring wind drapes her shoulders
She utters one small phrase
Just so she may hear herself
Just so the wind may hear

There is nothing to regret, she thinks
Flowers and grass grow free, under her feet
There is nothing difficult, she thinks
Step by light step she glides past

Why doesn't she wear purple or pink?
She wears nothing but black
Black clothes like a coffin
Shrouding all her scattered mistakes

She cannot bury the flickering images
The ones she intended to bury
Perhaps her aching heart is the earth
Where that heavy coffin is laid

Oh woman, life is not like that
Why do you foolishly bury yourself?
If you look up at the distant sky you will see
Spring trembling all over, anxiously trembling.

Translated by Martha Collins & Thuy Dinh

Vietnam

The Ghost

Ly Lan

'I tell you this, but don't be frightened. You are haunted by a ghost.' Miss Linh bites her lip as if she wants to take back her words. She waits for my reaction, but I'm not frightened. A ghost is the spirit of a dead person. A dead person can't rob me, murder me, or slander or imprison me. So why should I be frightened?

'I tell you this not because I have any desire for profit, but to warn you. This is a debt from a previous life. You must drive it away.'

I laugh. Among the six billion people who live on this planet, this ghost has chosen me. How can I have the heart to drive it away?

But my mother is worried. 'You look pale,' she says. 'Your soul and body seem not together. You seem lost, even when you are with others.'

To cure me, my mother takes me to the pagoda. We bring flowers and fruits with us. When we arrive, I prostrate myself before the Buddha, then join the others sitting cross-legged and listening to the Sutras.

'Antapha baphathuat datapha datmatapha batarami . . . '

My mother requests that I repeat the words. 'These True Words purify the three karmas,' she tells me. I repeat them. Pagodas on mountains are lofty places, and Sutras in Sanskrit are sacred, so it doesn't matter if, when I read them, I don't understand the meaning. Anyway, the Sutras are not for me; they are for the ghost.

'Batarami maphadata mahadatapapha . . . '

Listening to the Sutras, the ghost may be purified and freed from suffering. Or it may leave me, deciding to lead a peaceful existence at the pagoda instead. After finishing the Sutras, I walk in the garden. At noon I have lunch, then chant more Sutras into the evening. The plan is for me to stay a few days. The pagoda is a beautiful place, in the evening; from the back of the garden, I watch the sun set deep red in the west, then the skyline gradually turn a dark purple.

But on the second day of my stay at the pagoda, my younger brother arrives and angrily drags me home. He shouts at me, 'If you fast and pray like an ascetic, you will surely see your grave!' His recommended treatment is rest and invigoration. Meat, fish, chicken, duck, milk, eggs, cream ... and a can of beer each day—this is the regimen he suggests for good health. The next day he returns from work, announcing, 'My office is having a weekend in Vung Tau. Come there with me; we'll go swimming and sunbathing, eat fresh seafood. I bet you'll feel better.'

My mother is busy getting ready for the trip, but on Thursday the war in the Gulf breaks out. Friday evening, the entire family sits in front of the TV set.

'E-game,' my youngest sister cries. My mother ignores her and complains of how the prices going up make her dizzy. 'Those well-fed people know little about war yet. Let them learn!' my elder brother interjects. My father corrects him, saying, 'Nobody really knows. You and I have the experience of surviving the war, but only the dead know what war really means.' My younger brother announces, 'I have a bet with the chief of my office that Iraq can't last more than a week.'

He brought home a case of beer from his office yesterday. When the US issued its ultimatum, people in his office wagered whether Uncle Sam would fight—he fought and my brother won the bet. My brother now drinks beer and smiles at President Bush on TV.

I go to bed early so I will be able to get up to take the bus that departs for Vung Tau at dawn.

At Vung Tau the sea is oily; it foams as if boiling. I want to stretch out on the sand, but the beach is dirty. My younger brother rents a cot and umbrella for me. He dives into the surf with his girlfriend; later we will have drinks with his colleagues at a restaurant. The chief of his office sits beside me and offers me cashews and a Coke. I felt sick on the bus and still have a bitter taste in my mouth; I eat a cashew without tasting it. But the Coke makes me belch, and

I feel a bit better. My younger brother's girlfriend calls me to go swimming with her. 'I can't swim,' I call back. 'Come on, come play in the waves just for fun,' she teases me.

'Thanks, but I'm too lazy,' I tell her.

'Lazy?' The girl laughs and smiles. I smile too.

My plan is to walk along the beach to the other side of the mountain and rest there. But the chief of my brother's office comes back to sit beside me; this time he offers me crab and other seafood delicacies. I thank him and eat my crab with great attentiveness to avoid responding to this flatterer whose breath reeks of beer.

'Chief, may I have a cigarette?'

I look up at the speaker. It is a beggar with one leg and a stick who has been working the beach. I look right back down to the sand. The chief is annoyed.

'No,' the chief tells him.

'Then, chief, let me have five hundred *dong* to buy a cigarette.'

'What?' The chief grows angry at what he perceives to be the beggar's gall.

'Chief, five hundred *dong* is just the cost of one cigarette. Have pity on unlucky me.'

'Miss … ' The beggar turns to me.

I reach into my bag for money, but the chief stops me. He takes a pack of cigarettes out of his pocket and gives one to the man. I'm determined to look straight into the beggar's eyes this time.

'You are … ?' I ask him.

'Hoang,' he answers. 'And you are … ?'

'Forty,' the chief answers, cutting me off before I can respond. The beggar's face is rough and without shame; his look is savage and cruel. 'No problem,' he snaps back. I look down at the sand again.

'Please go away,' the chief says.

The beggar moves a short distance on his one leg and stick, then stops and looks back at me. The chief thinks to tease me. 'Acquaintance?' he asks.

I wonder if knowing a beggar devalues my personality, but I feel no need to satisfy the chief's curiosity. I shrug my shoulders; the chief turns and suddenly grabs the hand of a boy selling nuts. He stretches the boy's fingers out in his hand, and a pair of sunglasses falls out. 'I pick it up for you,' the boy tells him. The chief tells me to take care of my things as beggars and pickpockets are everywhere.

'Thanks. No serious losses yet,' I tell him.

The chief stands up and tells me to go on ahead to the restaurant.

My younger brother is already there sitting at a table. His face is fairly red. The men around the table are in the midst of a noisy debate. 'Who bets on Iraq?' 'Will Israel play the game?' 'Modern war is resolved in three days.' 'No, I bet this war lasts at least one hundred days.'

Are they war analysts, strategists, gamblers or drunkards? I tell them I'm sorry, but I have plans to visit the neighbouring pagodas. They try to call me back, but my younger brother shouts, 'Let her be with her ghost!'

Who is my ghost? I have tried to recall all the people I've known over the years in order to guess who might have died and turned into a ghost to haunt me. I have many old acquaintances whom I haven't heard from in decades. Classmates at high school, old neighbours ... countless men and women I once knew but have long since forgotten. Is the beggar named Hoang among my acquaintances? I can't say for sure. Is the ghost a lost soul following me by chance, or is it the soul of one who loved me but was forgotten? Am I so indifferent?

I stare at the empty space before me, begging, 'Ghost, who are you? Speak, please ... ' I hear my own voice speaking. I realize that I'm acting crazy and try to recover my composure.

The stairs up the mountain to the pagoda are steep. I climb fifty steps without stopping, nearly breathless. In the mountain there are caves where monks retreat and hide from the world so they may purify their hearts by seeking truth or the soul's salvation. I know of one of these caves because my mother took me there once, a long time ago, to collect the remains of my grandfather for cremation. Rats may well have been the only things living at my grandfather's side during his last minutes in this world. We found his bones, fresh and clean, scattered in the cave.

'Please come into the pagoda, miss.' The voice startles me. The woman seems to have walked right out from the cliff face; her face wears a smile of complete peace and contentment. Is she—was she—my acquaintance? Her look is very friendly. 'Come. Today the pagoda makes offerings of rice gruel for all souls,' she says.

I prostrate myself and make my offering to the Buddha. There are small dishes of sticky rice on the ground in the front and all along the sides of the pagoda. The woman puts small bowls of gruel next to the dishes of rice: these are for the lonely souls and wandering spirits. I grab her elbow.

'I'm really sorry, but who are you?' I ask.

'I was at the Mercy Orphanage.'

'What's your name?'

'Hoa An.'

Now I remember. My mother used to give alms to the pagoda and take me there to pray for my father at the battlefront. I was a little girl then, well dressed, holding two big bags of old clothes and toys and standing in front of a dozen children my age. The children stood at the end of the room, leaning against the wall, and stared at the visitors. My mother pushed me forward. 'Go and play with your friends.' I took some steps forward and gave a bag to a small girl. Her hand had just touched it when her face changed colour and horror filled her eyes. She threw the bag down, dragged me to a table in the corner, and pushed me underneath. The sound of an airplane grew near and then died away. The adults pulled us out from under the table and explained that the child was afraid of planes. She had been the only survivor of a bombardment during a mopping-up operation, and a soldier had picked her up out of a heap of corpses. She was named after the abandoned village, Hoa An.

'Why are you here?' I ask.

'It doesn't matter where I am,' she says, and smiles. In her coarse clothes and with her hair twisted into a bun; she looks like any other peasant woman.

'How have you been?' I ask.

'I've been doing chores for this pagoda and growing manioc up on the mountain,' she replies. After twenty years of swimming in the ocean of misery, she still remembers me. But I didn't recognize her. I am bad. I don't even recognize the ghost who haunts me. I spend the day with Hoa An, harvesting manioc on the mountain till evening. There are no visitors: the pagoda is not marked on tourist maps. When darkness comes, we hear the rhythmic sound of the bells and the wooden fish clanging as if to emphasize the quiet.

We are having dinner in the back room when I suddenly hear my name being called noisily from outside the pagoda. It is my younger brother and his companions. I say good-bye to Hoa An in haste so that the pagoda's peace will not be broken. Outside, my brother grunts at me and says, 'You really are haunted.'

It is dark as we climb down the mountain, and the way is difficult. My younger brother has a flashlight; I follow the round light as it falls on grass and bushes. Strong winds blow, and I shudder. The boys begin telling ghost stories, joking and laughing on the way down the mountain. The evening is cool. They say there are many ghosts in our country. After decades of war, who could count all the bodies killed in action or in accidents? Dying innocent, the thousands of young soldiers who didn't marry, who never loved, who never kissed a woman became ghosts with no great desire to go to Heaven. Still wanting a life in this world, they haunted young girls or unmarried women alone in bed. The chief raises his fist. 'I will settle the matter with *that* ghost.'

When we return to our hotel, another group of my younger brother's friends is gathering in the reception room. The words burst onto the screen: WAR IN THE GULF. The chief rushes in. 'Have the Americans landed?' he asks. He bets that the US troops would land today. My younger brother's girlfriend smiles at me and says, 'Come here. See who will pay the bill tonight.' 'Thanks, but I'm tired,' I tell her.

It is my younger brother who escorts me to my room. He has been drinking a lot, but he's not completely drunk. He tries to comfort me. 'Don't be frightened, Sister. Your brother is here. Have a bath and go to bed. Pay no attention to what these guys said. Don't answer the door, except if you hear my voice.'

Homesick and lonely, I take my bath, crawl into bed. Last night the whole family sat in front of the TV set. It was the first time in years we'd all talked about one topic. Though he had been a soldier, my father never spoke to us about war. He had fought in battles for at least twenty years. But he was a defeated soldier. When the war ended, he went to a re-education camp for six years. During those hard times, my elder brother joined the Young Pioneers because his law school had been dissolved. Later, he fought in Cambodia. He returned on one foot, with eighteen scars on his body and lots of medals and citations. Perhaps it was thanks to those citations and medals that he got to go to the university. Four months later, my father also came back home.

All three men in my house drink. My father drinks with old friends. My elder brother drinks with young comrades. My younger brother drinks with his office chief and colleagues. All those years and they had never talked about the war. If war just means fighting, then I know nothing about it, even though I was born and grew up during the war. But if war means women's sorrow, misfortune, helplessness . . . these things were absorbed directly into my bloodstream when I was in my mother's womb.

I hear a knock, then another.

Someone is at the door, which is locked. I remain in bed.

'Open the door!' a voice yells. 'I come to kill the ghost.'

I place a pillow over my head. My younger brother's voice calls from outside. 'Open the door. Sister. Your brother is here.' I open the door, and the smell of beer rushes into the room.

My younger brother staggers to the bed and throws himself on it. He slurs his words, dragging his tongue. 'No worry. I'm here.'

Then enters the chief. He is holding a long gun and stands in the middle of the room, shouting, 'Ghost, face the wall!'

The hotel manager enters, trying to stop the chief from shooting the gun. 'Don't joke, chief,' I say.

'I'm not joking! I said I would settle the matter with that ghost. I'll kill him.'

'But he was killed—he is already dead.'

'Let him die again. Stand aside, get out of my way.'

I step back to the window that opens onto the garden.

Laughing, my younger brother crawls on the bed. 'No worry, Sister. It's a toy gun.' He repeats the words reassuringly. 'A toy gun ... '

The chief raises the gun, aims, and shoots. *'Bang!'*

My heart is broken. I fall. The men all laugh, and then in a moment they're gone. The door is closed. The leaves are still falling in the garden.

Translated by the author & Kevin Bowen

South Asia

Bangladesh

Things Cheaply Had

Taslima Nasreen

In the market nothing can be had as cheap as women.
If they get a small bottle of *alta* for their feet
they spend three nights sleepless for sheer joy.
If they get a few bars of soap to scrub their skin
and some scented oil for their hair
they become so submissive that they scoop out
chunks of their flesh
to be sold in the flea market twice a week.
If they get a jewel for their nose
they lick feet for seventy days or so,
a full three and a half months
if it's a striped *sari*.

Even the mangy cur of the house barks now and then,
but over the mouths of battered women
there's a lock,
a golden lock.

Translated by Mohammad Nurul Huda and Carolyne Wright with the author

Bangladesh

Women Can't

TASLIMA NASREEN

Any man can unhesitatingly become exultant
By touching and kneading
Any woman's flesh and fat.
Any man can get heated
By suddenly opening up any woman from top to bottom.
Any animal can move towards any animal
During the season of passion.
Only animals and men can
Touch a body of flesh
Without love.
Women can't.

Those who can smell the bones and marrows
Can; women can't.

Women cannot caress skin without love,
Those who can, let them.

Translated by Fazlul Alam

Bangladesh

Irina's Picture

RIZIA RAHMAN

Dusk had barely fallen when the rounded moon floated up from behind the coconut tree. As soon as I woke up this morning, I remembered that it would be a full-moon night. At that time, the Poush dawn seemed full of mystery, enveloped in mist. Relishing the warmth of my quilt, I watched the faded glow of light through the frost-dampened window. Droplets of dew were sliding down the glass pane. My heart cried out in sorrow. I remembered my mother. It happens like this, nowadays. As soon as I am awake, my heart is filled with desolation. I keep remembering my mother. Until my mother comes, until she speaks to me, I remain suspended in emptiness. When I woke up today, I remembered how much my mother loved full-moon nights. The misty dawn as well. At that very moment, it seemed that my mother spoke: 'Oh Khoka, my boy. Get up and see the wonderful cloud of mist outside.'

I—Mahboob-ul-Hasan, who had once earned fame as a fiery professor of English literature at the University and as a rebel poet in the alternative tradition—I, that very same person, transformed in an instant into a little boy, an adolescent or a young man. Hearing my mother call, I would hide inside my quilt. My mother calls, 'Come on, get up, Khoka! Get up.' As though it's the childhood game I played with my mother—'Oh, Ma! Let me sleep, will you. It's terribly cold outside.'

'Why! It's hardly cold at all. Outside there's only mist and yet more mist. Get up and see, it looks as if the world is floating in milk-froth.' I can't help smiling. When it comes to creating poetic comparisons, there's no match for my mother. Of course, I know Ma loves reading poetry. At one time, so it is said, she used to write poetry as well. After her marriage, she didn't write any more. Perhaps that was because of my father. Baba was a doctor. When he was involved in World War II, he had earned the title of 'Major' that would be added before his name. The war had probably drained him of all passion. He had not liked the fact that Ma wrote poetry. Ma used to treat Baba with deference. Baba had married rather late in life, long after he came back from the war. The difference in age between him and Ma was considerable.

Ma repeated, 'Why, Khoka, not up yet?! I wanted you to watch the morning mist with me.'

'I'll be up right away Ma, in a couple of minutes.'

I kept my face covered with the quilt. All the same, I clearly saw my mother move around in the room, a dark green shawl wrapped around her body. The half darkness of dawn enveloping her. Ma sits down on the bed, next to me and places her moist, cool hand on my forehead: 'I never got to show you that vast, mist-covered river, my dear. If only I could have shown it to you!'

Taking my mother's hand in my fist, I turn over on my side: 'Don't be upset, Ma. I'll go see that misty river of yours.'

Ma lets out a soft sigh, 'You're crazy. Where would you find that river of mist! It's no longer there. Now, all around, there is only an expanse of sand.' My mother comes from a village by the river. The memory of that vast, expansive river would quite often make my mother nostalgic. Can Ma still hear the clamour of that vast, limitless, horizonless mass of water? I am about to pose the question when I stop myself. I say, 'Ma! Tonight is purnima, a full-moon night. Won't you walk in the moonlight with me?' Ma doesn't answer. Maybe she is weeping. Without making a sound.

I remain silent. Ma is probably not yet able to sever her ties with worldly joys and sorrows.

From the well of the staircase below, Chhoto Apa calls out: 'Hey Bulu! Are you up? Shall I send your tea upstairs? Or will you come down?'

Like a perfect circle drawn according to the rules of geometry, the full moon floats up in the sky. It scatters a handful of silver light into my room. I feel like laughing. This is hardly a room! It's a refugee camp. Pursued by war, I have sought refuge in this safe attic. My brothers and sisters have turned this house into a battlefield. Forcible occupation, conflict, jealousy and violence have turned Ma's home into a battlefront.

Of course, I don't concern myself in the slightest, about these matters. I am Bulu, the youngest son of this household, my mother's Khoka. Ma is still here with Khoka, her little boy, after all.

I remain standing at the window of the attic. Waiting for Ma to come. Just like those days in my childhood, she would say—'Let's go, Khoka. Let's walk in the moonlight.'

In the moonlight, we would walk in the garden, on the roof, on the veranda. Ma would hum a song to herself. It was Ma who taught me to love the light of the moon in its first quarter.

I remain standing, alone. Ma doesn't come. As if the clamour of pro-war human beings has blocked her path. I weep, clutching the window bars with both my hands. I weep in loneliness. In desolation. The universe has drowned in moonlight. A vast, endless river of light flows across the entire sky. Suddenly, my mother's face is visible up there. Her body is wrapped in a shroud of moonlight. All around her, silently, floats a cold, luminous mist. All of a sudden, the shroud woven from threads of moonlight unravels itself. Ma comes and stands next to me. She says, very softly: 'How lovely the moonlight is, isn't it, Khoka? Look. look, how the fronds of the coconut palm sparkle like silver!'

Holding Ma's hand, I return to infancy. I walk, stepping on moonlight-drenched bluish grass.

Ma says suddenly: 'Tell me the story of that book you were reading yesterday in the afternoon, let me listen to it.'

I start laughing. My mother has this one habit. As a child, I would return home from the school library carrying a bunch of storybooks under my arm. In the veranda, Ma would be sitting on a mora, a cane stool, knitting away. The books wouldn't escape her eyes. Eagerly, she would ask: 'What books have you brought, Khoka? Let me see, let me see.' Putting aside her knitting, she would leaf through the books to examine the titles in one breath—*Treasure Island, Uncle Tom's Cabin, Twenty Thousand Leagues under the Sea.* Handing back the books, Ma would laugh: 'Goodness! Will you be able to read all these books?'

Ma was extremely fond of reading. It was her secret and had not been hard for me to sense this. In the evening, my brothers and sisters create a hullabaloo as they play in the field in front of the house. I have ensconced myself on the terrace, with a storybook. A pale light falls on the leaves of the eucalyptus. The shadow of dusk has deepened on the cornices of the terrace. Ma comes upstairs. I feel the touch of her soft hand on my hair: 'What's this! You are still reading! You'll ruin your eyes, reading in such poor light. Let's go to my room. You can sit and read there.'

I accompany Ma to her room. The old-fashioned bed is neatly arranged without any creases. In a brass pot on the teepoy are placed a bunch of white roses, along with their leaves. The roses are from Ma's garden. Ma doesn't like red roses. She had told me: 'That nightingale in the fairy tale has turned the white rose blood red, by shedding blood from its own heart. I can't stand the colour of bloodshed.'

Lying on Ma's bed, I read *Oliver Twist*. Ma moves about, doing little tasks and listening to the story I read aloud. All of a sudden, Baba arrives. The chamber where he treats his patients is located within our house. In between examining patients, Baba often comes into this room. Seeing me, Baba's heavy brow creases in a frown. He doesn't forget to exercise his habitual authority. Addressing my mother, he says: 'You'll destroy this boy's future. It won't do to keep him tied to your apron strings like this, will it? Let him go out. Without roughing it out, playing, running about, how will he grow into a man?'

Baba snatches the book from my hands. Places it on the table, and orders me severely: 'Go! Go and play in the field. If you spend your time hiding in corners reading books, your future is doomed. Your life is not a rose arranged in your mother's brass pot. You have to win your life by battling with it.'

I didn't like the things my father said.

Baba advised us severely, every now and then: 'Be tough, be strong. Be ruthless like soldiers on the battlefield. Remember, life is a danger-filled battle ground.'

When he offered advice of this kind, the lines on Baba's face would become so harsh that he would look like a decisive army leader at the battle front. One day, Ma had said to Baba in great annoyance: 'Tell me, why do you always chant the mantra of "war" into the ears of these children? Is war a good thing? War means cruelty, violence, barbaric behaviour. War makes humans inhuman.'

At her words, Baba burst into a loud guffaw: 'So, in order to be human, must we only write poems about moonlight, early morning mists and the fragrance of flowers? Don't human beings have to survive? To sustain their existence, human beings certainly have to be heartless. They must learn how to be cruel.'

Arrogantly declaring his convictions, Baba repeated: 'I believe in the doctrine: Survival of the Fittest.'

After this, Ma didn't say anything more. But I could sense, sure enough, that Ma was hurt by Baba's words. Ma couldn't bring herself to accept those words as true.

There was a gust of wind, carrying with it a few fragments of cloud. It beat against the window-panes. Flashing in the light, the coconut fronds swayed. Ascending the staircase of clouds, the moon travelled across the sky.

Again, I hear my mother's soft voice: 'Khoka, won't you tell me what book you were reading this afternoon?'

All day, inside my heart, desolation has cried out like a weeping violin. Now, it grows calm. Once again, I feel the relief that comes from dependency. I am no longer plagued by solitude. My heart is filled with the familiar fragrance of my mother. I say: 'That was the immortal novel *War and Peace* by the timeless novelist Leo Tolstoy.'

Ma's presence instantly transforms itself into the restless breeze of youth: '*War and Peace!* Meaning 'war', and 'peace'?'

'Yes mother. War and peace.'

'In the novel, which does the writer favour? War or peace?'

I heartily enjoyed the eager curiosity in my mother's voice. Ma was my only friend. Ma despised war. So did I.

Ma's voice becomes restless again: 'Hey Khoka, tell me please, what does the immortal writer Tolstoy express a desire for?'

'I'll tell you, Ma. Tolstoy has expressed contempt for war. He has hinted at peace for the world to come. This happens at the end of the novel. The only survivors are a newborn infant, its mother, and a poet. Can you tell me Ma, what has the writer indicated by leaving these three alive?'

Ma remains silent for a while. Then, in a tearful voice, she says, almost whispering: 'The signs of love and peace. The newborn belongs to the future. For him, there remain the mother, a symbol of love, and the poet, a symbol of peace. Am I right Khoka?'

I am overjoyed: 'Ma you are great. You're a poet, too. Had almost forgotten that.'

'And you? Even you are a poet. Way back in time, when you were in college. I had shown you that picture of Irina. Seeing it, you had written a poem! Remember?'

Ma does not speak anymore.

Downstairs, the door to the stairwell opens with a harsh sound. Somebody switches on the light. The excited clamour of a host of people comes up and crashes against the attic walls. With a clatter of shoes on stairs. Chhoto Apa comes upstairs.

'What are you doing in the dark, standing like a ghost, all by yourself?' As she speaks, she switches on the light. Without any preliminaries, she delivers an angry complaint: 'See what an outrageous matter Bulu! Boro Apa and Mejo Apa have divided Ma's diamond earrings and diamond ring between themselves. Is this the right thing to have done? Tell me? Do I have no haq—no right—to Ma's things? Why should they not give them to me?'

I search Chhoto Apa's face for her memories of Ma. I search there for grief. There is none. Both her eyes are aflame with resentment and greed.

Gently, I ask: 'Didn't you receive anything at all?'

'I have. But is that called getting something! Just an old-fashioned lightweight gold chain of Ma's. I felt like throwing it away.'

I try to calm Chhtoto Apa down: 'So what if it's old-fashioned and light in weight. Still, it is a memento of our mother.'

Chhoto Apa is incensed: 'You have remained an ass all your life. As if all Ma's belongings are being divided up only to preserve her memory! Go and see what's happening downstairs. It's a free-for-all, do you understand.' Pausing a bit, she resumes: 'It's alright for you; having disrupted your domestic life to sit around like some sage or hermit, you may not require anything; but why should I give up on my claim?' It is almost three years since Samira left after obtaining a divorce. The wound has healed. The cut doesn't bleed any more. So it is easy for me to ignore the barb in Chhoto Apa's words. I say: 'I am part of Ma's household, after all. There is nothing new for me to claim. My mother is all I claim.'

'Ma doesn't belong to you alone.'

As soon as the words are out, Chhoto Apa falls silent for a while. She searches my face, with a deep, penetrating gaze. Slowly, her stance softens. Sadness appears in her voice: 'Really. Whatever happened to you! You gave up such a good job. You don't go anywhere. Don't mingle with anyone at all. Everybody thinks you're crazy. Mejo Apa was saying that you talk and laugh to yourself when alone. Tell me the truth Bulu, what's the matter with you?'

I give no answer. Chhoto Apa places her hand on my shoulder: 'You're grieving terribly for Ma, isn't that it?'

I gently remove her hand: 'Go away now, Chhoto Apa. I don't feel good.'

Her foot on the stairs, Chhoto Apa pauses: 'Bulu, let me tell you something before I go. Ma loved you the most. She has left you the keys to this house and the power of attorney—but that makes you everybody's enemy now.'

Having said these words, she leaves without waiting any longer.

I switch off the lights in the room. The moon is hidden behind the clouds. The moonlight has vanished.

In the darkness, I search for my mother. Ma doesn't come. All the sadness of the world descends on me. It pierces me with bayonets of agony. I scream silently. 'Ma, oh Ma, why did you go away?'

With all my senses, I try to bring to life the memories of Ma. With desperate single-mindedness, I recall only my mother.

The moon emerges from the cover of clouds. Light spreads, filling the sky, coconut fronds murmur in the gentle breeze. The fragrance of my mother comes wafting with the breeze. In an indistinct voice, my mother speaks: 'Khoka, don't be depressed. I am here!'

'Are you lost, Ma?' She laughs at my desperate query: 'Crazy boy! Who says that I'm lost? A mother is never lost, my dear, she lives on in the memory, in the heart. It's because of a mother's presence that humans don't forget how to love.'

'But Ma, humans are forgetting how to love!'

'What kind of statement is that Khoka? Aren't you a poet? Don't your thoughts include the creation of the whole world? Don't you seek out the secret of life, the survival of the animate world?' I am amazed at her deep philosophical words. Ma says again: 'Think of it: without a mother's love, would human beings, animals, birds—would any of them survive? They would be obliterated as soon as they were born. It's mothers who keep creation alive.'

There is soft, gentle moonlight all around us. The wind sings as it moves, laden with the fragrance of roses from my mother's garden. All bitterness vanishes from my mind. All agony is erased. In an instant I forget the sadness of not being loved by my wife Samira and the selfishness of my brothers and sisters.

Ma asks, suddenly: 'Khoka, do you remember Irina's story?'

'Yes, Ma.'

I become absent-minded.

The moonlit night becomes an album of memories. In it emerges Irina's picture. The background to the picture is clearly visible. World War II is over. Above the monuments of destruction, the lamentations, and the burnt earth, flies the flag of peace. Carrying war-weary soldiers from the Port of Aden travels a ship on its way to Mumbai. On that very ship, at the end of the war, Baba is travelling back to his own country. It was there that a French journalist had gifted Irina's picture to Baba. After their wedding. Ma had found the picture in Baba's cupboard. All this had happened long before I was born. All the same it felt as if Ma had kept that picture aside, only for me. She had never told me about it. The day she told me was the day I gave her my first poem to read and Ma had broken down and wept tears of joy. She had raised a storm of excitement in the house. She'd kept repeating, 'My Khoka is a poet, he's written a wonderful poem.' As soon as Baba returned from the chamber Ma handed the poem to him: 'Khoka has written this poem on his own, read it and see. What a beautiful poem!'

It didn't take a moment for Baba to reduce Ma's excitement, joy and pride to dust: 'What kind of achievement is poem writing, that you should create such an uproar in the house?'

Baba's features resumed the determined hardness of an army commander's face. Turning to Ma he said in a severe tone: 'Forbid him to write poetry and all that stuff. Do you know what a poet is supposed to be? A poet is a man with a single torn taka in his pocket, a rootless, rascal, good-for-nothing. Someone without a hearth or home.'

Ma looked up at Baba with wounded eyes: 'What's all this you're saying?'

'I'm speaking the truth. Writing poetry makes the mind soft, like mire. It makes you weep in sorrow, even for the blind kitten abandoned in the dustbin. The only benefit of weeping at others' misfortune is that the whole world will cheat him. They will take advantage of him.'

At this, Ma broke into a laugh: 'But that's the rule for offering love.'

Baba silenced Ma with a tremendous burst of rage: 'Forget your talk of love. You can't capture the world with love. To capture it, you must use power. Tell Bulu, it won't do to ruin his life writing poetry. He must be a soldier.'

On that very same day, Ma had shown me Irina Slovsky's picture. And told me her story, as well.

Eight years old, Irina Slovsky was a girl from a small town in Eastern Europe. She had no father. The bomber planes deployed in the war had destroyed their home. Crushed in the debris of that destruction was her little brother. There lay the tender infant's white teddy bear, stained red with blood. When the first group of German soldiers had marched into the town, they had taken Irina's mother away, along with the other young women of the town, at gunpoint. A terrified and bewildered Irina would stand on the broken pavement, holding a white rose. She stood at the place where she, along with her mother, used to sell flowers. In the midst of the debris, fire and sharp wind, the starved, tired and homeless child would stand, for hours on end. She would mutter: 'Take some flowers. Flowers.'

The darkness of death hangs over the main street, devastated by war. Irina's feet begin to tremble in exhaustion, and her head hangs down. Still, nobody comes to her. Nobody buys flowers.

The second troop of the occupying army entered the town with an array of tanks. The soldiers had marched ahead, the heavy sound of tanks making the empty high street tremble. Irina did an extraordinary thing. She ran into the street. Raising both arms she stood in front of the tanks. Waving her arms, holding bunches of white roses, she cried out: 'Stop, all of you! Take these roses with you.' An Austrian photojournalist had captured on camera a picture of Irina standing there, blocking the path of the tanks. That picture was said to have sold a hundred thousand copies in Europe. It was from Baba that Ma had heard all these stories. Irina's picture had moved me tremendously. I had felt contempt for war. Ma had said: 'Khoka, this picture will be kept aside just for you. You must write a poem for Irina.'

In the silence, my mother's voice rings out: 'Khoka! Do you remember the poem you had written for Irina?'

'Yes, Ma.'

'Will you recite the poem for me now?'

'But that poem isn't there any more. One day, in a fit of anger, Samira had burnt all the notebooks in which I wrote my poems. That poem was burnt as well.'

Ma is silent. She knows about that incident. Samira was not fond of poetry. Keeping house for a husband who was a poet had brought her no joy. After divorcing me, she married a man who ran a large business.

Breaking the silence, Ma speaks again: 'Can anyone kill poetry? Poetry knows no death. Search for it and see. Maybe it is alive in your memory.'

It is in my memory. I find the poem written long ago for Irina.

The hours of the night roll on. Having touched the moon, the clouds have flown far away. The moonlight has grown very bright. Slowly, I recite:

All those rows of battle tanks,
Fling them into the land of famine;
The starving people will break them,
Tear them into pieces, to be eaten
Like onions and bread. Afterwards,
They will become coloured toys
Infants will play with them.
Free of worry, mothers then
Will spread the sheets of peace
And sleep there, without fear.

I stop abruptly. Ma is weeping. The recitation comes to a halt:

'Why are you crying, Ma?' Wiping her eyes, Ma says. 'Oh, it's nothing. You complete the poem.'

I continue to recite:

All those bomber planes,
Let them become coloured kites
Or a flock of white pigeons.
Spreading their wings,
Strung on spools held by children,
Let them fly away in a cloudless sky.

Ma cries gain, silently. I say nothing. I know that Ma weeps for Irina and others like her.

I continue to recite to my mother the poem written for Irina.

All the lethal weapons of the world,
Sow them in flowerpots meant for roses.
Countless flowers will bloom.
In the abandoned boots of soldiers.
In the landmine-infested grain-fields.
Beside the destroyed bunkers.
Put down your weapons.
Pick up a bunch of white roses.

Ma weeps. I try to calm her down: 'Why are you crying Ma?'

Her tears overflow: 'Khoka.'

'Everyone says you're crazy. It makes me sad, my dear.'

I try to laugh: 'So, let them call me crazy.'

The doctor gives me medicines meant for crazy people. Once a week, I have to visit a psychiatrist. Of course, everybody would consider me crazy.

Ma gets angry: 'Be quiet, Khoka. Don't say such things. The people of this world are blinded by greed. They are rendered violent by selfishness. Aggression makes them mad. They are slaves to terrorism. I know, in the midst of all this, you're not able to adapt yourself to these conditions. How would you be able to adjust—after all, I have taught you to love.' I reach out, trying to touch my mother: 'You tell me, Ma. What am I to do now?'

Without answering my question, Ma says, very softly: 'Khoka. Make sure Irina's picture doesn't get lost. That picture belongs to you. It is meant to inspire all poets like you, to remain alive.'

The clamour of harsh voices crashes like a monstrous bomb into my room. I hear the sound of several pairs of shoes marching up the stairs to the attic. They shatter the presence of my mother, scattering the fragments into empty space. The tender breeze of the night turns into a violent storm. With their manes puffed out, black clouds come rushing up. They pounce on the moon. Ma is silent. She no longer speaks inside my heart. Boro Apa and my three bhabhis—sisters-in-law—come, and stand before me. As if they hold my arrest warrant in their hands. I know they will now force me to take tranquillizers and sedatives.

Boro Apa pierces me with a sharp gaze.

'Bulu, how many times have I told you to take your medication on time? What is this madness, sitting alone day and night in this room—who is to look after you, tell me that?'

A sharp-edged, mocking smile plays on the lips of Mejo Bhabhi: 'Oh my! Why would he be alone! Don't you know, Ma comes to guard him. Ma keeps chatting with him all the time, I believe.'

Sejo Bhabhi takes up from Mejo Bhabhi's words: 'All this is a clever trick. A ploy to retain possession. It is Ma who has left him in charge of the keys to this house.'

Boro Apa scolds lightly: 'Oh, stop this!' Holding the medicine and the glass of water in my direction, she says, 'Come and take your medicine. Dinner's on the table.'

It is truly an amazing situation. Ever since Ma left us, all her children, along with their families, have been living as guests in this house. Till now, they haven't returned to their own homes, not one of them. In all these days, not once have I been asked to come down to the dining room. I turn my face away from them. It is to Boro Apa that I address myself: 'Go away, all of you. I'll take the medication on my own. And I won't be taking any food tonight.'

Descending the stairs, Boro Apa turns her head to say, 'Come and give us the keys. This very night.'

'What keys?'

Mejo Bhabhi answers my question: 'Why, all the keys to this house are with you. The keys will remain with Boro Bhaiya. Give those keys to Boro Bhaiya.'

The three of them leave together.

Ma and I used to live in this, my father's house, purchased and registered in my mother's name. My sisters have left this house after marriage. My brothers have moved out to the houses they have built for themselves. As long as Ma was alive, none of them had the time to spend a single night in this house. This caused mother a lot of pain. Ma would say sometimes: 'It would be nice if all of them were to come here together, to stay for a few days as you did in your childhood.'

I would laugh: 'What an unrealistic whim of yours this is, Ma! Tell me, why on earth would your children leave the comforts of their luxury apartments in Dhanmondi, Gulshan and Baridhara, to spend the night in this antique, old-fashioned house!'

Ma would say: 'Why, what if they came! You stay here with me, don't you?'

'Maybe I stay here because I have no other option. If I too had a house of my own in Baridhara, Uttara or Banani, then surely I wouldn't languish here just to guard this "old castle" of yours either.'

Ma laughs: 'I know you can't leave this house to go and stay anywhere else. Do you remember? Once you wrote to me when you had gone to London for six months: "Ma, I feel terribly homesick for your garden with its eucalyptus, grapefruit and roses." '

Handing me the keys to the house, Ma had said: 'Khoka, I give this house to you alone. This house is a remembrance of your father and mother. The others have not learnt to pay the price for that memory. You alone have learnt it. You're a poet, that's why.'

Saying this, Ma had broken into laughter.

I had laughed as well: 'The memory of the two of you will remain locked away in the depths of my heart, all my life. I have no need for a house or any such thing. Don't you remember, Baba used to say: "There is just a single torn taka in a poet's pocket. They are without home and hearth, rootless human beings?" '

Ma has not changed her mind. She has left the power of attorney to me. Mejo Apa comes up the stairs: 'Here, Bulu! So did the three memsahibs come and brainwash you? You haven't handed over the keys, have you?'

'No.' Answering briefly, I turn to face the window. My mind is filled with incredible bitterness. Mejo Apa's arrival raises fresh fears in my mind. She settles firmly into a chair: 'Just the right thing to do. Well done. I knew all that "brainwashing" wouldn't be of any use.'

Without turning my head, I ask: 'Do you have anything to say, Mejo Apa? I feel terrible.'

Startled, Mejo Apa gets to her feet: 'Oh, I'd completely forgotten. You're an infirm person, of course. That's why Mejo Bhaiya was saying that it is not possible to grant a lunatic the power of attorney in property matters. That will have to be cancelled.'

Mejo Apa waves her hands: 'Forget it, all that is a load of nonsense. Are they not behaving like lunatics themselves? Mejo Bhaiya and Sejo Bhaiya want to mortgage the house to obtain additional loans for their industry. Boro Bhaiya says he'll give the house to a developer. They will demolish this house to build a multi-storeyed building.'

None of Mejo Apa's words touch me at all. Looking at her face, I search for my mother's image. Mejo Apa says: 'Listen, let me tell you one thing before I go. You mustn't hand the keys over to the brothers. Our brothers are meek lambs in front of their wives. Hand them the keys, and it's their wives who will take over the house. We will not be allowed to approach anywhere near the precincts. You must hand over the keys to me. The keys will remain with the sisters. Once they've declared our share of the property, only then will we give them the keys.'

As soon as Mejo Apa leaves, my head reels with violent, unbearable pain. A tremendous restlessness drives me out into Ma's rose garden. In my pocket I carry the bunch of keys. I fling the bunch out into the garden. Gradually, my shattered nerves grow calm again. I meander through the garden, aimlessly. Then I return to my attic. As soon as I step into the doorway. I stop short. Lights have been switched on inside the room. The cupboard doors are open. The contents of my chest of drawers lie scattered on the table and the bed.

It appears that somebody must have come in, hurriedly searched for something, and gone away. What were they looking for? The keys? Lying face down on the table is Tolstoy's *War and Peace*. I had brought it over from my mother's room yesterday. About to pick up the book, I am startled. Next to the book lies Irina's picture. Amazed, I pick up the picture in my hand. Who brought the picture into this room? So, was it inside this, my favourite novel, that Ma had kept Irina's picture? Perhaps it was for me that she had kept it there. About to place Irina's picture on the table—a picture faded by the onslaught of time—I stop short once more. At the back of the picture, written in green ink, are the words of a Bangla poem. Instantly, I recognize Ma's handwriting. Is this then a poem written by my mother? I start reading.

Destroyer planes
Have broken our home.
The soldiers have snatched away
My mother.
Stop, all of you. Come
Stand here.
Throw down your arms and take in your hands
These white roses.
In return, only wipe away the blood
From the body of my little brother's
Toy teddy bear,
And bring back our house
My brother and my mother.

I stand still. My attic seems to have transformed itself into a wintry town in war-torn Poland. The eight-year-old Irina Slovsky stands, blocking the path of tanks as huge as monsters. She holds up a bunch of white roses. I am startled again. Where is Irina? Blocking the path of the armoured tanks of the enemy forces stands my mother.

'Stop!' My mother's powerful cry of protest makes the entire house tremble. It shakes towns. Cities. The whole world.

It's not Ma. It's I who's screaming.

Rushing up the stairs come Boro Bhaiya, Mejo Bhaiya, Boro Apa, Mejo Apa—everybody in the house, they're all coming, to snatch and grab. To possess by force. Clutching Irina's picture in my fist, banging my head against the wall, I keep screaming: 'Stop! Stop all of you. Stop this.'

I keep on banging my head against the wall.

My forehead splits open, the blood rolling down onto Irina's picture. Her white roses have turned red.

Translated by Radha Chakravarty

Bhutan

Garba Lung Gi Khorlo and the Demoness of Nyala

KUNZANG CHODEN RODER

We are told that the Tongsa *penlops* or the governors of Tongsa were more or less able to maintain effective control over Tongsa and the surrounding regions even while the other governors were engaged in continuous power struggles among themselves for supremacy. Thus, the post of Tongsa *penlop* was not only prestigious but also important. Young aspirants from all over the country yearned to be in the service of the Tongsa *penlop*. These courtiers and attendants were said to be the brightest and the best. The elders tell us that a certain Tongsa *penlop* enjoyed the services of two truly remarkable men. They were his personal attendants or *garbas*. Garba Lung Gi Khorlo, which translates as 'Attendants with Wheels of Wind' was one of them. He was said to have been an exceptionally fast walker and, therefore, an excellent courier. He could walk so fast that he almost flew. Penjor was the other *garba* and he was an extraordinarily fast tailor. He was the *penlop's* tailor and could hand-sew a *gho* in one day, an incredible feat in those days when hand-sewing a *gho* usually took more than two whole days. The *penlop* was very proud of these two men and they were always expected to do a lot.

Garba Lung Gi Khorlo had to carry messages everyday and he had never let down his master. It is said that he could travel from Tongsa to Wangdiphodrang and back in a day. This journey is about 129 kilometres through rugged craggy terrain and would usually take an average person at least four days.

Those were the days of factions, conspiracies and plots. A single strong man had yet to emerge and the regional lords were constantly feuding, intriguing and scheming against each other. It was of the utmost importance that allies kept contact with each other and expediting information across the rugged terrain was crucial but at the same time a very big challenge. Garba Lung Gi Khorlo's services to the *penlop* were invaluable. But Garba Lung Gi Khorlo's real moment of victory came not so much from the distance he covered or the speed with which he completed his feat but when he was standing in the presence of his master and receiving the usual impassive 'Tubay' or 'all right'.

One day the *penlop* had a message of great urgency which had to be conveyed to the Wangdi *dzongpon* immediately. The *penlop* knew that he could rely on his attendant. The Zimpon handed the letter to Garba Lung Gi Khorlo and conveyed the *penlop's* order for him to speed to the Wangdi *dzongpon* and bring back the reply the same day. As Garba Lung Gi Khorlo left for the *penlop's* court, the tailor was just unfolding a fabric for a *gho*. It was at the hour of the first cock crow.

Garba Lung Gi Khorlo sped down to the Mangdi river and climbed to the other side of the Tongsa ravine and was soon climbing towards Pele La. He had done this trail many times and each turn and every ascent was familiar to him. But each journey now caused him more apprehension. It was no longer a challenge and a test of his own prowess as it used to be in earlier days. Each journey took more and more energy and effort. The soles of his feet hurt and his calves burned as if there was fire in them and his thighs grew heavier. Above all he dreaded the day he would fail his master, the day that his master would not say, 'Tubay'. As he thought of all these changes in himself, he passed through Nyala Lungma and he soon passed by the Nyala *dermo's phodrang* or palace—which is in rather an inconspicuous place not much different from the rest of the region. It is a small shaded ravine in the oak forest, it is dark, and hardly any sunlight reaches the place and it is wet although there is no stream anywhere. The most striking feature of this place is that it has an eerie atmosphere and you always feel the uncanny presence of someone that you cannot see. In a moment of impulsive recklessness, he looked towards the demon's abode and shouted, 'I am tired, I am so tired that I would rather take my life than do one more journey like this.'

Soon after midday he was in the court of the Wangdi *dzongpon* and after a quick meal he was ready and on his way back with the reply for the Tongsa *penlop*. By early evening he was already approaching Nyala Lungma and was looking forward to rest at the end of his journey. He took comfort in the thought that his wife would be waiting with a good meal and strong *ara* at his home in Tongsa. There were no human settlements anywhere in the area although he occasionally met one or two people on the way. They were sometimes travellers like himself, herders or pilgrims. He would greet them and ask them a few questions but never stopped to actually talk to anyone. But today it was different and he had to stop and look carefully. For there was a woman wearing the region's famous *tarichem kira* which is a black woollen *kira* with bands of red and blue. She was bending towards a little stream and washing a basket of meat. A closer look revealed that the basket contained what looked like entrails of some fairly large animals. The woman was completely preoccupied. She had her back towards the road and was bending down towards the water trough and washing the contents of the basket. Garba Lung Gi Khorlo wondered how it was possible that in the middle of nowhere there was this woman washing meat. So he asked, 'It looks like a big animal. Is your cowherd nearby?' The woman continued to wash the meat and did not turn to answer him. She simply said, 'This is not an animal's entrails. Garba Lung Gi Khorlo gave me his life this morning. These are his entrails.' As if in a dream, she then disappeared, leaving not a trace of her having ever been there. The emptiness and the silence seemed to envelop him, a shudder ran down his spine, and his skin rose in goose pimples. He seemed to float for the rest of his journey. He had no thoughts or pain; he just felt a lightness in his being.

The conch shell was being blown from the monastery to mark the end of the day as he entered the Tongsa *dzong*. Darkness had fallen and one could no longer read the lines of the palm of the hand. He felt a sense of calm and satisfaction but there was a sadness that transcended everything. He saw that the tailor had completed stitching a *gho* that he had cut out in the morning and was folding it. Garba Lung Gi Khorlo did not stop to greet anyone. He went straight into the inner chambers of the court and presented the letter of Wangdi *dzongpon* to the Tongsa *penlop*. The *penlop* seemed to have a trace of smile on his face and there was perhaps a hint of emotion when he said, 'Tubay'. The *penlop* then pointed to a large bowl of rice on which were placed portions of dried meat and a large roll of butter. A servant stepped out nimbly from behind the *gochor* or screen in front of the door, picked up the gifts, and indicated to Garba Lung Gi Khorlo that the audience was over. The two men then stepped backwards until they were behind the *gochor* and left the *penlop* to read the letter. Garba Lung Gi Khorlo had once again not failed his master. He went home, quietly ate his meal and followed it up with a cup of delicious strong *ara*. As he ate his meal, he calmly related the incident to his wife. After the meal, he lay down asleep and never woke up again.

Anyone travelling the lateral highway across Bhutan has to pass through Nyala Lungma. It is the area between Chendibji and Thumbidrak. It is always dark and always somewhat damp. There is no abode in the true sense of the word. But the demon lives here somewhere. Once you have heard this legend the place seems almost forbidding. Do stop and remember her, for she appreciates acknowledgement but do not call upon her to do anything. One can never be sure; she might just take you seriously.

India

Giribala

MAHASWETA DEVI

Giribala hails from Talsana village in the Kandi subdivision. It had never struck anyone that Giribala might have a heart and mind of her own. Our Giri is neither beautiful nor ugly, just ordinary. But her eyes are full of life. She'd catch your eye because of those eyes.

In their community, even now, it is customary to pay for the bride's hand in marriage. Aullchand had handed over eighty rupees, heifers, calves, so much stuff, to Giri's father. After that, he had married Giri. Truth be told, Giri's father had also presented his daughter with four *bharis* of silver, pots and pans, floor mats and a cartload of bamboo. And why not? Giri's father owns several bamboo groves. Aullchand had said, 'It's only because the hut's burned down that I'm leaving your daughter behind. Give me some bamboo, I'll build a home, then I'll come to fetch my wife.'

Aullchand left and was never seen again. After a few days Bangshi Dhamali, the ED peon, came to Giri's house. Bangshi Dhamali is ED peon at the Nishinda sub-post office. Because he can't support his household on a hundred and forty-five rupees, Bangshi spends his evenings helping the doctor at Nishinda treat his patients. The doctor is attached to a hospital and so of course he lures patients away for his own private practice. As a result Bangshi too has plenty of clout over the neighbouring villagers. They know, it's only via him that anyone can get to the doctor.

Having watched the doctor at work, Bangshi has himself begun to spout words of medical wisdom. As a result, he is now held in even greater esteem.

Bangshi addresses Giri's father as Mama. Nobody can remember exactly how this came to be. Bangshi Dhamali said, 'I'd been to Bethuadahari. A couple of other places as well. What do I hear? You've gone and married off your daughter to Aullchand?'

'He came along and I agreed.'

'Indeed! And how much has he paid you?'

'Eighty-one rupees, and some things.'

'Can you handle the risk?'

'What risk?'

'What can I say! I'm a government servant, the doctor's right-hand man as well, couldn't you have asked me just once? Aullchand's not a bad sort. Smoked a lot of ganja with him, that's not to be denied. But that money and that calf—it all belongs to Chan'an. Chan'an's marriage was fixed for Kalhat. So Aullchand, being Chan'an's paternal uncle, went to pay the bride-price.'

'What!'

'Well, Chan'an's mother was in tears. She'd begged and borrowed to get her son married. What kind of man is this fellow, tell me? Neither land nor property, lolling about Chan'an's house all the time...'

'No land or property?'

'No, no.'

'He took a cartload of bamboo to build a hut.'

'That's what I'm trying to tell you. After selling the bamboo to Chan'an's pishi, his father's sister, for a hundred rupees, he's gone off to the Banpur fair.'

Giri's father sinks to the floor in despair. Bangshi Dhamali continues to list Aullchand's exploits. Finally he leaves, saying, 'The boy isn't bad. But just like I told you. No land or property. Roams about from fairground to fairground, singing. Otherwise, he's not bad.'

'But Mohan never told us any of this. It was he who proposed the match, after all. He never breathed a word.'

'Why should he? They're best friends.'

Giri's mother said, 'I'll get my daughter married all over again. Cheat, scoundrel. I'm not sending my daughter to him.'

But when Aullchand turns up a year or so later, he doesn't give them a chance to refuse. He brings an enormous sweet tuber, new clothes for his bride, a stool made of jackfruit-wood for his mother-in-law, four new jute sacks for his father-in-law. Of course, Giri's mother does repeat all the things Bangshi had told them. Aullchand merely beams magnanimously and says, 'Can't live in this world by Bangshi-dada's words, Ma. Your daughter's going to live in a new hut now. That's not a lie, is it?'

Giri's mother braids her daughter's hair, dresses her. Then she says, weeping, 'This man, my child, is like the tree with a thousand roots. Growing right in the heart of the house. Every time you uproot it, it grows back again. Every word he speaks is a lie but oh, how cleverly he plays with those words!'

Giri says nothing. The groom is supposed to first pay bride-price to the bride's father. All this is true, no doubt. But still, she's a girl. A girl's by fate discarded, lost if she's dead, lost if she's wed. Giri senses that hard times lie ahead. She sobs silently, alone. Then she sniffs, wipes her eyes and says, 'Bring me home when the deity is worshipped. You will, won't you? Feed the brown cow. I've chopped the straw. Don't forget to water the hibiscus.'

And so, at the age of fourteen, Giri goes to keep house for her husband. Her mother packs pots and pans for Giri's new home. Aullchand says, 'Just add a bit of rice and dal, Ma. Got a job with the babus. Have to report for duty as soon as I get back. Won't have time to go to the market.'

Giri takes rice, dal and salt. Then leaves home. Aullchand walks at a rapid pace. Says, 'Now let's see you move those legs of yours.'

Aullchand takes her to a hut made of brick, once they enter the village of Talsana. Mango, jamun, guava, all kinds of trees in the babus' orchard. In one corner is a ramshackle hut meant for the keeper. Aullchand says, 'I'll build us a place to live in, sure enough. Ever seen anything like this? There's the pond, over on that side. Let's see you nip down to fetch some kindling, and put some rice on the boil.'

'But it's getting dark! Isn't there an oil-lamp?'

'Lamp? Now where would I find a lamp?'

The babus' maidservant, arriving suddenly, comes to Giri's rescue. The woman swears at Aullchand, gets an oil lamp. Takes Giri to the pond. Says, 'Have your parents hearts of stone, tell me? To leave such a tender little girl in the hands of that ganja fiend? What's he got to feed you? Grazes the babus' cows, works as a day-labourer. Hardly earns a pittance every month. Works sometimes, sometimes goes off, god knows where. Girl, if you've got even a grain of good sense, then listen to me, go to your parents' tomorrow itself, leave those bits and pieces of silver there.'

Even then Giri doesn't run back home the next day to keep her jewellery. She is seen instead lovingly plastering clay on the ramshackle hut, its frame protruding, at the corner of the orchard. From the babus, Aullchand gets hold of a piece of tin sheeting. Fashioned with a bamboo frame, that becomes the door of the hut. Very soon, Giri gets to work in the babus' household for a meal wage. After a few months, Aullchand says, 'Wife, made a householder out of me, you have. No parents, never known a home and family, drifted from one place to another.'

'Get help from the babus to build your own hut, get hold of some land.'

'You think they'll give?'

'Why not? A newcomer's expected. Will he be born in another's home? Even the wretched *boshtoms* have dwellings of their own.'

'You're right. My heart too aches for a home of my own. Never felt this way before, though.'

A home, how they yearn for a home of their own. But their first daughter, Belarani, is born right here, in this same hut. The girl is barely a month old when Giri returns to the pond to wash the babus' mosquito nets, sheets, rugs. The mistress of the babu household can't help commenting, 'That girl's quite crazy about her work, I must say. Works well, too.'

Overcome by an immense magnanimity, she gives her boys' old clothes to Giri's daughter. She tells Giri, 'Let your work be. Let the child have your milk. Or how will you cope?' Belarani, Paribala, Rajiv, are born to Giri at intervals of one-and-a-half to two years. And when the youngest daughter Maruni is born, Giri has an operation to prevent future childbirths.

Meanwhile Aullchand has prodded and pleaded with the babus and acquired two *kathas* of land. Even built a hut of sorts. Now he wanders from place to place, working as a day-labourer. He is enraged. 'Had an operation, did you? That's a sin. Why did you do it? Go on, tell me?'

Giri remains silent. Aullchand grabs her by the hair, hits her a couple of times with his fists. Giri suffers the beating silently. Then she says, 'They said for you to go to the panchayat. They're building a road, men are needed. They'll give grain.'

'Why don't you go to your father, tell him to give us some bamboo.'

'What for?'

'Dying for a home weren't you, and look at the mansion you live in! Some bamboo would give us a house to speak of.'

'We'll work hard, make our home.'

'How?'

'We'll have to try.'

'The silver, if we were to pawn it, or sell ...'

Giribala stares, unblinking, at Aullchand. Aullchand lowers his head before her gaze. Giri has placed her few *bharis* of silver in the hollow of a bit of bamboo, entrusted it to the mistress of the house. Even now, she works at that house. From the age of eight Belarani has been running a thousand errands at that same house for a meal wage. Even she is ten years old now. Fed on the rice of the babus' house, the girl grows rapidly, flourishing like a weed in the rains. To get the girl married, that bit of silver will be required. That bit of silver, and twenty-two rupees earned through hours of bone-wearying toil.

Giri says, 'I won't sell the silver to build a house. Baba gave all he could. Provided a cartload of bamboo for the hut. The price of that bamboo, even in Nishinda, was then a thousand rupees. One hundred and sixty-two bamboos.'

'The same old story.'

'Won't you get our daughter married?'

'A daughter means a female slave for someone else's house, after all. When he read my palm, Mohan had said that the fifth time onwards there'd be only boys. You've gone and turned barren, you want to go astray.'

Giri had gripped the *bonti* tightly. She'd said, 'Speak such evil and I'll slash the children's throats and then my own.'

'No, I didn't ... I won't say such things ...' Aullchand had quelled his tongue. He spent the next few days worried and anxious. Perhaps it was then that Aullchand began hatching his plan. The root cause of this too was Mohan.

Mohan appeared out of the blue one day. Lots of work in every village with the bus route from Krishnachowk to Nishinda now to be an asphalt road. Both Giri and Aullchand have been going to work. They earn grain, the mouths are fed. Mohan has also been working. Still the same vagabond, hasn't married, hasn't settled down. He sells the wheat and buys rice, pumpkin, fish. At night, he sprawls out on Giri's verandah. Wandering through cities, drifting through villages, a complete *bohemian* in speech and manner. Looks at Aullchand and clucks sympathetically, 'Stuck in the mud, are you, pal? Clean forgotten the life you had?'

Giri says, 'Stop your churlish nonsense.'

'My friend had such a great singing voice.'

'That he did. That brought money too. But that money never got home. Wouldn't buy food for the children.'

It was Mohan who said one day, 'No girls at all in the land of Bihar. Yet the bride-price's very high there. So, those folks are coming here, taking our girls away. Paying so much! Sahadev Bauri got five hundred rupees for his daughter.'

'Where is that?'

'Would you know if I told you, pal? Very far away, indeed. And they don't speak Bangla.'

Aullchand said, They paid five hundred rupees?'

'Sure.'

The conversation ends there for the moment because just then a fire breaks out in the cowshed of Kali-babu of the panchayat, sparked off from a pile of smouldering hay, the smoke from which acted as a mosquito repellent. A huge uproar. Everybody rushes in that direction.

Giri forgets the conversation, Aullchand does not. Who knows what Giri was thinking, for her husband's words caused her no alarm. Because one day, Aullchand said, 'Who wants your jewellery? We'll get Bela married, then fix our house with brick and mortar. Fed and fattened in the babus' house, how nice my daughter looks!'

Even then, no warning bells rang in Giri's mind. She said, 'Looked for a boy?'

'Just watch how it all takes care of itself.'

Giri said, 'The hut's sagging to one side. Need to prop it up a bit. How else will it stay up?'

It was with this idea in mind that Giri went to visit her father for a few days. Carrying Maruni in her arms. Holding the hands of Pari and Rajiv. Bela had wept a lot. Because she was leaving her behind, Giri had pressed eight annas into her hands. 'Buy yourself some sweets, girl. You want to visit your grandparents, you can go another time. Now work hard. We're gone four days at most.'

How could Giri know that she would never see Bela again? If so she'd have taken her daughter along. If so she'd have clasped her, kept her so close. Making the girl slog at the babus' since she was seven, was that mere fancy? Couldn't feed her, couldn't clothe her. A kiss on Bela's forehead and Giri left for her parents'.

A girl's by fate discarded, lost if she's dead, lost if she's wed. Still, their daughter, after all! The father has bought three bighas of land with his profits from the bamboo trade, been apportioned another two bighas as his share of property. The father says, 'Couldn't bring you home, *khuki,* but stay a few days now that you're here.' The mother says, 'Let me fry some *muri,* pick some arum. What kind of a marriage is this, child? How your skin used to glow. And now, turned soot black! Your lovely hair gone, your bones sticking out! Spend a few days looking after yourself. Let your health improve.' The brother says, 'Why not stay, didi. Even for a month—I'll make sure there's enough to eat.'

Lots of pampering, lots of care. The father says, 'Bamboo? Of course. You're here for a bit, take some when you go. How can you have good in-laws without a good home? They'll see the house, know they've married into a good family.'

Giri could have gotten more out of her father if she had wept and pleaded. The mother said, 'Girl, just ask for a maund of rice.' But Giri hadn't asked. Why should she? Give, if you've a mind to. Why should I ask? Giri had slowly walked over to the hibiscus bush. See, so many flowers. She had planted that bush. How nice the courtyard looked, freshly plastered with cow-dung, the roof newly thatched. If her mother agreed, Giri would leave Rajiv here so that he could go to school. She bathed her children, scrubbing them with lots of soap. She bathed too, washed her hair clean. Then she'd gone for a walk about the neighbourhood. This little respite, as though unimaginable bliss. The mother had sent her brother to the canal to catch fish. A single irrigation canal had transformed the area. Raise two crops a year, catch fish all the year round. Giri was content. Her mind at rest, at peace.

Bangshi Dhamali had come. 'Poor, poor Giri! How you suffer at the hands of that Aullchand! Doctor-babu's built a house in Baharampur. The sons study there, the wife lives there too. Had Aullchand been a man, he'd look after his children. You could work there, kept your youngest with you. A part-time job in the neighbourhood too, after your work at the babu's. Could have set up house with your children. All of them could've worked for a meal-wage. Can city ways be village ways?'

Giri had smiled a little, 'Dada, let those things be. Now tell me, all the riff-raff are getting land, so can't your Rajiv's father get some too?'

'Has he tried? Come to me? Said anything about it? I work for the government, I'm the doctor's right-hand man, sure enough I could have done something.'

'I'll send him to you.'

To Giri it all seemed like a dream, unreal. They're to have a house, perhaps some land as well. She knows only too well that her husband's an absolute vagabond. Yet her heart filled with pity as she thought of him. No home, no land, how can such a man be a householder? How can he settle down? 'Tell me, dada, should I send him to you?'

'Can't you see your father? As good as gotten into the panchayat. And Mama, what about you? Surely you should arrange for Aullchand getting a bit of land, first of all?'

'I'd tried, but he insulted me in public and stalked off. Said he could get it on his own.'

Giri knows nothing of all this. 'Oh Bangshi-dada! I beg you, please tell me what needs to be done. He knows no better. A roof over our heads true, but through which the moon shines at night and the sun mocks us in the daytime. No leaves to thatch it with, no straw. Bela's to be married, but where will the groom's folks sit? Find us a match for her.'

'There is a boy, haven't you noticed? My own paternal cousin. What a nice shop the boy's set up. Sells groceries.'

Giri was relieved at this news. Rajiv had said, 'I can go everyday to Jamai-dada's shop then, get oil and salt on credit, right, Ma?'

Giri had rapped him sharply on the head. 'Growing to be your father's son. Eat on credit and twiddle your thumbs.'

The two days rolled into six. As they depart from her father's home, Giri dressed in a new sari, the children clad in new clothes of the Bangladeshi brand 'Nilam! Nilam', stamped with the dead-sahib symbol, a bundle of rice on Giri's head, Bangshi Dhamali floats in like a straw in the wind, breaks the bad news. 'Disaster or blessing, call it what you will. Tremendous news, oh Mama! Aullchand said, 'Come Bela, let's go to your Mama's.' Took her to Kandi on that pretext, with Mohan's connivance. Married off that mother's pet, that timid twelve-year-old girl there, to a stranger from another land. They're strange folks, live in Bihar. Five of them have married five such Belaranis and gone back to their land. It's all part of the girl-trafficking business, oh Mama! All the addresses they've left are fake. It's a common racket nowadays. Aullchand's got four crisp, hundred rupee notes. Now Mohan and he are sitting at home, getting drunk. Aullchand is weeping 'Bela! Bela!' and Kali-babu from the panchayat is swearing at him, calling him names.'

Giri's world falls apart. She bursts into wails of despair. Her father says, 'Let's go, I'll take some men with me. We'll find the girl, thrash that father of hers. Cripple him for life. And we'll fix that Mohan for good as well.'

Mohan is nowhere to be found. Aullchand boxes his own ears in remorse and laments loudly, occasionally blustering, 'It's my daughter I've married off, so what's it to any of you?'

They search high and low. Giri goes crying to the babus with her silver necklace. 'Please speak to the police, oh Babu! Tell it on the radio. My Bela knows nothing beyond Talsana. You also know that my man's a monster. Why did you leave my daughter to him?'

The babu explains to Giri's father, Thana-police is lots of trouble, very expensive too. The damage is done. This is a new racket that's begun. All this talk of marriage is just a front for girl-trafficking. The racket's in full swing all over Murshidabad. They come, give a few hundred rupees. A few crisp notes are enough to make the beggars lose their heads. The police won't touch a case that's full of holes.

They'll tell you, if the father gets his daughter married, what can the thana do? Poor Bela, curse her fate!'

Father, neighbours, the babu's wife, everyone offers the same explanation to Giri. 'Fate rules over everyone. What can you do? It would have been good were you fated to keep her with you. She's a girl, not a boy. A girl's by fate discarded, lost if she's dead, lost if she's wed.' Her father sighs, says, 'Your daughter's sacrificed her own life, as if she's given her father the money for the house.'

Crazed with grief, Giri sighs, 'Don't you send any more bamboo, Baba. Let the devil do what he can.'

'No use going to thana-police, child.'

Giri leans against the wall and sinks to the floor, silent. Shuts her eyes. Amidst this numbing grief, the truth suddenly flashes across her mind. Nobody is willing to give much thought to a girl-child. She, too, should not worry. She, too, is female. Her father too had surrendered her to a monster without making any enquiries first.

Aullchand senses the change in the air. So he says, 'Your daughter's not all that innocent either. To hunt for the girl, the necklace is produced. If she'd given her jewellery earlier, the house would have been built, daughters would not have to be sold. And look, what a shameful thing to have done. She has an operation, comes back barren. Says, 'You can't even feed us, what would you do with a son?' Well, I've shown what I would do. Even the daughters can yield so much profit, see how much money I got ...'

Giri beats her head against the wall overwhelmed with rage, with grief. Everyone rushes to stop her.

Over time the uproar dies down. The babu's aunt is a wise lady. She says, 'An adolescent girl's her father's property. What use is it for you to shed tears?'

Giri doesn't sob any more. Grim faced, she leaves Pari at the babus' house. Says, 'If your father comes to get you, I'll chop you to pieces if you go with him.'

And if Aullchand tries to speak to her, she doesn't answer him at all. Just stares unblinkingly at her husband. Aullchand gets scared. He says: 'It's a-l-l for the house. So we can build a home, right?'

'Right. Tell Mohan to find out where they eat human beings. Why not sell off these three also? Enough money then for a cement house. Can't Mohan find out?'

Aullchand says, 'Never met someone as heartless as you, wife. Asking me to sell the children? No wonder you made yourself barren. Or else how could you speak this way? And your father was willing, so why didn't you take the bamboo?'

Giri leaves the room, sleeps on the verandah. Aullchand whines for a bit, then falls asleep.

But time's a great leveller after all. Over time Giri accepts everything. Aullchand buys bamboo matting and makes a hut. The roof remains thatched with palm leaves. Rajiv becomes Kali-babu's apprentice and Maruni grows up, playing about the courtyard. Looking at Pari, Giri cannot stifle the fire in her heart that burns so. Just like Bela. The same smile, the same gaze, the same tilt of the head. The mistress says, 'What a good girl she is. Loves her work so.'

Because she loves her work, Pari sweeps the babus' huge rooms and verandahs ten times over, carries the paddy-sacks to the pond for washing, plasters the courtyard, so huge, like a field, with cowdung. Giri feeds Pari some *muri*, fried chickpeas or sweetened chickpea balls, then roams around in the babus' orchard collecting leaves and branches. In the middle of the afternoon, she is surrounded by rustling leaves, scurrying squirrels, a gentle breeze ruffling her unkempt hair. She remembers then, the plaintive appeal in Bela's voice, 'But Ma, you're frying *muri* today! When they call from the babus' house, will you tell them that Bela will go to work tomorrow? Today she'll stay home?'

Such a big girl, and she still liked to sleep with her face pressed into her mother's bosom. The low wooden stool on which the babus' aunt used to sit for her oil-massage had fallen on Bela's foot, grazed it. In the end, warmed-up oil from the lamp had been applied to soothe the pain. If Giri had fever, Bela would ask for time off from the babus' house to run home and cook the rice before going back again.

Bela, Belarani, Beli
Not discarded, our dear Beli
Beli's her name I said
Lost if she is dead,
Lost if she is wed.

Gone, gone where? How far? Which place? Remembering, wondering, Giri would whisper in memory of her lost daughter. There, there! Wherever you may be, stay well, stay safe, my girl. If I knew where you were, I'd fly to you like a bird. But I don't know, little one! I took the address and had Babu write a letter. That address was fake, my dear!'

Back home, Giri cooks rice. Eats with Maruni. Aullchand's rice stays in the pot. The days he doesn't go to work he lies stretched out on the verandah. The days he does, it's mostly on small-time jobs. Buses now ply on the Krishna-Chowk-Nishinda busway they had built. Get onto the bus, and you'll reach Kandi in an hour-and-a-half. Now there's work going on, digging a drainage outlet from the irrigation canal. The babu's son now throws his weight around there. Working as an overseer, he has managed to extract a bus-permit as well.

It's there that Giri catches sight of Bangshi Dhamali. With quite genuine concern, Bangshi exclaims, 'Oh dear, Giri. I didn't recognize you. You look like such a wreck! Pining after that daughter of yours I suppose … well, what can you do about it, after all?'

'Oh that's not it, dada. It's because Pari is ten years old now.'

'Ten years?'

'Why! The time your doctor-babu built a brick-and-mortar building, the time *electiri* came to Nishinda, that's the time Pari was born.'

'True enough.'

'If we'd only listened to you then, moved away, all of us! Even the boy's working as an assistant. If we'd moved then, they could have gone to school.'

'Don't know about school. But the *town* is like an ocean now. Your children would have been working by now.'

Giri understands that Bangshi is angry at the suggestion that her children could go to school.

'Let it be, dada. They'll have to earn by the sweat of their brow. What's the use of some two-bit reading and writing? So why don't you find a match for Pari?'

'I'll let you know, let Aullchand know.'

'No, let me know.'

'This is an empty grudge you bear, my dear. He's done something foolish once, can there be no forgiveness for that? Can wedding arrangements be discussed with a woman? The other party will wonder if there's something wrong with your family, When you arrange a match for your son, his prospective in-laws would listen to you. But will they listen when it's your daughter's marriage in question?'

'I should know what happens.'

'Let's see. There's a chap, plies a rickshaw at Keshtochowk. Quite old, though. Say about twenty-five.'

'That's okay.'

'The girl will live in Keshtochowk itself. No land or property, but the rickshaw's an asset. Even that brings in money for four or five days. In the evening, the chap rolls bidis. But she'd have to keep house. Got no one to cook and clean for him so he wants a wife.'

'Let's see. If it works out, we'll fix the wedding for this Magh itself.'

The heart that had broken over Bela's loss now sees a ray of light. A glimmer of hope. Giri says, 'Whatever I've got, I'll give it all. No point keeping it. I'll worry about Maruni later. My own daughter, how can I sing her praises! She slogs at the babus' house true enough but a meal a day and see how pretty she's grown. Who'd take her for a ten-year-old? Come dada, have some tea.'

Sipping tea, it's Bangshi who says, 'So Mama's got two more bits of land, two more granaries. Really, Mama has done well for himself. Such a feast for the eyes. But they never come here, after all, never bother to find out how you are. It's a painful thing for you to hear, sister, but even your own folks aren't always your own. Mama mixes with his equals now. Not with someone in your station in life.'

Giri sighs. Undoes the knotted corner of her sari tucked at her waist, takes out some money to pay for the tea. Says, 'Oh dada, remember Pari.'

'I'll remember.'

Aullchand meets Bangshi, they speak about the rickshaw-puller. Aullchand is delighted. He says, 'Dada, it's a rickshaw-puller that I've in mind as well. He plies a rickshaw at Baharampur. Head-full of hair, complete with beard and bristling moustache, all dressed up in *coat-pant* stamped with the dead-sahib brand! Don't you worry about this any more.'

Later, when Bangshi meets Giri, he says, 'I've spoken to Aullchand. You don't have to worry any more.'

Aullchand goes in search of Mohan. Mohan's is the brain that guides Aullchand. Lalbagh, Dhuliyan, Jangipur, Ziaganj, Farakka—is there any place he has not been? In Delhi, Meerut, Dhanbad and Tatanagar, the flesh trade is rampant, flourishing. A great demand for nubile young girls from West Bengal. The rich clients, the traders, are fond of tender flesh. If fed and fattened, a girl can be used to recover all costs within a few years.

Mind you sir, the wedding game needs to be played. If you offer money outright the village folks will mob you. So it needs to be said, 'Girls are scarce in Bihar ...'

The wedding ceremony is performed, priest and all. Then one must say, 'I'll complete the remaining rites and rituals back home, and then we'll have ... what's called conjugal relations. With your kind permission, let me take away the bride.'

There have been several instances when girls have been taken away with the excuse of, 'I've come from Bihar to get married.' Now a new ruse is required. The local *tout* can locate the girls. Even he doesn't get to know the full story. Although he senses that there's something fishy afoot. But he'd rather not know where exactly the fraud lies. He's been asked to supply brides and that is all that he does.

The parents-brothers-uncles of the girls don't suspect a thing. All they know is they're giving the girl, they're getting the bride-price. The groom's a foreigner and so the need to keep it secret. People are no longer well-meaning, after all. If they know how much money we're getting, they'll throw a spanner in the works. A foreign groom is best for us. Bengali grooms pay the bride-price still, in communities where that's the custom, but then they ask for a watch, a bicycle, a radio—five-seven thousand rupees gone before you know it.

Aullchand goes looking for Mohan. After the Belarani debacle, Kali-babu had said, 'No more odd jobs for you any more. You won't find work at the panchayat.'

Armed with his education (up to fourth-grade), Mohan has now set up operations around the Nishinda Block Office. Selling off fertilizer as soon as the farmers acquire some, grabbing a share in the agricultural debts—now he has a lot to do.

Aullchand's tale has him shaking his head in vigorous denial. 'No thank you. Mohan Mandal wants nothing more to do with your affairs. Done with charity, enough's enough. Getting a girl married is an errand of virtue. You got the money, what did I get? At least those folks gave me forty rupees. And you? Took the money and built a house of bamboo-lath. I'm scared of your wife, mister.'

'Don't worry, she's the one who's suggested this.'

'Is that so?'

'Just you listen,' Aullchand says, 'Why the rickshaw-puller from Keshtochowk? You keep to the background. Send out feelers. Aren't there rickshaw-pullers in the city? Wished for the longest time to have in-laws in Baharampur *town*. Increases my esteem in the village, also gives me a toehold in the *town*.'

'A rickshaw-puller from the *town*?'

'Yes, mister. Give it a try. But make sure you look in Baharampur. No more folks from that Bihar place. Must be a rickshaw-puller from *town*, my daughter will stay in *town*. We'll come and go, bring her home sometimes. Bela's mother is still grumpy with me. Now her doubts will finally vanish.'

'You want to get friendly with your woman? It's better that way. That bitch doesn't think I'm human. I want to prove that I can get a daughter properly married, too. I can't manage that without your help.'

Mohan laughs. He says, 'Go on, then. But I won't be seen anywhere. I'll just provide the contacts. You're asking for a son-in-law from the *town*, what if he hands you a list of demands?'

'I'll have to borrow money.'

'Got it, now go.'

Mohan realizes that this time he'll have to tread very carefully. The 'just-arrived-from-Bihar' *party* will remain backstage. In the forefront will be the rickshaw-puller. He will be the groom at the wedding. And a good thing, too. This time, five girls must be procured. Rickshaw-puller ... rickshaw-puller ... now, who can do the job? A visit to the *town* is on the cards.

The business of Pari's marriage brings Giri and Aullchand a little closer, once again. Finally Mohan tells Aullchand, 'I've found a groom.'

'What's the deal?'

'Has a watch. Owns a radio. Plies a rickshaw, so he doesn't want a bicycle. Groom's clothes, bridal wear, mat-umbrella-shoes, hardly very much.'

'Will he pay bride-price?'

'A hundred rupees.'

'Any place to live in?'

'A rented room. But the rickshaw is his own.'

Aullchand and Giri are delighted. When the boy comes to see the girl, Giri stays out of sight but looks him up and down carefully from her hidden vantage point. The boy's name is Manohar Dhamali. Sturdy of build, bearded, and a moustache too. There really is a rickshaw-puller called Manohar Dhamali in Baharampur. This boy is actually Panu. Just acquitted for lack of evidence in a robbery case. Even Aullchand doesn't know this. After coming out of jail, Panu has married two Paribalas, one in Farakka and one in Jalangi, and handed them over to his new masters, the 'we-are-from-Bihar' gang. For five weddings he is owed five hundred rupees, not bad at all. Panu's next stop is Siliguri.

Last time, for Bela's wedding, they couldn't invite the relatives. This time Giri's parents come. The conch shells are blown, the women ullulate. Giri, oily and seating, cooks rice and meat in the kitchen. She's dressed Pari in the jewellery she'd kept safe with the babus. Her mother has given her new clothes to wear. The babus have offered fifty rupees by way of help. Her father has brought rice. The groom arrives at the wedding in a bus, with five companions. Smeared with turmeric and *alta*, Pari looks very much like Bela.

The next day they hail a bus from the main road and leave.

When she left, that's the last time they see Pari. The next day, Aullchand goes with Rajiv and Giri's brother to *town*, to see his daughter. They're gone for the longest time. Afternoon turns into evening. Then night. The hours roll by. Giri hears the scrunch of shoes in her courtyard. At once, warning bells ring in her mind. She opens the door to see Bangshi Dhamali. Bangshi's clutching Rajiv. Rajiv sobs, 'Ma!' And Giri knows at once that disaster has struck again. She gazes at him, silent. Her brother says, 'Didi! I'll explain.'

There's not much to tell. The Manohar Dhamali who lives in *town,* he's a middle-aged man. They'd tried asking around. 'Didn't find your man at his address? How will you? Sounds like Panu. Yes, yes, he's been going around, getting married quite a few times these last few days. Seems to have joined some kind of racket.'

Giri interrupts, asks, 'Isn't Mohan involved in this?'

'He's the ringleader.'

'And Rajiv's father?'

She runs off to find Mohan. Everyone says Mohan's made five to seven hundred rupees out of Pari's wedding. Need girls, want money, he's lost his head as well!

A big crowd collects in Giri's courtyard. 'Get hold of Mohan, thrash him.' 'Get the thana-police involved.' 'What about the law of the land, after all?' Many words, much noise.

Aullchand returns in the wee hours of the morning. Overwhelmed by the gravity of the situation, Aullchand has come back drunk. Where did he get the money? 'Yes yes, my name is Aullchand Sardar, sir! Could Mohan escape me? I wrung his neck and squeezed the money out of him. And why shouldn't I, tell me? Isn't the girl my own daughter? Didn't you go sell her off on false pretences? And you want to take the money? Why should I let you? Where is Pari's mother? Why did you have that operation, wife, the more daughters you produce, the more money you acquire. If I don't build a thatched house for you ... Pari my child!' Aullchand bursts into loud sobs, then lies down on the verandah and is asleep in an instant. Her mouth dry, Giri forces out the words, 'Please go back to your own homes.'

Everyone moves away, goes home. They wonder what Giri will do. Maybe she'll die, maybe she'll drown herself. Everyone says, 'Maruni will have the same fate. What a scandal over a girl's wedding, I tell you! Go, Giri, plead with the babus, tell the thana-police.'

Giri stares at them, her eyes widened in surprise. Shakes her head, no. No, she won't do anything.

Aullchand's made money, let him do something. Giri shakes her head, disagreeing, 'No, no.'

Bangshi Dhamali says, 'Who knows what God had in mind. One daughter got them walls of bamboo and the other, a thatched roof.'

Giri stares at him.

Aullchand thatches the roof even as he weeps for his daughter. The more his eyes fill with tears, the more Giri's eyes stay dry.

The babu's pishi says, 'She's the mother of a girl-child, after all!

They say, a girl's by fate discarded, lost if she is dead, lost if she is wed. And your fate, no different. Don't I know why you shed no tears? Small sorrows make you weep but great grief turns you to stone. Let's see you get to work. You'll get used to it all, my girl, but you've got to feed that mouth at the end of the day.'

Giri stares at her as well. Then says, 'Speak to the mistress. Give me my dues.'

Giri takes the money and knots it into the corner of her sari. Returning home, she stands in the courtyard. Not a bad house. Walls made of bamboo plastered over with clay, a thatched roof, not a bad home. Just the kind of house she'd wanted, after all. Perhaps she had wanted too much. That's why Beli and Pari had to be handed over to the pimps. To be prostitutes, to those men, pimps. Were any of those girls bought to play wife? Never.

What a house! Aullchand glances at Maruni furtively. Then carries on with his work. Giri stares at him, unblinking. Aullchand thinks to himself, no matter how sad she is, she must love the way the house is now.

When they get up in the morning, everyone is dumbfounded. How extraordinary, how very extraordinary. Giribala has gone to *town,* boarded the bus from the main road in the early hours of the morning. Maruni in her arms, Rajiv's hand clasped in her own. Later they come to know that getting off at Nishinda she'd told Bangshi Dhamali, 'Tell Pari's father, he can rot for all eternity in his house.' Giri will work in the *town* as a maidservant, bring up her children. If Aullchand tries to look for her, Giri will lay her body across the railway tracks.

The news amazes everyone, sets their heads shaking in disapproval. What happened to Bela and Pari was common practice these days. But why leave your husband and go away? What kind of woman was that?

Everyone is convinced that it's not Aullchand but Giribala who's at fault. An indescribable relief fills them, all of them, when they reach this conclusion.

And walking through the streets in *town,* Maruni clasped to her bosom, Giri thinks to herself, 'If the heart'd mustered up courage earlier, I'd have left then, long ago. Would Pari have been lost to us then, or Bela?'

Tears stream down her face as she remembers. But she walks on.

Translated by Radha Chakravarty

India

Caves

Jyoti Lanjewar

Their inhuman atrocities have carved caves
in the rock of my heart
I must tread this forest with wary steps
eyes fixed on the changing times
The tables have turned now
Protests spark
now here
now there.
I have been silent all these days
listening to the voice of right and wrong
But now I will fan the flames
for human rights.
How did we ever get to this place
this land which was never mother to us?
Which never gave us even
the life of cats and dogs?
I hold their unpardonable sins as witness
and turn, here and now,
a rebel.

Translated by Shanta Gokhale

India

Cow-dust Time

P. SATHYAVATHI

One Sunday afternoon, caught in a drizzle, as I stepped into our house, I noticed father and mother feverishly busy in the kitchen, engaged in cooking something and arguing with each other. The debate didn't concern cuisine—it was about our educational system—she is a lecturer—and he, of course, a professor. She had put the deep fry pan on the fire and had poured oil into it; she was now kneading the Bengal gram flour in a basin. Sniffling his nose, wiping his eyes, he was slicing onions.

I put my arm over his shoulder and said, 'Need some help?' Instantly, my mother pushed the dough basin towards me, and said, 'Fry the pakodis—I have to mark the scripts.'

And quit.

Any other Bharat mata, Indian mother, wouldn't have shoved me, exhausted me, engaged as I had been in research at the university for the last four years, to the kitchen fire in this way—but then she is a different sort of mother! Can't help it!

'Could you please help me with these onions,' father said, and almost bit off his tongue; he even wiped his eyes immediately. He had taken a vow at a very young age, I believe, that—no woman in his family should shed tears, he won't allow it—not even while shredding onion. He wouldn't permit either mother or me to cut onions; if he had to go out of town, he would first cut up a half-kilo of onions and store them in the fridge, and then only leave, my dear beloved father. And thereby hangs a tale.

Actually, my father is known in his village only as Tank Tulasamma's grandson. Not professor so-and-so. Tank Tulasamma is the very Mahalakshmi, the great Goddess of Prosperity of my father's place.

Of course her given name was Mahalakshmi only: but she is remembered only as Tank Tulasamma.

Mahalakshamma garu had been married at the age of eight; the groom, I believe was just sixteen—when this eight-year old baby would come of age, when she would begin family life, for that kept waiting not only her wedded husband, but also the paternal grandmother of her husband, and two of his paternal aunts widowed and returned home to their parents, as did of course his mother. At the age of fifteen, just beginning to cover her shoulders with a paita, girl's uppercloth, she stepped (right foot first) into her mother-in-law's house, commencing family life. Even at that tender age, her husband, and his grandmother, and his paternal aunts, and his mother kept roasting her the whole day like a brinjal or a sweet potato—bone-tired with household chores, and heckling and harassment the whole day, when by night, pouring a little warm water on herself, she longed to hit her bed for a few winks, even this was made impossible by the great man's amatory assaults. Inexplicably—she should not understand the reason—fear—pain—hatred—who could she confide in? How could she write to her mother without having learned even the alphabet—nor did that lady know how to read-only if someone arrived from their village she could communicate her feelings.

Waiting and waiting, at last it was the festival of Sankranti—her father came, and fetched them both to their home—for god's sake, she thought, why this man also, but it couldn't be avoided, could it—the very evening after her arrival, she poured her soul out to her mother, and shed tears, and her mother laughed it away. Life in the mother-in-law's house, did you imagine it's like playing a girl's game of physic nuts? That is the way women's life is, of course—haven't we all suffered the same way. You will get used to it, no doubt, she said, and she cooked a whole lot of fried snacks for her, chegodi—arisalu—madata kazalu—that's it, after that the girl did not confide her woes to anybody. By evening, completing all her chores, she would sit before the tulasi plant in its brick work in the backyard, and would weep to her heart's content—making a submission of all her travails to that benign mother tulasi—that every evening the daughter-in-law of the house was seated before the tulasi brick platform, lost in dhyana, deep meditation, this came to be known not only to the family members, but everyone outside in the village. They all believed that seated there, she was meditating on Mother Tulasi. As she sat there every evening for ten years, sitting and sitting for ten years, her tears formed a tank around the tulasi brickwork—for the family members as well as for outsiders, it was nothing short of a miracle—the prayers of this lady Mahalakshamma they came to believe melted Mother Tulasi and created a tank. The lady's prestige grew; meanwhile came four children. The two old paternal aunts passed away, as well as granny. Giving birth in quick succession to three sons—causing a tank to form in the backyard brought good fortune to our father's granny—her prestige grew, at home and outside—the great pativrata, husband-devotee, as the Tulasamma of the Tank she became famous even in the neighbouring villages—earlier the women of the village had to trudge all the way to the tank outside the village to celebrate the lamp festival in the month of karthikam—now the womenfolk began visiting this tank—a mere glimpse of granny's face was sufficient good fortune, they believed. In this tank, the housewives bathed, washed their sacral cloths—children went swimming—but the water was too saltish to drink—because it was the type of village home with a thousand square yard living area and a backyard as large as Lanka. Even when a tank formed there, or when there were floods, it could withstand anything. If such a thing were to happen in cities, people would move around their rooms in boats, thought my father, and had taken, early in his life, this vow of onions.

The oil was simmering—mix the onion slices in the Bengal gram dough with a dash of cooking soda in it and roll them into small balls—drop them in the boiling oil and fry them to a nice shade of brown—that is, until they acquire a golden hue—drain them in a perforated ladle and take them out (in the process, if hot hot oil drops fall on your body, jump and hop around a bit). Now nose tingling—sorry—crispy crisp pakodis are ready.

'You and your stupid vows.' Mother was scolding him fondly—

'Look at your face and nose—go and wash and then eat these pakodis—'

'Father's nayanamma was truly great,' I said, putting a plate of pakodis before mother—she gave me a look, and went on marking her scripts, munching pakodis.

'I too will mark your scripts—but first, on a Sunday like this with a drizzle outside, please tell me about your own nayanamma,' I said.

If it were father, asked or unasked, he would have gone on non-stop recounting things about himself; this lady is different. She wouldn't say a thing until she is requested again and again—but isn't the asker a creature deserving of contempt from the teller? 'Tell me, thalli, dear mother, please won't you—what kind of miracles has your nayanamma performed with the glorious power of her husband—devotion? Tanks? Rivers? Or oceans?' I said.

'None of those stories of miracles in their family,' chipped in promptly the respected professor.

'My nayanamma considered tears inauspicious—except when my grandfather passed away, she never shed a tear. Even at that time, she hesitated for a moment or two whether it was propitious or not, and when someone advised that it would be inauspicious not to weep on the occasion, she gave herself a quick cry, they say.'

'She probably had no problems—mothers-in-law, paternal aunts—husband's sisters—husband himself—everyone treated her well, I presume—'

'Not at all—she too suffered from all those—but when she was being sent off, to lead family life with her husband, her mother counselled her cogently. That if the lady of the house sheds tears, the Goddess of Wealth will quit the place forthwith—that Goddess, Goddess Lakshmi hates snivellers—that a woman should always keep her hair nicely combed—with the auspicious mark on her forehead in place and—keep smiling, keep laughing ever and always—shedding tears is inauspicious—therefore nayanamma even as she came to start family life she took a vow first not to shed tears and then came to live with her husband. Besides, she believed in several other things, any number of them—early in the morning when it was time for Goddess Lakshmi to knock on the door, the whole house should be kept spick and span—all the people therein must keep smiling—then the afternoon was work time—evening, dusk, asura sandhya, lamp-lighting time. In this manner, she had a 'time' for everything—and during those 'times', no one should weep, or abuse, or use foul language against anyone—shouldn't utter inauspicious words—there hover around us gods, tadhastu ('be it so!') gods, who would promptly make such things happen—if we curse somebody, these gods will utter, 'tadhastu', 'be it so!' 'amen'—that's why, we should ever keep uttering auspicious words—if you don't have anything else to do, pour some raw rice into your winnowing tray and keep uttering the name of 'Rama' each time you pick out an unhusked grain and put it aside—and those unhusked grains of Rama's Name you give away as alms—My paternal aunt lost her husband even in her childhood, and so returned to us—she has no children—'

As she attempted to rise from her chair as though she had given me enough, I forced her back into her chair again, 'Not enough, more, tell me more—'.

She resumed. 'Among my nayanamma's favourite topics there was one, "cow-dust time"—that I can never forget—nor can you.' As I looked eagerly into her face, waiting for her to tell me about it—she got up, brought more pakodis in a plate, 'you both eat these', she said, as if she was imposing a sentence on us.

'Why don't you eat?' father said, demanding to know. *'Have I said I won't eat? Have I? Any time?'* she crooned in the rhythm of an old cinema song.

'Nayanamma did not know the alphabet—nor did she know the numerals—they were of little use to her—if she needed anything for the home, she would tell her children, who would then pass the word on to the grandfather, her husband—on the instant he would fetch them and drop them at the threshold of the kitchen—she had nothing whatever to do with cash transactions—she couldn't even identify the denominations of currency. Once a ryot brought a bundle of ten rupee notes and gave it to her and asked her to put it away safely—and this lady put it in the eaves—and when on the third day her gentleman asked her for it, it had been nibbled badly by rats—those were the days when just one hundred and fifty rupees fetched ten sovereigns of gold, I believe—naturally the grandfather danced the furious dance of Shiva and when she attempted an explanation he gave her a resounding slap—at 'midnoon time'—she went straight to her winnowing tray of Rice of Rama's Name and settled down—when my aunt approached her and sought to condole with her—'Father has gone too far'—my nayanamma shut her up—'Don't utter a single word against that maharaju, that great man—if an error is committed, wont even God punish?' She was extremely fair skinned—looking at the pink welts on her cheek she was filled with anger—and grief—if she were to weep her mother would rebuke her, so she got up and went away—'

'Great!'

One evening, surrounding herself with ten hurricane lanterns, and sundry little lamps, with a rag and a handful of lime wash powder to wipe the glass chimneys, my aunt settled down in the hall.

She conducted this programme every day for an hour. During this period, mother was busy in the backyard, either cutting the vegetables for the evening meal, or serving a meal to the field hand who had returned from the fields—or supervising him grinding horse gram paste—nayanamma would keep sitting there, leaning against a pillar, next to my aunt. Both of them would go on chatting, sometimes back-biting mother, or sometimes gibing at each other, at times criticizing or praising someone in the village. That was an extremely 'hectic time'—and also the time when we returned from the school. 'Shall I also clean the lanterns, aunt,' I said, having just returned from the school, having 'swallowed' whatever mother had to 'give' me, as well as a snack, karappoosa.

'Enough of nonsense, go take your bath,' said aunt.

'Don't say such things to a girl child at any time of the day—that's wrong,' said nayanamma.

'Whatever I say is wrong for this lady,' muttered aunt to herself.

'Have the cattle returned home?' enquired nayanamma all of a sudden. Everyday when the cattle returned home, it was her custom, she went to the cow she worshipped daily and milked her all by herself—to give it to our grandfather at night—he drank cow's milk along with his ayurvedic medicine. It was her belief that the field hand didn't know how much milk he must leave for the calf and how much for our use—our grandpa needed one glass of milk, for offering to god, another for himself—you should only milk that much and leave the remainder to the calf—she even had a measuring mark in the chembu, the brass vessel to indicate when two glasses had been milked—she wouldn't even tolerate a spoon this side or that—you are murdering the calf, she would charge.

'What is the time when cattle return home called, nayanamma?' I said, for fun.

'It is called *godhooli vela,* Cow-dust Time—you don't know even that much—continuing your education even after puberty?' she said, mockingly—among matters which were not to her liking was my continuing my education.

'What does it mean, nayanamma?'

'While cows come trotting home eagerly at dusk—their hooves raise dust which colours the sky red, it appears—that is why it is called cow-dust time.'

'Is it the cows alone—even the oxen come home—she-buffaloes return too—don't they—why don't they say cattle-dust time?'

'It is important for the cows to return home on time—the calves wait for their milk—we have to milk the cows in time, sufficiently early—after nightfall, there could be creeping things in the wood-pile—cows have a lot of things waiting for them at home—and it is necessary for us also that they should return home in time. That's why they return trotting home on their own exactly on time,' said aunt in a sort of commentary.

'That means cows are more useful than oxen, that's why we worship them—right, nayanamma?' I said.

Nayanamma didn't agree. 'Oxen plough the field for us—draw the carts—without them, where will you get your food! Therefore, oxen alone are superior—the cow—another name for patience, Mother Cow, we say—like a mother it is—Goddess of Patience—that's why we worship it,' said nayanamma—and left to check if the cows had returned to the byre.

'Cow-dust time'—the term just stuck in my mind—I can never forget it—'Even the marks in these scripts—mark the totals—have an appointment at five'—It's impossible to hold her back even for a moment.

All this had happened two years ago.

*

The last lecture period was still on—those of us who had finished for the day, sat around in the staff room—some were chatting about the share market—some others about the Principal. Political Science Lecturer Sandhya Rani kept looking every now and then at the clock next to the main gate; she had to change two buses to reach home; in the rush hour you couldn't get a bus; she had urgent chores always waiting for her at home. 'Botany' Pushpalata was saying that her son's fever wasn't coming down; it transpired they had an appointment with a specialist today. When she asked 'Telugu' Siva Rao garu, he was telling her that he wouldn't be returning home direct; he had to give a tuition in Sanskrit to someone on the way, he said; he wouldn't be home before eight; until he finished his shopping, until he looked up his circle of friends, he wouldn't return home, he was telling her conclusively. 'I agree with you, brother,' said another gent, 'Going home and returning, it will be a lot of petrol wasted—better get done with everything on the way and reach home—after all, once you arrive home, all that you need to do is eat and watch the TV.'

Sandya Rani kept looking at the clock. Pushpalata slumped heart-sick in her chair—rushing home and picking up her son and rushing to the hospital, it could be too late, probably—if she were to miss the appointment time, she would have to wait until the last patient had had his turn; only then would the doctor call her in—and it would be after ten p.m. How could she manage cooking the evening meal, etc?

At last, the bell rang—having got her bag ready, Sandhya Rani crossed the gate in one bound. Pushpalata requested 'English' Subbarao who had just come back from his class for a lift up to half the way, and, looking triumphant, perched on his pillion seat. Sundara Rao and Suryamukhi who had been talking about the share market until then, joked about Pushpalata's request for a 'lift' and sniggered—'Telugu'. Sunanda and I walked down at a leisurely pace to the bus-stop. The place was overflowing with women—their faces writ with perpetual anxiety—on the road—even the vehicles plying frenetically belonged to women—must reach home—and as early as possible—chores waiting to be done at home—children—returning from school, office, college, university—why have you taken so much time to reach home! What have you been doing all this while! Don't you know you should arrive sharp! When so many others could get a bus, why not you! Shoving and trampling, Sudha Rani squeezed herself into a bus.

Ammayya, whew! Serious trouble averted for one more day—

'In this mad rush we cannot board a bus, I say—let a couple of buses go—catch a bus later—meanwhile let's get a couple of corncobs from that parked trolley,' said Sunanda, making sure that no students were around. But then a not-so-packed bus came along—we both clambered into it.

At this 'time' of the day, wherever you turn it's women! Women—we have acquitted ourselves of our official duties for the day satisfactorily—without palpitations, let's return home—even for calling on a friend on the way, no poise palpable on anyone's face. Hurry—hurry—vegetables on the way—snacks for the children—if you take an hour for buying medicines for the elders, there will have to be an explanation—if you don't get a bus—if you call on a friend—no explanations allowed—March—Forward—Pushing ahead, March—Treading steadily, March—March into your buses—climb in sharp—umm, still faster.

'What is this rush—these women frantic to return home,' I said as if to myself.

'Cow-dust time, of course!' said 'Telugu' Sunanda in an absolutely laid-back tone.

Translated by Ranga Rao

India

Dead-end

AJEET COUR

The darkness outside was dense and impenetrable. Only the howling of dogs ripped across the dark shroud of the night.

I was unable to sleep.

Ever since my brother Kewal was murdered, sleep had eluded both of us—me and my mother, who was numb with grief. But we both pretended that we were sleeping, so that the other should keep her eyes closed. Sleep sometimes quietly slips into closed eyes, they say.

They think my brother was killed by extremists. I have no idea. He had never hurt anybody. Why should anyone kill him?

Actually it was difficult to say who murdered him. Extremists, or anybody else. How long does it take to kill a human being anyway?

It takes months for a human form to take shape in the mother's womb. It then takes years to bring him up. The longest any living being takes to grow up is the human child. And then, just one metal bullet and everything is over in a fraction of a second. Like a full-blown balloon pierced with the tip of a pin.

After all a human being is a fragile thing walking on two legs, breathing, with his heart beating rhythmically inside the rib-cage. Just pierce him with one bullet, and the blood spurts out. What is left is a dead body. Just a handful of dust! Everybody waits impatiently to take the body to the crematorium. 'It is just *mitti,* a handful of dust. Send it to its destination. Why delay?'—that's what everybody says.

It happened just four weeks ago. But I feel as if centuries have gone by.

When the sparrows start singing heralding the morning, I don't feel like getting up. How can they go on singing like that? I wonder!

Both mother and myself would like to continue with the pretence or sleeping. Getting up forces you into a meaningless routine. We don't feel like cooking, but I force myself to cook so that my mother pushes a morsel or two down her throat. She too does the same, to make me eat. Each one of us pretends to eat so that the other eats too.

Sometimes I wonder who the killers were. It is quite possible that Sarla's brothers killed him. They had threatened to. Not once but many times. Sarla? Didn't I tell you my brother was in love with her? She was his classmate in college in the city where he was studying. Sarla's parents and brothers were convinced that Kewal had no right to be friendly with their Brahmin daughter. Yes, they are Brahmins and Kewal was from a low-caste Kamboh family.

I could never understand how Kambohs were low caste, simply because their traditional occupation used to be dyeing clothes. How can the people, who make ordinary, drab-looking clothes come alive with rainbow colours, be low-caste? For that matter, how can people who create beauty by weaving cloth, by dyeing it, by stitching it, by transforming hard, foul-smelling dead hides into beautiful footwear and bags, by moulding ordinary clay into beautiful pots and pans, be low-caste?

Our forefathers were dyers. But my grandfather had departed from the traditional occupation; he was a school teacher. And my father was an employee in the postal department. He was very keen to give both Kewal and me a good education. He always told us, 'Nobody is born high or low. All these divisions of caste and religion are man-made. They might have been useful at a certain point of time, but they have lost their relevance today. It is only one's deeds and achievements and human values which make one high or low.'

When I told this to my friends, they smiled condescendingly. And my classmates, who were outside our intimate circle, didn't hesitate to say openly, 'All the low-caste people say that. They just try to fool themselves. But they can't fool the others.'

Anyway these things never bothered me. Life was so full and satisfying because of the books, warm relationships, and all the newly-discovered secrets of life that I never wasted my thoughts or time on such irrelevant things. My father was the best father in the world; my mother was affectionate and warm; my brother and I were on the same wavelength; and I was lucky that I was studying in high school. That was enough for me.

But ever since Kewal has been murdered, strange thoughts keep buzzing in my head. They keep coming to my mind inadvertently. And they don't occur to me in any clear sequence. They are even vague and out of focus. They just keep buzzing inside my skull which seems hollow after so much crying. I can't cry anymore.

Our father told us once that one of our forefathers used to dye Maharaja Ranjit Singh's turbans. The Maharaja was so pleased with their vibrant colours that he gave him a large *jageer,* a few acres of land. That is how the following generations drifted into farming. But the family kept multiplying and the land kept getting divided. My uncles still farmed their land, while my grandfather gave his fields to a sharecropper. That sharecropper's family cultivated our lands and gave us our fair share of wheat, rice, lentils and vegetables, which was a great help of course, because my father's salary was not enough to see us through school and then college.

I was in the final year of school when our father passed away. Kewal was still in B.A. first year. He wanted to give up his studies and take up a job but my mother said, 'No, you must fulfil your father's dream.' So he continued. Since I had nothing to do after school, I just waited for Kewal every evening. When he came home, he taught me whatever he had learnt during the day.

We were very close to each other.

And now he is no more. My life is a yawning abyss, and so is my mother's.

Why do people have to go on living even after they lose the will and desire to do so?

*

That night I had a strange premonition that a horrible danger was hovering over my head. These days I often get this feeling. A strange, nameless fear grips me. Two bloodthirsty eyes of a carnivorous animal glare at me through the darkness around.

What sort of danger can it be? Danger was a living, pulsating presence while Kewal was alive. Every morning, both my mother and

I struggled with the lumps in our throats when he left for college in the city nearby. It was only when he came home safe in the evening that the lumps dissolved.

But now that Kewal is gone, what sort of danger can threaten us? It has lost all its horror and relevance for us. There is no greater danger than death, and death has already visited this house.

Hearing the howling of dogs in the distance, I felt as if they were lamenting for us.

I got up and walked on my toes through the three rooms of the house. I got down on my knees, and peered under the cots. Only the shadows of the cots were discernible in the faint light of the one *diya* flickering in front of Kewal's portrait. These shadows had a sinister presence, and I felt they were threatening to pounce on me. I felt terrified, though the refrain: 'What danger? There can't be any more dangers. They have already killed Kewal. What else can happen?' kept humming in my head.

I came to the back of the house and stepped into the courtyard. In a corner, from the water-tap, a drop of water kept falling at regular intervals on the cemented patch where we clean the utensils and wash our clothes. In the eerie silence even a tiny drop of water can sound deafening.

Darkness can produce its own sinister horrors. The brass pitcher lying in a corner looked like a man sitting on his haunches, with his head between his knees. Someone could be hiding in the bucket even, or under the haystack, or behind the pile of firewood.

At the far end of the courtyard, near the back door which opens on to the back street, there is a small room in which we keep all the useless stuff, and also the wheat and potatoes and onions that our sharecroppers give us after every harvest. There are a number of old boxes too in which quilts and *durries* and *khes* are stuffed, and also lots of old clothes which nobody ever uses.

I hated these old, colourless wooden and tin boxes because they smelt of bygone ages and dead ancestors. But at this unearthly hour, during which people slept and grappled with their nightmares, and dogs kept a vigil and wailed, a few grief-torn people, like my mother and I, wandered like lost souls in the twilight zone between life and death, between sleep and wakefulness. People like us are neither alive nor dead, because both life and death are decisive, and all decisiveness had deserted us.

We were not even waiting, the way all sad people wait: for a better tomorrow, for the wheel of fate to turn, for a ray of bright sunshine to enter our lives! For us, everything was over.

Without thinking, I pushed open the door of this back room and peered into it. It was dark. I switched on the light. A zero-power bulb came to life. I was a bit surprised because I was almost sure that the bulb would have fused long ago. Nobody ever came to this room at night, except when some unexpected guests dropped in and we needed extra bedding. It was ages since anyone came to stay with us, especially after my father's death.

Moving listlessly in the room I was thinking of all these guestless years, when all of a sudden ... I received a rude shock which was like touching a naked electric wire.

I saw his eyes. They looked like the eyes of a wounded deer whose neck is caught in the powerful jaws of a tiger. Both death and fear of death seemed to be frozen in those eyes.

After the first rude shock, I realized that his eyes reflected pure innocence.

I tried to relate those eyes to his face, which looked tense with terror. Even his short curly beard was trembling with fear.

He was terrified of me, and I was afraid of him. Both of us stood still.

I felt my legs shaking under me. Who was he? How did he come to our house? What was he doing here? What did he want from us? Did he want to kill us? The way the others had killed Kewal!

And then I realized that he was clutching his leg with both hands. Blood was oozing out of a small, red, raw wound.

He whimpered,

'Water ... !'

*

He was wounded and was begging for water. These were the only two things that my mind registered clearly. Nothing else mattered.

I went to the kitchen and came back with a glass of water. My hand was probably shaking when he almost snatched the glass from me. Was I still afraid of him? I don't know. Perhaps, I was, even though I knew that he was at my mercy.

He gulped the water down in one go. I could hear the sound of gurgling in his throat. He emptied the glass and stretched his hand towards me. I again went to the kitchen, refilled it, and took it back to him. This time he drank slowly, and kept the half-emptied glass beside him.

He looked at me. Now he was a little relaxed. The naked terror in his eyes had receded giving way to a dark emptiness. A few purple dots of anger seemed to be floating in those two black pools of silence. But the anger was evidently not for me. He was angry at his own helplessness, at the open wound from which blood was still flowing.

'Don't be afraid, sister. Rest assured, I'll go away silently as soon as I can.'

He spoke, and the mountain of ice between us began to thaw. The lump of terror in my throat also softened. The throbbing fear in my ribs subsided.

I again went to the kitchen and filled a glass of milk from the earthen pot that my mother always kept on the slowly dying embers and hot ashes of dung cakes, throughout the night. He sipped it slowly, looked at me softly, and said, 'Do you have a piece of cloth to tie this wound with?'

I opened an old wooden box, took out Ma's old *dupatta* and handed it over to him. He wrapped it around the wound and tried to tie the edges into a knot. His hands were shaking. I sat beside him, caught hold of the edges and tied them into a double knot.

'It's a bullet wound,' he said softly.

'Bullet?' I shuddered.

'Yes, bullet. Those police dogs ...'

'Police?' I was in the grip of fear once again.

'No, don't misunderstand me, please. I am not a thief. Nor a smuggler. I ...'

'An extremist?' I tried to keep my voice from shaking, but the effort was beyond me.

'Extremist? Is it some kind of extraordinary species of mankind, *bibi*?' he smiled.

Suddenly his face contorted, his teeth clenched, and his jaws jammed. I could see anguish in his eyes. He clutched his leg, just above the wound, and doubled up over it.

I was feeling helpless.

'Go and sleep, bibi. Let the pain subside a little, and I'll leave.'

'You won't go anywhere.' I suddenly felt responsible for him. I almost ordered him, 'You are not going to leave in this condition.'

I got up, locked the room from outside, came back to my cot and lay down.

I was acutely aware of all the sounds coming from the street. The night rumbled on, moving slowly like a frightened black cat on its padded paws.

After a long, long time the day dawned. Almost terrified by the daylight that would soon crawl in, I got up and rushed to the backyard. I filled a small *lota* with water and unlocked his room. I heard him moaning softly, without making a noise, as if a shaft of solid air was slicing through the stillness in the room.

I said softly, 'Day is about to break. How will you manage to go out for your … ? Well, here's some water. Try to get up and I'll take you outside. Near the outer wall. I'll stand guard. Nobody passes this way at this hour.'

He bent double with pain as he got up. I held his arm, undid the bolt of the back door, and pointed to a place in the shadow of the wall outside. I kept the water jar near him, and with my back towards him, I spread out my veil like a protective tent.

I was like a hen, protecting her helpless, fledgling chick, because black kites and eagles were hovering in the sky above, searching for their prey with bloodthirsty eyes.

I felt like a mother protecting her wounded son. A flood of tenderness heaved gently in my breast.

I heard the splash of water after which he got up by holding on to the wall with one hand. I helped him get in, bolted the door, took him back to the room and made him sit behind the boxes. I took out a quilt, folded it and kept it under his wounded leg. I gave him two pillows and a khes to cover himself with.

In the morning two policemen came to our house. It was not unusual. Ever since Kewal had been murdered, police kept coming to our place on routine investigative rounds. But that day, seeing those two in police uniform, I panicked.

They said, 'Last night there was a minor encounter between a police patrol and a group of extremists on the outskirts of this village. You must have heard the firing.'

Yes, we had. But these days the sound of firing is a routine thing. It is a part of the familiar sounds emitted by the night: cicadas, frogs, dogs, and bullets.

They said, 'We suspect it was the same gang which murdered Kewal. In the crossfire nobody was killed. They escaped under cover of darkness. But we are sure that at least one of them was injured. We could clearly see the trail of blood leading into the village. He must be hiding somewhere. You shouldn't worry. We will nab him soon and unearth the mystery of Kewal's murder too. We won't let the bastard escape.'

'In fact, the trail of blood enters this very street and then ...,' said the other. 'But you shouldn't worry. Just keep the house properly bolted from inside. We're going to search each and every house.'

The words hit my ears like thunderbolt. Like a whirlwind they engulfed me, and I stood frozen near the door. I could hear the mad rush of my blood racing through my veins.

It was midday. The sun was like an angry eye looking down on earth. With my mother moving from one room to the other, I couldn't go to the room at the back. Ever since Kewal's death my mother has taken to roaming around aimlessly, as if she has lost something, she can't remember what, but has to find it nevertheless.

After eating, my mother sat down on her cot and opened the *Gita* in her lap. I knew the words would keep floating around, getting lost in the air, and she would keep seeing Kewal on the open page before her.

I had made four extra *rotis* for the boy in the backroom. I put some cooked brinjals and potatoes on the rotis, covered them with my *chunni*, and took them to him.

He looked younger in the daylight. He was lying there, with his head on the pillows, his eyes closed. His innocent face looked helpless, contorted with pain. His beard was a mere splash of light brown hair, short and curly. I was sure that under the curly hair, there would be a dimple in the middle of his chin.

I touched his elbow softly. He opened his eyes. Black pain floated in them. His eyelids were a little swollen and red. Perhaps, he had been crying in the darkness last night. He was hardly eighteen. Thinking of him crying didn't surprise me.

I extended the rotis towards him. He said, 'I'm not hungry.' He held his wounded leg with both his hands. He tried to stretch it and get up, but collapsed with pain.

'You have to eat even if you're not hungry,' I almost ordered him, the way you do with small children.

He held the rotis and started eating like an obedient child. I looked at the glass, it was empty. I went to the kitchen and brought him water.

He was eating silently. I saw that the cloth with which I had wrapped his wound last night, was soaked with black blood. On either side of the 'bandage', I could see his leg, swollen and red.

'It must be hurting like hell,' I said softly.

My tenderness touched him. His eyes were moist when he looked at me and said, 'Yes, the bullet is still inside.'

I shuddered. An ugly bullet, made of solid metal, concealed in the soft flesh of the leg, poisoning the blood! Visualising this horror, I experienced a strange painful sensation searing within me.

He needed medical treatment. But what sort of times were we living in, when getting medical help meant exposure to death!

For him, all the doctors and surgeons had become irrelevant because their instruments had rusted with the curse of these times.

I came out of the room and looked around.

In the backyard the afternoon sun slumbered. I walked across and entered the room where my mother was still looking blankly at the open pages of the *Gita*. I took out a soiled 50-rupee note from the small basket in which my mother kept needles and threads, covered my head with my chunni, and came out into the street.

I looked around, from one end of the street to the other. On the left, outside the grocery shop, three policemen sat on a long bench, engrossed in gossip.

I started walking the other way, came out of the street, and walked to the chemist's shop. This chemist used to be quite friendly with my father, the way people living in small villages usually are with each other. I said, '*Chachaji,* I need a packet of cotton wool and a bottle of Dettol, and some gauze too.' Though my voice was hoarse, I tried my best to sound natural.

The chemist, whom all of us called 'doctor', asked with concern, 'Is everything all right? I hope *bharjaiji* hasn't hurt herself.'

Everybody was particularly concerned about us after Kewal's death.

I said, 'No, nothing much. She just didn't see the grinding stone and knocked her foot against it.'

'Should I come home and bandage her foot?' he asked.

'No, it's nothing, really. I can do it myself. Don't worry, Uncle,' my voice shook as I said this.

He looked at me from behind his eyeglasses, and quietly handed over the bottle of Dettol, a packet of cotton wool, and rolls of bandages.

How will I carry all this?—I wondered, thinking of those three policemen sitting outside the grocer's shop in my street.

'Do you have a carry bag, Uncle?' I asked hesitantly.

He took out a plastic bag and stuffed everything into it.

I carried the bag to the grocer's shop nearby, bought a packet of salt and put it neatly over the other things, and walked back home.

The three policemen were still there, gossiping as usual.

❋

My mother had dozed off. I went to the room in the back courtyard, and unlocked it. He was moaning, bundled up with pain. I removed the dupatta from his wound. It was an ugly, blackish gash, swollen, with clots of blood encircling it. I soaked the cotton wool in Dettol, and as I started cleaning it, I was painfully reminded of a similar wound that I had seen on Kewal's back which didn't need any cleaning because he was already dead.

A black whirlwind was moving in mad circles inside my head. I was trying to push it back with all the force of my willpower. In my ears I could hear the buzz and beating of my own blood, but I was trying not to listen to its mad fury.

He was biting his lips, trying not to scream. When I kept a large pad of cotton wool soaked in the antiseptic lotion on his wound and wrapped a bandage around it, I could see a thousand black furrows of pain on his face. He was holding his leg in a firm grip with both hands. And his eyes were moist with tears of anguish that he was trying to hold back.

I felt like pulling his head onto my shoulder, patting it and saying softly to him, 'Cry, my child, cry. Cry out your pain. Don't push your tears back because they freeze inside, and become big rocks weighing your soul down.'

But I didn't. I couldn't say anything.

I went to the kitchen and brought him a glass of hot milk. I locked the room from outside and washed my hands with soap to remove the pungent odour of Dettol, but it lingered on in the pores of my skin.

I went to the kitchen and prepared tea. Took one glass to my mother, sat on my cot with the other one and started sipping.

I was oblivious of my surroundings. Only that black swollen wound kept floating before my eyes to be replaced sometimes by those three policemen gossiping out there in the street.

I don't know when I lay down and went to sleep.

Even in sleep, a part of me was wide awake, trying to catch any sound which might signal danger. I was keenly aware of the threat lurking around, ready to pounce on the person in there whose name I didn't know.

In my fitful sleep I saw vast deserts, frightened rabbits running for their lives and ferocious dogs chasing them, snarling, howling, panting, with their bare white teeth flashing, and their red tongues hanging from their black jaws.

*

It was the howling of dogs which made me get up with a start. I was soaked in cold sweat, frightened. Evening shadows were lurking ominously in the corners of the room. Mother was not on her cot, and outside in the dark the sound of barking in the distance was audible.

I got up and came to the backyard. Mother had lighted the fire in the kitchen and was looking at the leaping flames with her chin resting on her knees. There was a pan on the *chullah* in which *daal* was being cooked.

She sat there, unaware of me, unaware of the pan on the fire, lost in thought, deep down in the dark well of her pain.

And then she looked at me, trying to focus her thoughts, and said slowly, 'Do you have a headache? You slept for so long. It isn't good to sleep in the evening when day and night meet.'

Could anything worse happen to us than what already had? I wondered.

I silently looked towards the locked room at the back and said to my mother, 'You should rest now. I'll make the rotis.'

Ma pressed her knees with her hands, sighed, got up, and went out.

After serving my mother, I kept four rotis in a thali, put some daal in a bowl, poured piping hot butter on the daal, and took it to his room.

He was probably sleeping, his mouth slightly open, like a child. I touched his arm, it was hot. I put the thali down and touched his forehead. It was burning hot, and moist.

He didn't open his eyes. Every breath of his was a soft moan. I looked at his leg. The swelling had increased. Black blood had oozed out of the bandages.

Feeling dejected and helpless I came out and locked the door again.

I couldn't eat.

*

At midnight I again went to him. Opened the door and switched on the light. He was doubled up, bent over his leg. His helpless moans were heart rending. I touched his head. He didn't look at me.

The food was lying in the thali, untouched. A white layer of butter covered the daal.

I lifted his head and forced him to take some water. I don't know if he was aware of my presence or not, but he did gulp down a little water, and again bent over his leg.

Behind the old wooden and tin boxes which contained age-old abracadabra, he looked like a bundle of soiled clothes. And outside, all those people were looking for him.

Next day he was delirious with fever. Almost unconscious. He only took a few sips of water whenever I managed to go to him, lifted his head and touched his lips to the glass.

It was evening, and his fever was blazing. I soaked a towel with cold water and kept it on his head. A strange smell emanated from his wound. I changed his bandage.

With the cold, wet towel on his forehead, he opened his eyes. I gave him some hot milk. He sipped slowly and then said, almost in a whisper. 'I don't want to die here. If I do, how would you take my body out? *Bhain*, I have already been such, a great bother. I don't want to put you to any more trouble.'

I felt like crying. I placed my hand on his head, the way mothers bless their young ones when they go to school for the first time. And came out.

I looked around. Where could I sit and pour out all the pain flooding my soul?

Just then, there was a loud knock on the outer door, the door which opens onto the main street. I was startled. My mother asked irritably, 'Who can it be at this unearthly hour? They should know there are two lonely women here.'

I went and opened the door. Outside stood the same two policemen who had come the previous morning. They said politely, '*Bibi*, we know we needn't search your house, but every time our dogs sniff the drops of blood, they stop here. Can we take a look inside?"

I was terrified. Real, naked terror was churning inside my belly. I said, '*Ma* has just dozed off after eating her food. You know she hardly sleeps. If you can ... if ... after an hour or so ... perhaps?'

'Don't worry. Let *Maji* sleep. We'll come back after an hour. There is no hurry. But we hope you won't mind our coming in at night.'

'No, it doesn't matter. You are like my brothers. You have been looking after us after Kewal's death,' I said softly.

They left.

'Who was it?' asked Ma.

'Some policemen. Wanted to search this house. They are looking for someone, and they think he is hidden in one of the houses in this street.'

'Have you bolted the door properly?' asked Ma anxiously. I assured her that I had, and she lay back on her cot.

On tiptoe I quietly walked to the back room.

Perhaps he had also heard the knock at the outer door. How could he, in the condition he was in? I can't understand it even today.

He was aware. His face was alert and his eyes full of terror.

'Who was it?' he asked.

'Policemen. Wanted to search the house. They'll come back after an hour.' I wanted to offload my entire burden. He had to know. The moment had finally arrived when he should know.

He immediately made up his mind. How can one arrive at such decisions in a fraction of a second? A decision that would probably land him straight into the jaws of death!

'I must leave,' he said, and staggered up.

I didn't ask him to stay. I couldn't. Both of us knew that we had reached a dead-end. All roads were blocked. Escape now was next to impossible.

The danger lurking outside for the last two days was about to cross the threshold and enter.

With his face contorted with pain he tried to take a step forward. With clenched teeth biting into his lips, he took another staggering step. And then another. And stepped out of the room.

I opened the back door. Stepping out into the street, he halted for a moment, a very brief moment, and looked at me. So many different emotions were mingled in the dark pools of his eyes—affection, gratitude, and also the shadow of death. There was so much more for which I can't find any words. Human language hasn't yet found words for all those other emotions floating in the dark pools of those eyes.

I only know that his eyes, and all those silent emotions in them, will haunt me all my life. I will never be rid of them. They will come and nestle close to me in all the silent moments of my life.

He went out. I bolted the door from inside and stood rooted

there trying to hear the muted sound of his departing footsteps, trying to smell the danger in the air.

Suddenly the dogs barked. Many of them. They were barking in a mad fury. And then, the sound of bullets pierced the stillness of the night outside and blew my soul to shreds.

I am telling you the truth. Believe me. I didn't hear his cry. Only heard the sound of bullets, loud enough to rip the earth open. But no human cry.

I could also hear echoes of heavy shoes running up and down the street.

*

Ma was probably in that azure zone of half-slumber when the body sleeps but all the senses remain awake and alert. Perhaps, she was seeing Kewal in her dream, floating in the twilight zone of no-man's land that lies between sleep and wakefulness.

She heard the sound of bullets and got up.

Abruptly, in a frenzy she rushed towards the front door, opened it with a thud and ran barefoot into the dark street outside, crying in a heart-rending wail, 'Don't kill. Don't kill him. Don't kill my Kewal. Don't kill my little one. Don't fire at my innocent little baby, don't fire at him! He is my only son, my Kewal!'

With her arms raised, her dupatta trailing behind her, her hair dishevelled, she ran barefoot on the naked bricks of the street, begging, imploring the darkness, 'Don't kill him! Don't kill my little one!'

Translated by the author

India

Laila's Call

SUKRITA PAUL KUMAR

(Dedicated to Mahmoud Abu Hashhash)

O Qais, the eternal lover,
If only you could come out
Step out of your mystical yearnings
Walk out of your longings frozen in verses
And see your Laila, hear her pounding heart
Feel her lamenting soul

If only, Qais, history could release you
And geography could bind you
You, camouflaged in clouds of love
Travelling through time and space
Century after century
Blowing images of Laila into caves and tombs

You fettered in words and epitaphs

Laila stuck forever on the potter's wheel
Rotating between the cups of your palms
Your fingers chiselling and shaping her forever

But Qais, Laila is whole
As the complete circle of the full moon
A planet amongst planets

Your poems are the gurgling waves of the ocean
Leaping to reach the skies
And withdrawing merely with the reflection
Tired and limp on the surface of the placid waters

Love is a blessing
Says Laila, not a curse
My Majnu, my Qais,
Says she, come to me,
Fear not death,

Your wish *for* immortality
Keeps us apart.

India

Silence

TEJI GROVER

This silence
spoken out
would grow denser.

Peels, tossed away in the wind
Inside, the fruit ripening with juice.

On the screen of the eye
around the flame
Wavelike, a rising breath
should sweep off my words

There, where the ebbing waters
ferry breath for the fish

Let my words be there
in the retreating wave
where fish rise, leaping for breath
to the surface …

Let the words be just those words of mine—
spoken out—
the silence would grow denser

Translated by Arlene Zide & the poet

India

The Stigma

PRATIBHA RAY

Sarami was seized with a shameful bout of hysteria yet again. She clenched her fists, flung her legs about obscenely, rolled her head and yanked out her hair, shook her body and stuck out her tongue, threw her sari off her breasts. One moment she lay limp, exhausted, her eyes closed and the next she was up, fiercely rolling her eyes, hissing like a snake and frothing at the mouth. It took four or five stout young fellows to restrain her. Alternately she laughed like a shameless hussy and wept like a wretched waif. Sad like a silent grey afternoon one minute and riotous like a crazy sunset the next. Then the spell was over just as suddenly as it had begun.

Except for these periodic bouts, Sarami was every inch the typical shy bride, sensitive like a mimosa creeper. She never revealed herself, neither her moon-like face from behind her veil, nor her mind. The ankle chains she wore on her reddened feet tinkled ever so faintly when she tiptoed around. She was so gentle, so serene, so unruffled that she often resembled a sculpted image. It was of course quite another matter that despite her damnest efforts to smother her youthful figure under layers of clothes, her voluptuousness was apparent. Her brother-in-law devoured her with his eyes; even Sudam, the young unmarried nephew of her husband, unabashedly ogled her, mentally mapping her exciting contours. When a lovely flower blooms in somebody's garden, it belongs to the garden owner but don't others get to feast their eyes on it and inhale its fragrance? The same held true for Sarami: she might have been Raghu Tiadi's wife but there was no earthly reason why others could not appreciate her beauty or flirt with her a little. It was accepted social behaviour that a young brother-in-law could banter and take some verbal liberties with the new bride in the house. Even if Raghu Tiadi didn't like the idea, he would have to put up with it. To think that in the beginning he had even tried to shield his wife from Sudam, his nephew, the orphan of his own elder brother! Hadn't he raised him since he was a little boy? If Raghu's first wife had borne him a son instead of a daughter the son would have been the same age as Sudam! What evil stars! The wife passed away in childbirth and the girl grew up, got married and had three girls herself. It had dealt a blow to Raghu's pride to be a grandfather to not one but three young girls. His second wife was a shade better: she bore three sons, but God alone knows what sins she had committed that she and her sons should have died when the evil goddess of smallpox visited the family. Sudam's father too fell to the scourge. Raghu's stars were bright, maybe he had the benefit of accumulated merit from previous births; he managed to claw back from the jaws of death, though losing an eye and developing a lame leg in the process. And of course plenty of tell-tale pockmarks on his handsome face. Young Sudam and his mother were away at his maternal uncle's place and had thus escaped unscathed. The mother had lived a long life and had died only two years ago.

True, Raghu Tiadi had lost an eye and his good looks, as well as his erect gait, but he had not altogether been robbed of his manhood. He had the grave responsibility of preserving the family line from extinction. Sudam, already on the threshold of adulthood, could have been trusted to keep the line alive but Raghu Tiadi couldn't bear the thought that his name would be completely wiped out. No wonder he had seriously toyed with the idea of a third marriage. His well-wishers too had egged him on, and a search was mounted to hunt for young brides for both the uncle and the nephew. Regardless of the difference in age both wanted young girls and nubile young things were not exactly in short supply. But there weren't many from respectable, well-to-do families. And what did 'sweet sixteens' from poor families amount to—nothing! Sudam had made it clear that he had no qualms about tying the knot with a girl short on looks but long on dowry. Paragons of virtue and beauty from humble homes could try their luck elsewhere. Why take on the eminently avoidable responsibility of providing food, clothing, jewellery, children and conjugal bliss to a girl from a poor family! There was only one way out for a good-looking girl from a poor family: she could escape the curse of spinsterhood by hoping to be accepted as a second or third wife of some doddering old man.

When the matchmakers brought a proposal for Sarami, both Sudam and Raghu Tiadi went to inspect the prospective bride. Sudam took a shine to the girl but not to her father, who was as poor as a church mouse. Flowers and fruit were all such a man could offer as dowry. Agree to the match? No way. The girl had great looks, but so what? Her father didn't have enough money, he could never come to the son-in-law's rescue in his hour of need, and what's a father-in-law if he couldn't do that? Neither Sudam nor his uncle could give the go-ahead.

Sarami's father, who was blessed with not one but three millstones around his neck (grown girls were, proverbially, worse than fire; one never knew when they'd burn the good name of the family to cinders), grasped Raghu Tiadi's hands and begged: 'Gosain, you're a big man. You command respect in ten neighbouring villages. Surely you do not lack for anything that you too will look for a dowry to fill your house! Please accept my daughter as your wife and I'll remain eternally grateful to you. You will be doing a good turn, for which the gods will reward you. My daughter has strong stars in her horoscope and she will bring prosperity to whichever home she goes.'

Raghu Tiadi was not easy to melt—he had heard enough spiels and sales pitch before—but a lingering look at the exquisite face of the girl touched a chord in his heart. On a sudden impulse he consented, and the wedding date was fixed on the spot. Sarami's eyes briefly met Sudam's. There was a flutter of gratitude in hers but all Sudam's piercing gaze held was the hint of an erotic welcome.

'Aunt,' he gushed, only a few days after the wedding, 'aren't you breathtakingly beautiful! The aunts before you were not equal to your toes! Uncle is one lucky man!' The new aunt had looked into the nephew's eyes: was he being facetious? A bitter question flashed through her mind: What about your new aunt's luck? Or are girls from poor families not supposed to have any? But her face remained as serene and her lips as tightly shut as ever. It was her first lesson in deceit in her husband's place and in the days ahead she would need it aplenty. She would have to learn to stifle her innate candour, honesty of opinion and easy and open manners. She was an aunt to Sudam and must continue as such, and as nothing else, in the young man's eyes. He could afford to behave like a lecher; society wouldn't condemn a man as much as a woman. One little scandal and Sarami would be handed a one-way ticket to purgatory; no amount of penance would absolve her of her crime.

Sudam married shortly afterwards and got a fat dowry. He kept it all but sent his wife back to her parents before the year was out. Obviously she wasn't as handsome as the dowry: she was toothy, squint eyed, pitch dark and loud mouthed. 'Display one girl and palm off another? They dare do this to me?' was what Sudam alleged. God alone knew the truth. Not long afterwards he married again. His second wife was not half as beautiful as Sarami, although in a manner of speaking, quite nicely put together, but that hardly mattered anyway, for a few days after the wedding she drowned in the family pond. No one knew whether it was an accident or suicide. Evidently Sudam wasn't lucky in marriage. Nonetheless there was no dearth of girls, and the young man was still in his prime.

Meanwhile it warmed Raghu Tiadi's heart no end that his nephew had taken to his wife regardless of her aloofness and unmistakable display of annoyance. Of late she had badgered her husband one time too many: 'Why don't you break with Sudam? Just because I'm around to work myself to death and keep the house, the fellow doesn't seem to bother whether his wives live or die, stay or leave. I can't be expected to look after him forever. In the future our own family will grow ...'

Raghu Tiadi turned a deaf ear. Weren't women proverbial house-wreckers? Why start worrying before the family has expanded? Cross that bridge only when you come to it. Moreover Sudam wouldn't be without a wife for long. His horoscope indicated a bad patch for three years but after that everything would be all right. Split with a nephew? No way, a nephew was as good as a son. The trouble was that Sarami was not prepared to look upon Sudam as one. Petty, jealous, selfish woman! Take Sudam. He never complained about his aunt. On the contrary, her name was on his lips all the time. Ten words from him would fetch a monosyllabic reply from her. Never once did she pull the sari off her head and show him her moon-face. Why be so stiff, so standoffish? After all she was his aunt, wasn't she, although some seven or eight years younger? And wasn't an aunt the same thing as a mother? Besides Sudam was such a help. What would Raghu Tiadi do without him? He was freed from everyday cares and anxieties only because of this young man who looked after the land and farming, the farmhands and harvests; he made it possible for the old man to devote his time to worship, adjudication meetings, teaching Sanskrit, and reciting scriptures. Raghunath Tripathy, alias Raghu Tiadi, was a learned person who had a name in society; people stepped back when he passed by. Wasn't Sarami a lucky woman to have become his wife? What did it matter whether she was the third or the fourth? She must thank the good karma of her previous births.

A woman's good fortune was judged by the social standing of her husband, the amount of jewellery she could laden herself with, the quality of food she ate, the weave of the clothes she wore—her state of mind, happiness, emotional fulfillment, wishes all counted for nothing. Better that way, otherwise poor Sarami would have chosen to drown herself. She had learnt not to reflect, not to mull things over, not to dwell on her condition; she had painfully acquired the habit of not thinking too much about herself. The abyss of darkness within her was fathomless and frightening. Sometimes she wondered what would happen to her if she lost her looks and turned into an ugly toad. Anything could happen. As long as she lived with her parents a fire had been in her stomach, but ever since she moved into her husband's home it had moved to her heart. The fire in the belly could be extinguished with food, but neither food nor clothes nor jewellery could douse the flames in her heart. On the contrary, the tongues leapt higher and higher. Sarami would gaze at herself, her beautiful body in an exquisite sari and bedecked with jewellery and her face would darken with anguish. She had everything, yes she had everything she wanted. Raghu Tiadi never denied his wife the good things. To say that she was virtually like a queen was no exaggeration. Nobody ever caught Raghu Tiadi being harsh to her. As the saying goes, he kept her on a pedestal. If despite all this she wasn't happy, she had no one but herself to blame. Admittedly Raghu Tiadi was a lot older and had lost his looks because of smallpox, but that didn't mean he was any less a man. Why, he was in the pink of health, his manliness undiminished. Although he favoured his lame leg, the ground literally shook when he walked. His emergence from his doorway—lines of shining sandal paste across the wide forehead beneath his bald dome—reminded many of Lord Jagannath's pahandi during his ceremonial chariot ride. He had successfully impregnated his young wife not once but twice, and in quick succession too; the blighted woman had only herself to blame for the miscarriages; they were no reflection on Raghu Tiadi's masculinity. Yes, yes, Sarami was squarely to blame. Particularly when there was no comfort under the sun that she lacked—she had plenty of food, clothes, jewellery! Perhaps all that had made her too lazy to even hold on to the foetus in her womb. Whereas her own poor mother, waging a daily battle against hunger and poverty, had ritually delivered babies every second year until she finally dried up. Sarami, on the other hand, had become too pampered in her husband's home. Even she herself sometimes tended to agree with this view. How she wished she had had two or three children! Then there would have been no free time to look into the depths of her soul. Everyday cares would have ensured that life pass faster and the hungry looks, the suggestive gestures, the audacious flirtations of her brother-in-law Dibakar and nephew-in-law Sudam wouldn't have troubled her so much.

To think one time she had nearly married Dibakar! The match had come unstuck at the last moment because her father could not scrape up the two thousand rupees Dibakar had demanded. The same fellow who had rejected her for the blessed money was now so full of love for her, the scoundrel!

But no matter how hard she steeled herself, how rudely she behaved towards Dibakar and Sudam, she couldn't hide from herself that she secretly relished the advances of the young wastrels. Sometimes when she served Sudam food, the fellow made a point of grasping her hands to say 'Enough, enough, aunt!' and although she jerked her hands free and scolded him sternly 'Why do you have to grab my hands? It's enough if you speak. I can still hear very well', she did feel giddy and delirious at the touch, her face aflame, her heart pounding away like a husking paddle. 'My dear lovely aunt,' Sudam would flirt outrageously, 'I'm forced to hold your lovely hands because I'm afraid my words don't ever enter your beautiful ears!' Sarami would shriek, a flaming snake of desire slithering inside her entrails, 'There's God above, Sudam. He's watching. You're going over the limits of decency. An aunt is like a mother.' Sudam would burst into a guffaw: 'You wouldn't have become my aunt if your poor father had been able to scrape up a good dowry. Don't think I didn't notice the look in your eyes the day Uncle and I turned up at your place to see you. Don't tell me you didn't feel attracted toward me, that you didn't find me desirable. Listen, ours is a quiet household and there's no one around to spy on us. It's an open secret that you don't get enough physical satisfaction from your husband.'

Turning crimson as much from anger as from contempt, Sarami would rush into her bedroom, slam the door and throw herself on the bed, sobbing convulsively. A wild desire to spit at Sudam in the face would seize her. When it was a question of marriage the fellow hadn't thought twice before rejecting her, but now he was so eager to start an affair! He might come to no harm but what would happen to her? Society would denounce her as an immoral bitch, a whore, a sinner. But who could she tell all this to? Once or twice she had tried to tell her husband ever so subtly, but the old man had retorted, fixing her with a hard, one-eyed stare, 'Don't ever talk against our innocent Sudam. If he wanted to have you for himself he could have had got you on a platter. What was there to prevent him from marrying you? Remember, I decided to step in only after he had turned you down. How can you insinuate these things against him?'

More than Sudam it was Raghu Tiadi who was responsible for her unenviable plight. He had damned her by his kindness. Surely her father could have found a young man for her, even if only from a nondescript family. She would no doubt have had a tougher life, maybe she would have had to work like a donkey, but anything was better than the kind of deprivation she was condemned to. Raghu Tiadi could give her the moon but not the physical bliss and pleasure for which she ached and ached no end. Their cohabitation was and would always remain an act of deceit, a sham, a pain. On the other hand, although with one part of her mind she hated Sudam and Dibakar, with another she feasted her eyes on their handsome, muscular physiques. A stray touch sent her pulse racing wildly, her heart beating furiously. Sometimes when Dibakar playfully tugged at the end of her sari she was scared she might swoon; she could hardly speak, she stuttered, stammered, became tongue tied. True, she was able to fend off their advances but could she dam the surging tides of desire and passion in her heart? When her marriage with Raghu Tiadi was being finalized, her parents should have realized that the man was old enough to be her father and could give her no physical satisfaction. But did they give it a thought? Raghu Tiadi too should have given it one. But did he? All of society should have protested against the mismatch. But did it? And now there were the likes of Dibakar and Sudam hovering around her to take full advantage of it. How they ogled her and propositioned her at every turn! Leave alone the most virtuous woman, if you work on a goddess ceaselessly, sooner or later she'll give in—it's as simple as that. In fact, the deeper the need the faster the opposition ended, sweeping aside the barricades of taboos society artfully clamped on relationships between a sister-in-law and a brother-in-law, an aunt and a nephew, and between cousins. Swept away like dry leaves in a torrent. Hunger made a person lose all sense of morality, drove him to beg crumbs from any source, compelled him to leftovers on the sly. No matter what little saints, holy men, Sati Savitris people posed as, deep inside they were tormented souls on fire. Hungry, tormented souls, driven by lust.

There were examples galore, many of them from that very village. Similar events might well have occurred elsewhere, in other villages as well. Nothing under the sun can remain forever under wraps. Yet the ones who ate the forbidden food nonchalantly wiped their lips and continued to pretend they were holier-than-thou, purer than the sacred waters of the Ganges, more sacrosanct than the consecrated prasad of the gods. Many clandestine affairs were embarked upon. Take the relationship between a man and his wife's sister, for example, or between a woman and her husband's brother, or between a woman and her god-brother. On the outside it was all very prim and proper, very correct, with just a whiff of flirtation maybe but nothing discordant, displeasing to the eyes, but inside it was all body. Something society was only too well aware of. At times the body drove one so crazy that he or she broke even bigger taboos. Perhaps, in the ultimate analysis, there was only one relationship which remained beyond the pale of corruption—the relation between a mother and her child. Everything else could prove rotten, even the relation between a father and a daughter, oh the shame of it! Man was nothing if not an animal underneath his clothes. Not long ago in this neighbourhood one wretched girl had chosen to hang herself because of the persistent attentions of her own father. There was a clandestine affair between a widowed aunt and her nephew which produced a child, whose dead body was discovered under the screwpine bushes at the edge of the village. In another incident, a man split open the skull of his brother because of the brother's carryings-on with his wife. For many a woman the loving attention of their devoted god-brothers had taken the sting out of their long separations from their husbands, who had to remain away from home on work. There were many, many more instances. But not a ripple on the surface—all was very placid, fine, within bounds.

Sarami was not the only one of her kind in the village—there were quite a few second and third wives, and none of them badly off either; in fact, they lived quite happily with their decrepit husbands, who were also dark and ugly in the bargain. How outrageously they flaunted their clothes, jewellery, authority and offspring! But were they really happy? Didn't they have regrets? How was it that not a shadow of their internal turmoil showed on their faces? How did they manage to look so serene, calm, collected? What were they made of—flesh and blood, or wood, stone and metal? Where had they put their minds—in a cave? And shut the mouth of the cave with a slab of stone? Did their bodies clamour for nothing besides food, clothes and jewellery? That was hard to accept. Why, Sarami was afraid that her mind and body were ready to betray her at the slightest provocation. How her mind yearned, hungered, lusted! Were there any tricks to wish one's mind away?

If only she could ask those women on the quiet, 'Do you really find the social canons as sacred as the scriptures? Don't you ever feel tempted to break them? Don't you ever feel tormented? How do you manage to put on such serene expressions? If you are above all torment, what's the secret?' But she knew she could never bring herself to ask these questions. She could do so only at the risk of revealing herself, rendering herself vulnerable to tongue-wagging. The whole village would be abuzz with gossip: Sarami's got a filthy mind; all she ever thinks of is sex; she can't be too far from the path of adultery and infidelity. Without committing any wrong she would be roundly condemned as a whore, a sinner and an immoral woman, her reputation in tatters. Just as society sometimes dismissed the truth as idle gossip it could seize a rumour and hammer it into a truth. Truth and rumour were like two sides of the same coin, and how quickly both travelled through the air! Better to keep her thoughts to herself. Thank God, thoughts were invisible. What total chaos there would have been otherwise! Would it ever have been possible to maintain even one perfect relationship, be it between a man and his wife or between a sister-in-law and a brother-in-law, or between cousins? All of society would be turned on its head. The flaming red vermilion dot on a woman's forehead was only a facade; she sinned enough in her mind to be damned to perdition until the end of eternity.

Sarami's self-flagellation often left her mind lacerated and badly bloodied. Her conscience was like a shark-tail whip—sharp, thorny, stinging. Ultimately that was what kept an affair away, though starting one or even several at the same time would have been terribly easy. A lonely house, the quiet afternoons; a deserted back yard, the dark evenings. She could get as many men as she wanted. A tiny nod from her and droves of brothers-in-law, nephews-in-law, uncles-in-law, stiff-lipped village elders, pontificating priests, stern-faced guardians of morals, men of high principles would have descended on her back yard, barnyard, pond-bank, cowshed, seeking trysts; and no one would have been the wiser. They could come and go, each at his appointed hour, without bumping into one another. There wouldn't have been a blot on their reputation. Not a blot on Raghu Tiadi's either. And of course Sarami's virtue would be left as dazzlingly bright as ever. Everything would continue smoothly, just as the hidden lives of all others did. But who prevented her? Who stopped her from crossing the strait of morality and fidelity? Sometimes she suspected that even her revered lord and master too was encouraging her to stray from the straight and narrow path. Why else did he leave a young and beautiful wife alone in the house under the care of a virile young nephew and stay away for days on end on the pretext of arbitrating disputes, giving scholarly advice and what not? Didn't a worldly-wise man like him know the consequences? Sudam might be his nephew, his blood relation, but he was nothing to Sarami. A little change in the script and the young hound could well have become her husband. A towering rage would possess her at times—a rage directed as much against herself as against her parents, her husband, society, the gods, everyone; her tortured soul sometimes taunted her to go whoring around to her heart's content. But a stern voice from within would stop her—what was it, her ego, her samskara, her notions of self-respect, her ideals of perfect womanhood? Adultery, she knew, was like a bowl of borrowed curry—good enough only for a gulp or two, it could never amount to a square meal. It would never fully sate her appetite, but leave her reputation in the mud. Even if it remained under wraps, she would never be able to hold her head high the rest of her life, forever ashamed to face herself.

But those who erred the most, those who made a profession of seducing and bedding women other than their wives, were the first to vilify an erring woman: 'There goes the adulterous whore, pity her poor husband!' Sarami could never in her dreams bring herself to be reviled by these lowlifes. Even Sudam, who never ceased his broad hints, was scared of her. One frown from her petrified him into a block of wood. If she gave in to the temptations of her flesh even once, this very same Sudam would start treating her like a doormat. Once he was past the first flush of the fling he would seize every opportunity to rub her infidelity in. Life would become intolerable.

In fact, although her physical craving was as deep as an ocean, her mental resolve was as hard as a mountain. One pitted against the other in a no-holds-barred fight; no quarter given or expected. Sarami was a battle-scarred ground.

Just as the molten fire in the womb of the earth sometimes flares—the fiercer the fire the greater the intensity of the tremor—and breaks free, spitting smoke, lava and ash, burying green vegetation, ruining nature, underlining its own ugliness, so too the repressed sexual desires smouldering within Sarami would sometimes erupt like a volcano. It was then that she went into sobbing hysterics, uncontrollably, unpredictably. Raghu Tiadi, with his slack, ageing muscles and slothful manhood, completely failed to rein her in and would steal away like a thief into the farthest corner of his verandah, subdued, crestfallen, morose, his copper-coloured face turning bitter black, ruing the day he had wedded a girl who was to bring him shame one day.

When Sarami was in the grip of hysteria, even the entire womenfolk of the neighbourhood could not curb her. It took five or six stout, strong-bodied hunks to pin her to the ground, their eager hands groping, probing, squeezing, caressing, assuaging her body. After the spell passed, she would sit up, chastened, her face back behind her veil, biting her tongue in regret. Much as her blood boiled at the sight of the lusty young fellows crowding around her like vultures around a carcass, she had only herself to blame for making a spectacle of herself. What evil spirit had gotten into her and prodded her into such a shameless show!

In the beginning Raghu Tiadi and the relatives thought that perhaps an evil spirit had temporarily possessed Sarami or a sorcerer had cast a spell on her. Some said it could be acute stomach ache or some kind of extreme physical pain. But Sarami didn't respond to any cure—neither medicine nor exorcism. The doctors proved as helpless as the exorcists. In the end, people came to only one conclusion: 'The girl is shamming! Can't you see how quickly her pain vanishes once four or six young men hold her down? What does that mean? She's dying for you-know-what, the bitch, the immoral bitch! Poor Raghu Tiadi, he brought shame on himself by marrying a third time. But a wife who isn't satisfied with her lawfully wedded husband, be he old, ugly or pockmarked, is a whore to the core.'

Sarami couldn't prevent tongues from wagging. The only way out was to stop having hysterical fits, but that was something over which she had no control. The bouts came over her with embarrassing regularity, sometimes three or four times a month, in spite of having hardened her mind to stone. The stronger her resolve, the more determined her efforts to avert her eyes from men who made eyes at her, the more intense her afflictions. The very young men she kept at bay were the ones to feel, fondle, caress and squeeze her back to her senses. Could she ever tell them the truth? Why couldn't she keep her mind in check? Why was the mind so devious?

Time passed—weeks, months, years, decades; and Sarami's afflictions lessened and then suddenly disappeared altogether. She became normal. Her life became normal. In due course she became a mother, then a mother-in-law, and finally a grandmother. But the scandal of her youthful disgrace was not entirely forgotten or forgiven.

Sometimes when there were quarrels, the relatives and neighbours did not shy away from rubbing it in. Sarami couldn't answer back, for she indeed had had that horrible disease when she was newly married.

*

The other day when the young second wife of old Manu Rath was wallowing in the grip of hysteria, the whole village turned up to witness the drama. Four or five hefty young fellows were told to hold her down. That's what she needs, the immoral bitch, people openly commented. Poor Manu Rath's fair name was in the mud.

Sarami, old, bent, shrivelled, stood a little straighter, as if to get a kink out of her back, and looked around. She knew them—the ones who had their saris over their heads and easy judgements on their eager lips. She knew them all inside out, the depth and extent of their chastity and fidelity, or rather the lack of it. Gathered here to castigate Manu Rath's wife, eh? That was a crime in Sarami's eyes. If it was a crime on the part of a young woman not to be satisfied with her old, decrepit husband, it was a bigger crime to expose her sad failing in public.

'Listen you all!' She faced the crowd, her brittle voice catching from rage. 'The young woman here is suffering from an abominable affliction. Pity her by all means, but give her the respect she deserves. Praise her for her conviction, for she didn't give up the principles of chastity and fidelity and rush to seek solace in clandestine affairs. That's why the fire within her drives her crazy sometimes. There are many women present here who took the easy way out to douse their fires, but not this poor girl. She did not want to open her doors to other men and keep pretending she was as virtuous as a Sita or a Savitri. You dare denounce her just because she didn't? Come on, ladies, come, come my pretties, my beauties, come and swear on the heads of your husbands and sons that not a single dirty thought ever flitted across your minds!'

She paused and added, 'Society is cruel to women. Like cattle, girls are given away to old men against their wishes. They have no say in the selection of their mates. Why? Don't women have minds? Are they all body and no mind? Have they been made only to eat, work and bear children? Yes, the body can be satisfied, but not the mind. And a dissatisfied mind can never extinguish the fire raging within. So in the end it's society which compels a woman to acts of immorality. A few who decide not to fall from their convictions convulse occasionally like this girl here. All you Sitas, all you Savitris, all you virtuous whores—have you no pity that you dare assemble here to castigate this poor little thing? Why are you so eager, so enthusiastic to witness her shameful plight? Get going. Go away. Leave before I give out all your dirty little secrets. Do you think old Sarami doesn't know what each of you has been up to?'

The women were hushed. The contempt in Sarami's old withered face was as dark and dense as their hidden sins.

The poor young wife of Manu Rath lay like a wick burnt from end to end—alone, away from the crowd, aloof as it were from society itself. Sarami hobbled over to her and sat down by her side. With her dry, decrepit, wrinkled hands she gently wiped the stains of the stigma from the forehead of the young woman. But could she be rid of a stigma for a sin she had never committed in the first place?

Translated by K.K. Mohapatra, Leelawati Mohapatra & Sudhansu Mohanty

Pakistan

The Grass Is Really Like Me

KISHWAR NAHEED

The grass is also like me
it has to unfurl underfoot to fulfil itself
but what does its wetness manifest:
a scorching sense of shame
or the heat of emotion?

The grass is also like me
As soon as it can raise its head
the lawnmower,
obsessed with flattening it into velvet,
mows it down again.
How you strive and endeavour
to level woman down too!
But neither the earth's nor woman's
desire to manifest life dies.
Take my advice: the idea of making a footpath was a good one.
Those who cannot bear the scorching defeat of their courage
are grafted on to the earth.
That's how they make way for the mighty
but they are merely straw not grass
—the grass is really like me.

Translated by Rukhsana Ahmad

Pakistan

Who Am I?

Kishwar Naheed

I am not that woman selling socks and shoes

I am the one you needed to bury alive
to feel fearless as the wind again
For you never knew
that stones can never suppress a voice.

I am the one you hid beneath
the weight of traditions
For you never knew
that light can never fear pitch darkness.

I am the one from whose lap you picked flowers
and then poured flames and thorns instead
For you never knew
that chains cannot hide the fragrance of flowers.

In the name of modesty
you bought and sold me
For you never knew
that Sohni* cannot die braving the river on a fragile pot of clay.

Translated by Rukhsana Ahmad

* A famous Punjabi legend. Sohni would cross the River Chenab on a baked clay pot every night to meet her lover. This pot was substituted by her sister-in-law for an unbaked one, causing her to drown.

Pakistan

To Be or Not to Be

ZAHEDA HINA

Darkness had spread itself over the trees, descended into the scent *Raat ki Rani*, mingled with the cold of the air.

I was feeling tired out sitting in the smoke-filled room. My shins down to the soles of my feet were saturated with fatigue. This is why I apologized to my husband and his friends and walked barefoot on the cool verandah floor.

All the windows of the drawing-room were open and shreds of light were scattered on the verandah floor. This reminded me of a childhood game when we would frolic, jumping over these bright spots and any of us who stepped on one was declared the fool and had to hop on one leg to catch his or her scampering companions. In the mêlée all the shreds of light were over and our shrieks filled all the dark corners.

That night when I was walking barefoot in the verandah it felt as if the drawing-room windows had swallowed everything up and then spewed it out.

I stood rooted to the spot. I caught sight of my husband turning on the stereo switch. The screaming voice of 'Boney M' rose into the air … Ra Ra Rasputin. I stared into the room in fear. There were four of them inside, blind drunk, laughing uproariously. On the bookshelf facing me there was a photograph of a hillock with base white stones. One side of the hillock had been sliced to look like a wall. In the wall there was a gate with iron bars, heavily locked. Beyond the gate was an arched tunnel, leading to a narrow dark cave, and beyond it was eternity and an unending sleep that distinguished between the living and the dead.

I was also in this picture, holding on to one of the bars, peering into the tunnel, facing the cave with my back to the camera. And next to this picture was a bronze statue, the statue of the prisoner in the cave. This statue I had bought from the same city. When I had this photograph taken and bought this statue I had never imagined that a night would come when for a moment a man would look at this photograph and say something as I heard it, and darkness would swallow up all the fragments of light. My gaze wandered and came to rest on a TV set opposite the book case. On the TV cabinet stood a military decoration in a black frame, Only a few weeks earlier my husband had been given this award for meritorious services.

This moment was now congealed inside me like an eternity. And what gave rise to it was the voice of my husband's friend. 'This photo with the steel bars, what does it stand for?' And my husband replied, 'This is the prison cell of the old philosopher who spent thirty days and thirty nights here waiting for his cup of poison.' My husband's friend guffawed, 'What a contradiction of symbols your darling wife has brought together, the old philosopher's statue and prison cell on the one hand and your military decoration on the other!'

'Hush!' said my husband, 'if my wife comes to hear about it there will be hell to pay.' His voice seemed to be coming from another planet.

'Are you trying to tell me that your dear wife doesn't know anything about your job?' The drunken voice said.

'No. She doesn't know a thing.'

'But she was present at the award-giving ceremony.'

'Yes she was but she knows nothing about the background of this award or the nature of my duties.'

And the man who said it was dearer to me than life itself. They kept on talking and complimented my husband for crushing a movement I had been attached to since adolescence. The black framed decoration was in front of my eyes and so was the face of a man with whom I had discussed problems of history and literature for hours together, who loved the arts, and was an ardent student of the philosophy of history. Were they talking about the same man?

Suddenly my legs gave way and I sat down where I stood. Were these human voices or the growling of snarling wolves? They mentioned names, many of whom I knew, with whom I had often talked of literature and politics, visited slums of the poor and the destitute whose bleak lives the affluent of the town could not even imagine, these men whom I was hearing about and had come to live with and share their suffering.

And then I went abroad for higher education and that is where I met this man who had also gone there for some training course. I fell in love. When I mentioned the subject to my brother who knew my political views, he expressed grave doubts about my picture as the wife of an army officer. His misgiving amused me. Hadn't Socrates also taken the oath of a Greek soldier and sworn that 'I shall never betray my weapons, nor leave the battlefield while another soldier stands by my side, and I shall fight faithfully for God and men.'

I had read that a man's profession did not change his nature or his frame of mind. I said all this to my brother and at last he fell silent. Love can defeat all arguments and my brother was defeated.

And so, shortly afterwards we were married and returned home. I had been away for five years and in spite of my wishes I wasn't able to restore the same relations with my erstwhile friends. Political oppression had increased, old political ties had broken up and above all old friends would not trust me any more. They now regarded me as a Trojan horse who could not be admitted into the front line ranks. This brought me such intense suffering that I could not even express it. And I retreated within myself. I realized that my friends were justified but perhaps so was I because I was afflicted with love.

The names being mentioned in the drawing-room were arrested one by one and the news appeared in the press a few weeks after our return. Then it was given out that their case had been handed over to a military tribunal. I tried to talk about it to my husband but he avoided the subject. He knew that I had friends among the accused and he didn't wish to hurt me with details.

Later I heard that one of my companions had died under torture and had been buried in some obscure graveyard. His grave carried no inscription. It was a grave of an unknown soldier. Some brief single column news of his lamenting young widow and aged mother appeared in some newspapers and was soon forgotten as if nothing had happened. I wept over the news for many days.

How could someone like him die so young, I kept wondering to myself. Someone so brilliant of mind, so noble of soul. A tongue rolling in gems of wisdom, how could it be deprived of speech. Those hands that always upheld truth, how could they be buried in the dust.

The molten lava of their voices was slowly penetrating my hearing. These men kept repeating a name I admired so much. They were jovially telling each other how they tortured him, how his finger nails were pulled out, for how many hours he was stretched out on ice, how many electric shocks convulsed his body. Then I heard that he had been finished long before his death, he was made to crawl like a beast, immersed in excrement, hung up with heavy weights tied to his feet and wrists. Torture, he and his companions were subjected to, every conceivable torture, merely because they differed with the rulers who had reduced the lives of their people to hell on earth, the rulers who regarded themselves as vice-regents of God and were dealing out divine justice. And the overseer of these tortures was sitting there and laughing. When he was ordering these tortures I had waited for him impatiently every evening and spent every night in his arms.

How many books, pamphlets, reports and documents I had in mind. Amnesty reports on torture, Universal Declaration on Human Rights which carried the signatures of my past and present rulers and the assent of my husband. The first article said that all men and women were born equal and were entitled to equal rights, article nine said—but why talk of first or ninth, or the twentieth article—it carried so many articles, did none of them ever trouble the minds of those who signed them?

These questions and their answers sprouted so many seeds in the field of conscience but this field had long been mortgaged to an inhuman race with stone-coloured eyes and bodies of copper line.

These war voices all around me, and fire and smoke and the stink of rotten bodies. Suddenly I felt sick and vomitted what was inside me, all that had been purchased from the proceeds of these tortures and I kept sitting by this mess. I sat there I am not sure for how long. Then I got up, went to my bedroom and cleaned up this mess. But inside me there was still the dead foetus of my dearest relationship.

I wiped the lipstick from my lips and looked at my hand, at my hand ending like every other hand in my fingers, beautiful fingers with their pink polish and an opal ring on the index finger sparkling with all the colours of the rainbow.

Then I remembered the fingers I had seen years before, strong masculine fingers with clean manicured nails pulsating with the pink blood underneath, with nicotine stains on the second and third one. I had seen those fingers turning over the pages of an article and those lips reading those pages.

That was the last time I saw those fingers and heard a voice from those lips. Today I came to know for the first time that when those strong hands bid farewell, they had been reduced to wooden splinters and those sensitive fingers and pink finger nails had been crushed into nail-less pulp.

Those hands that wrote poetry, and authored a book on the dialectic interpretation of history and the social evils of our times had been swallowed up by dust.

Once again the sound of the song of 'Boney M' rose ... 'He was the steppe's wolf. I stood up again as I was in a trance and my eyes pictured the strong body of the wolf whom I had fed on the pleasures of my body.

I stand in the semi-dark arch of the drawing-room door. The persons are not yet aware of my presence. The moment they are they will change their masks from wolves to sheep and their growling will change into piteous bleating.

They say that ignorance is a bliss. Today I have reaped from the field of ignorance the crop of nothingness.

They have heard my footsteps and they are hurrying to change their masks. I look at the face of my husband. Perhaps he has forgotten to put on his mask. I stand alone in the arena with all lights turned on me and all my sins, committed and uncommitted appear to be crowding in on me with their bloody jaws gaping.

Translated by Faiz Ahmad Faiz

Pakistan

Soul-weary

Bano Qudsia

This was the first time.

After that it happened twice—exactly as follows:

My left foot was on the last spindle of the bamboo ladder and my right foot was six inches above the wet earth when Ma grabbed me from behind by my hair just as a kite pounces on a newly born chicken. I lost my balance and tumbled down on the wet ground like a bale of clothes. Ma didn't have to give me a shove, as I had little energy left, coming as I was after separating from someone. Even a breath of hot wind would have been enough at the time to tilt my balance. And Ma had pulled me by my hair!

'Just tell me where are you coming from in the middle of the afternoon? Where have you been, you wandering strumpet? It's so hot that one cannot bear it even under the shade, and you were wandering on the roof. What were you doing, you whore?'

I was quiet.

'Tell me who's there on the roof. There's no attic and no shade up there. Then what took you there? I'll drink the blood of the fellow you had gone to see. Tell me his name.'

I was mute.

My papa was also a quiet fellow. But his quietude and his silences infuriated Ma. He liked to tease mother no end. He would keep smiling in his jumbo moustache, not caring to reply to Ma's questions. He would never say a word in his own defence. His honour and his triumph were hidden in his silence. When Ma got tired of abusing him, and her yells, curses, four-letter words did not yield any result, she would pull up the cot leaning against the wall and throw herself on it face down. Her face at that moment showed innumerable marks and stains as on a stale bread. I felt pity for her.

But Papa was different. When there was a face-off with Ma, he would simply sling the check wrapper across his shoulder and leave the house in the manner of a wrestler who had just vanquished his adversary. Ma was like a ball bouncing erratically between me and Papa. She hit her head against one wall and bounced back to the other. Ma's entire life was spent in this futile game of one step forward, two steps backwards. She didn't realize that this would simply exhaust her to her very bones.

When Papa returned late at night Ma would be sleeping peacefully like a mother who had just given birth to a baby. I would open the door for him, Papa would run his hand affectionately over my head and go in quietly. I could understand Papa even if he didn't utter a word. As for Ma's incessant harangue, I could never understand a word of it.

Papa was a quiet fellow. But his quietude was part of a well-thought-out strategy.

I was also quiet, but not like Papa. There was a great difference between Papa's silence and mine. He was like a lofty mountain at whose foot the waves strike and then go to sleep. My silence was like the lava that boils underground, then gets stale and flows away.

'Tell me. Why are you dumb like your witless father? Tell me whose bed have you warmed, you bitch.' It was because of such outbursts that Papa had decided to take recourse to silence some years ago. Thus he had freed himself from the obligation of providing explanations. What could I have said to Ma? Where could I begin and where end?

'Bitch! Our roof is the lowest in the *mohalla*. Many must have seen you going and coming. Since how long has this been going on? Come on, tell me how many months' pregnant are you? I can get a doctor or a nurse before our honour is ruined.'

Tears began to trickle down my eyes.

Just a while ago *he* had also held me by my hair and said the same thing. Could I have told Ma that I had just heard the same words from him?

'Why don't you tell me? Why are you crying? If there's any need of a doctor I'll pay for him. Why don't you say anything?' I could say nothing either to him or to Ma. I had this fear from childhood that no one could understand me if I told them about my feelings. Rather, they would misunderstand me and become my enemies.

I got up from the wet ground and went into the bathroom inside.

Ma kept on banging at the door for some time. Then resorted to curses and imprecations. When she exhausted them, she kept crying for a long time leaning against the wall. Then she resorted to her old 'technique'. She lay down on the cot in the courtyard and began to rattle off all the events since my birth to the present in a loud voice: how difficult it was for her when I was in her womb, what unbearable pain she had to suffer while giving me birth, and how she had me clasped to her lap for nineteen days when I had chicken pox. In other words, she unloaded her countless privations upon those who were at hearing distance. By the time she was through with her litany, it was almost evening.

When I came out, Ma had let out all her steam and was sleeping like an innocent baby. The ropes of the cot had left their marks on her left cheek. Innumerable birds were chirping in the *neem* tree, but Ma was totally oblivious to them. She wouldn't have known if I had eloped with someone at that moment.

But with whom would I elope? Only God knew what sort of women got men to run away with. No one bothered to ask girls like us to run away with them!

I sat quietly leaning my head against the cot. Who was there in the world to call my own except Ma? Papa too had no one except Ma. He walked out on her a thousand times but ultimately came back because there was no treasury that would accept a counterfeit coin like him. My father was a totally useless fellow. He used to eat very little as he did not like to chew his morsels. He wouldn't have the patience to rub soap on his body, for which he was unwilling to take a bath. In winter he would sleep in bed without the quilt over him, in summer he would be seen dripping sweat but wouldn't fan himself with the hand fan. He was somewhat like the hole that boys make while playing *gilli danda,** which remained gaping all the time except in the rainy season when it got filled with water.

Ma gave him company throughout his life, talking to him, taunting

---

* Indian version of tip-cat.

him, cursing him, and sometimes crying for him.

Hitting her head against the two walls—Papa and me—she had grown old. What could I have said to this wounded, half-alive woman? Where could I begin and where could I end?

In our house we badly lacked the things that animated and enlivened life, that is, wealth, honour and love. We had just enough to keep us alive, and nothing more. When I was three years old Ma had started going to a nearby factory for work. Papa and I stayed at home. We were prisoners of our own silences and were too far from each other even though we stayed close. When Papa was at home it seemed as though he had gone out somewhere, and when he was out I thought he must be somewhere quite close!

I went to school for a short period. Then it was stopped for reasons of expenses. In a way it was good, because I never liked the school. There all the girls looked so happy. They had so many things to share with one another that even while the teacher was teaching they would pass on bits of paper with messages on them to their friends. The girls in my class teased me for my taciturnity, but I never retorted. I couldn't participate in their carefree world of ecstasies and taunts and stayed by myself most of the time. When I left school I became really a frog in the well—the same mornings and evenings, the same dull rituals of daily life without any variety, any excitement.

Then one day Papa died.

That night he wore the chequered blanket, wore the cloak of his silence and became quiet forever. Ma was stunned. She neither howled in lament nor hit her head against the walls. She just sucked it in like a piece of barren land sucks water. No relatives came for condolence, no readings from the Qur'an were held, and no other rituals could be adhered to. The people of the mohalla contributed for the expenses of the funeral and helped Ma lay off her burden. After the third day, Ma resumed her work in the factory.

Now Papa was in the house all the time.

Frightened of him, I sometimes climbed to the roof. We didn't have tall railings on our roof; only small mud parapets on the sides with straws gleaming on them. Sitting on them I could see Ma taking a turn at the corner for home and came down immediately. There were many girls in the mohalla who had tried their best to break my silence and finally given up. Now, the parapets on the roof were my companions, along with the kites flying in the sky, the droves of pigeons from the neighbourhood and the rows of crows returning home in the evening.

One day I heard somebody whistling from the roof of the fourth house. I didn't know then that it was Qadir, the street vendor who was whistling. I also didn't know that he had five children and that his wife was the most beautiful woman in the village. I could only see that Qadir's house was the tallest and the most impressive in the mohalla. There were curtains on the windows and lattices on the walls. On the roof was a room that seemed very airy; its windows had been freshly painted in light turquoise green.

This room turned out to be my first home. It was there that Qadir had offered me a Coca-Cola that he had brought from his kiosk. He had also given me plastic clips, artificial earrings, glass bangles and a glittering but small nose ring. Everything about Qadir reeked of his vending box: he was accustomed to buying a lot of goods by paying a pittance. He didn't sell things on credit; nevertheless, he didn't allow any customer to leave his shop discontented.

I don't know if I went there for fear of Papa.

I don't know why the loneliness in our youth drives us to such burrows.

God knows whether it was the quest for excitement, the hunger for eating and laughing to one's heart's content, to grab some pleasure of life that drew me there irresistibly. Perhaps, it is not always necessary that there must be a reason. Human beings just go on getting themselves more and more entangled in the web of life like a length of silk cloth around the wheel. Qadir loved his family dearly. He would never tire of talking about his *maasis, phuphis* and co-brothers. He also loved his wife greatly as she was an important part of the family. Even at intimate moments when I was in his arms, he would be taking her name. His love was like that of a starving man who made my mercury soar in the skies.

He just loved to talk about his children. He laid great store by family traditions, the reputation of the mohalla and the honour of his community. As a matter of fact, Qadir also was a stranger to extravagance. His whole life was spent in the effort to maintain a balance between social mores. He had been a vendor for such a long time that his life had come to symbolize an empty vending box. Yet he used to see me in some style. He would bring only those things for me from his box that did not deprive his children of their rightful share. He gathered the pleasures of life with studied caution, like an old woman makes her *paan* with exact amounts of lime, *katechu* and just a pinch of *zarda*. His emotional life was also measured; there was no extravagance or impulsiveness. He would immediately extract the price of whatever he gave me.

How could my garrulous mother understand all this?

When she opened her eyes in the late evening, she kept staring at me for a few moments. I thought that she had gone out of her mind because of the intense sorrow. But the next moment she struck me on my shoulder and asked, 'Which month is it, you hussy? Come on, tell me.' How could I explain to her that with such keepers of accounts months do not matter. There's neither profit, nor loss. Life's account book is filled with such numbers as no one can read.

'Will you meet him again? Tell me.'

She gave me a stinging slap that left the mark of all the five fingers on my cheek. How could I tell Ma that I had no particular attraction for Qadir. If I tried to explain it to her or Qadir, probably both of them would have killed me.

'Will you meet him again? Tell me, you tramp.'

I clung to her feet. It was not my grief that I was concerned about. I had no personal grief. But I could not bear to see her so distracted. If she had beaten me, probably I wouldn't have felt so uncomfortable. Now she was hitting her own face. It pained me greatly to see her inflicting pain on herself.

I took a thousand oaths that I wouldn't meet Qadir again. I took oath on the Qur'an. After that I never went to Qadir's house again. But as Ma spent the whole day in the factory she was not sure that I stood by my oath. She had become suspicious of my movements. When I slept she would steal over me and pull up my shirt and poke my belly with her fingertips to see if a child was growing in my womb. Sometimes, in the last hours of the nights, she would sit by my head and break into tears.

Qadir did not open my accounts again. Neither did I go to him. He was not accustomed to wasting time on a sinking concern. Even after so much familiarity, our relationship ended with no profit, no loss. Life went on in its trivial way. I was neither excited, nor contented. It's just that I survived.

Then one day Ma returned from the factory very happy. She had a big packet of sweets in her hands.

'Come on, Hajera, take some sweets. Fate has smiled on you … I've returned after arranging your marriage at Badami Bagh.'

It was Qadir who sowed in me the seed of this desire. He used to talk so fondly about his wife. I also yearned that someone should talk the same way about me. I expected that some day people would come to 'view' me. Then a groom would come wearing a crown. I would leave my house looking at his shining boots. I longed to go over to the other side of the jungle.

'Come. Don't just lie there on your face. Allah has settled your affairs. Manager sahib's wife had come to me herself.'

'Are you listening, darling. Are you listening to me?'

'I'm listening, Ma.'

'Then why don't you look happy?'

'I'm happy, Ma.'

Ma came over to my side and said secretively, 'Manager's wife said that it was about her sister's son. He is not educated, but the only heir to the family property. We can't even utter the word "property". You're going to possess it. I had gone to Badami Bagh myself in Manager sahib's car. I saw the house, which is a yellow two-storeyed *haveli*. There were fans, radio, television, carpets and everything else. Come, take some sweets. The boy lives upstairs. It's a large house. You'll wear silk your whole life. And you won't have to suffer the discomfort of this mud hut. Be happy. The Lord comes to the rescue of those who have no one to turn to.'

After what seemed a long while I asked, 'And he … how is he?'

'Well, the inhabitants are known by their houses, aren't they? Low-class people do not live in such houses.'

'How does he look?'

'Going by his beautiful mother, he must be very handsome. She is spotlessly fair and has a sharp nose. Her wrists were covered in bangles.

And Hajera, she talks so sweetly—"come sister", "take your seat sister", "please help yourself, sister" ... "will you drink something hot or cold", and so on. I didn't feel like leaving the place. That's the truth, Hajera.'

I kept quiet.

'Listen, Hajera. She told me that they just wanted a girl who would keep their son pleased and will look after him well. They don't expect anything else. In fact, she said, "God has blessed us with everything else. If we were greedy, we could've got a girl from a rich family long ago. But it is our belief that among the daughters of poor families one can find self-respect, love and honesty." '

I laughed to myself. The woman from Badami Bagh didn't know that poverty results in the loss of just those three things. Lack of wealth produced poverty, but what really sustained it is the lack of all those three things.

'Here you are. Take some; they're real *motichoor laddos.*'

Ma was very happy that day. She hummed to herself while cooking. Then she went out to share the news with the people of the mohalla. When she returned she had a beaming face. I had never seen her so happy. She was the same bubbly self, laughing and humming till the last night before the marriage. A day before the marriage when she returned from Badami Bagh in the evening, her face looked pale and she was unusually quiet. With effort she pulled in the suitcase containing dresses and jewellery to the courtyard. And then without calling out to me went straight into the bathroom. She didn't say anything to me, nor showed me the dresses and the jewellery. After that night Ma never said anything to me.

At midnight I was awakened by her sobs. She had opened the box and was staring at the clothes. 'What's it, Ma?' 'Nothing. Get back to sleep.' 'Why are you crying?' 'Nothing.'

Ma hugged me. Her curses, abuses and taunts made me feel that she was alive. But when she clasped me to her chest I felt as though her life was going out of her body. I thought she was mourning my imminent separation, though my own heart was emptied of all kinds of emotions. There was no pleasure of union, or pain of separation. The months and years of my life were only measured by the inanimate numbers on the calendar hung on a wall. And when the year is out the old calendar is replaced by a new one.

Ma kept on crying till morning. When my wedding day began and the first light of the dawn began to emerge in the sky she said, 'Look Hajera, you can't fight your fate. Fate determines a woman's life. Just look at me—I was married when I was thirteen and my husband never earned a single pie in his life. Neither did he give me a bit of his love. But I did not complain about my fate. Had my luck been good, I would have been blessed with everything and without effort. Are you listening to me? If Allah blesses one with wealth, he may not have children, if there are children they may not be in good health. The sorrows of life are as numberless as the stars in the sky. Everyone is bound to the sorrow of his star.'

I began to have a nagging doubt that Ma was hiding something from me. She was telling lies. And both these things were foreign to her nature.

'Ma, what's the matter?'

'Nothing. Every mother gives something to her daughter while she leaves the house. I cannot give you a dowry, but can't I give you some words of solace?'

I broke into tears and clasped her to my chest.

'On my way to the factory, I find several manholes lying open on the road. In the dark of the night passers-by often fall into them. Hajera, imagine that our dear Lord has laid out manholes of different sizes and depths in the world. How long can you play safe, after all? Human beings are fallible, and life is long and bleak. They must fall in one hole or the other.'

'Why don't you tell me clearly what's it? What has happened?

'Nothing has happened. Nothing at all. You are going to a new house, among new people. Your mother won't be there, but neither would be our poverty. Everywhere there's happiness as well as pain. A girl who keeps on thinking about the comforts in her parents' house cannot be happy at her in-laws.'

'Ma, someone must've told you something. Why don't you tell me?'

My mother kept quiet. Her silence was even deeper than Papa's or mine. On the second night of the marriage my mother passed away from this world quietly. The people of my husband's family buried her secretly and didn't tell me anything. They didn't want me to bear two shocks at one time.

As immature babies are kept in the incubator to help them acclimatize with the world outside, the people at my in-laws' house kept me wrapped in comforts, luxury and flattery so that I should first get used to them before my encounter with Guddu. As long as the guests were there I was told that Guddu was ill and was staying in his mother's room downstairs. I often felt the strong urge to go down and see how he was doing but could not muster enough courage to do so.

My mother-in-law was exactly the opposite of my mother. She was spotlessly fair, plump, quiet and incredibly patient. Sometimes I felt that she was not a creature of this world. Her eyes were filled with so much sorrow that they gave me a scare. After my mother's death it was she who had won my heart. I felt sad whenever I saw her sitting quietly, like my mother.

On the night of my first meeting with Guddu my mother-in-law sat beside me for a long time. Her hands were on my knees, patting them now and then. She would start saying something, but would leave it halfway and begin to stare at my face.

'How is Guddu sahib now?'

'He's all right now. Will come to you tonight.'

The anticipation of seeing my husband lit up my heart.

'Hajera, it often happens that the image that girls form in their minds of their husbands turns out to be different from reality. But it all depends on the way you look at it. It is women who give birth to children and sustain families. Men are, in any case, outsiders.'

I began to have apprehensions for the first time. Then I thought, probably Guddu was ugly and that is why she was saying all this. That could also be the reason they did not allow him to come to me yet. Perhaps my mother-in-law did not know that I had grown really anxious by then. I desperately wanted to see my husband.

My mother-in-law kept on sitting by me for a long while without any reason. Then when she was going out she said, 'Listen Hajera, we'll be very grateful if you look after Guddu. He is our only son, the only brother of five sisters. You just have to tell me anything that you need. There is nothing more precious to me than Guddu.'

I was trying to fathom what she was driving at.

She was speaking as though she was trying to cool the fire burning in her heart with her tears and her words. 'There is no lack of girls among my relatives. But I deliberately went for a girl from a poor family because one can find sympathy and love among the poor. Whatever Guddu is, he is yours and yours only.'

So saying, my mother-in-law left hurriedly. She was right that Guddu was mine only. But the pity is that I couldn't be his, not even as much as I was Qadir's!

Late at night Guddu entered my room. First there was some whispering outside, then he entered the room. Immediately he clung to me as bats cling to the branches of trees. Behind him were my mother-in-law and my two older sisters-in-law.

'Mother, my bride ... my wife ... my lovey-dovey bride.' My mother-in-law and sisters-in-law quickly separated him from me.

'What're you doing, Guddu!'

'Just see, my bride! They didn't allow me to come to you, saying that you'd run away. Will you? Am I so bad? You tell me. Shall I bring my *Reader* and read out to you? Where is my *Reader!* Why don't you bring it? I'll read out to my *dulhan*!'

When my mother-in-law wanted to silence him, he began to cry. 'Everyone treats me badly and says that they're doing it for my good. Why shall I shut up, *badi aapa!* You shut up and leave me alone. She's my bride and I'll talk to her ... I will ... I will.'

To hang a loose mosquito net on bamboo poles is a difficult job. If you try to tighten the poles on one side, the poles tied on the other side get displaced and slip under the bed. In the same way, it proved to be a futile endeavour on the part of my mother-in-law and sisters-in-law to present him before me as a normal human being. After sometime they just threw up their hands in despair and left the scene. They thought that the danger would disappear if they stayed away from it. This was the beginning — the beginning of my descent into terror. It was the beginning of my married life with a half-mad fellow. Till then I had spent my life without the good things of life. Had he been a commonly mad person, I could have lost myself in a life of comfort and luxury. But, despite his madness, Guddu was a man of romantic temperament. He liked to touch and hug, kiss and cuddle me all the time. He wanted that I should stay lying in bed with him all day long. He would start dragging me from the table at breakfast.

'Guddu, let Hajera have her breakfast.'

'I've something in mind, Mother. Very private. It can be done only in my room.'

'At least let her finish her toast,' my oldest sister-in-law would say.

Then he would sidle up to me and whisper something into my ear that could be heard by all. He would mention body parts that are not usually mentioned in public.

'Come on, Hajera. Be quick.'

'You go. She'll come in a minute.'

He would then start pulling me by my dupatta. 'Hurry up.'

Once in the bedroom, my reproaches and pleadings were of no use. He would be bounding like a monkey over me and kissing me all over. If I showed reluctance to take off my dress and jewellery, he would start howling. At such moments he would have me in total control. To see that golden-haired boy crying stirred some deep sadness within me and I felt like taking him into my lap.

I was in a delirium, as it were. The days and nights passed in a trance. I was not aware whether the days were sunny or the nights were dark. My mother-in-law was very considerate about me and looked after my comforts. She bought me new jewellery and dresses. My sisters-in-law looked embarrassed in my presence and would avoid me. Only my father-in-law would sometimes seat me by him and tell me about the uncertainties of life.

Guddu had his lucid moments and days when he looked transformed and that would make me optimistic. I would expect a miracle to happen. In those days no one could tell that it was the same Guddu. Donning the cap on his head and holding the prayer rug in his hands he would come to me and say with a smile, 'Hajera, I'm going for my *isha* prayer. Take your meal and go to sleep. Don't wait for me.'

Seeing her son, the only brother of five sisters, behave so nicely, my mother-in-law would be overjoyed. 'Of course, she'll go to sleep. Don't you worry. You go and say your prayers.'

On his return he would greet everyone before coming to our room. He would take a long time brushing his teeth, like an old man. Then he would sit on the sofa and in the light of the headlamp turn the pages of books which were difficult for him to read. Late at night he would climb on the bed, and turning his back towards me, go to sleep. Once he recovered from his ailment, he had very little to do with me.

He would go to the factory regularly with my father-in-law. On his return he would take his meal quietly, talk about the day-to-day affairs at the factory and then go to see movies without bothering to see me.

In those days, my mother-in-law would be walking two feet above the ground.

'Hajera, we've made over all the properties in Guddu's name—the bungalow, landed property and the factory. My daughters will be married off and leave us. Everything belongs to you and Guddu.'

Those days were very peaceful.

If I even touched him by mistake before anyone, he would be upset and say aloud, 'What're you doing, Hajera? Don't you see that my grown-up sisters are watching us?'

But those days were few and far between. On a fine morning Guddu would get up and appear in his former self. When he was well there would be rolls of laughter reverberating through the house. There would be talk about the marriage proposals of my sisters-in-law. The whole family would go to see some movie in the matinee show. Relatives would be invited to dinners and lunches. My mother-in-law would introduce me to all and say benevolently, 'Sisters, it's all due to Hajera's magical powers. She has succeeded in doing what the doctors could not. Guddu has been suffering for ten years, but now he's perfectly all right. Hajera has given him a new life. She has made a man of him.'

I felt embarrassed by her compliment. She was a mother and her maternal emotions were genuine. But I was a woman and my needs were not fulfilled. Hence, I couldn't feel deep down in my heart what I showed outside.

Had it been in her power, my mother-in-law would have liked to be his wife herself and protect him from the harsh realities of life. Sometimes, when Guddu wet his bed, she would promptly wash the sheets and mattresses before anyone could notice it. I was not burdened with the responsibility of looking after Guddu. Looking at her, I would often wonder how a human being could so skilfully draw a veil on another's handicaps, how one could so totally accept another despite all his inadequacies. Sometimes I felt that God hides human beings behind the veil of death so that the devil may not make fun of the inadequacy of His creations.

My existence seemed to me so phoney in the presence of my mother-in-law. All the comforts and luxuries in which they had wrapped me proved fruitless. I could not make a place for Guddu in my heart. I tried my best, but it was obvious that one stitch wouldn't do where thorough mending was necessary. Occasional cuddling wouldn't do where total dedication of heart and soul was needed.

Only God knows if it had happened on account of Guddu.

God knows, after Ma's death my heart had gone absolutely blank.

Was it God's will that my life did not move on the straight path for long? Rather it preferred narrow, barren pathways strewn with stones and pebbles. People travelling through lush meadows delight in getting entangled in thorns. In wealthy people's lives there are always doctors, as there are sorrows and running sores.

It had happened for the second time!

When my left foot was on the last step of the staircase and my right foot was six inches above the white marble floor, my mother-in-law pulled me from behind by my hair. A person suffering from the pangs of guilt like me could hardly stand steady on her feet. She didn't need punches and blows to knock her down.

'Bastard, tell me where are you coming from at this time of the night?'

My head hit the floor, like a golf ball.

'There's neither a room nor toilet on the roof. What were you doing in the attic? Answer me, you strumpet!'

My heart, brain and soul had all turned into a stone.

'Speak! Who was it that played with our honour?'

My mother-in-law was sitting on the stairs going up to the third floor and crying bitter tears. In the attic my father-in-law, wrapped in a blanket, was getting into a cold sweat in the chill of December. How could I tell my mother-in-law that I was not playing with her honour, but was trying to preserve it. But some words sound so false when they come on the lips!

'Who was up there? Who broke into my house? Say something, you ungrateful bastard?'

I was lying on the cool floor and wondering what I could tell her. Where could I begin and where, end? Could she even begin to understand such a tangled narrative?

'Listen, Hajera, either you tell me his name or I'll get you divorced straight away.'

I had grown fond of my mother-in-law. How could I've told his name to her?

'I've looked after your comforts in all possible ways, and this is how you pay me back, you black-faced one? Come on, give me his name. Look, I haven't ever lifted my hand to strike anyone, but ... Just don't try my patience anymore, and give me his name.'

How could I have told my mother-in-law that it is because of her kindness to me that I had taken to this sinful ...?

It was in the beginning of winter that my father-in-law had come to see me one day. On that day all other members of the family had gone to a shrine along with Guddu to distribute consecrated food among the devotees. I could not go with them as I had fever. There was a light knock at the door. It was as though a bird was hitting against it to find its way through.

After what seemed to be a long while a feeble voice came, 'Hajera'.

I opened the door. He was standing outside.

'How do you feel now?'

'I'm fine.'

As I was turning back he caught my hand and asked softly, 'Did the doctor come?'

'Yes, he did.'

He sat on the sofa by my bed for a long time scrutinizing the medical pamphlets. Probably he was preparing in his mind what he was going to tell me. Getting tired, when I was going to turn on my back, he cleared his throat and said:

'Hajera, I wished to say something to you. I don't know how you'll take it.'

'Please go ahead.'

'Guddu is my only son, the heir to all my property.'

'God willing, he will be all right. Ammi has gone to ... How can he be all right? We had to return from America empty-handed. There's just one way ...'

What was that? I kept staring at him for a long time. All of a sudden, I saw tears trickling down my father-in-law's eyes.

'If only Guddu had a child then my honour would be saved. There must be an heir to this family.'

I didn't know why the family must have an heir. But I felt pity for my old father-in-law.

'Save me. Save the happiness of my family. My family's honour, its name and fame are all in your hands.'

*

Sitting on the staircase going up to the third floor my mother-in-law was enumerating the favours that she had bestowed upon me in the short period that I was with the family. Shopping at malls, dinners at hotels, films at theatre houses. Somewhere far away, a cock was crowing to declare the break of dawn. My mother-in-law appeared to me like a bouncing ball that had got bruised because of her love for her mad son. She reminded me of my own mother at that moment.

'Tell me, Hajera. For God's sake, tell me who was it? He who wants to rob my Guddu of his happiness cannot escape me.'

I couldn't possibly have told my mother-in-law that I was a sinner and the person who sinned with me had also sealed my lips. I couldn't have explained to her why a relationship that had begun on the plea of saving the honour of the family continued even after I was pregnant. Many incidents in life appear to be like incidents in history. You could find all kinds of theories or explanations for them but it becomes almost impossible to arrive at the truth.

'Tell me, Hajera. I'm asking you for the last time to name the fellow who's playing with our happiness.'

My mother-in-law, my poor mother-in-law was lost in her love for her son. How could she have understood that from the beginning of this world human beings had been playing this game, the only game that was real and true. If human beings had not associated honour with this game then they would have progressed much beyond the present stage. Now if one ever strays beyond the established conventions, he is crucified in the name of honour. God knows which enemy of love had initiated this process and tied up the concept of honour to the process of human reproduction. God knows which new thinker had decided the code of love and in which century, by combining religion, love and the physical needs of human beings.

'Hajera, I'm asking you for the last time — whose child are you carrying in your womb?'

I felt like screaming to tell everyone that no one had yet expressed happiness at my pregnancy. All they wanted to know was the identity of the father. Isn't the child important on its own? Could one be happy only when one knows that it is legitimate? If it were a natural law, then a mother would have felt no love for her illegitimate child.

'Who is it Hajera? Come on, tell me. If you tell me then I promise to accept the illegitimate child. If not ... then ... then I'll get you divorced.'

I was on the point of telling her, but my love for her prevented me. I felt deep empathy with her and couldn't bring myself to ruin her world in a single stroke.

Quietly, I returned to my own house.

Here, my father used to give me company all the time. My querulous, voluble mother was lost to me.

Today, this has happened after twenty-two years ...

And, for the third time!

My right foot was on the last step of the staircase and my left foot was suspended six inches above the ground when someone pulled me by my hair. I was already huffing and puffing from the effort of climbing down the stairs, and I tumbled down on the ground instantly. I felt a thin stream of blood flowing down my temples.

'Where are you coming from at this midnight hour? Tell me what business did you have upstairs at this time of the night?'

I kept quiet.

How could I tell my adult son what difficulties a mother had to face bringing up a son?

'I've heard many things from other sources. Tell me what kind of relationship do you have with the landlord? What is Sheikh sahib to you? Speak!'

I was mute.

Did I need to tell him that Sheikh sahib was our benefactor. He had supported us for years. Never charged rent from us. Besides this, he had helped us in many other ways.

'I ... I looked upon you ... as an angel in paradise ... a *houri* ... I ... I often told myself ... it didn't matter ... if my father was mad ... my mother is ...'

Tears flowed down his eyes in a stream. He was telling me of all the deprivations of his life since childhood. He was in conflict with himself and the world.

'Tell me who was with you up there. What's your relationship with Sheikh sahib?'

I spoke out for the first time. From the frightful realm of silence came the voice, 'Son, I have never had any relationship with any one!'

Indeed, I had never had any bond with anyone.

Translated by M. Asaduddin

Nepal

A Strange Temple

Manju Kanchuli

The idol behind the shut door of God must be
arrayed with vermillion and rice
That I don't know
Before meeting the deity I've seen
nothing but naked figures on the struts above
I've read so many times
'Behind the locked temple door there's no God at all'
A long time has passed ... these days
I haven't opened that temple door with flowers of hope
Its inner wall might have transformed into a mirror
blossoming in the mirror the priest's aroused mind
might have bulged outward,
the mirror on the torso turned toward his mind
might have melted with immense shame
That I don't know
Out of shame I haven't till now
parted that mirror's curtain
Encountering yellow sunlight everywhere
the priest's robe of black clouds
might tremble
Tangled in the loincloth of a hurricane
It might be hovering above some gorge somewhere
That I don't know
I haven't forced that cloud to land

In the theatre of the earth
I haven't harassed it with bright sunlight
History, upon a wall of mud, has been written with lines
In the vacuum of space, with voices
over the forehead of Earth, with blood
In the ink of the heart, with red
Into the pen of the human, with a cry;
beneath the layered soil of Earth, with bones
Into layers of sedimentary rock, with coral
Inside black coal, with illuminating diamonds

But I've never understood
the meaning of the blank paper smeared with spider shit
In the piled garbage bin near the temple
An old wall might have been changed into a new mirror
that new mirror crawled upon by a snail
Into parchment of fresh slime
That I don't know
I've taken those walls, mirrors, and blank sheets
to be your undershirt
and have never in front of anyone else
parted them till today
I haven't opened the temple door
I haven't disrobed the priest
The image inside the closed door of God
must still be arrayed with vermilion and rice
That I don't know
Before meeting the deity I've seen
nothing but naked figures on the struts above

Translated by Wayne Amtzis & the poet

Nepal

Illicit Connection

Banira Giri

Let my son
be a Hamlet
and wear a medal
coated with doubt and qualm
Let him live a Trishanku in limbo
between to be and not to be
Let him sharpen or shine the sword
on the whetstone of ill-fate
and dip the point
in a potassium cyanide cup
and let him just touch with it
in my neck
and
compel a betraying woman like me
to die wriggling
a poisoned death
because
having deceived all
I have established
An illicit connection with my age
An illicit connection with my age.

Nepal

Untitled Poem

Benju Sharma

For years, a tatty picture is hung up in my room
the picture my grandmother has ever been idolizing
that my mother had hung there with a sense of pride
A moth-eaten disfigured shape
with an erect tattered silhouette
that strikes only an accustomed eye
Faith has a limitation
belief has boundary, too
this picture is becoming an eyesore for me now
Having covered all its corners completely
I would like to smudge this
with the colour of fire, and
put a burning matchstick in the centre
exactly in the centre,
that's all.

Nepal

It Has Already Been Late

MAYA THAKURI

'Who else is there in your house?' The old woman enquired of him as she was stoking the fire-wood in the kitchen oven.

'It is just my mother,' the man with a gentle and impish smile in his lips replied in brief. 'Just a mother and no one else?' The old lady again asked giving a final turn with a spoon to the rice that was being cooked in the oven and then covering the same with a lid.

'Is it the *kavro's** chutney that you're preparing?'

The young man, as a ploy to escape the old woman's volley of questions, asked her back with his eyes on the kavro leaves that were lying piled up on an aluminum plate beside her and were ready to be seasoned.

'Yes, you are right my son. I brought these leaves from the forest today when I found the local kids plucking them from the tree. Truly speaking, these sour and acidic stuffs do not at all suit my health but it is my tongue that always desires these hot and piquant sort of tastes to swallow my food. The leaves are already boiled. All it needs now is mixing a little bit of salt, chilly-powder and a few drops of mustard oil in them.'

'I am sure you are very hungry with those two days' of walks, and god knows, how many more days are still there for you to walk!' She was just blabbering away by the side of the oven.

But the young man with all gratitude for the old lady expressed, 'You are wrong, mother. I feel all my tiredness gone now that I am seated here by your side. What greater happiness can there be for me

---

* Kavro—Kind of tree whose tender buds and sprouts are used to make chutney or pickle.

than sitting here by your side and getting this opportunity of eating the meal that is being prepared by you?'

'The rice is just cooked and while it is fluffing I am herewith getting a fistful of *gundruk* boiled. And I will serve the food to you right away,' said the old lady as she put the blaze out on the piece of firewood by sprinkling some water on it. The young man was consistently gazing through the smoke at her loving and wrinkled face when the old lady was talking. Many kinds of thoughts crossed his mind as he was watching the white-haired lady at her chores.

'I am going to season the pickle and then I will boil the gundruk. Your taste, I am sure, is accustomed to all sorts of delicacies,' she said as she removed the rice pot from the top of the oven and re-entered the firewood in the oven.

'No matter whatever we eat in the town, it is the taste of Nepali gundruk and *dhindo* that outdoes all others. It is told that they only eat dhindo in the villages but how is it that I see you cooking rice this time?' The young man expressed himself with a note of seriousness and curiosity in his voice.

'You are indeed right, my son. Folks like us have to wait for the festivals to eat rice. You can never say when you are faced with exigencies so I have the habit of saving whatever amount of rice that I can get as a part of my wages for the help that I offer to the others. It is just some amount from this saved rice that I have cooked for you now, my son. As for myself, I am going to cook dhindo. It won't take long,' the old woman answered.

'No mother, never. I am not going to eat this rice alone. You cook dhindo first. And how about we two sharing this rice and the dhindo equally and eating?' The young man asked her looking affectionately at her face.

'Oh good graciousness! What is this, you just said? Why are you so kind to this old woman? Please for god's sake, I entreat you, do not show this gesture of your affection to me.

'The man who was supposed to show his care and affection for me left me at the prime of my age and disappeared somewhere in the sea of this world. And it is not just he alone who is gone. He took along with him my only child who was then only about one year of age,' the old lady's voice quavered as she was speaking.

'I am sorry, mother. I am really sorry. I never meant to hurt your feelings. It is just that I wanted to eat together with you ...' He was at a loss for words as he was trying to speak further.

The young man looked in his late thirties and he had a robust health.

It was two days ago when he had got off the bus and after crossing many streams and rivulets and walking over many hills and ridges he had reached the old lady's house late this evening.

'It's getting dark. Will you please let me in so that I can pass my night in your house, mother?' He had asked in a very loud voice standing at the courtyard outside the old woman's house in the dim light of the dusk.

'Who are you and who sent you? I am all by myself here. You go further south. You may get refuge at Karki Danda which is not very far away,' the old lady had answered from inside the closed house.

'On reaching the place called Nag-Pokhari this afternoon I enquired where it was possible for me to find a place to pass my night. And an old farmer I met there told me of this house of yours. I am very tired of walking for the last two days. My stomach is writhing because of hunger. It is fine if you open your door for me or I will be compelled to lie down here in the veranda of your house and pass my night,' the young man had spoken in a rather presumptuous voice.

'What a dilemma I am confronted with!' With the words coming out of her mouth the old lady, at last, opened the door of her house.

The young man then saw in front of him an old and fragile face standing with a dimly burning oil-lamp held in her hand.

As soon as his eyes fell on the old woman he could not help falling down and bowing at her feet as a gesture of his veneration to her.

'Who are you and what are you up to?' The old lady exclaimed in astonishment.

'I am just a passerby. I am here begging before you for a night's refuge, mother,' the man repeated with his eyes fixed on her.

'Then why are you at my feet? I am ...' the voice of the old lady, he felt, had pierced right through the middle of his heart as a chilly draught does in winter.

With a brighter look on his face the man replied, 'Why, is it not in our culture that we venerate out elders by bowing at their feet?

Compelled though we are to spend our days in a distant land yet we do everything to conserve our customs and practices.'

'But you gave me a scare. Step in then,' the old lady welcomed him in.

'I think I should leave my boots outside here, right?' Saying this he took his boots off and left them outside the house.

'No, you would do well to bring them in. The time is not so safe these days. If your boots are noticed by them they are very likely to draw their own conclusion and they will not hesitate to cause us any kind of harm,' the old lady very softly uttered the words. She further muttered, 'May be taking this old woman's age and the solitary life into consideration they have spared this life of hers till this day.'

'Why, mother, why should anybody be causing us any harm when we have done no harm to anybody?' The man asked her with a furious note in his voice.

'See, my son, you don't have to do any wrong to be their target. There is no telling how many innocent people from this village had to lose their lives for no fault of theirs. The family members of those who are killed are living very miserably now. This is, I guess, what our ancestors called a "catastrophe". I am afraid it is all nothing but a total catastrophe on its way,' the old woman said in a grieved tone.

The man then thought of his father and very regretfully said in his mind, 'Father, you were very late in disclosing the facts about my mother.'

Truly speaking the man was not aware of the fact that his mother was still alive. His father had lied to him when he was very small and had told him that his mother had been long dead due to some illness. But it was about a month ago that his father lying in his deathbed had told him the truth saying, '... and may be she later started a new life. She may also now have some issues from her new husband. My son, if you like you may very well go and meet her.'

This disclosure from his father had made him very sad and infuriated him against his father but the pitiable condition of his father on his deathbed compelled him only to shed tears quietly and calm down.

And in a very tender voice he said to the lady, 'May be your husband did not at all marry again and may be he brought up your son to be an educated and worthy man.'

'God knows what he did to my son. He caused me big harm by taking my milk-sucking son away from me. What a big relief it would bring to me if only I could see my child once, just once, before my death!' She began sobbing before she could finish her sentence. 'Mother, please see here. Please look at this ...', the man told her holding in his hand a photograph that he had taken out of his pocket.

'Open the door. Open it immediately' were the words that came suddenly from outside the house.

The old lady turned pale on hearing the voice and she replied meekly, 'I am all by myself here and why do you want me to open the door?' She said this while at the same time gesturing to the man standing before her to keep silent with her fingers on his mouth.

'We know very well who else is there with you. Open the door or else we are going to break your door with our boots,' the voice scolded her.

'What are we waiting for? Kick the bloody door open.' Somebody ordered and within a second the door lay open before her with a crashing loud sound.

'Mother, this picture ... this' the man had only been able to open his mouth when he was snubbed by those uniformed men who spoke, 'So you are here to wheedle this old lady into offering you a haven in her house. We are well informed of your ulterior motives and plans. You come out with us. Move on, you son of a bitch.'

'Let me tell you. Please let me tell you I am not the one that you are suspecting me to be ...' He was pleading before those gun-men.

The old lady was dumbfounded with fear and panic and was seated trembling in one corner of the room.

'Please spare my life. I beg of you, please have mercy upon me. Let me just once ... my mother ...'

'Bang,' the man's voice was suddenly cut short by the sudden sound of a gun-fire that was shot at his temple by one of those uniformed gun-men.

Then for the last time he uttered, 'My mother ...'

The man's hand that was clutching the photograph then reached out to the temple where the blood that was gushing out of the wound blotted out the face in the photograph.

Translated by Damodar Sharma

Sri Lanka

Wedding Photographs

JEAN ARASANAYAGAM

'Have you any wedding photographs,' I ask achchi,
'No, nothing,' answers my mother-in-law.

It all happened well over half a century ago,
No, there are no reminders of traditional poses
Framed behind glass but I see them both,
Pata, achchi seated on that velvet-covered divan
Beneath the flower decked manaverai,
Achchi's slender neck, she was only sixteen and small,
So fragile, weighed down by that thali of twenty
Gold sovereigns.

That marriage bed, once strewn with flowers
Vacated by Pata's death, the bed dismantled,
Cast aside, its purpose over.

In that dawn, so distant now,
Childbride my mother-in-law woke from sleep
Still swathed in folds of vermillion marriage silk
Her jewels warmed against her body,
That heirloomed heritage adorning flower-fragrant
Flesh, her loosened hair with its crushed jasmines
Flowing over her shoulders, wandering alone in the garden
Dew glistering on her white feet
Silver toe-rings misted over,
Whispering below her breath
'Now I am a woman

I will carry on the sacred traditions
Worship the gods and goddesses at my shrine
Bring forth sons and daughters.'

Did she regret that her playtime was now over?
We sit face to face, musing over each other's
Lives, thinking of gnarled feet stepping over the shambles
Of a ruined house, of our spent lives, of age and passing time.
'I was an orphan,' achchi said,
Who then gave her that ritual bath of milk and honey,
Who braided her hair with fresh white jasmines,
Who painted henna patterns on her hands and
On the soles of her feet?

'Jewels I had,' she continued,
'Attiyal with rubies, emeralds, brilliants,
Gold bangles, earrings, mukutti with pearls,
With rubies and diamonds, houses, I had properties, so much land,
I lacked nothing, I followed the sacred rituals,
Walked round the yaham with its everlasting
Flame, I remained faithful unto death to Pata,
He was handsome with his milk white skin
And slender limbs, I was so young,
He was twenty years older.'
'Your stepmother and that uncle, your guardian,
What did they do for you?' I asked.

'My uncle squandered all that wealth,
My stepmother married again. Went away.
For my wedding, nautch girls, devadasis,
Came and dressed me, they were dancers
In the temple, rich men kept them.
They, those beautiful women, put all the jewels
On me, braided my hair with flowers,
Wrapped the vermillion and gold silk round my
Body, prepared me for the nuptials.

'And so my new life began,
I lit the lamps at my own shrine
Worshipped the deities at my own altars,
Fasted, prayed, chanted the slokas,
Brought forth sons and daughters,
I was both dutiful and auspicious,
My fortunate womb fertile,
When Pata died, part of my life too
Perished on his pyre,
With his death not a thread remained in his ashes
Of his silk veshti, his shawl, his garlands,
Not a strand of hair, from that once luxuriant head,
Only memory remains of his noble mien
And the seed that springs from his loins
In my sons, my daughters.'

Sri Lanka

Telephone Conversation

JEAN ARASANAYAGAM

My daughter hangs up on me, abruptly.
There is nothing she can do, she feels
To help me change my mind.

I am an old has-been,
Can't think of a future like her,
Remain behind in the past
A derelict soul on a lonely park bench
Feeding pigeons who speak a different language
In a far-off country.

Listening to the brass bands
While the trumpets glitter in the late
Autumn light, the poppy wreaths red
The plush uniforms like scarlet tulips.

I slept then in a forgotten city
Sometimes lonely, stepping into the Welcome
Caravan in George's Square, dragging other
Strangers with me to drink hot coffee in paper
Cups, eating oat cakes, asking strangers for
Directions.

Soon the roads grow so familiar that
I become the guide,
Lead others to find a way.

I walked into cold churches with soot-covered
Walls, hearing ghost-echo sermons
Thundering fire and brimstone from
The strict presbytery of their theology.

Mike was different, picking up each
Blessed morsel, crumbs of the communicants,
The hot line was always ringing
For the desperate would-be-suicides.

We wept at parting
Giving each other the kiss of peace,
Feeling, as we held each other close,
Close, the chilled flesh and bone
Pressing through the warmth of flesh
To feel the beating heart.

Outside, the snow was high, knee deep,
The fir trees mantled
The ice-topped mountain summits
Merged into the peerless whiteness of sky.

We built a snow-woman I remember,
Mike did and decorated her with berries
Decked her with leaves like some ancient
Earth mother in fertility rites.

Yes, Mike, he was a priest
Filled with love for all strangers and
Wanderers, feeding the hungry who begged
For sandwich money.

Yes, my thoughts wander,
So many cities, so many journeys
Changing views from many windows,
I watched the birds.
Divined their auguries

Spelled their omens,
Read Aristophanes in simple lines.

Exchanging the patois, the argot
With this one or that as if I am on a silk
Route caravan travelling through history.

I meander, pause at market-places
The epics now become folk tales
Simplistic, of a return country
And the terror heads choreograph my nightmares.
I have no dreams left except of death.

Her words, my daughter's words, recur,
'Do you think you'll feel humiliated
If you ask for political asylum?
If you have to beg to cross that bridge?'

'No, I don't give a damn,' I say.
'You remind me of the past,' she says bitterly,
'You always said possessions are
Of no importance.'
The dialogue continues
'I've left your sister behind,
I am responsible for her.'

How else explain my cowardice?
My daughter wept, her voice trembling,
The child, this woman, who took a
Different trail, crossed a frontier,
Sheltered with nuns in a night stop
For transients, waifs, drug addicts.

Memories plaster the walls of my
Mind-room with stark black and white
Photographs.

'It's not your other daughter that
You want to return to,' she says,
'You're still shackled to your past.
What do you want to hold on to?
A heritage you never had or a martyr's
Death at the stake from which
There is no guarantee for your return
Or your escape.'

Sri Lanka

Death by Drowning

KAMALA WIJERATNE

Bang …
Running feet …

'Nona Mahattaya …' 'Nona Mahattaya …'

I put down the book I was reading and became immediately attentive. *'What's it?'* I was irritated. I had just got to the most interesting point in Solzhenitsyn's *1918* … Caught up in its grim drama in fact. Nine long years in this lonely, parched land had made me turn more to books for company. My husband wouldn't be home until dusk or even later. I had the house and day all to myself.

'Nona Mahattaya …' He was prevaricating … Always prevaricating, as usual … My little servant boy …

'What is it now … Where have you been?' Looking closely at him, I became very angry. He looked as if he had been wallowing in the muddy pools of the tank which skirted the front garden … Enjoying himself as usual. One of these days, he will drown: and I will have a whole chain of ugliness unleashed on my head … Police inquiries, witness boxes … irate parents … I will send him home this week-end, send a telegram to the mother … Sad … the woman lived on the boy's wages. But I can't keep him any more. No … I can't … at this rate …

He came in and stood on the carpet (My Wilton and Axminster! I had bought it only three months ago from an expatriate returned from England).

He wriggled about on the Wilton with one foot over the other. Soon, the carpet was caked with mud …

He seemed to be drifting around for something to say … He started haltingly …

'Nona Mahattaya knows Wimalawathie?'

Almost pleading ... He saw me looking at his feet. He knew I was angry.

'What Wimalawathie? You know I don't know many people in this village.'

'Oh you know her ...' he persisted. *'She is that woman who stands outside her door and combs her hair all the time.'*

Impelled by the blank look on my face, he went on, compelling me, forcing my memory. *'Oh you know her!'* he said impatiently. *'Can't you remember when we went to the co-op on Saturday. She was standing on the steps of that big red-roofed house ... Where they have a hedge of red hibiscus flowers? You said you thought it disgusting that a woman should be combing her hair on the doorstep at midday, looking at the road.'*

I seemed to remember faintly, yes she was a big woman with a big full body. Her cloth hugged her buttocks and the silk jacket blew up her bosom. She had a round face too, I remember, like a flat moon. She was lighter in complexion than most people in that hot scorched land. And she had long black hair which flowed down in waves to her knees. She combed it gently, caressingly, as if it were her most prized possession. I remember how taken aback I was by the figure of that woman, and the kind of boldness she had. With all my education, with assurance born of urban culture, I was timid in front of the brash. I could never do the unconventional.

'She is the retail dealer's wife, isn't she?.

'Yes.'

'So what happened to her'?

'She is dead.'

'Dead? How? She seemed to be young enough to live for another fifty years.'

His face had the look of someone who was sharing a terrible secret. *'Well, she drowned in the lake. You know, Nona Mahattaya, the people say that it is her Karma.'*

'I can't believe it,' I cried. *'That big full woman. She seemed to be born to live for ever and ever. How did she drown?'*

'She was picking the Olu seed.' Clearly, the boy was enjoying his role as a reporter. *'You know they cook it like rice,'* he said, with an inquiring look at me, and when I nodded, he went on, *'At this time of the year nothing will grow on the chenas. Everything is burnt up. So they go on the lake and gather the Olu and Manel seeds from the dried up cages of the flowers.'*

'How sad. But how did the retail dealer's wife happen to be at the lake?' They were rich enough, I thought. She did not have to go collecting food from the lake. *'Well, the villagers think she was mad. She thought it fun to waddle around in the lake. She wanted to do better than the other women, go to the deepest parts of the lake to collect the biggest pods. It was very slimy in there.'*

'I am sorry,' I said.

'But the village is not sorry, Nona Mahattaya. Gunawathie Akka says this is what happens to people who show off.'

'It is not nice to talk ill of a dead person,' I remonstrated with him. *'But this is what the people say, Nona Mahattaya.'*

'Why do you listen to all the village gossip?' I asked him. *'You should have dug up the garden and made the beds for the vegetables before the rains.'*

But I was curious in spite of myself. For the past three years I had been in this big glass-windowed bungalow, with its front to the lake and its back to the village. I had kept aloof from the people, and was a stranger still. I felt ill at ease with the villagers when I met them on the road. They would smile at me when I went to the co-op with the servant boy, and ask timidly, *'Nona Mahattaya is going to the co-op?'* just to be polite. I would shyly answer and move on. I could not have spoken half a dozen words with any of them. They were shy with me. Something shrank within me when they did talk to me. I found their attempts to be polite irritating. I did not go about much, I had very little contact with the village. The two places I visited frequently, the co-op, for the weekly provisions, and the temple for weekly worship, were formal occasions for me.

I think it was part of my upbringing. My parents came from the village but had settled in the suburbs of K ... town. They had not belonged to the community they lived in with its small-time businessmen from the lowlands and migrant professionals. I remember the inordinate note of superiority my mother adopted when talking about them. My parents were first cousins and descended from two branches of an old family which owned land, now mostly overgrown with jungle—tea, cardamom and assorted spices flung over the hills. Altogether they were proud, aloof and overbearing.

My mother had almost a phobia about people. I was sheltered fiercely and continuously, permitted no contact with people she thought not good enough for us. Twelve years in one of the sophisticated girls' schools in town, surprisingly ending in a university career, had left me with a qualification that could have made me shake off the shackles of my heritage, if I had wanted to. But I could not, and would not, offend my parents. For a while they condescended to let me teach in my old school, but permanent employment of any kind was anathema to them. Then they found a partner suitable for me, not the ideal—because there was some question of pedigree—but very good on the whole. He was of wealthy parentage, educated in one of the better known schools, had done a university degree and was holding a prestigious post in the administrative service. I married and he was appointed an AGA in this arid tank-riddled district, which was scorched for the greater part of the year: Leonard Woolf Country.

I was a princess in a single-pillared castle. My husband's position in the district assured me the respect of the men who worked in the co-op. As soon as they saw me, they would shove the villagers aside and hurry to serve me. That did not help matters either. Outwardly, the villagers did not show any resentment. But I could see the glint in their eyes at unguarded moments, the whispers in corners. Well, I did not care.

In the temple, the priest fawned on me and my husband. A big official was an asset to the temple. And my weekly alms were a welcome change from the villagers' simple fare.

I did not mingle with the crowd at the temple. As soon as I entered the compound, the chief monk would invite me in. Then he would discuss the next Poya day programme or the renovation plan. The shrine room was opened specially for me. I liked to make my offerings and worship alone, unobserved by those rough, inquisitive people.

But now I was curious about this woman, this woman with a zest for life, who had dared and drowned, her life so rudely cut short. The boy had been waiting patiently throughout my reverie. He was apparently waiting for me to go on.

'What did you say Gunawathie Akka said?' I was interested in spite of myself. All this is beneath me, I thought. I who had such superior tastes in arts, in literature, in conversation. How could I break that circle of Pirandello, Solzhenitsyn and Kurosawa? Was it debility of some kind, the stagnation forced on me by countless days of lassitude and ennui. I was really falling.

'That she was very free with men. You know it is not usual in the village. She would wait combing her hair, they say, to attract men. Then she would go on talking with them.'

'What is wrong with talking to people?'

'Oh! I don't know. The women seem to think that was not proper. You know, Nona Mahattaya, they say she speaks in a certain coquettish manner. She wants people to think she is pretty.'

'She was pretty,' I exclaimed. An unusual voluptuous beauty, I thought, like the red hibiscus blooming on her hedge, a beauty of the flesh—so different from me with my bone-China look, thin, ivory, and bony. My friends did say I had an aristocratic look which I felt was an indirect way of saying that I was too thin, flat chested and stern.

'I have heard some fellows calling her Sarungale. She used to wear lurid colours like the flowers of the Mara tree.'

He was right. She was overdressed. She was almost always overdressed to go to the temple. Normally women wore white to go to the temple, or very light shades. But this woman was different.

I let him go on. I succumbed to something low and petty within me. Perhaps I was long in need of exhilaration of some kind, denied as I was of theatre recitals, art exhibitions or the like.

Well, I was another woman after all and gossip was tasty to someone ravenous for novelty, for a break from the humdrum, the monotony of a life lived from day to day.

'And she smelt so nice. Like jasmine flowers,' he chortled.

I was really angry with him then. The crudeness of the remark, and the way it was said about the dead woman, broke something within me. He was like the rest of the village, like most of human society, ready to laugh, to ridicule and to condemn.

'Why shouldn't she smell nice? She had enough money to buy nice perfume?'

'But,' he said, almost in a state of shock, *'to go to the temple? To the temple? You go to the temple to worship. She did not go there to worship.'*

'Why not? Can't you worship in pretty clothes with sweet smelling scent on you?' But he went on vehemently, not taken aback by my outburst. *'It is not proper.'*

'Maybe not. But she had to wear those pretty clothes somewhere, poor woman. This is a small place. And the only place people gather at is the temple. If I were as pretty as she, I would want people to look at me.'

He laughed at that. He seemed to find the thought funny.

'What Gunawathie Akka says though is that she brought it all on herself because she had led a sinful life.'

'How so?'

'Well,' he said. *'She was married before, she says. You know in the town ... to a man who carried sacks of flour from the big godowns to the lorries. He was poor. So she had run away with the retail dealer. She was a bad woman, Nona Mahattaya ...'*

I did not answer. The boy, small as he was, was picking up the black and white morality of the little community he lived in.

And I felt a curious sadness. Like all women, this woman too craved the nice things of life ... pretty clothes, perfume, attention. She had never had them before. So when she got them, she wanted others to see, appraise, admire. Well, that was immoral!

Encouraged by my silence, the boy went on, *'Gunawathie Akka says that this had to happen. She was spoiling the young men in the village.'*

I reacted to that immediately.

'What a nasty world. What horrible people.'

Inside me, I was boiling. I let out my anger on the boy.

'I think you have picked up a lot of rot from the street,' I shouted at him. *'You should have dug up the garden before the rains.'*

But my thoughts went back to the woman. I had merely seen her in passing. I had never spoken to her. Never known her. But I was weighed down with a terrible sadness.

A hard, hard life. Denied the nice things that her voluptuous nature craved. When she found them she wanted an audience. But she had overreached herself; trying to make people notice her. She waded into the deepest reaches of the tank to pick the biggest Olu pods.

'Maybe, there will not be many people at her funeral, Nona Mahattaya.'

The boy was disturbed by my long silence. He was trying to get back my attention.

'Well, Martin. I think you should clean off that mud. You smell like the rotting weeds of the tank. Wear your clean sarong and shirt and don't come in until you are really clean.'

'Yes, Nona Mahattaya.'

'And Martin. When you come back, can you please scrape the coconut and do the things to prepare dinner. I have half an hour to read this book before the sun starts slanting.'

'Yes, Nona Mahattaya,' he said humbly. I can't send him away. I need him.

What would I do without him?

'Now go,' I told him kindly. *'Go and have that bath.'* He was moving on. Then he paused and asked me curiously.

'Nona Mahattaya. Are you going to the funeral?'

'Well, I don't know ... I suppose I will.'

Central Asia and Russia

Azerbaijan

Sparrows

Afagh Masud

Her hands shook, or she lost her concentration. Whatever the reason, she fell down again while carrying the teacups, and the cups broke. With the cups her heart broke too. There was sweetened tea in the cups.

In the hallway her mother's angry face appeared. Her mother's face was frightening when she was angry.

Her mother entered her dream with the same frightening face. With this strange face, her mother walked over her with heavy ironlike steps ... like a storm. With the shadow of her mother night fell and everything sank into darkness. Under the spell of her mother's rage she was left alone in the darkness. Her trembling heart turned into a small drop of water. Then her mother passed over her with her big heavy feet. She beat her and smashed her and dragged her on the floor. She tried to call for help with her weak voice ...

She woke up with goose bumps on her body, and while trying to clean up the broken pieces of the cup, she wondered whom she had been calling for help in her dream. Then she remembered. Her grandmother. Yes, that's it. Her mother's mother. With her heavy body, her grandmother used to try to take her from her mother's skinny hands that were shivering with nervousness. Her grandmother would hold her and press her to her heart, and she would start crying in her arms.

She missed her grandmother. She wished she could curl up in her grandmother's arms again. She thought if she could get into her grandmother's arms she would never come out. She would remain there, she would do her homework there, she would sleep and wake up there. Grandmother's arms were deep and huge like an ocean. If she had wanted, she could have even floated in that vast ocean …

Her mother was still looking from the end of the hallway. It was as if the more she looked, the more her teeth pressed together, and she would make a fist, and the hair would stand up on her arms.

It looked like her mother was coming to beat her again. She was coming to pull her hair and pinch her to the bone. She thought, why didn't her mother get tired of beating her? On the contrary, the more she beat her, the stronger she became and the more relieved she seemed. It was as if her mother were getting back at someone by taking it out on her and her small, skinny body. Whom was she trying to get back at? she wondered.

Ha, she thought, cleaning up the broken pieces—maybe, her mother was trying to get back at her wretched body. Why? she wondered.

At times when her mother could not beat her, she would walk around the room and curse someone. It looked like her mother wanted something badly but could not get it. What did her mother want? she wondered. As she was cleaning up the broken pieces, the sharp glass cut her hands and they started bleeding.

Her mother looked at her from a distance for a while and took a deep breath. It seemed like she did not have the desire to beat her. Maybe she was tired, or maybe the blood on her hand had calmed her mother's anger.

'Did you hurt yourself?' her mother asked with her usual dry, cold voice.

Shaking, she stood up and went to the kitchen carrying the broken pieces in her skirt. As she walked she felt the arrows of her mother's hateful words. She would always throw the same arrows at her when she was in the other room as well. Sitting in her own room, her mother would bang angrily on her black typewriter, and every bang on the keys seemed like a bullet that her mother was shooting at her.

Her mother would shoot her even in her dreams. She would ride on her black typewriter like it was a roaring tank and run over her. Pressing the keys of the typewriter, she would riddle her body full of holes like a strainer. Then she would look at her body and notice the things that had pierced it were not bullets but the painful words coming out of the typewriter. She would run to hide from her with the same words all over her body.

She went to the kitchen, carrying the broken pieces in her skirt, rubbing her knees together. There she pulled the garbage-can lid up and poured the broken pieces inside, with her ear tuned to the hallway. She got rid of pieces of glass as small as dots. She poured the pieces from her skirt into her palm.

Her mother was still in the hallway, her breath roaring with anger like a huge wave coming to pull her under.

Once she had seen her mother in a dream. It started with her mother sitting with her face toward the window and her back to her. She approached her mother on tiptoe. Her mother was silent, her hands on her knees. She was gazing off somewhere in the distance ... then she held her mother's shoulders. As if she were empty inside and made of cardboard, her mother fell to the floor and moaned. Her mother was like her headless doll. In tears, as she tried to lift her mother, her arms came off and her head fell. With all her body shivering, she held her mother's body parts and took them to her own room, and there, with her hands shaking, she hurriedly tried to put her mother's pieces together and mend her. Her mother did not mind any of this at all ...

The door to her mother's room slammed. It did not take long before the angry sound of the typewriter was heard again. She took a deep breath and calmed down. She thought, what is all this her mother is writing? She had once entered her mother's room in secret and had read from the pile of her writings and had not understood a word of it. Her mother was writing something about sparrows.

She thought, maybe her mother likes sparrows. Or maybe her mother is a sparrow herself, and that's why her mother does not like her. Or maybe she doesn't like her because she is not a sparrow.

Or maybe her mother did like her. Yes, sometimes it looked like she did. This was usually when she was sick, especially when she had a high fever. It was then that her mother would not bang on the typewriter and she would not groan; she would focus her eyes on one spot and stay still, and once in a while she would touch her with her cold lips to check her fever. At those times she would not feel any warmth from her mother's lips. With the same cold lips, she would also check the heat of the iron and the wetness of the laundry. She thought maybe if she died, her mother would like her more … then she imagined how she would die, how she would be put into a coffin, how her mother would throw herself on the coffin and cry hard.

Her mother would throw her whole body over the coffin. Then she would feel the weight, the warmth, and the smell of her mother's body. Then sleep overcame her.

She had been imagining this a lot lately. It was nice … If she was not afraid of death, and if she could be sure that she would come back to life, she would die. Yes, definitely, she would die.

She thought about this and sighed. She hugged her knees and for a long time thought about death. Death was very strange. It wasn't dark. It was cold and white as a foggy spring morning. There, what could she do in that fog with her small body? Would she be sitting or lying, or would she fly like a small sparrow? How would she go from this clear room to that foggy place? She didn't know. Would any part of her body hurt, or would she grow short of breath, or would all her body parts be cut into pieces as if processed in a meat grinder? The thought scared her.

While she was deep in her thoughts, night would fall and the room would sink into darkness. She got on her tiptoes and turned on the light.

Her mother would be crying for her. She would go mad with sorrow for her … She had seen her mother crying like this when her grandmother had died. She had held on to the coffin and with a sorrowful voice had screamed, 'Mother …'

Then she imagined her mother's death. Her mother would be lying in the coffin with the same make-up and the same kohl on her eyes and the same bored look on her face. She would sit next to the coffin and caress her mother's pale cheeks. At this point she could not control herself and her tears rolled down her cheeks.

Her mother went to the kitchen silently from the hallway. There it seemed like she was making coffee for herself. With the cup in her hand, she returned to her room and started typing again.

She thought, how strange, it looked like her mother was not alone. Being in her room for hours, or passing through the hallway pensively, standing in front of her, it always looked like her mother's mind was involved with something or someone. That's why she never felt the slow passage of time or the murdering silence of the house.

She curled up in the corner of the sofa and thought, what could be occupying her mother's mind? There was silence in the other room. She wondered what could her mother be doing there now? She thought, maybe her mother was not doing anything at all behind that closed door. She was just sitting there, looking at the wall.

Her mother would go into her room as if she were hiding from someone. She was hiding either from her or from her father, she wasn't quite sure. But once when she was arguing with her father, she had said violently, 'Let go of me. Let me die!' Then she had hidden her face in the pillow and cried.

She thought maybe her mother was right. She had gone to that other room to die. But her mother wanted to die. She was one hundred per cent sure of this. Then she wondered why. Maybe the cause of her mother's gradual death was what she wrote about so madly day and night ...

Her father also hated these wretched writings, she was sure of this. Her father had once said this himself. In the middle of the night he had gotten up from bed, gone to her mother's room, opened the door and said, 'I hate your writing.' She thought this was strange since her mother was not doing anything to her father, but it looked like she was hurting him. Yes, it was strange. Then she thought, maybe her mother was also shooting her father with her typewriter from behind the door of her room.

Her father had lately been looking at her mother with such painful eyes, as if he had a toothache. Then, having no other choice, her father would contract a fever. He would lie in bed and would look at her mother and say, 'Don't you feel sorry for me?' Her mother would not feel sorry for him, even when he was sick, and not even if ...At this point she got goose bumps.

Even if her father had died, her mother would not have felt sorry for him. Once, when her father had been very angry, he had said, 'If I died, I would be free,' and her mother, with a cold look on her face but not raising her voice, had said, 'But you are not dying.' It was obvious from her mother's face what she wanted. These thoughts made her shiver. The silence was deafening.

Once when there was such a silence in her mother's room, she had gone on tiptoe and had opened the door silently and had been surprised by what she had seen. Her mother was sitting on a chair and quietly looking at herself in the mirror. Her mother looked at herself for a long time and put her head on her arms and started crying silently. Ever since that day, she kept thinking about why her mother was crying but could not find an answer.

She thought maybe her mother was crying again right now. She thought she was hearing her mother's moaning. Her heart started pounding. She got up and, on tiptoes, went to the hallway and opened the door to her mother's room slightly. Her mother was standing at the window, leaning on her arms and watching something. She noticed her presence.

'What is it?'

'Nothing. I thought you were crying.'

'I am not crying,' her mother responded coldly. 'Enough with spying on me.'

The window in front of her mother was filled with sparrows. So, her mother had been watching the sparrows all this time ...

She went out into the hallway and closed the door. She stood in front of the mirror and looked at herself for a long time. She looked at her eyes and her mouth. She definitely did not look like sparrows.

She thought, her mother should at least kiss her once a day. She used to kiss her when she was a baby. Maybe she had been fed up with kissing her. So be it. She had gotten fed up with kissing her. At least she could sit face to face with her and talk to her. She would only sit face to face with her mother at breakfast and talk, and their conversation would go something like this:

'Your face looks like a spoon again,' her mother would say. She would smile and shrug her shoulders.

'Why aren't you eating properly?'

'I am not hungry.'

'Did you get any grades yesterday?'

'I got a five in literature.'

Her mother's facial expression would not change with this response.

'Well done.'

Then her mother, with the same expressionless face, her thoughts with the sparrows perhaps, would go to work. Or maybe she would go to be with the sparrows.

In the evening, her mother would be the most angry. She would first change and lie down for a while with her eyes closed. Then she would eat something hastily and go to her room and perhaps write about the sparrows again.

She thought her mother had wanted to do something for a long time. What was it that her mother had wanted to do? Maybe she had wanted to increase the number of sparrows. She then thought, what would be the use of that? She hid her head in the arm of the sofa and cried silently.

It didn't take long for her to hear the typewriter again. It looked like this time her mother was shooting at someone else. It was as if her mother would forget everything once she was behind that typewriter. Her nails would look like the tip of a sharp pen, and she herself would look like a wild animal.

Yes, that's it. She would look like a lion. Her mother would look like a lion whenever she was writing. She got up and moved closer to the window. It was getting dark. In a short while her mother would say with a cold voice, 'Time to sleep,' and would lie down on the sofa gazing at the ceiling for a long time, waiting for sleep to come to her.

No sooner was she overtaken by sleep than her mother would come to her. Every once in a while her mother would be kind in her dreams. She would work with a sewing machine instead of a typewriter and she would be making pink and orange dresses for her. She would then put these dresses on her and seat her on her lap and comb her hair, and her hair would fall as she combed it. Her hair would fall on her knees, on the floor, and would remain in her mother's hand ... it was strange. As her hair fell, she would never feel any pain; on the contrary, she would feel sleepy.

The door opened with a bang. From the hallway a beam of light poured inside. It was her mother coming. She first entered with her head, then she tiptoed across the room. She came and stood above her head. Her mother stood there for a while. It looked like she wanted to check to see whether she was sleeping.

Her heart started beating fast, and she didn't dare open her eyes. After a few minutes, her mother bent over and whispered in her ear, 'Are you still spying on me?' Frightened, with her eyes closed, she nodded. Then her mother held her nose and mouth with her hand so that she could not breathe and jumped up. The book slid from her knees and fell on the floor. Was she asleep?

She felt cold. She put her hands under her arms. She suddenly jumped up. Excited with the thought that had come to her, she went toward her mother's door. She opened the door and looked inside.

Her mother was writing something again. She had a kind look in her eyes. She didn't notice her coming.

She felt courageous and went in, drew closer to her mother and stood face to face with her. As soon as her mother noticed her, the kindness in her eyes disappeared.

'What is it?' she asked and put her glasses on her head, looking at her with an angry face.

'I am sick.'

Her mother took a deep breath and put her cold lands on her head.

'You don't have a fever,' she said, with the same expression.

'Maybe I should take my temperature.'

'It is not necessary.'

'Then maybe my fever is going to rise,' she said and looked her mother in the eye. Her mother's expression did not change; instead the colour of her eyes did.

'Then when it rises, we will do something.'

She bowed her head and wanted to leave, but then she thought of something and returned.

'I feel bad … I am nauseous, I am cold.'

'Eat a lemon and put on warm clothes.' Her mother uttered these last words like a robot.

She left the room and closed the door. With her small hands, she had made a fist. She went back to her room and opened the window.

Knowing there were lots of sparrows in front of the window, she tried to frighten them. They flew away. Although spring had come, it still felt cold.

For a while, in her light dress, she shivered, and as the wind was blowing through her hair, she thought of getting so sick that her fever would exceed the measurements of the thermometer. Or perhaps she could throw herself down. Then her mother would come to her, running down the steps in tears. Or maybe she would not come down at all. She would just take a look down from the window, and with bored eyes she would sigh and put on her glasses and continue writing madly. On her toes, she rose to look down. She grew dizzy, and she felt like her feet were losing contact with the floor and going down with her head. She held on to the frame and got her balance back. She closed the window, her heart pounding. She returned to the sofa and curled up.

In front of the window there were lots of sparrows eating the bread crumbs her mother would put there for them every morning. They were turning their heads from side to side, jumping over one another. It looked like they were doing the Anzali dance. Sometimes it looked as if they were peering at her through the window, laughing at her.

Every morning her mother would get up and, before doing anything else, with her sleepy face, would rush to the kitchen to get some dried bread. Then she would go from one room to the other, crumbling the bread and putting the crumbs on the window-sills. Then, with the same sleepy face, she would watch the sparrows eat the breadcrumbs. The mixture of the chirping of the sparrows and the banging of the typewriter made a strange music.

With goose bumps, she got up and, like a cat stalking its prey, slowly approached the window.

Quietly she opened it. The sparrows were very close. They were chirping.

All of a sudden she stretched her hand out. The sparrows turned and flew away.

Her hand was not empty. She had been successful in catching one of the sparrows. She could feel the warm body of the sparrow in her hand, its small head was out. It was gazing at her with its small black eyes. It looked like the sparrow was laughing at her.

From her body a poison oozed out and poured into the hand holding the sparrow. Her hand started squeezing the sparrow so that its lifeless head dropped to the side.

She flipped the dead sparrow in her hand and looked at it. The sparrow still had the same smile on its face ... that's why. She turned the sparrow's head like a key and pulled it off. She took it to the kitchen and threw it in the garbage bag. Returning to her room, she felt her knees shaking. She sat on the sofa and looked at her hands. Her hands were shaking too.

After a while her father came in. He was angry again. It looked like he was drunk. He kissed her with his hairy face and then sat in front of the television, as usual. She came and sat next to her father. She put her head on her father's shoulder. Her father's shirt felt wet.

'It is very cold in this house,' her father said, and then kissed her on the head. Her father's body had a bad odour.

*

In the morning the typewriter was silent. The television also could not be heard. It seemed as if no one was home. She got up, put on her shoes, and went into the hallway. The door to her mother's room was open. She went in.

The room looked different. The typewriter was not there. The typewriter stand was pushed to the side, like an unnecessary piece of furniture. The mirror in which her mother used to look at herself for hours was not there either. Nothing belonging to her mother was in the room. Her mother's chair was in the middle of the room, and her father now was sitting on it. He was hiding his hairy face with his hand, smoking a cigarette. He felt her presence. She then noticed her father's bloodshot eyes.

'Where did she go?'

Her father shrugged his shoulders and looked at her with a miserable expression.

'I don't know,' he said. Then father and daughter embraced and sat next to each other.

It was very quiet in front of the window. There was no sound of sparrows. She knew her mother had left them, her eyes filled with tears. Her mother had gone with the sparrows.

Translated by Shouleh Vatanabadi

Mongolia

Untitled

G. Delgermaa

Sought Freedom, Couldn't find.
Caught under control, Couldn't get apart.
Ran away from parents, Couldn't escape.
Searched an abandoned land, Couldn't reach.
Wished peace. Nowhere. Couldn't rest.
Induced in fright, Couldn't survive.
Thought of my idea, Wasn't right.
Waited for death, Wasn't taken.

Tajikistan

A Letter

GULNAZAR

Whatever I see—
like waves on the water's surface,
leaves no trace on my mind.
Are you me or am I you,
that you never leave my mind for a moment?

I pick words from the eagle's footprints,
I take my paper from the mountain snow,
My heart is the abode of caring and hope,
I tame the wandering breeze.

So that you hear my voice for a moment,
I borrow the melody of the streams.
Although the lover's tears are a tempest,
I will send you a drizzle.

In Badakhshan,
where rubies are rare,
I will seek out many rubies for you,
so that you know how resolute a heart is
in sincere fidelity toward you.

My heart's condition resembles
a waterless desert beside a river.
One day the desert will be in bloom,
but my life will pass away like a mirage.

I compose a letter to you
in which my words are my country.
Images of plains and mountains and rivers
are my heart's gift and solace.

I don't know where your home is,
I don't know where you might find a homeland.
Are you me or am I you,
that all my letters are addressed to myself?

Translated by Sunil Sharma

Afghanistan

What the Scar Revealed ...

ZOHRA SAED

1977, Afghanistan: A girl born on Lailatul Qadr, holy night of Ramadaan.

Her mother tilts her head back to face the sky. The night is smoother than her amber skin. Young mother sees spirits walking across the sky with stars blossoming at each step.

The stars join as a single thread of daylight
A gold streak across twilight.

Grandmothers tell the story of healing; how wounds heal only after they have memorized the moment of hurt. A newborn's navel is the same as any wound. To heal, the cut navel swallows the city and remembers its fragrance. Turquoise domes, spice vendors, pomegranates like hearts, and the adhaan in her ear are consumed by this bloody wound.

April 1978: A revolution tangles ribs and spines with iron and steel.

Smuggled under veils and old pots, she ties borderlines into knots. After suckling her mother's fingers for days in the desert, she throws a tinselled veil up to the sky and catches lapis-coloured doves. Quartered and roasted, the doves whisper God back into the wanderers' sleep.

1998, New York City: In an apartment overlooking a blue-gray street, her mother's veil hangs on the wall like a talisman. Her lapis doves and tinselled mountains are misplaced and glorified behind plates of glass at museums. She visits them weekly and cleans the glass between them.

When Lailatul Qadr comes again, she is over a bridge between Brooklyn and Manhattan. While the night is threaded in gold, the lost city in her navel unwinds itself from swirls of skin and slips over this new city like a fog.

Afghanistan

Voices: Archive of Spines

ZOHRA SAED

I serve a tray of pine nuts, dried apricots, thin slivers of chocolate and cups of perfumed tea for the guests who have come.

Laughter slips from mouths.
Carefully, I archive their round existence.

Father entertains with accounts of his children's brilliance. My sister blushes by my aunt's side. She holds the hand of the one she resembles.

For years I have traced their voices, arranged them into stanzas only to see the lines eventually overwhelm them, confuse and lose each other in the stretch of long-distance phone calls.

They reach for sweets   one after the other.

Daintily raising tea cups to their mouths, they welcome the coils of steam that whisper against lips and cheeks. Here and there, a tale of escaping war, of the texture of tents in refugee camps ...

Aunts who have embroidered history onto the hems of sleeves and skirts, exchange coy glances with me, eldest daughter, seeker of stories. I wait until the warmth of the pink tea has coaxed out family legends, still aching from its closeness to their hearts.

Their voices evaporate to the ceiling, then fall on my lips like snow.

I taste the past from which we have escaped with our lives.

Afghanistan

The Ugly Face of Power

DONIA GOBAR

They all shine,
sinking in soft velvet seats,
where ruby-coloured drapes
mark the theatre.

We all watch,
in the face of undeniable reality
the dissolving process of the '*Nobodies*'
whose lips
have not touched the tips
of *golden skirts*;
whose hands
have not polished *spotted shoes*
of '*somebodies*'—
in the murky halls of power.

We all sigh,
hearing the sound of imitated wisdom,
as twisted images fall into the mosaic
of popular subjects;
as hollow ideas bubble out
of a suffocated marshland,
where the bodies of truth and wisdom
have been slaughtered
and abandoned.

My thoughts—
the misplaced peaceful observers
struggle in dark,
as the *lefts* and *rights* lie in wait,
camouflaged,
in the battlefield of contradictions,
to entrap
the scattered feverish emotions;
and,
as the distinct smell of rotted facts
marks the unmarked marshlands,
quietly, we house
the wounded images of the intellect
and of the innocent
in the concentration fields of survivors;
so that the great ugly powers may not ridicule
the hunchbacked carriers of freedom,
as we gasp for truth
at the edges of unmarked marshlands
in the battlefield of our lives.

Afghanistan

'Ariana'
(dedicated to the country of my birth)

Donia Gobar

Such a sad silence ...
This bottomless whirlpool of grief
Oo ... the gasping airless senses
and the old dry tears
still burning,
running
on dusty ruins of Beloved Ariana
Did I hear her bitter laughter?
Did I hear Her whisper?

'I Will Never Be Gone ...
I will never be gone ...
I will never be gone ...'

Russia

I Am Called a Woman

MARIA ARBATOVA

Memories of my childhood are full of chilling stories about the witch Baba-Yaga,* while my youth was petrified by the mere utterance of the word—*gynaecologist.* All our pedagogical gaffes and the entire folklore wisdom concluded with the fact that the more beautiful and coquettish girls amongst us met their doomsday right there in the gynae's room.

A written-off dentist's chair used to be lying in the garbage behind the dispensary, which was under construction, and the entire sixth standard students, divided into groups of girls and boys, would go there to catch a glimpse of it: the boys used to unscrew the nuts and the bolts. The girls were happy rehearsing their future feminine roles by sitting on this chair with knees tightly pressed together, their chins exerted upwards and their hands folded on their torso. One and all had the conviction that the chair in the gynae's department was of the same height as that at the dentist's and you are made to go through the same kind of nightmare at both these places.

The senior girl students had worked out a system, which was passed down by word of mouth, of escaping the annual medical check-ups. For quite a few did not want to make an issue of the loss of their virginity, while the majority, due to their cultural background and training, felt uncomfortable about their bodies. Hence these check-ups caused them a lot of distress.

The long and short of this story is that I had to visit the gynae being quite pregnant.

My mom, who herself worked in a hospital took me to the doctor,

* Baba-Yaga is a witch in Russian folktales.

bypassing all queues. My eighteen-year-old insights could grasp the mountain of tribulations that lay ahead, as well as the necessity to overcome them. This awareness was exactly what distinguished me from the opposite sex.

'I give a damn to your tears!' A horrible looking female, who was washing her hands in rubber gloves, was shouting at the pale, young blonde woman with a big stomach and big dark circles under her eyes. 'I refuse to answer on your behalf! Whom do you think you are going to give birth to? An abnormal? As a doctor I can tell you this for sure that you'll give birth to an abnormal child!'

The doctor swiftly moved away from the sink and taking a seat, she began to dig into the ankle of the blonde woman with her *rubber* fingers. 'Do you see the swelling? A hand till the elbow can sink into it.' 'I can't be hospitalized,' said the blonde crying. 'I have nobody to baby-sit for my child! My parents live far away and my husband is—a drunkard ...'

'Big deal—husband is a drunkard!' Turning towards my mother, the doctor said, 'And whose husband is not? So this is your daughter?'

'Yeah, mine,' my mother said proudly and with some embarrassment added, 'I hope she is not pregnant.' Her tone was that of a physician talking about a patient—'I hope it is not pneumonia', or 'it isn't heart attack.'

*

'Other people's children grow really fast! I still remember your daughter prancing around here in her school uniform! Take off your clothes ...' the doctor waved towards the chair with her hand in a rubber glove.

'Doctor, please, I can't be hospitalized for a long time, he beats the child when drunk,' whimpered the blonde.

I carefully began taking off my sweater.

'No, not the sweater, take off your jeans, stockings and your panty,' Mom whispered to me.

'You are simply bugging me!' screamed the doctor at the blonde and turned towards me. 'What are you doing just sitting pretty; you think you are in the Bolshoi Theater? Haven't you ever sat before?'

'No, never,' I admitted in the tone of a bad student.

'Open your legs apart!'

'How?' I was scared.

'As you did when you were making love!' yelled the doctor and came to me.

'So, who is the one responsible for her pregnancy?' asked the doctor digging into my genitals.

'Well, he is also a student but they have already given the application at the registrar's office.' Without any enthusiasm my mother tried to defend me. She would have wanted a more respectable man for a son-in-law.

'And where is he studying?' asked the doctor again.

'He is training to become a singer, an opera singer,' emphasized my mother.

'Oh! These singers, they are all like that,' the doctor summed up her knowledge on the subject. 'And what about your daughter?'

'She is studying in the University,' added my mother.

'Which course?'

'Philosophy,' admitted my mother somewhat embarrassed.

The doctor and her hands stiffened as she examined deep inside me and with a mix of disgust and curiosity she asked: 'What kind of a specialization is this, philosophy? And do they, these philosophers work? Pray, what kind of a family would they make—a singer and a philosopher? All my life, I am yet to come across such a combination.'

'That's the trouble,' said my mom. 'I would've rather she had gone for medicine or a course in law.'

'I am recommending an abortion,' the doctor concluded.

'Of course, an abortion, what else!' Mom added, 'It's too early for them to start a family.'

'That's right,' said the doctor and barely having washed her hands, sat down to make the report.

'One should first complete the university, then—children,' my mom declared as if she was being consulted on what to do after what, or as though she was ever concerned about my knowledge of sex and contraception.

'Oh, these youngsters have a non-serious attitude towards life,' sighed the doctor.

'Strange, that the doctor did not try convincing me to carry on with my pregnancy,' I said as we came out of her cabin.

'How could she, she herself must have had fifteen abortions,' informed my mom.

Such a thought never even occurred to me that the pregnancy of an eighteen-year-old girl, marrying her beloved, could result in the birth of a child. The heights of the philosophical reflections attracted me more than the anxieties of Soviet reality, which combined motherhood with studentship. Neither my fiancé nor my mother thought of continuing with our genealogy. My fiancé understandably did feel guilty, bogged down and upset; but the ambition, associated with our future professions, multiplied by infantilism, fed by over-protectiveness, united us and together we turned out to be a useless couple for procreation purposes.

The next day I was in the queue with my hair plaited and wearing a terrible out-of-fashion blue coloured hospital gown. The scene was full of dispirited women sitting on the stools in the operation room ... screams of a momentary victim and she being escorted out with all the picturesque details ... she slumps down, the nurses make her stand against the wall feeling ashamed of her.

'Hey you woman, think you are the only one here? See, a whole queue is waiting over here! Fast, get into the ward and better put the pad under you, the blood is flowing still and there is nobody here to wipe the floors! You will not come and clean it for us, isn't it?'

The everyday reality is industrious; expecting women proficiently looking at the clocks to see what else, apart from this abortion, they could squeeze into their schedule for today; tired and fretting nurses; heart-rending screams from behind the door of the OT. From the appearance of the people it seems that everything is moving as it should have and grown-up people habitually go about their adult chores. I was the only immature creature perceiving all this very tragically!

'Do they do it under anaesthesia?' trying to sound as natural as possible, I asked the fat elderly woman.

'High hopes, under anaesthesia!' answered she, yawning noisily.

'Then how?' I asked frightened.

'You should thank your stars if they even give you a Novocain injection.' The elderly woman looked at me carefully and turning around with disgust said, 'Still a baby herself and ready for an abortion!'

'But then why are they screaming, if they have been given the injection?' I turned towards the young woman wearing fascinating earrings.

'Why? Because Novocain doesn't work on everybody.' She smiled at me. 'You'll be better off sitting calmly counting the elephants than analyzing the medical procedures.'

'Counting which elephants?' I almost begged, well recognizing my total ignorance and unworthiness of my being in the same queue with such experts.

'Well, in the same way, when you don't get any sleep. Keep saying to yourself "one elephant and one elephant plus—two elephants, two elephants and one elephant plus—three elephants, three elephants and one elephant—four elephants". Just as you finish counting up to a thousand elephants, the abortion procedure will also end. Of course, if there isn't any complication.' As I sat counting the twenty-seventh elephant, my turn came.

'How old are you, my child?' The elderly Armenian doctor in a short-sleeved gown with his strong hands folded on his chest, covered with thick hair, asked me.

'Eighteen.'

'Is this your first abortion?'

'Yeah.'

'The boy refuses to get married?'

'He wants, but career and children,' I simply blabbered to drag time.

'Your mother is alive?'

'Yeah.'

'What does she work as?'

'A doctor herself.'

The doctor gave a long abuse in Armenian. 'I will not do the abortion today. Often termination of first pregnancy results in infertility later. You have a whole night to think about your decision. I really want you to think it over.'

I looked at the doctor with dog-like loyal eyes and said:

'I shall think over. But please remember I am allergic to Novocain.' This was a literate lie taught to me by my mom, who did not teach me ways of contraception.

'I can go through abortion only under general anaesthesia.'

'We, as a rule, do not do it under general, but since you promised me to think over your decision, I shall personally arrange it for you with the anaesthetist from the other department, if need be.'

'I dashed out of the OT, shining bright and the whole queue of women followed me with their hard, ailing eyes. Of course, at that time I was only thinking about the fact that under general anaesthesia I shall see nothing and hear nothing. Morally I am not a very conscientious person and the value of the life that I was going to end, was associated only with my own personal physical discomfort. But the decision to do so was done in the company of people who taught me that this is how it should be. According to me they were equally responsible for this action of mine.

'So you have come back?' asked the Armenian doctor with hostility.

'Yes, come back,' I blabbered.

'As you know, yesterday the abortion was on my conscience; today it is already on yours.'

More than this I do not remember, except that later my fiancé came to meet me and we hugged each other. Without realizing that it may harm me, we even took a walk in the rain.

The most terrible thing was over and now one could prepare for the wedding, have fun, visit the cafés with the money sent to us as a wedding gift. One could love each other and try out being partners together, while living in marriage. In reality this was just some kind of teenage fun of living without parents. It seemed that I paid for the right to get married to the person in the white coat called the gynaecologist, guarding my admission to adult life.

'Again, don't tell me that you are pregnant?' After a few months later that very terrible doctor asked me in that very same clinic in the presence of my mom in her white coat, which gave her access to enter all cabins bypassing the queues, but did not empower her to enlighten her grown-up daughter.

'Again there'll be toxicity problem negative Rhesus factor; I'll recommend an abortion.'

'There is no need for that,' I said quietly but firmly.

'So what do you plan to do?'

'Give birth to the child.'

'Have you gone crazy?' The doctor was so shocked with my answer as if I was a man. 'And what do you think you'd deliver for us, you are so thin, pale and with such low haemoglobin.'

'I will deliver for myself and not for you ...' I would have continued but Mom, realizing that I was no longer frightened of the gynae's cabin and was quite capable of giving back for all the indignities of the past, covered up flatteringly:

'What can you do if she has made up her mind to have the child! I would request you to examine her, as our local doctor is quite a novice, still a student.'

'And he will die a student, can't even properly look at a woman, wonder how he could make his wife pregnant,' answered the doctor. 'But a rule is a rule, so only he shall examine your daughter.'

The young male gynae seemed to be a little older than me. Both of us were feeling equally embarrassed. We felt like two small school kids punished and made to stand next to each other naked.

'Motherhood—is a very serious responsibility,' he was blushing thoroughly as he said this while filling up the medical card for me in his childlike handwriting.

'Yeah,' I answered.

'Has somebody already checked you up? In that case I will not examine again. Here is the recommendation for further tests. Are you feeling sick? You can take this medical certificate for leave.'

'Ok,' I answered.

'On Friday I am giving a lecture for first-time mothers-to-be ... well nothing great about it. All that is useful is when the labour pains begin you should give a massage like this ...' he pulled up his gown, turned to show his back and vigorously with his fist began massaging his jeans near the tail end of his spinal column.

'And how can you massage if you are lying on your back?' I asked surprised.

'Wonder how, but that's what we were taught.'

My pregnancy was not an easy one; everyday uptil mid-day I would be throwing up and flinging myself on people as somebody who's just back from war! In between I would read the classics to intellectually influence the child in my womb though all the classics would get lost in the sea of scares and frights, as I would be hearing about somebody or the other dying during delivery. The young gynae having got accustomed to me, began yelling at me, having acquired the mantle of chief preacher.

'You woman, what are you doing with yourself? Why are you putting on so much weight? You'll have to drastically cut down on salt. Not even a gram of it. By the way what did you eat today?'

'Bananas and a packet of tooth powder,' I answered very honestly.

'And, pray, how do you eat it? Do you mix it in water?' The gynae looked seriously interested.

'No, just like that with a teaspoon.'

'But it is tasteless,' he insisted.

'I also thought so, till I got pregnant.'

'I am afraid, I will have to hospitalize you, and the mortality rate of pregnant women is increasing in the country.'

'What's that got to do with me?'

'You have a high level of water-retention. What would you deliver? Nothing! Your baby has already dissolved in water.'

The whole night after my visit to the clinic I cried. Later I decided that the less I see of these doctors, the better I would be with my baby. But this male gynae happened to be one of the conscientious types and with the enthusiasm of a new convert he would drop in at home or catch me in the courtyard. Once my husband and I bumped into him in the street and we almost ran across to the other side of the street. The doctor kept shouting behind us.

'Hey, you woman, you have oedema, blood pressure! You'll die in your labour if tomorrow itself, you do not get hospitalized! Then you'll remember me! If something happens to you, I shall be stripped of my degree. As it is we do not have enough gynaes in our country!'

After this incident in the night I almost aborted. The ambulance came and the elderly woman doctor gave some injections. She looked at my toxic face with disproportionately big eyes due to my thinness; examined my belly, covered with blue, red patterns like on the globe, outbalancing my nineteen-year-old body a step forward and said, 'Ask your husband to punch that male gynae right on his face, when he comes again with his diagnosis or he would maim you and many more women. And look for some pull to find a good doctor; it seems to me that you are going to have twins.'

During those days the ultrasound machine could only be found at the Institute of Gynaecology. My mom managed to find her way there. The sprightly youngsters in white coats applied some cream on my stomach, moving the apparatus over with a pad and the image of two small babies of impressive size appeared before my eyes on the screen.

I was gripped with an overwhelming feeling of disbelief. So far I had failed to logically feel the living beings within myself. All this while I had comprehended my pregnancy in a fragmented manner; I was pregnant, soon a baby would appear and I would become a mother. My awareness levels prohibited me from perceiving these as related facts. The cultural upbringing in my country did not prepare me for this. 'You are a girl, a future mother and hence should not …' this was followed by a whole list of unfounded limitations, a step to the other direction was considered dereliction of duty. As often and with the same amount of disbelief from the days of my childhood, I had been hearing that army service is the moral duty of every citizen. My mom had always made an issue of her being 'a mother', whenever she was doling out disgusting punishments to me. Such role-model mothers made from cast iron and stone were spread along the length and breadth of the country; their prototypes squabbled in the queues, lamented over their drunkard husbands, willingly put their children under the mercy of the crèches, hospitals, young-pioneer camps and schools. I had no intentions whatsoever of joining the ranks of such mothers. The Soviet-style role model of motherhood did not much inspire me enough. I was far away from the idea of my transformation from a bohemian university student into that of a mother of twins. As a matter of fact I was not concentrating on the transformation as the front line of physical survival that passed through the gynaes' cabins.

Finally I was hospitalized. The maternity ward was situated in the building of the casualty department. There was no hot water and only one toilet for all the women on the floor. A queue of pale women clutching on to their stomachs stood opposite the toilet. There were thirty beds in the ward and in order to save on space, one side-table stood between two beds. The atmosphere in the ward was hardly encouraging for the arrival of healthy descendants. If one woman with a pathological condition could raise hysteria around herself, imagine thirty of them creating a ruckus! In the hospital the women almost had to wage a civil war to get the *fortochka** opened when the temperature rose to 30° C. The commotion ended with the nurse coming and putting all the agitating women on sedation.

The bedtime stories of 'Scherezade' in the pioneer camps after the all-clear signal reminded me of the terrible stories about maniacs, vampires and the visiting sprits. Here the ignorant gynaecologists, drunkard husbands, mean bosses and soulless mothers-in-law, however, played the role of the villains. Brought up on the university culture of the small groups, I tried to hold on to my different self of an adult woman. I even tried to absorb the nonsensical talk around me, which provided for useful data for psychologists and historians. But this atmosphere was ruinous for a young woman about to deliver her baby.

'This is an obvious Caesarean case,' said the broad-shouldered, rude doctor doing the rounds, poking her finger into me. Such kinds of doctors heading the gynaecology department were fit only to sit at the vegetable shops.

'Why a Caesarean?' As she was the head of the gynaecology section, I ran after her to confirm.

'As if you do not understand why, woman!' The doctor expressed surprise. 'Measure your hips in centimetres and think about it. The baby needs space; you'll die yourself and torture the baby also. I am marking in red pen in your card, so that it is clear that yours is a Caesarean case and you are sent only to me to deliver.'

'But I do not wish to come to you.'

'Why? You do not like my section?' The doctor was offended.

'Yesterday in our ward a woman went into labour pain but the nurse asked her to wait as there were only two tables and both were busy.'

'So, what's the problem?' The doctor expressed surprise. 'And what

---

* Small-hinged windowpane used for ventilation.

happened? Well, she must have screamed a bit. For your information my mom delivered me in the fields. She was cutting the hay and there I was born.'

'I would prefer more comfortable arrangements than your mother.'

'In that case you may send a telegram to Brezhnev himself and tell him that you are special over here. Let him have you deliver on his writing table! In any case I am overworked for the salary I get here.'

In the general discussion in the ward, it was resolved that a Caesarean was much better than a normal delivery. The reasons being, firstly, that you do not feel the pain and secondly, the doctors are always around you. In case of a normal delivery you may just not see them. Thus all the stories relating to deaths due to a Caesarean or in absence of it, that were there in the repertoire of those twenty-nine, terror-stricken souls, were narrated. And when everybody had calmed down, started breathing normally and then snuffling and snoring, I lay there crying in the darkness and rotating the Rubik block of my future. Of course there was the strong allure of the anaesthesia, as well as of the image of two cute kids wrapped up and tied with a bow. But being a university creature I had read through heaps of material on this issue and my readings suggested that the vegetative vascular system of the children born through Caesarean is not well adapted to the changes of atmospheric pressure.

However, the gynaecologists had so deeply ingrained my psyche with the idea that the Soviet women with wide hips were capable of happily and coolly delivering a child in the hay, in the cot and in the lift, at the mill, near the blast-furnace, and so on, that it seemed to me as though I, with my twins and also with a negative-Rhesus, toxicity, narrow hips and baseless pretensions was the only bohemian black sheep amongst them.

Somehow I survived this hospital along with its scheduled morning ice-cold baths in the small bathroom; its three-litre-full jar tests prescribed by Dr Zemnitsky; its food, the smell of which was enough to terminate any pregnancy; its dirty windows opening into the morgue and all its other *accessories,* with which a pregnant woman had to put up in the twenty-first century.

From the hospital I was referred to the All Union Institute of Gynaecology, where the wives of diplomats, astronauts, privileged top men and women with a pathological medical history delivered. I fell into the last category. Mom's acquaintance, who worked there, warned her:

'You see, we have better conditions here than other maternity clinics, but if you feel that your pains are coming you should call me up. I do not guarantee anything if you fail to do so.'

The wards in this institute were, either six-bedded meant for the commoners or single-bedded for the much-privileged astronauts, generals' wives. The ward woman came carrying a dull-coloured ashen gruel for the commoners and restaurant delicacies for the not so common. They were allowed to have their guests in the wards, whereas we were supposed to make do with exchange of chits, telephones or through-the-window talking. Though my husband wearing a doctor's coat and with all his artistic nuances did make his way to me to the fourth floor, where I stood hiding in the dark corridor to meet him. We hugged each other like the underground revolutionaries since towards the end of my pregnancy, the feeling of humiliation and insult almost turned into a belief and along with the administration I also began to think that a meeting with my own husband, while being pregnant, was violation of the rules. And if caught I deserved the justified punishment to be discharged immediately and having to deliver under less comfortable conditions. The vulnerability and inadequacies of the pregnant women are such that they easily metamorphose into the best of the zombies of the world.

The Negro woman, fed up of the Russian food in the Institute, used to fry bananas in sunflower oil and the Koreans stewed herrings. These soul-irritating smells coupled up with my toxic perceptions aroused racist feeling. The only relief was in terms of the hullabaloo that was created by the regular visits to the long-legged Negro woman by three other wives of her diplomat husband.

This Institute was also distinguished amongst other similar centres because of the presence of a large number of dark and yellow-skinned students. The smart professor with a bunch of papers regarding the history of the ailment would enter the ward with her crowd, irrespective of the fact that I could be eating, sleeping or dying and would start blabbering to one of them pointing at me:

'See, this an interesting case, nineteen years old, twins, negative-

Rhesus ...' with this all those twenty-eight students took turns to feel my stomach with the airs of high professionals.

'Don't you think that for once I may deliver in the midst of these lecture-demonstrations?' I asked.

'Nothing will happen, in fact we even intend to have a report on your case,' she answered.

Once during my pregnancy I lost consciousness as I lay on my back. As the room containing ammonium chloride was at the end of the corridor at quite a distance, I was slapped on my beautiful (according to me) face to regain consciousness. Again when I lay back on my back I lost consciousness. The doctors stood around me for long, discussed the situation and left shrugging their shoulders. The whole night was before me and I was paranoid about getting into a horizontal position. So that whole night I sat like an orphan hugging a pillow, but in the morning I collapsed and fell asleep. This is how the energetic professor, who was brought to me by the crowd of puzzled doctors, found me. The lady-professor was angry, gave my face a tight slap, made me sit up and turned to the group of doctors.

'What did you study in the Institute? Who gave you the degree? Look at this woman—a typical case of twins, the babies with their heavy weight are pressing the hollow vein. This is not to be learnt in pathology, but to be observed by those who call themselves specialists!' The doctors were all looking down. 'And, you woman, remember that until you deliver you shouldn't be lying on your back at all.'

'And how would I deliver?' I was bewildered.

'Lying on your side. The French women traditionally deliver lying on the side, and the Koreans deliver while squatting down.'

'But an obvious Caesarean is mentioned specifically on my card,' I said. 'How am I going to deliver sideways or squatting?'

'Give me your card,' demanded the lady professor. 'You see, woman, I am striking off the Caesarean bit and instead I am diagnosing the syndrome of the vein in your case.'

'But the baby will not be able to come out off such narrow hips!' I starting yelling.

'Who put this nonsense in your head? You have ideal hips for twins. It's just become fashionable to go for a Caesarean! No Caesarean! Cut it out! Well, if you are in labour for three days, you may have a

Caesarean!' And she went out making a noise with her heels and waving my card. I was totally confused and could only hope for God's mercy.

At times I would look at the lump of my naked belly in the mirror, which moved and was raised up like Solaris—heads, knees and elbows appearing from it. Rationally I could not understand that these were babies and I related to it as an abstract comprehensible mass with which I was communicating, to whom I was complaining about life, to whom I addressed my request not to hit at my internal organs during sorting out, which had started between them. I must say that my requests were taken care of. My basic instincts told me that now I was not alone in the frame of my own skin. But guided by my scholarly experience I knew that the responsibility for the survival of all three of us was entirely mine. As the happy day, which was almost like the judgement day for me, drew closer such thoughts made me tremble like an aspen leaf.

Suddenly one day I woke up in a pool of water—a phenomenon that nobody had ever explained to me. It would have been foolish to wake elderly women around me to satisfy my silly queries. So I softly walked to the attendant's desk only to see the nurse was snoring, having taken some diluted spirit the night before. The water kept on flowing.

'Excuse me, please,' I shook her by the shoulder, 'I need help.'

'You, woman, why don't you calm down and sleep at night,' the nurse on duty growled.

'I do not know but some kind of water is flowing,' I mumbled.

'It's some problem or the other ... what's the time?'

'I do not know, don't have a watch.'

'Then go and see. Who needs to know the time? Me or you?' Like a fool I tiptoed to the clock at the end of the corridor feeling guilty equally about soiling the linoleum floor and having to wake somebody in the middle of the night.

'It's 5 o'clock,' I conveyed to the nurse.

'Ok, fine, let's go,' said the nurse, lazily getting up and walking along the corridor with difficulty.

'Where to?'

'To the "where-to" mountain ... where else woman? To the labour room!'

'For the delivery?' My feet were trembling beneath.

'Hey, you woman, get into the lift, why are you standing like a log of wood?' I entered the self-operated lift and the nurse shoved in a stretcher.

'Lie down on the stretcher.'

'But why?' I could barely whisper.

'Such are the instructions. Your water bag has burst, so you must lie down.'

'Then why did you make me run up and down the corridor?'

'Well, you may give these lectures to your own child soon. For the seventy roubles that I get here, I am not supposed to run after each one of you and listen to your sermonizing. What do I get from you? The foreigners at least give presents ...'

The labour room was a big hall with beds and other apparatus, where women were screaming in terrible voices. 'How sad it would be to die so young, so beautiful and so talented!' Thinking about myself I wept bitterly.

'You, woman, will you finally lie down like a human being on your back!' hollered a young lad in a white coat.

'I can't. I have the hollow-vein syndrome, it's written in the card,' I quipped very categorically and firmly.

'Such a vein does not exist in the human body and I am the doctor here. Lie down! They have to put the apparatus for you!'

The young nurse began to enmesh my body with all sorts of tubes and put a belt on my forehead with metallic strips, connected to the apparatus.

'Here is the switch, woman, if you turn right, it increases and left, it decreases. Understood?'

'No,' I answered. All that I understood was that these people would not let me die in peace.

'Well, if the pains are strong then increase and decrease as they go.'

'And what is it?'

'Well, I do not know. Some kind of current, scientific work. Later fill up the questionnaire how much relief from pain you got.' I turned the switch and shuddered from the shock. The unnatural position that I was in, where I was trying to look as though I was lying on my back and simultaneously fulfilling the previous instruction of not to lie on my back, added to the theatrical scene. The doctor on duty was flipping through the pages of a detective novel in a blazing cover. In any other ward it would have been normal to find a person reading a book on duty. But here the howls and cries were blending and multiplying in the high ceiling as the northern lights: the frail Korean was weeping quietly, the long-legged, broad-shouldered blonde was howling loudly, the fat woman with her hair plaited was crying and my neighbour with her forehead burning due to the pain-relieving current was shouting in a heart-rending manner.

'You've a stone instead of a heart! I wonder how your wife manages to live with you?' My neighbour started a conversation with the doctor.

'Woman, what a fuss you're making of yourself? You are not the first or the last woman who is delivering a baby here,' the attendant doctor retorted snapping over the flipped page of his book.

'Oh! You, a creep in pants!' declared my neighbour, 'and what do you know about all this? I am delivering my third child. You would have known better if you were to go through even one menstruation a year—you would've prepared a whole nine months for it!'

'Enough,' said the doctor, 'you are getting on my nerves!' He banged the book and left.

'Stupid,' the long-legged woman shouted at her neighbour, 'why did you do this? Who will now handle my delivery, you?'

'Yeah, he would have paid attention to your delivery, if you were to deliver straight in his book,' the neighbour retorted back.

All this reminded me of a spaceship ruthlessly left alone with women, who do not have either the possibility to call anyone for help, or are capable of helping themselves. Everything inside me was twisting and the force of the pain was thwarting this spaceship towards devastating heights. I came to my senses because of a deep cry and a hazy forehead, which, later I recognised were my own. With great difficulty I forced myself not to turn the switch button of the current to maximum while the pains came and I unsuccessfully tried to restrain from howling. The lower half of my body seemed to have disentangled itself and was floating under the roof, brandishing the bed sheets as wings, while the upper portion of my torso kept on clinging to the cot, trying to reflect upon the situation in between the howls. The time sense was lost; the din and semi-darkness filled up the room. I began to bid farewell to everything that was close to my heart in this life.

The sound of heels could be heard and a woman in spectacles, with an air of fastidiousness but looking tired in her swollen face, exasperatedly said to me:

'You there, woman, why are you quiet if you are having labour pains? With your twins we have to record the indications. Move over to the stretcher.' Though at that moment I could have been anything but quiet, but I was already in a trance and was unable to get into any discussion. I crawled over into the stretcher like a crab and could only hazily comprehend how in the other room, which was chock-a-block full of monitors, that woman pushed the data tubes into the various parts of my body. She was running between the various screens and her notebook, where she was noting down the indicators of my left-over existence.

'All that you are doing, is it for my children or me?' I asked almost in a buzzing whisper in between my labour pains.

'This is for the benefit of science, woman,' proudly answered the woman. If she were standing closer to me I would have kicked her powdered face on behalf of all the women having to give birth during Soviet times.

Somehow I regained consciousness on the delivery table situated near the window covered with sunlight and saw a huge round clock ticking away. It showed that it was 9.40 a.m.

'There is nobody as it's time for change of duty,' a woman from the next table said softly. The quietness resembled that of a crematorium though outside the window, the birds were making a hubbub. All the bulbs were bursting in my head and in my heart because of the emotional overstress. Blissfully distanced away from everything, I was awaiting my end.

Two elderly women entered the room. After seeing me they started scolding everybody and the whole ward started running up and down. I overheard, without any interest, that my delivery should have happened an hour ago; that I had been torn wide from below; that it was unclear how I would deliver; that for this lapse all the employees could be chucked out but not before their hands were cut off.

'Don't worry, everything will be fine! What is your name?' The elderly woman summed up, turning me on my back and was almost over me. As during the last couple of months I was not used to being addressed otherwise, but simply as 'woman', I just did not have the energy to tell her that I had categorically been advised not to lie on my back; as I felt this moment to be my much awaited 'end', capable of liberating me from this torture; I uttered in a soft voice:

'My name is—Woman—' and I lost consciousness.

I opened my eyes still dazed due to the effect of the anaesthesia and saw an incredibly dark-haired huge screaming baby.

'Just see, what a beauty,' said the woman chirpily.

'Can I feel the baby?' I requested. Frightened, I touched the baby who was brought to me. The baby seemed hot like a cookie, as though taken out of an oven.

'Do not let yourself go, soon you'll have to deliver the second one, which is very impulsive and has already sucked some foetus water,' said the elderly woman.

'Can I rest a bit?'

'No, we have only five minutes to go about it all. Fast, put the drip in the hands and the feet!' A whole battery of obstetricians (it seemed that there were not many according to the timetable) began to fix my hands and feet to the drip, creating a lot of hubbub as in the fish market. Within five minutes I saw another baby, who started to shout more than the first one when slapped.

'Is this also mine?' I babbled in a state of excited idiocy.

'Of course, yours,' answered the nurse as she removed the drip, 'you should be thankful to Professor Sidelnikova, who accidentally came in, otherwise you wouldn't have had even one of them!'

Subsequently, for two hours my neighbour and I had to keep on lying on the stretchers in a cold, ragged corridor with our stomachs lying on top of us like blown-up airships. Robbed of everything and feeling humiliated, we kept on staring towards the ceiling.

'Hope they look after these at least? Or is it like us about whom they do not bother?' I asked.

'They won't say,' my neighbour answered sadly.

'Women, you shouldn't sleep!' Everyone passing by us would shout this to us.

'Why aren't we being sent to the ward?' we queried, almost collapsing.

'As you should not be sleeping for two hours, so as to keep a check on the internal haemorrhage; the attendants are provided only to the foreigners.'

'But it is cold here!'

'That's intentional so that you do not sleep off.' After two hours I was on the operation table.

'Will you be able to tolerate the anaesthesia? One would have to stitch you for almost an hour, as you are in shreds.'

'Yeah, I will,' I answered and finally disconnected from the world under the mask.

'Tell your husband that I did my very best to make it new almost. He owes me a treat! But why did he bring you here so late for delivery. For almost half a year you won't be able to sit properly because of the stitches,' said the lad after an hour on completion of the job.

'I have been here for a month ...'

'Well, all kind of things happen. We are also mortals here. And where do you work?'

'I am studying.'

'What discipline?'

'Philosophy.'

He probably wanted to say that not all is in order even in philosophy but perhaps thought over it and said: 'Well, you may philosophically take all this.'

Seems like these words were the last straw and all my built-up howling broke loose out of my system, which resembled the dance of St. Vitus's.

'Please calm down, calm down ...' the doctor rushed up and down, trying to hold me on the table and looking into the adjacent room from where the surgery-nurse was missing. 'Oh! You will break your stitches if you cry like this! It will take another hour to stitch you. Come on now! Everything has ended so well for you, you've such splendid babies! Why do you cry, my dear?' The doctor began to fill up the syringe from the ampoules while shouting into the corridor: 'Lena, Lida, where the hell are you?' The doctor poked the syringes into my, already blue with injection, upper arm. And everything started to float in front of me: blinding bulbs, the nurses who finally appeared, green walls, and so on. In the twilight caused due to the cocktail of drugs I saw myself running naked through the long, cold corridors of the Institute of Gynaecology; passing through the formation of doctors spitting and throwing earth at me; towards the open, bright door, simultaneously trying to cover my huge belly with my palms ...

All this I experienced seventeen years ago just because I happened to be a woman. This will continue to happen with every other woman as long as there are such people who do not wish to discuss this issue. For in our world being a woman is not a respectable thing, even at that moment, when a woman does that one single job, which the man is simply not capable of doing.

Translated by Ranjana Saxena

West Asia

Iran

Zarrinkolah

SHAHRNUSH PARSIPUR

Zarrinkolah was twenty-six years old and a prostitute. She was working in the New City at Golden Akram's house. Akram had seven gold teeth and was also called Akram Seven. She had been there since she was a child. At first, she had three or four customers a day. By the time she was twenty-six, she had twenty to twenty-five or even thirty customers a day. She was tired of working. She had complained to Akram several times, and was yelled at and eventually beaten, until she shut up.

Zarrinkolah was a cheerful woman. She was always cheerful, whether she had three or four customers a day or thirty. She even turned her complaints into jokes. All the women liked her. When they ate lunch, Zarrinkolah would start joking and dance around the table, and the women would die laughing.

Several times she intended to leave the house, but the women wouldn't let her go. They said that if she left the house it would be dead. Perhaps all the women encouraged Akram Seven to beat her. Zarrinkolah never really intended to leave, for if she left this house, she would have to go straight to another house. Once, when she was nineteen, she received a marriage proposal and had a chance to leave. The suitor was an ambitious construction worker who dreamed of becoming a mason, and who needed a hardworking wife. Unfortunately, before they could decide what to do, someone cracked open his skull with a shovel during a fight.

Although she complained sometimes, she had accepted her fate. But now, for six months, she had not been able to think clearly. The problem started one Sunday morning when she woke up.

Akram Seven shouted, 'Zarri, there's a customer, and he's in a hurry.'

There weren't many customers early in the morning. Usually just a few who had stayed over from the night before and had the urge in the morning. That Sunday morning, Zarrinkolah thought, so a customer has come. So what. She wanted to shout out, so what, but Akram Seven yelled, 'Zarri, I'm talking to you. I said a customer has come.'

She left her breakfast and angrily went back to the bedroom, lay down on the bed and opened her legs, The customer entered the room. It was a man without a head. Zarrinkolah didn't dare scream. The headless customer did his business and left.

From that day on, all of the customers were headless. Zarrinkolah didn't dare say a word about it. They might say that she was possessed by a demon. She had heard about a woman possessed by a demon, who would start shrieking at eight o'clock every night. For a while this scared away the customers until they kicked her out of the house.

Zarrinkolah decided to sing every night at eight o'clock so that she wouldn't shriek like that woman. She did this for six months. Unfortunately she couldn't carry a tune. A guitar player said, 'You bitch, you don't even have a voice, you're giving everybody a headache.' After hearing this, she went into the bathroom every night and sang there for half an hour. Akram Seven ignored it. After all, Zarrinkolah took care of thirty customers a day and was still cheerful. She was always cheerful.

Then they brought an innocent young girl to the house. One day Zarrinkolah took her into her room and said, 'Kid, I have to tell you something. I have to tell somebody. I'm afraid I'm going crazy. I have a secret that's making me miserable.'

The girl said, 'Everyone has to tell their secrets to someone. My grandmother used to say that the poor Imam Ali, who couldn't talk to anybody, used to go out to the desert and put his head in a well and pour out his grievances.'

'That's true. Now I'm going to tell you. I see everyone without a head. Not the women. The men. They're all headless.'

The girl listened kindly. She asked, 'You really see them all without heads?'

'Yes.'

'Ok, so maybe they really don't have heads.'

'If they really didn't have heads, the other women would notice.'

'Well, that's true. But maybe they all see them without heads, but like you, they don't dare say anything about it.'

So they agreed that whenever Zarrinkolah saw a headless man she would let the girl know, and if the girl saw a headless man she would let Zarrinkolah know.

Zarrinkolah saw all the men without heads and the girl saw them all with heads.

The next day, the girl said, 'Zarrinkolah, maybe you should pray and make a vow. Maybe then you'll see the men with heads.'

Zarrinkolah took two days off work and went to the bathhouse. Instead of going to the public section like she usually did, she went to a private room so that she wouldn't have to talk and joke with the other women. She hired a bath worker to scrub her back. She washed herself from head to foot. She ordered the bath worker to scrub her three times. The bath worker scrubbed until Zarrinkolah's skin was raw. But she wasn't satisfied that she was clean enough to pray.

The bath worker finally broke down crying and said, 'You poor woman, you must be crazy.'

Zarrinkolah paid the bath worker well so that she wouldn't tell anybody about her, and asked her how to perform ablutions after sexual pollution.

When the bath worker left, Zarrinkolah performed ablutions. She did them fifty times. Her entire body was burning from the chafing of the sponge.

She intended to get dressed and go to the shrine of Shah Abdulazim, but she had a sudden urge to pray. She decided to pray naked, but she didn't know how to pray. She decided that if Imam Ali was so sad that he went out to the desert to pour out his grievances to a well, it would be all right for her to just repeat his name as a prayer. She prostrated herself in prayer, naked in the bath, saying, 'Ali, Ali, Ali, Ali, Ali, Ali, Ali, Ali, Ali ...'

As she was saying this she began to cry. She cried and called out to Ali.

Somebody knocked on the door, and then banged on it. She came out of her ecstasy and asked, sobbing, 'Who is it?'

It was the bath attendant. She said they wanted to close up the bathhouse.

Zarrinkolah put on her clean clothes and gave her dirty clothes to the bath worker. She went out and walked to the shrine of Shah Abdulazim.

It was night time and the shrine was closed. She sat outside in the yard and cried quietly in the moonlight.

In the morning when they opened up the shrine, her eyes were swollen shut. She stopped crying, but did not enter. Her body felt like a piece of straw.

She ate breakfast in a diner. She asked the owner, 'If a person wants to drink cool water this time of the summer, where should she go?'

The owner looked at her puffy eyes with pity and said, 'Karaj isn't bad.'

There was nothing in her face to show that she had once been a prostitute. She had become a small woman of twenty-six with a heart as big as the sea.

She went to Karaj.

Translated by Kamran Talatoff & Jocelyn Sharlet

Iran

O Bejewelled Land

FORUGH FARROKHZAD

I did it
I got myself registered
dressed myself up in an ID card with a name
and my existence was distinguished by a number
So long live 678, issued from precinct 5,
resident of Tehran ...
Now my mind is completely at ease
The kind bosom of motherland
the nipple of former ages full of history's glory
the lullaby of culture and civilization
and the rattling of the rattle of the law ...
Ah
Now my mind is completely at ease.

*

With utmost joy
I walked to the window and fervently, six-hundred
seventy-eight times, drew into my breast
air grown thick
with the dust of dung and the stench of garbage and urine ...
And at the bottom of six-hundred seventy-eight IOUs,
atop six-hundred seventy-eight applications, I've written
Forugh Farrokhzad.

*

In the land of poetry, nightingales, and roses
living is a blessing, yes, indeed
when the fact of your being, after so many years,
 is approved —
a place where I
with my first official glance see six-hundred seventy-
eight poets through the folds of the curtain—
impostors, each in the strange guise of beggars
searching for rhymes and meters in heaps of rubbish.
And from the sound of my first official step
suddenly, from the dark and slimy marshes, six-hundred
seventy-eight mysterious nightingales
who have donned for fun the form of six-hundred
seventy-eight old black crows
flap lazily off toward the edge of day
And my first official breath
is imbued with the smell of six-hundred seventy-eight
red rose stems,
product of the great Plasco factories.

*

Living is a blessing, to be sure
in the home of Mr Fool-son, instant fiddler
and Mr O-Heart-Heart of the drum, clan of drums,
city of superstar champions—legs, hips, breasts and
glossy covers of Art,
cradle of the authors of the philosophy, 'Hey man,
what's it to me?'
source of Olympic scholastic games—ay!
a place where from every broadcast you turn on,
in vision or voice,
there blares the bleating horn of some young ingenious genius,
and the nation's intellectual elite
when they gather in adult classes
each has arranged upon his breast six-hundred seventy-
eight electric kebab grills

and on each wrist six-hundred seventy-eight
Navzar watches, and they know
that impotence comes from an empty purse,
not from ignorance.

*

I've done it, yes I've done it
Now to celebrate this victory
I proudly light, at the foot of the mirror,
six-hundred seventy-eight charge-account candles
and leap to the ledge to deliver, by your leave,
a few words on the legal advantages of life
and to the resounding of thunderous applause
I strike the first blow of the pick-axe for building
the lofty edifice of my life
right on top of my head.
I am living, yes, like the River of Life
which once lived too,
and I'll take my share from all that exists
in the monopoly of living men.

From tomorrow on I shall be able
to walk along, strolling
through the city's streets abounding in national blessings,
through the shadows of unburdened telegraph poles,
and I'll write, six-hundred and seventy-eight times, proudly
on public toilet walls:
I wrote this to make asses laugh!

*

From tomorrow on I shall be able
to hold in heart and mind
like any zealous patriot
a share of that profound ideal everyone pursues
passionately and anxiously

each Wednesday afternoon—
a share of those thousand fantasies born
   of each thousand-rial bill
which you can redeem for curtains, furniture or fridge
or give some night,
in exchange for six-hundred seventy-eight natural votes
to six-hundred seventy-eight sons of the native land.
And in the shelter of their shining skies,
   in their utter safeness,
six-hundred seventy-eight immense plaster swans
in alliance with six-hundred seventy-eight angels
—they too made of earth and clay—
busy themselves from dawn to dark
launching plans for stillness and silence.

*

I've done it, yes, I've done it
So long live 678, issued from precinct 5,
resident of Tehran,
who in the shelter of perseverance and will
has attained so high a standing as to have settled down
in a window sill
six-hundred and seventy-eight metres above the ground
And she has this honour:
she can cast herself headlong from her perch —
not by the stairs —
madly into motherland's kind lap
And her last wish is this,
that in return for six-hundred seventy-eight coins
the great master Abraham Sahba
exalt her life with an elegy that ends in nonsensical rhymes!

Translated by Hasan Javadi & Susan Sallée

Iran

I Will Greet the Sun Once Again

FORUGH FARROKHZAD

I'll give greetings to the sun once again,
to the stream that flowed within me,
to the clouds that were my tallest thoughts,
to the painful growth of aspens in the garden
who endured the seasons of drought with me,
to the flock of crows
who as a gift
brought the fields' nocturnal scent to me,
to my mother who lived in a mirror
and revealed the figure of my old age,
and to the earth, whose burning womb I've filled
with green seeds in my lust for repetition —
I'll give greetings once again.

I come, I come, I come
with my hair exuding the smells beneath the earth
with my eyes, thick with experiences of gloom
with the bouquet of greens I picked from the wood,
on the other side of the wall ...
I come, I come, I come
The threshold fills with love
and I, on the threshold, will greet once again
those who love, and the girl
still standing on the threshold filled with love

And it is thus
that someone dies
and someone remains

In the shallow stream that flows into a ditch,
no fisher will hunt a pearl.

I
know a sad little fairy
who takes abode in the ocean
and plays her heart on a wood-tipped flute
softly, softly …
a sad little fairy
who dies from a single kiss at night
and will be born with a single kiss at dawn.

Translated by Hasan Javadi & Susan Sallée

Iraq

My Silence

NAZIK AL-MALA'IKA

You may reproachfully provoke
   my guilt
Would I retreat?
Would the sharp icicle of your plaque
   cut through my flames?
Would I yield,
   and not go mad?

No.
I should revolt,
I scream inside.

But
were I to trespass
darken the air
with some bitter phrase
   perhaps a misplaced word
You would be offended
turn dry like sand
Rise
and quietly
disappear.

Don't ask me why
I am gagged.
Here, I remain
a bed of roses bent
   under your snow;

a puzzle of unanswerable questions
in some corner of your heart.
It is destiny's prescription:
Adam is the ice
Eve the fire.

Translated by Kamal Boullata

Iraq

Washing off Disgrace

Nazik al-Mala'ika

'Mother!'
A last gasp through her teeth and tears.
The vociferous moan of the night.
Blood gushed.
Her body stabbed staggered.
The waves of her hair
 swayed with crimson mud.
'Mother!'
Only heard by her man of blood.
At dawn
If her twenty years of forlorn hope should call
the meadows and the roseate buds shall echo:
She's gone
washing off disgrace!

Neighbourhood women would gossip her story.
The date palms would pass it on to the breeze.
It would be heard in the squeaking of every
 weather-beaten door,
and the cobbled stones would whisper:
She's gone
washing off disgrace!

Tomorrow
wiping his dagger before his pals
the butcher bellows,
'Disgrace?

A mere stain on the forehead,
now washed,'
At the tavern
turning to the barman, he yells,
'More wine
and send me that lazy beauty of a nymphet
   you got, the one with the mouth of myrrh.'
One woman would pour wine
   to a jubilant man
another paid
washing off disgrace!

Women of the neighbourhood
women of the village
we knead dough with our tears
   that they may be well-fed
we loosen our braids
   that they may be pleased
We peel the skin of our hands washing their clothes
   that they may be spotless white.
No smile
No joy
No rest
for the glitter of a dagger
                              of a father
                        of a brother
               is all eyes.
Tomorrow who knows
what deserts may banish
you
washing off disgrace!

Translated by Kamal Boullata

Israel

What Am I Speaking, Greek? She Said to Him

SAVYON LIEBRECHT

Eliyahu Yitzhakov, the real estate agent, donned his professional welcoming demeanour for the woman; she had attracted his attention from the moment she alit from her car, scanned the signs on top of the building, and made her way to his office. A picture immediately popped up in his mind: a black marble floor, a wide staircase leading all the way to the roof, French windows in the Salon. Quietly closing the door behind her, the woman walked in, bade him 'Good Morning' in a pleasant voice, peeled off her gloves and glanced at the office walls. Eliyahu Yitzhakov eyed her with pleasure as she quickly took in the photographs presented to him by building contractors to hang in his office, pictures of unfinished structures, surrounded by scaffolding, photos of completed buildings, and one photograph of a house undergoing renovation—draped in purple plastic sheets, like a gigantic gift-wrapped birthday present—that he himself had snapped somewhere in Germany. It did not escape him how her eyes lingered on an enlarged newspaper photograph in which he and the mayor were shown shaking hands at a presentation ceremony of 'Business of the Year' awards.

When she sat down facing him and turned her eyes on him, he shot a quick look, like a seasoned hunter, at her fingers as they trailed the gloves across the desk, and said hurriedly, 'I have something just for you, Ma'am. Exclusively handled by my agency. It's a penthouse not far from the beach. Imported tiles, black marble floor, completely furnished, leather upholstery in the front room, irrigation system on the roof—super luxury!'

The brim of her hat shaded her eyes a little when she turned her head politely and smiled furtively, a smile that made him uneasy, as if she were remembering a private joke. A slight hostility arose in him, but he quickly allowed himself to be seduced by her pleasant voice.

'I'm interested in the flat on 34, Ha-Mered Street.'

He recoiled in his impeccable imitation leather executive chair, his face registering insult, his mouth contorting in an affected disgust leaving no doubt as to his reaction. 'Ha-Mered Street! It's nothing but a dump next to the junkies' park.'

'I saw your agency's sign on the window.'

'34 Ha-Mered Street.' He correctly read the determination in her voice and now tried another of his tactics: he leaned forward in a gesture that suggested intimacy and intoned mellifluously, '34 Ha-Mered Street is not a place for a classy woman like you.'

'Why is that?' the secretive smile was back on her face.

'I know how to read people,' he explained earnestly, ignoring the amused smile that lingered in her eyes. 'Like a good matchmaker who knows how to introduce the right people, I know, as soon as I see someone, which flat will suit that person's soul. I once saw a woman from behind; she was standing nearby, looking at a jeweller's window. There and then I knew I had the flat for her. I went out and asked her if, by any chance, she was in need of a flat. To this day, whenever she passes by, she comes in and thanks me for the flat I found for her. So you see, even by looking at a person's back, I can find them the right flat. Ha-Mered street is not for you. Look—' he spread the palms of both hands in front of her, as if to underscore his total honesty, 'I'll tell you the truth: the owner of the flat on Ha-Mered came to me and said he had this flat on Ha-Mered street. As soon as I heard Ha-Mered I said to him: I don't want it. Go to another agency. But he insisted and gave me exclusive rights. So I said to him: I'm not committing myself. I once handled a flat on Ha-Mered street—I told him—and couldn't get rid of it for half a year. Finally sold it to a couple of blind people. But you—you'd be wasting your time going there. Better let me show you the penthouse.'

Twenty minutes later he stood in front of the ground floor flat, struggling with the old lock, applying his weight in an attempt to force the door open. The door gave suddenly, and he was hurtled inside the flat, immediately assaulted by an overpowering mouldy odour. He hurried to a window, fiddled with its rusty handle, and opened the shutter.

Only then did he turn to her to invite her in, except that she was already inside the flat, at the entrance to the room adjacent to the kitchen, her gloved hand still on the doorknob, tilting her head upward to study the ceiling.

Even before discovering her motive, his senses told him that this did not bode well. 'Let's start with the salon,' he suggested, trying to steer her toward the best room in the flat, but she did not react and just stood there, looking upwards, focused, her neck stretching. Then, without moving her head, she removed her hat with her free hand, and the fair hair that was trapped under the hat, fell straight onto her shoulder, like plastic fibres, the strands in the middle of her back amazingly long because of the backward tilt of her head. He wondered what was drawing her attention up there, so he came closer and peeked and immediately realized where the mouldy smell was coming from, and also knew he would have to lower the price of the apartment.

'It doesn't look good, but it's only a minor plumbing job. Nothing serious. It wasn't here a month ago,' the smell of her hair hit his nostrils as he craned his head above hers.

She grinned, remembering the first time she had seen those stains.

'Just one month?' she said unable to contain her derision.

'One month and one hour,' he tried to impress her with an old joke that often stood him in good stead.

She did not respond; her memory became clearer and sharper, carrying her back to the moment that had haunted her for many years: the morning following that awful, sleepless night. As soon as her parents had left the house, she leaped out of bed and sneaked into their bedroom like a thief, looking for the stains she mentioned while sobbing. There were two grey spots in the corner of the ceiling, resembling two unmatched eyes with pale pupils, perhaps the result of a shoddy painting job.

Across the ceiling, she now noticed some black, sooty squiggles surrounded by flecks in all shades of grey that looked like a series of x-ray pictures laid side by side.

'This looks older than one month,' she said in a broken voice, devoid of any argumentativeness. Her neck still craning, she wondered how her mother was able to predict the longevity of those stains as she wept on that terrible night, long after midnight. 'How can you tell me that it will disappear? These stains will be here long after I croak.'

'You can trust me, Ma'am. I have experience in such matters. This happened a month ago—two months tops.'

'More likely twenty years ago,' she chuckled, her head still tilted backwards.

He stood behind her, sensing his anger welling up at her persistent examination of the stains. Suddenly, it occurred to him that her purpose in lingering there was to bring down the price of the apartment, which was already low.

'Listen,' he shouted in her ear, 'I'm going to see a house nearby. I have some business there. I'll be back in half an hour. You can look around as much as you want in the meantime.'

At the door he heard her say, 'What, you're leaving me alone here?' Before slamming the door he announced harshly, 'I have a good eye for clients. You'll end by buying the penthouse. But if you enjoy peering at stains on the wall, Ma'am, be my guest.'

As soon as he left she was overwhelmed by an eerie sensation. Alone in the empty flat, the silence suddenly became oppressive, like the silence she recalled from the nights at the rural summer camp when she used to lie on a mattress she could never get used to, listening intently to the ominous silence, imagining beasts lurking in the dark, moving swiftly, furtively, on padded paws, making their way toward the innocent, unsuspecting prey smelling in its dreams. Now she found herself roaming gingerly around the apartment, feeling her way, absent-mindedly caressing the walls, the panels, the bathroom tiles, searching for old clues, for kind regards from the girl who used to live there, who dreamt a lot, secretly imagining her future, not knowing that the imagined future awaited for her in the bosom of coming years, never guessing that one day—like a visitor from another planet—the heels of her boots would click on the very floor she used to wash every Friday after school, and that she would recognize the exact spot where water had stubbornly gathered in the dining area near the crooked tiles, but would then search in vain for the pale squares left on her bedroom wall by her kindergarten and elementary school pictures, for marks left by hooks that supported shelves laden with her textbooks and the Junior Encyclopedia that her father bought second hand. Only the stains that her mother mentioned in her weeping remained. She went back to the old bedroom and stared at the ceiling.

Had she not requested a reading lamp for her fifteenth birthday, she would have never heard the weeping. But she did request a reading lamp, and when they brought the lamp home, wrapped in brightly coloured paper, they realized that the light socket was hidden behind the wardrobe. Her mother immediately declared, in her razor-sharp voice: 'The Wise Men of Chelm: first they buy a pig, then they find out it isn't kosher.'

Her father hastened to say, before her face could register her disappointment: 'Actually, it's time we shifted this wardrobe. I always thought it was in the wrong place.'

She emptied the shelves and the drawers of the wardrobe, and her father strained, his face flushed, to turn the wardrobe around and push it toward the opposite wall. Light burst from the window that had been hidden behind the wardrobe for years, and filled the room. Without much effort, the two of them moved the bed to the wall where the wardrobe had left a pale square. Her father plugged in the lamp and turned it on. Like witnessing a magic trick, the two of them marvelled at the bright shaft of light that fell on the sheet.

She spent that afternoon replacing her belongings, one by one, in the wardrobe, in a meticulous new order: one drawer for socks, one drawer for stockings, another drawer for underwear, another for handkerchiefs and her white scarf, a shelf for school shirts, a different shelf for everyday shirts, and a shelf for the two dress blouses. Then she got down on her knees and diligently polished the floor tiles, placed a small rug near the bed, smoothed its fringes, laid her slippers precisely in the centre of the arches in its pattern, shampooed her hair, combed it until the strands looked like flax stalks, then snuggled under her blanket and lay in bed reading until late at night, her face turned to the window, her eyes above the book, observing the drapes, puffed by the wind, like a pregnant belly.

At midnight the voices started coming through the wall; she reread the last line on the page and her heart sank at the thought that the neighbours might be turning up the volume on their radio, as they had been doing since their last quarrel with her mother. But then she recognized her mother's voice, and then her father's, and even before catching the words, she was horrified at the realization that all those years the wardrobe had served as a buffer that absorbed their voices, and that from now on, she was doomed to hear them.

'I need it, Marrila.' her father was saying.

'I can't today,' her mother's voice sounded sharp and metallic.

'That's what you said last week, too.'

'I've told you before and I'm not going to repeat myself like a parrot.'

'You won't even have to take off your nightgown.'

'No.'

'Do it tonight and I won't ask again until next week.'

'Cut it out.'

'I'm begging you, Marilla.'

'No, period.'

Even before she connected the words together to understand the exchange between his failing voice and her relentless one, she knew what they were talking about, but part of her kept on reading, pretending to her own ears, clinging to the letters sliding down the page. When she reached the bottom line she realized that she had not understood anything and started all over, struggling hard to be engrossed by the story, terrified by the voices now rising anew beyond the wall.

She scrunched up in bed and turned off the reading lamp, hoping that the darkness would drive away the sounds, but the voices only got louder and stronger.

'I don't know what to do anymore. I can't restrain myself any longer.'

'Then don't. I can't stand the pain.'

'You said you'd see the doctor.'

'It's not going to help. You don't go to the doctor for something like this. It's a question of age. We should quit doing it. Full stop.'

'I had a minor accident with the new machine today.'

'This too is my fault?'

'I've been edgy the whole week.'

'You're edgy? Well, I'm edgy too! You think I should do things for you—while you do nothing for me. I can't stand these stains. I told you so a month ago.'

'What stains? There are no stains here. It's something in the plaster. The painter must have done a poor job.'

'I must be speaking Greek again.'

She tried to force herself to fall asleep, conjuring the image that always brought her calm before slumber: she is swimming in placid water, with measured motions, gliding like a dolphin on the smooth, shimmering face of the water over a murky bottom, and then sinking, sinking into the inviting blue, forever deepening and darkening.

Suddenly she was roused from the depths, wide awake, all her senses alert. For the first time in her life she heard her mother crying, and immediately recognized the sound as if she had heard it often. In the dark she saw the curtain float into the room and heard her mother's sobbing and her father's voice: 'Now it's the stains. Last month it was the tap in the bathroom.'

An unidentified sound came from beyond the wall, like people wallowing in rustling sheets unrolled from huge bolts; her mother's voice declared, harsh and devoid of tears: 'And paint the ceiling, for God's sake. You can see these stains in the dark.'

Silently she got up, went into the bathroom, locked the door, filled the tub, muffling the gushing water from the tap with a towel, undressed and submerged herself in the water. She washed her hair, dived and surfaced, rubbed her ears, her nape, her temples, scrubbed her skin so raw that it looked infected. She combed her wet hair once more, then tiptoed back to her bedroom, wrapped herself in the blanket, pulling the cloth over her head. She lay thus for several hours, waiting fearfully for the voices behind the wall, but she heard nothing and fell asleep only to wake up alarmed, watching the window getting lighter and brighter. In the morning, when her father came to wake her up, he found her lying in bed, her eyes open, red, and he said immediately, 'I can tell by your eyes that you've been reading the whole night. So this is what will happen with the new lamp? You'll just read on and on and on?'

'I want to put the bed back,' she said, her voice sounding sick to her.

'Now, when the wardrobe is finally standing in the right place?'

'I want to sleep on that side,' her high voice, sounding foreign even to her own ears.

'But there's no socket to plug in the lamp,' he contended logically.

'Then I won't read!' she rebelled.

'You must read a lot,' he said softly, lovingly, caressing her hot forehead. 'There are still so many things you have to learn.'

In the mornings after the recovery she would sit with her parents in the kitchen, the three of them eating silently, their elbows touching, her eyes focusing on the bread, the butter, the jagged knife, not daring to look her parents in the eye.

On Saturdays, breakfast was even harder for her, but as she sat hunched over her slice of bread, diligently spreading the margarine, she was surprised to hear them discussing mundane affairs in their normal tone of voice, 'This notice from the post office about a parcel has been lying here for two days. You've got to go to the post office.'

'Maybe it's not a parcel. Maybe it's the tax authorities again.'

'We got a letter from the tax authority just last month.'

'So maybe it is a parcel.'

'Don't they have anything better to do at the tax authority than to write to us? They must employ a special clerk just for us.'

Her knife stopped spreading the margarine and she froze, somehow expecting to hear a continuation of the previous night's conversation with her father saying again, 'Just once'. And her mother immediately shooting back, 'That's what you said on Monday. It took you half an hour.'

'Why don't you see the doctor?'

'I should see the doctor? I must be speaking Greek.'

The door to the kitchen porch, long exposed to the rain, was peeling and its pane was cracked. She tried to open the blind, pulling hard on the threadbare cotton strap, but the blind refused to budge and remained stuck crookedly in its rusty casement. She peeked through a gap in the slats and saw the back of the neighbouring house, a patchwork of peeling plaster; her eyes were drawn to a line of striped kitchen towels hanging out to dry along the ground-floor balcony.

Sometimes she would remember the young couple that used to live there at the time, their bedroom window facing hers; she remembered the laughter that emanated from there in the nights, sending strange shivers down her body, from her throat to her toes. Sometimes, in the morning, on her way to school, she deliberately stopped and waited for them to get to their motorcycle that was always parked in the same spot, leaning against an electric pole. She pretended to busy herself with the buckle on her schoolbag, watching them from the corner of her eye as they climbed on the bike, the woman hugging the man from behind, clasping her hands over his fly, the two of them becoming one unit, like stars in a movie preparing for the final scene when a helicopter rescues them from a jungle thicket. Many years later she used to talk about them to men she loved, always whispering, always with the longing that accompanies a belated realization.

The first time she heard their laughter, she was sitting with her mother in the kitchen: she was peeling cloves of garlic while her mother was furiously chopping cabbage for pickling, her hand clutching the big knife firmly, pounding the sharp blade very close to her fingers. Suddenly a peal of laughter was heard, sounding fresh and surprising. The two of them fell silent at once. Her mother stopped in mid-motion, pricking her ears as if she had been issued a declaration of war. She stood still for a moment, then braced herself and said to her daughter, 'Don't go out.' She burst out of the kitchen onto the adjacent porch.

'There are children here,' she heard her mother's voice outside, and she quickened the rate of her garlic peeling, 'You should be ashamed of yourselves!'

When her mother came back into the kitchen her eyes were glaring, her face flushed with fury.

'Who were you talking to?' her daughter ventured to ask.

'Talking? Can you talk to them? Animals!'

'Why did you tell them to be ashamed of themselves?'

'They know the reason very well.'

Outside a young voice was heard derisively, 'Lady, we are terribly ashamed!' The blood rushed to her mother's face.

Another peal of laughter was heard and her mother rushed outside to the porch, brandishing the knife in her hand. The girl rose, the garlic skin in her palm, gingerly walked to the door and peered out. On the balcony opposite she saw the man and woman, looking like a pair of high school kids. The woman was hanging out laundry, bending toward the taut washing lines, intoxicated with her laughter, curls cascading over her face down to her neck. The man was standing behind, bent over her, hanging the laundry above her head.

The girl stood there, half hidden, smiling at the sight of the handsome couple hanging laundry together, like a four-armed creature: two arms placing a blue T-shirt on the line, and two arms clipping clothes-pins on it, moving .in unison, like synchronized rowers in a rowboat.

'Pigs!' her mother shouted at the top of her voice, flailing the knife; the girl, recoiled and sat back in her chair in the kitchen. 'Only pigs carry on like this!' Her mother slammed the door, her eyes bulging in her face.

Years later, while shaking a rug over the balcony railing, her husband came behind her, lifted her skirt and pressed against her bent body, whispering in her ear, 'We're like Napoleon, capable of doing several things at the same time.' In that instant, the scene flashed through her mind, as if splashed on a giant screen, and for the first time she realized why the skirt had flown up the young woman's back and why the laughter burst from behind the curls. 'What's the matter, lady? Come over and look. All we're doing is hanging out the washing together. We're trying to save precious time.'

The bottom cabinets and the marble counter in the kitchen had already been replaced by subsequent tenants, but the upper cabinets, ordered by her mother a few years before they left the flat, were still in place. One by one she opened the cupboards, finding them empty, and remembered the flowery wax paper her mother used to replace every spring, and the muslin ribbons along the middle shelf behind the glass door where the beautiful crystal goblets were displayed. During Passover holidays, she would help her mother in the kitchen, polishing silver candlesticks, peeling the old wax paper off the shelves, scraping hardened glue with a knife, scrubbing the shelves with a wooden brush and laying them on the floor to dry. During the hours they spent together, her mother worked diligently and efficiently, her lips pursed, constantly carping about the glue that dried too slowly, about the inferior paper that could not be cut straight, the dishonest merchant who had sold her defective lace ribbons. Bitter and cantankerous, she would settle accounts with the greengrocer who sneaked a rotten eggplant into her bag; with the neighbour who saw a sheet blowing by his car but did not bother to pull it out of a puddle; with the insolent couple—new neighbours who had no shame; day and night you can always tell when they are at home, carrying on loudly; with Father who would not lift a finger around the house, and look at the grimy door frames that he claims are perfectly clean—

When her father's name was mentioned, she bent herself further over the shelf and worked more industriously, shrinking as if to protect herself, listening to her mother fuming: 'He doesn't understand anything; it's as if I'm speaking Greek to him'.

Now, standing in front of the empty cabinets, she felt sorry for her father, for the pointless bitterness her mother had injected into her life, for the poison she accumulated in her heart all those years, letting it fester and bubble like boiling lava, bolting her heart even against rare moments of sweetness ... Suddenly she remembered one Saturday night:

her father came out of the shower, clean and fresh, a towel around his shoulders, looking like an advertisement poster for a summer holiday; his face was so happy and he looked so handsome with his hair brushed back, his hands stretched out, singing an aria from some opera loudly and terribly off-key. He approached her mother, hugging her from behind; but her mother recoiled from him crossly, wiped her nape where he had dripped on her, smoothed the blouse he had wrinkled, and snapped, 'Why are you shouting in my ears?'

Even in old age, her father never ceased to woo her mother: always bringing her flowers and small gifts, never begrudging her refusals, and all the years trying to reconcile his daughter's heart to her, telling her, his voice full of affection, 'You have no idea how beautiful your mother was. Even after the war, when sometimes you couldn't tell who's a man and who's a woman, only she, with her grey eyes—like a butterfly.'

So why does she cry in the night? The question tore from her but halted at her twisting mouth; in its stead another sentence came out, with a smile that replaced the contorted lips: 'Daddy, I'm sure you don't mean to say "butterfly".'

'But it's so hard to love her,' her father continued his train of thought. 'So don't be angry if at the end she won't let you have a party here. She doesn't know how to give of herself.'

In her parents' bedroom, her eyes staring at the ceiling, she heard the key turn and there was the real-estate agent standing in the doorway.

'You're still looking upwards?' his eyes rounded in amazement. She stared at him and suddenly burst out laughing, the kind of carefree, gay laugh she used to emit when her children were small and surprised her with newly invented words or an unexpected, clever act. It was the first time he saw her shed her sardonic grin, and he joined her mirth.

'At this rate, it'll take you a month to inspect the apartment,' he said, glad to hear her laughter now.

'And maybe six months to inspect the penthouse,' he was encouraged by the laughter which had become obsessive. The anger he had felt towards her disappeared and he was filled with kindness. 'Now I have all the time in the world for you. I'll show you the apartment tile by tile. I can see that you like ceilings, so I'll show you ceiling after ceiling.'

'I really want you to show me something,' she said, her laughter slowly subsiding. She leaned forward, lifted her right leg, and standing thus on onę leg, her chin touching her knee, started to undo her bootlaces. Her long fur coat hid her hands, and he could see the golden curtain of her hair part, exposing dark roots.

'Everything alright, Ma'am?' he asked, amazed, trying to fathom her actions.

'Perfectly all right.' She did not raise her head to him, looking like a big polar bear hugging its raised knee, her bootlaces pooling longer and longer under the fur coat Suddenly one boot was in her hand, and she put it on the floor next to her foot in a sheer nylon stocking. She lifted her left foot and again bent to unlace the other boot.

'I was thinking about this stain in the ceiling,' he said, ill at ease, trying to divert his attention from the woman who was doing her bizarre act with such determined motions, his eyes, lured, following the bootlaces dangling from under her coat. 'Something pinching in your boots, Ma'am?'

She lifted her head, her face lit by a surprised smile. 'You could say something was pinching,' she agreed pleasantly.

'Concerning the stain,' he grasped something familiar, trying to extricate himself from the confusion she caused him, 'it can't be dampness, because in the apartment upstairs, the bathroom and the kitchen are on the other side.'

'You're selling the apartment upstairs, too?' She placed the second boot next to the first.

'No ... I just looked ... from the outside ... judging by ... ' With burning eyes, he followed her motions as she stood in her stockinged feet, took off her coat and laid it on the floor, its clean white lining resting on the dirty floor that had not been cleaned for many months.

'Judging by the windows ... Isn't it a pity to ruin your coat like this?'

'There's no choice,' she said. 'I could hold it for you,' he offered. 'You'll soon see that it's not so simple,' she smiled, stood on the coat, bent her knees, and again, standing on one foot, started taking off her stocking. He stood there, his eyes mesmerized by the things briefly exposed beneath her skirt when she lifted her leg to remove the stocking that was held by a wide lace garter. The stockings rolled down her legs, and then she unzipped her skirt and let it fall at her feet on the white fur.

'Ma'am,' his eyes were riveted on her short muslin slip, 'Are you all right?' His eyes followed the skirt that now joined the boots, followed by the delicate slip.

'We shall soon see, it depends on you,' she looked at him amused and saw fit to increase his embarrassment by explaining, 'Usually I begin to undress from the top.' She watched his eyes roll in his face.

'What are you doing, Ma'am?' he muttered confusedly, fearing her, yet fearing even more that the magic sight would disappear before his eyes. She asked, 'Is the door locked?'

At that moment it dawned on him and he rushed to the door, his hands reaching to open his trouser belt. By the time he came back, he had managed to undo his belt—his fingers struggling with the loops and with the buckle—she was already lying on her white fur coat naked, her legs stretched straight forward, one foot resting on the other, her head supported on her hand, watching him undress with hurried motions. His trousers dropped to the floor revealing a small belly, surprisingly tanned legs and dark purple shorts, the colour of a velvet dress she once wore on Purim when she dressed up as a gypsy. He quickly dropped his shorts to the floor, but when he noticed her eyes following him, he thought better of it, picked them up, folded them neatly together with his trousers. When he bent down she saw .a tiny, flower-like spider tattooed on his shoulder in pink and turquoise. The sight made her laugh, a pleasant, surprised laugh, as if she were making a mental note: a man with a tattoo—now that's a first for me.

To her surprise, she felt neither embarrassment nor strangeness. She watched him as he laid his pile of clothes next to hers, and naked, stretched by her side on the fur that her husband had given her for their tenth wedding anniversary. The fur now lay, face down on the gray pavement-like floor, in the exact spot where her parents' double bed used to stand. The touch of his body, she noted, felt familiar, and her palm stroked the inside of his arm as if she had done so many times before, and the scent of his after-shave also smelled familiar, and so was the way he slid his hand from her waist to her shoulder and bent his head in search of her mouth. She jerked her head sharply and he found himself burying his face in her neck. With his sharp merchant's sense, he grasped what it was she was trying to convey to him so he heaved himself and took her by storm and she received him without protest.

Her eyes closed, she felt herself drawn inward, ignoring the hard floor underneath and the man above. Clear, cool water swirled around her and she traversed it in a straight line, spreading her arms, then joining her palms together, swimming forward in long, measured motions, cutting through the encompassing azure that glimmered like silken cloth. A sense of well-being engulfed her, infusing her body like a stream. And all the while—even when the blue light began to recede slowly outside the water, like a shining neon light, and she made to dive away from it—she remembered the man crouched on top of her, and a faint voice, like a call from afar arose inside her: 'Mummy, Mummy,' not in panic, or desperation, or supplication or demand; 'Mummy, Mummy,' the voice came out of her in love, like an experienced person trying to impart important knowledge to a young and very dear one: 'Mummy, Mummy, it could not be that awful with a man who truly loved you, who even in old age remembered you as he had first seen you, with the bond of war uniting you. Here I am, Mummy, with a strange man I met by chance, a man without any distinction or merit, and he is pinning my head to the exact spot where your head used to lie, my eyes facing the stains which give off a terrible, musty smell, and I wonder why you never accepted the consolation of the body, why you never taught me this great conciliatory gift, this immeasurable pleasure, and I had to learn all this by myself, as if I were a pioneer. I always remember your rasping voice: "Greek, I must be speaking to you in Greek." What were you crying about all those nights, a bitter and dull woman, so harsh and cruel to your loved ones, so totally devoid of charity toward yourself and others?'

She opened her eyes and saw the agent's face close to hers; his eyes were closed and he crouched above her without burdening her, supporting his weight on his elbows on either side of her body and all the while—she suddenly noticed—whispering in her ears endearments he must have heard in movies and assumed that a woman of her sort is used to hearing at moments like this. She felt a wave of warmth toward him, for his naïvete, for the words he whispered into her neck, for the lightness of his chest against her. Grateful, she smiled, realizing how tender his actions were, how unexpected for a man whose tattooed spider was bouncing up and down in front of her as if threatening to pounce, then reconsidering and withdrawing.

Above his bouncing head she suddenly noticed the ceiling with two stains in the shape of butterflies: one huge and grey with yellow specks on its outstretched wings which covered half the ceiling, hiding another butterfly, small and slightly lighter in colour, and both butterflies were flying away from the corner towards the window, as if trying to extricate themselves from the plaster, assume bright colours and fly away. Her eyes wide open, she followed the man's face in front of her as he groaned, shifted his body and then relaxed, still hovering over her, supported on his elbows, opening his eyes.

'Next time we go to the penthouse,' he panted in her ear, 'there's a bed and a Jacuzzi in the bedroom there.'

'Greek,' she told him softly in her heart. 'Who needs a Jacuzzi? Does the penthouse have butterflies on the ceiling?' she said derisively.

'Who needs butterflies when you have a penthouse?' he said seriously.

She smiled at him affectionately, with the kindness of someone to whom a secret has been revealed, and she thought: You don't even know, Mr Eliyahu Yitzhajcov, what pearls of wisdom are emerging from your mouth.

'I'm the only one who has the key to that flat,' he smiled in return. 'If you wish, I could draw butterflies on the ceiling.'

Without warning, tears rose in her throat and gathered at the corners of her eyes, despite herself, and she thought: You will also never know that you were the first man to see me cry naked. It is your uncanny tenderness, your warmth. Things one is unused to break one's resistance easily; she could feel the tears streaming down her face.

'Lady.' Alarmed, he lifted himself on his hands, 'What's the matter? Why are you crying?'

She spread her fingers on her face, smoothing it and removing the hair from her face.

'Is something wrong?' the tone was that of a person used to rendering service.

'You did very well,' she heard herself giving him a grade, like a teacher to a student. Supporting herself on two straight arms, she lifted herself to a sitting position, facing him, leaning against the wall, and wiped her eyes with the back of her hand, fingers straight as if in a salute.

'Lady,' his voice sounded hurt and he narrowed his eyes, 'You wanted it. Don't tell me you didn't. A friend of mine was once tricked like this. A woman seduced him and then went to the police and accused him. His name was in the papers.'

'Don't worry,' she reached for her panties. 'I won't go to the police.'

His face turned red at the sight of the sudden cold, aloof expression on her face. 'You dragged me here,' he fumed, humiliated. 'As soon as I saw you get out of your car, with your blond hair and all your rings, I knew something was not right.'

She got to her feet, her stockings in her hand, all matter of fact, her eyes dried. She peered at him and saw the large shoulders, contracting their muscles, extending the turquoise spider's legs. All at once she realized that he was offended because the roles had been reversed and he could not accept it. While putting on her stocking, stretching her toes all the way, she glanced at the rings on her fingers and at the white fur spread on the floor, and for the first time was gripped by genuine fear. A man of his sort, her alert sense told her, you can never tell how he may react when crossed. She smoothed the stocking and adjusted the lace garter on the top of her thigh, and then saw him approach her on his knees, naked.

'And then,' he raged, 'when you walked into my office and told me Ha-Mered street, I had a feeling about you. From the beginning you wanted to drive me nuts!'

His eyes were covered with a thin film, as if hypnotized, and she glanced nervously at the door, her mind rapidly calculating: if she grabbed her blouse and skirt and dashed to the door, he would not pursue her in his state of nakedness. But he seemed to have read her mind and grabbed her arm. He glimpsed her free hand reaching for her blouse and clamped his other hand on her outstretched arm. With her hands thus imprisoned, she peered closely into his eyes, admitting to herself that she could not decipher their expression. She looked for clues in his face: its language, too, was foreign to her.

She decided to gamble, assuming that his reactions were slower than hers, and the sooner she acted, the better her chances to win this battle that was waging between them and whose rules were not known to her. She moved her arm gently, letting the pain climb from her wrist to her shoulder, and seemed to feel his grip loosen. She continued shaking her arm, until she realized that her hand was free and wondered at the ease with which she had accomplished it; she knew that now she must plan her moves wisely so, one by one, she lifted his fingers from her other wrist. With both hands now free, she picked up her blouse, straightened, and with knees aching from the strain, stood over him and put her arms through the sleeves, fearing all this while that he might toy with her a little more, and in a minute would pounce on her and nail her down again.

But then she saw his eyes.

His eyes, she noticed, looking down on him as he stood on his knees, naked, were sad—her fear dissipated at once. She bent down facing him, without a skirt, her blouse still unbuttoned, and cradled his face in both her hands, the way she used to treat children when they got bruised and cried. Like them, he too let her wrap her hands around his large, stubbly cheeks, and remained thus, obedient and placid as she bent her face and kissed him on the cheek and said, 'Don't be angry, I don't want you to be mad at me. I will always remember you with great affection.'

He seemed confused, hovering between his anger and the realization that these were words of farewell. The hurt still lingered in his eyes, his cheeks were still flushed but his face already registered reconciliation and wore a childish expression. 'You women drive us nuts, that's all,' he said, putting some distance between himself and his present predicament, as if this were not something happening between a particular man and woman, but a conspiracy of all women against all men.

She burst out laughing, with a great sense of release, buttoned up the delicate pearly buttons on her blouse, gathered up her skirt and said, relieved, as she watched his eyelashes twitching rapidly, 'You won't have any problems finding tenants; this is a very good flat. Just make sure you paint over this ceiling—then everything will be okay.'

Translated by Marganit Weinberger-Rotman

Lebanon

A Girl Called Apple

HANAN AL-SHAIKH

Apple had not married. She was almost forty and she had not yet married. Neither was her dark skin the reason (many girls with her colour had married) nor was it her name. That is the least important matter in marriage, and anyhow oasis girls are sometimes called by the names of fruit: her girl friend Banana had married last year.

Fate? Accident? Or was it Apple's obstinacy which had refused and continued to refuse to raise the wedding flag on the roof? Even though its hoisting upon the occasion of the girl's first menses was customary in the oasis. But Apple had refused. She had begged and cried, hiding her face, saying to her father, 'Daddy, please don't. I don't want it.' Her mother had thought that Apple was embarrassed that everyone—old and young in the oasis—should learn that she had reached womanhood. So she shook her head at her husband, who understood and left Apple alone.

A month later when the matter was forgotten, her father was about to plant the red flag in an earth-filled container. But Apple ran up to him, begging him with tears streaming from her eyes, 'Daddy, I don't want it.' And he didn't understand. He asked her in obvious confusion, 'You mean that you don't want to get married?'

And when she answered, he did not understand what she meant despite the fact that he heard her say, 'I want to get married, but I don't want the flag.' And her weeping increased.

Her father clapped his hands together and repeated, 'There is no power and no strength save in God.' How was it possible? Her grandmother, her mother, all her aunts, and every woman born in this oasis had been married by means of the flag. The importance of raising the flag had not been explained to them, but they knew as well as they knew their own faces that the flag was probably the only way to get married. Indeed this oasis was the only one that had not relied on the services of a matchmaker for generations—in fact, not from the time of Hind, who separated more than she brought together, and who used to describe every bride as a model of virtue, every groom as the moon of his age, a cavalier. The girl was said to be an enchanting dark-skinned innocent and the groom owned ten camels. The families would agree quickly to these descriptions, and Hind would swear solemnly that this was the truth. And on the wedding night the screams could be heard. Moreover, many strangers came to this oasis. They would halt their caravans, letting their camels drink for a couple of hours. Surely the idea of marriage would not occur to anyone in such a short period, and yet the flags fluttering above the roofs would tickle the men's hearts, enticing them to marry in this oasis.

Apple refused the red flag, although her father had tried to plant it in some sand in a can whose shiny surface rust had dulled. He tried to hoist the flag without her knowing. But Apple did not let the night pass with the stars guarding her flag. She pulled it down, and then she knelt and kissed her father's feet, weeping and saying, 'I don't want it.' Her father could not understand the secret of her refusal, but believed that an evil fortune had chosen his daughter, Apple, to be this generation's oasis spinster.

Scandal tried to whisper to her mother, but how? For Apple, like all the girls of the oasis, never left her home, day or night. And if ever these girls did leave their homes, they would be enveloped in *abayas,* their faces covered and they would be accompanied by someone. Days passed and Apple continued to help her father dye the sheep skins at home, bring water from the well, sweep and cook. Then she sat at her loom and with her woollen threads wove a carpet of camel hair. She thought about herself and wondered why it was that she refused despite her ardent desire to get married and to have a house of her own. And she loved children. She wanted to have lots of them. When she had really asked herself the reason, she discovered that the answer was easy: she was mortified at the thought of the flag and its fluttering on the roof. When she said this to her father, his wrinkles smoothed out and his hopes rose. Without further ado he got up and set off to plant the flag on the roof of the house of her bachelor uncle, after saying to her happily, 'Rejoice, for whoever knocks at your uncle's door will be sent here.' And to her amazement she found herself refusing adamantly. She was surprised by her refusal, especially since the red flag, the one that was used for the under-twenties, was about to pass her by; the blue one was good until age thirty, and then finally came the yellow one. Apple thought: 'God willing, I shall marry under the shadow of the blue flag.'

But she did not. The days passed, never to return, and the blue flag was about to disappear with her years. And Apple refused to let the flag flutter over the roof. And whenever she passed by the mud houses of the oasis and saw the coloured flags playing with the breeze, she laughed to herself and said, 'Crazy, stupid women.' And yet Apple envied the bride when she dyed her hands with henna in preparation for the wedding, choking whenever she saw her sitting like a princess, surrounded by singing and dancing in her honour. Whenever she heard the cry of the newborn babe she would run to the house, pick up the infant, put koḥl in its eyes, and bathe it in oil, wishing that it were of her own flesh and blood.

The red flag flew away, and then the blue one, as she jumped past thirty. And although Apple shrugged her shoulders as though she did not care, she began to know depression. She had never before found herself grumbling about helping her father and doing the housework. She sat behind her loom, pulling the threads through and tying them nervously and in annoyance. She kept asking herself, 'Why do I refuse marriage? I long for a husband to be the crown on my head, and for children to skip around me. I am hiding the beautiful clothes and the turquoise stones and the heavy rugs until the day of my marriage.' She turned and saw the shadow of a date branch on the wall of the living room. She saw her mother's dress next to the prayer garment, and suddenly she was filled with tenderness for everything she saw, and she felt that this time she had found the answer. And she said out loud, 'I don't want to leave this oasis.' And she hurried to her father and said, 'I don't want to leave you or the oasis.'

And her father's wrinkles smoothed out: 'May you never leave my sight, Apple. If the man who marries you is a stranger to the oasis, I shall give him three camels and I shall build you a house in our oasis.'

He got up and, stretching under the bed, dragged out a palm leaf basket that Apple had made. When part of the yellow flag appeared, Apple ran to her father and kissed his hands, weeping and crying, and her head was almost rent from her body to fling itself against the walls. And she sighed and wept for herself because she had refused, because she could not control her obstinacy.

The following day after a sleepless night, she compelled herself to accept, and she hurried to tell her father the news, having seen with pity the grief and sorrow which had inscribed themselves in his wrinkles. But no sooner did she see the yellow flag in her father's trembling hand than she fell to his feet, once again begging his pardon and again refusing the flag.

Apple changed as though the black sickness had hit her. She began to frown much more, becoming thin and sad. She was annoyed by her mother when she wished her good morning and by her father when he wished her good evening. But she never let her annoyance cross the bridge to her inside.

One evening, she was holding the thread in her hand and was asking herself the question that she had thought about every moment of her life when she held her breath and heaved a deep sigh. And this time she grasped the true answer and it was so simple: the flag might flutter for months on end, and no one might come. I would be like mutton or old dates for sale. And she found herself for the first time coming to grips with her fear: 'Maybe no one will come. And everyone in the oasis will see the flag wherever they go, and they will feel so sorry for me because I am unsaleable merchandise.' Again she blamed herself, defeated: 'But why was this simple, clear reason so hard to find before age forty?' Apple found herself leaning under the bed and carefully dragging out the basket, making sure not to wake up her mother. She took out the flag that no house in the oasis needed, and she climbed the stairs up to the roof while her mother and father and the oasis were sound asleep. And this after everyone was sure that marriage had passed Apple by forever, because it would not be long before even the yellow flag would be gone, and then no one would open the path of marriage to her. Indeed, it was felt that this was already the case.

In the starlight, Apple raised her face to the heavens and called upon God to be her witness. Then she knelt and fixed the flag in the container, thinking all the while that the oasis was small, that there were few men and that there was no matchmaker. She went downstairs and, sighing, sat down to await a knock at the door.

Translated by Miriam Cooke

Jordan

Untitled Poems

Mona Sa'udi

I

Blind city,
In its streets my visions multiply
In the chaos of objects
In the labyrinths of insomnia
I hear voices of silence
The stillness of time and sea
The death of night.
I warm myself with weeping pavements
There, life glows in an instant
Born in a puddle of light.

2

Through galaxies of stars and planets
I sail
in vessels of salt and crystal
navigating across black bareness
and deserts within. In
the habour of dreams I find
myself. The world
is reduced to the size of a toy.
A blind singer begins with a song
I hover in the dark of the night
I fall in love
with All
now blind.

Tonight, I am born
Tonight, I die.
Greetings to all the living
and all the dead.

3

When the loneliness of the tomb went down into the marketplace
dropped into nameless objects
and ascended as funeral sounds
I grew harder than tears
tears turned to stone
and stone was a passing friend I could not place

I shatter in all my dimensions
I multiply
I take on shapes like water.

4

In her heart she planted a tree
and said to sorrow:
Come forth.
Together we shall cross a distance
immeasurable but
by the heartbeat;
Stretching over a thread of light
we shall penetrate desolation.

Overwhelm me
she said
to the dream
that I may be reborn
without a road
save the shivering of the heart.

5

Darkness is
A field of past visions
Where fire of the primal creation
Burned.

Love and the heart of stone
Dwell in the dream
Of transferring realities:
Our First Water.

Women of the world:
        Take over my dream
        Plant it in your womb:
        As you leave darkness behind
        Beware of becoming
        The captives of daybreak
Dwell in the page and erupt from the stone
As on Earth, so let it be.

6

And I erase the face of your immense love
    in this totality of nighttide
        as the place is overtaken by slumber
That I may forget

and you may no more be my chain.

And I shall love you
in the water's movement.
I shall flood into a sea
which does not flow in you.
Inasmuch as I love you
I erase your love.

For you want me a reality
and I want you and want me
   in vision, a child
   of fire that danced
   and was lost
   in
   whirling ...

Don't stop.

7

Why don't I write in the language of air? master a new tongue
   with a different taste, a language that dances,
that goes drunk through the streets, embraces trees, walks
   on water ... that cries? a language
that burns the world, and gathers autumn leaves?
If I tell the sea to become a word—will the sea consent?
If I tell the word to die, If I pile up the words of the ages
past, present, and future, and say to the sun:
   Burn heaps of words
and say to the earth: Bury the ashes of words
and say to the ashes: Word-ashes
bring forth a sorcerer's tongue
   to tell fire: Be word
   and word: Be a poem
without words,
which can neither be read, nor seen, nor heard.

Translated by Kamal Boullata

Palestine

The Path of Affection

LAILA 'ALLUSH

On the startling road seized from the throat of new accounts
On the startling road seized from this century's earrings
reaching the bloodied neck
On the surprising road seized from old Jerusalem
and despite the estrangement of signs, shops and graveyards,
I gather my fragmented self together,
to meet my relatives in the New Haifa.

My companions on our smooth trip in the minibus
know nothing of my suffering
But I am an authentic face, well-rooted,
while their seven faces are alien.

This land is still the old land
despite pawned trees on the hillsides
despite green clouds and fertilized plants
and water sprinklers spinning so efficiently
On the startling road seized from the throat of new accounts
the trees were smiling at me with Arab affection
In the land I felt an apology for my father's wounds
and on all the bridges,
the shape of my Arab face
echoed there in the tall poplar trees,
in the winding rings of smoke.

Everything is Arabic still, despite the change of language
despite the huge trucks, and foreign tractors.

Each poplar and the orange grove of my ancestors
laughed to me, my God, with Arab affection.

Despite changes, dismissals and revisions,
despite the modern tunes,
commercials slapping visitors' faces
despite the flooding seas of light, despite technology
the many psalms, the many nails
and all the goings and comings of foreign peoples,
the land continued to sing an affectionate Arab tune.

Even with propaganda wavering in the air
languages mingling, multiplying,
around the strange outgrowths
of modern buildings,
the land was gently defying it all.
Oh my grandparents, even in the stark light of noon,
the red soil was shining
with Arab modesty
and singing, believe me,
affectionately.

Translated by Lena Jayyusi & Naomi Shihab Nye

Palestine

From The Diary of an Almost-Four-Year-Old

HANAN MIKHA'IL 'ASHRAWI

Tomorrow, the bandages
will come off. I wonder
will I see half an orange,
half an apple, half my
mother's face
with my one remaining eye?

I did not see the bullet
but felt its pain
exploding in my head.
His image did not
vanish, the soldier
with a big gun, unsteady
hands, and a look in
his eyes
I could not understand.

If I can see him so clearly
with my eyes closed,
it could be that inside our heads
we each have one spare set
of eyes
to make up for the ones we lose.

Next month, on my birthday,
I'll have a brand new glass eye,
maybe things will look round

and fat in the middle—
I've gazed through all my marbles,
they made the world look strange.

I hear a nine-month-old
has also lost an eye,
I wonder if my soldier
shot her too—a soldier
looking for little girls who
look him in the eye—
I'm old enough, almost four,
I've seen enough of life,
but she's just a baby
who didn't know any better.

Palestine

From The Siege

MAI SAYIGH

Buildings stick to each other, hug each other. It was a city of cement and steel, they said, of shops and banks, of millionaires and their deals, of middlemen, and peddlers of goods and ideas.

It had sea and sun, they said, tourists, hotels, cafes and amusement centres, money-changers, smugglers, and smokers of pot.

Beirut was jam-packed with people, they said, and surging with an ocean of cars. It had theatres, art galleries, poetry readings, and speech-making. It had book exhibitions, publishing houses, a press that was sometimes free and sometimes bought. Some writers were bought and sold off by auction. Political parties sprang up like weeds after the rain. There were weapons everywhere, to defend the political estate, to distinguish the factions, to demonstrate joy or anger or grief in the streets. There was an immeasurable spirit of rebellion.

It's ringed with wretchedness. Houses of tin and mud. Hunger. Poverty. The camps of Palestinian refugees, of defeated nationalities: Arab, non-Arab, Turk, Armenian—brought together, in a journey of want and misery and exile, by the instruments of oppression, and holding the memory of a lost land.

Alleys of mud. Open drains. The stench of filth and vermin. Children grow up on charity, on a diet of bread, salt, and onions: malnutrition and a variety of diseases. The relief agency. Boys selling chewing gum. Begging.

Poor workers flood in from the south and from the mountains, seeking a livelihood in the labour market, but denied social security and the services of the state. Their shoulders it is that have raised the other Beirut. They've built the tower blocks, they've paved the roads. Deprived, racked by hunger, they stand outside the brightly lit hotels and cafés and swimming pools and restaurants. Away from the blaze of elegance and excess, it's their hearts and hands and feet that have borne the strain.

In the south people worked in the tobacco fields. They were skilled at reading the face of the land and the secrets of the meadows. They observed the seasons and the festivals. They toiled for the sake of food for their little ones and for the sake of company profits. They resisted the state and the feudal princes who tried to snatch their livelihood from their mouths. Stubbornly they stood up to successive assaults of the Zionists on their homes and villages. The fishermen became browner and more confident as the sun of each new day shone on them. For they are the ancient friends of waves and rocks.

How well we knew the land, the stones, the lanes, and the orange trees! The heart of downtown Beirut with its narrow streets, its lights, its stalls of vegetables, its trays of sweetmeats, the good nature of its people, recalled for us the narrow streets of Gaza. Beirut brought us together and treated us as Beirutis.

Beirut lies sprawled on the coast and reaches up to the mountains; and the shore and mountain trees are the frontiers of my heart.

Beirut's old quarters fill my mind with their houses and faces. This is a land of children and oleanders, of joy in chains, of households awaiting a new dawn. One community stretches from Tel al-Zaatar to the southern suburbs and Sabra and the Arab University. The poor and the revolutionaries have one religion, one sect, and one banner.

Where shall I start my story? I know it well and I can recall the agony. Time passes as I pause amid the pain and the inspiration. The lie of the land has been shattered. I see bloodshed whenever I gaze on pavement and balcony.

The war took place in the streets, before every window; and the Arab nation from the Atlantic to the Gulf followed the fighting as if reading chapters of a novel or watching a film. It held back its weapons and continued to bow its head to the police, to be constantly beneath the heel of the secret services and those in the seats of power. The Arab homeland is no homeland, it is a port of constant departure, a place of hunger and harassment, of fear for the future, of successive disasters, of surveillance, purges, and prisons. Oil swamped us and devoured our obligations, our honour and our self-respect. Patriotism was now a matter of choice, and treason a point of view. This was the era of the 'Pax Americana', designed to make the world safe for rulers and kings with a common interest in the shibboleth of national sovereignty. We were polluting the Arab atmosphere. They were preserving their territories immaculate—ready to admit the enemy.

While their frontiers remain calm, our children fall like burned moths; their toys and shoes and little trifles remain after them, while the whole world's busy forming organizations for the Protection of Animals. They proscribe our blood, and friends and loved ones leave us while posters carrying their pictures remain on the walls, and in our hearts, till the rain and tears wash them away. Their blood falls drop by drop over the Arab cities, but they kindle only the echo of words in the newspapers; while the streets remain imprisoned, and spring remains slain, and the whole Arab nation forgets.

But we go on, counting our wounds, checking our blood group, totting up our soaking bandages and drugs—alone, always alone.

For the Arabs, time stands still. They do nothing about the retreating armies and the feet of the invaders and the endless progression of graves. Victory is postponed 'till further notice'.

They killed Kamal Junblat* ... They wanted to crush the will of a nation. Beirut was fashioning new streets and landmarks. Quarters were marked by barricades and given the names of the martyrs. But in spite of the war Beirut still celebrated and mourned. Beirut swelled till it took in the whole of Lebanon.

During nights of air raids when buildings collapsed, when power was cut off and we could hear the cries of the wounded, I'd feel lonely and depressed. I saw the brains of my neighbour, the pilot's wife, spattered and scattered at the crossroads. Another neighbour, Haji Abdu, collapsed

---

* Kamal Junblat was a porminent Druze leader, a socialist who was assassinated early in the Lebanese Civil War.

on his balcony playing trick-track with his son. He'd diced with death as if it were all a game.

Here they mutilated the corpses of Zaatar, and here we took in the children and the martyrs.

But in spite of the deaths, life went on. The bombing would cease for a while, funerals would take place, and then the streets would fill with people. The bread shop would open, so would the other stores, so would the cinemas. Sellers of milk and licorice would go their rounds. Abu Khalid would sell his sweetmeats in the light of a candle or a gas lamp. The loudspeaker in the mosque would work from a generator. Neighbours would sip coffee on the balconies.

The road to Cola and Sabra was always open. Unless bombs cut the road on Cornichc al Mazra'a, unless snipers dogged your steps or took aim at balconies and passers-by, life revolved around the spirit of the Qu'ranic verse: 'Nothing will happen to you unless God decreed it.'

'We should stay where we are,' Laila once said, as the building across the road was engulfed in an explosion, burning the neighbour's clothes and children. They killed her sister, Khaldiya, and her sister's husband in their house ... A stray bullet killed Lena in her house, near her child's bed. One of Ruwaida's brothers was killed, with his neighbours, at the front door. Another brother's missing.

Beirut made us feel bombardment was a phenomenon of nature, that sniping and the stray bullet were like the weather, and death a human requirement like sleeping, eating, drinking, and moving. Cruel Beirut! How often I grew weary of it, hating it because of the bombs and the deaths of friends.

Cruel Beirut! ... It's part of me, my lost bastion with its bright, smiling face that refuses to acknowledge death, the face that's a part of all of us ... Life flows out of the houses to those passing in the street, sparkles and blazes away. Liveliness brightens the faces of the fighters at night, when vigil's kept till dawn. Everybody knows everybody else. Beirut's a sea of relations, an arena of political and literary ideas in conflict. Coffee houses are absorbed in supplying coffee and attacking ideas and their holders. You can find everything on the pavement stalls: from fruit and vegetables, clothes, cigarette lighters, cassettes, and songs to news about the Sino-Soviet conflict, or disputes about the row that broke out just yesterday between two local factions, or arguments about whether Fatah's* petty bourgeois or upper bourgeois. From the outset, ideology permits neither error nor conjecture. History's full of wise sayings and answers ...

Everything's subject to analysis. Every statement has to be proved. A rumour goes round and round and round until it ends up where it began. Jokes and quips are the property of all. There are no secrets. Alliances, friends, enemies, and armed camps are well defined ...

Heroes march out from the base camp side by side with men of the intelligence forces who work by barter, blowing up one building in exchange for another, one car for another.

The Jamal 'Abdul Nasser hall is full of smoke and sweat. The bodyguard of the leadership fills the place, and curses against imperialism, and particularly against America, are common. Differences of opinion as to whether the Soviet Union is at the head or merely in the vanguard of the socialist camp. Banners hang calling for total liberation. Or half of it. Or a quarter of it. Calling for establishing a state of what has remained of Palestine—or hasn't remained of it. The PLO (Palestine Liberation Organization) is the sole representative. Imm 'Ali dances. Press photographers, foreign journalists, and solidarity groups take pictures of her.

The illustrated press, fifty or sixty magazines, papers, and publications: are they all alike in production, pictures and subject matter? Some say, 'Yes.' Some say, 'No.' Others are lost between Yes and No. Radios and car horns spread their messages. Posters and wall sheets and graffiti in all colours and scripts. Down with ... Long live ... Victory to ...

On the back page of the newspaper, *Al-Safir,* the Palestinian child continues to turn his back on the world in the daily cartoons of Naji al-'Ali.**

---

* Fatah is the main wing of the PLO (the Palestine Liberation Organization).

** Niji al-'Ali was a famous Palestinian cartoonist who was assassinated in London in 1987 because of his struggle to expose, through his art, Israeli aggression and intrigue against his own country and people, and the indiscretions and deviation of some of his compatriots. His memory is revered by all loyal Palestinians.

Patches grow on the garb of his Arab toiler. As he gets ever thinner, he grows in wisdom and knowledge. Pride thickens the necks of the lords of oil and rule. Their bellies and their cloaks are filled with wind. Meanwhile the Arab nation shrinks and dwindles in the face of open aggression against its possessions and the things it holds sacred.

Beirut is all this and more. And so they burnt it, they destroyed it, they killed its children.

The enemy has no respect for anything, from Dair Yasin, Qibya, and Kufr Qasim to Sabra and Shatila.* A history heavy with hatred, enmity, and bloodshed.

In the Old Testament, the children of Israel came, primitive nomads from the wilderness, and destroyed the civilization of Canaan under the leadership of their prophet, Joshua, at the behest of their God, Yahwe. They were given a free hand and killed everything in the city of Jericho, 'Both man and woman, young and old, and ox, and sheep, and ass, with the edge of the sword.'** On the seventh day the city was a furnace for the Lord. 'Only Rahab the harlot shall live, she and all that are with her in the house.'†

'And the Lord said unto Joshua, "Fear not, neither be thou dismayed; take all the people of war with thee, and arise, go up to Ai ... And thou shalt do to Ai and her king as thou didst unto Jericho ..." And so it was, that all that fell that day, both of men and women, were twelve thousand, even all the men of Ai.'††

The pine trees cast their shadows on the courtyard of the Children of Resistance Orphanage in Tel al-Zaatar. A green light filters through to the dining room. A sweet fragrance drifts in from the balconies and

---

* Names of four massacres inflicted upon the Palestinians in recent times, Dair Yasin by Zionist factions, Qibya and Kufr Qasim by the Israeli army and Sabra and Shatila by the Lebanese Phalangists. Qibya is a village whose inhabitants were attacked at night in 1952 by Israeli troops who blew the houses on top of its sleeping people; Sabra and Shatila are the two camps where the hideous massacre of the Palestinians took place during the Israeli occupation of Beirut. According to the latest statistics, at least 1700 people were killed in cold blood.

** Joshua, Chapter 6, verse 21.

† Joshua, Chapter 6, verse 17.

†† Joshua, Chapter 8, verses 1-2 and 25.

mingles with the talk about the role of women in the Palestinian revolution, and about the children. We're seated around the lunch table, and it's a quarter to three.

Here's Qasim Aina, the Director of the orphanage, the Egyptian poet Zayn al-Abdin Fuaad, Dr Fathiya al-Saaudi and Anush, her Algerian friend. Zayn al-Abdin was due to leave the following day for Cairo. Pleased to be going back to Egypt, he's come to say goodbye. Anush wanted to know exactly where I stood on the feminist issue. She belonged to a woman's group preparing research papers on the position of women in the Third World, and was working as a volunteer in the Palestinian revolution.

The workers had the day off, so the children were cleaning up and getting the dining room ready. The older ones arranged the distribution of food to their younger brothers and sisters. Then they all went off to play in the front yard.

The planes came from nowhere. The hands of the clock pointed to a quarter to three, and the planes came from nowhere.

There was a noise like a frightful clap of thunder. The sun swooped down. The sky swooped down. The peace was destroyed. Speech and food were all over the place. The spectre of death and fire shut out the light of day and created terror and despair.

We rushed to pick up the little ones who couldn't yet walk very well and hurried the older ones down to the shelter. As I hugged a child to my breast, I picked out the words, 'I don't want to die! I don't want to!'

'You're not going to die. Death's a long way away.'

I see terror in the eyes of the little ones. Two hundred children between the ages of one and seventeen. Time marches slowly, like some fabulous beast threatening destruction to the innocent who aren't aware of what's going on.

The city flows in my veins—its alleys, its old roofs, its trees, my friends and loved ones. As we stagger to the shelter we're drowned in the flames and smoke …

My mind wanders off by chance, as if to grope around the streets and look for people one by one, and ask about my husband, Muhammad; and I wonder, where has death struck? I pull myself together.

'We must get the children away from the walls.'

'No. Let them be protected by the walls.'

'This is no shelter.'

Qasim embraces the children with his hands, his eyes and his heart.

'If only they'd given us time to move the children up to the mountain.'

'But the other children in other quarters and camps of the city, where can they go?'

I pick out the voices of Jamila and Butros.

'They're targetting their raids on the Sports Stadium and our area of Bir Hasan.'

The two young imps didn't come down to the shelter with us; they'd gone to the upper floors to watch the raids.

These children came to us, having narrowly escaped, as if by the distance between the blade of a knife and the wound it makes, between the head and the body from which it is severed. They've come out from among the pieces of torn flesh and limbs, from the seas of blood. They've plunged into the depths of death and come out to us, frozen pieces of humanity, their faces expressing only terror or apathy.

Jihad was not yet a year old. For a whole year he offered no response to anything. The doctors were sure he was retarded. He was transferred to the Children's Deaf and Dumb Institute ... Suddenly he came out with complete sentences. Rashida Taha, the Director of the orphanage at that time, shed tears of joy when she told us the story. We celebrated that day. Jihad was born anew.

Ahmad came to us with a swollen belly when he was eighteen months old. He'd been living on grass for a week before people discovered him and brought him to us. A lorry took him to Damour. When the other passengers got down, nobody claimed him. The will to live is stronger than death.

When they drew pictures, they drew pictures of tanks and cannons, black airplanes, houses that had been demolished, men who looked like crows. The black was very black. When they added colour, they used deep red. They painted blood on faces and on walls. Wounds were everywhere.

The older ones made up words, to the tune of a popular song:

We can drink water mixed with blood,
Tel al-Zaatar, O my beloved,

They envied me for your defiance.
        At night, O Zaatar, at night.
We can eat lentils for all we care,
We can drink water mixed with blood,
                At night, O Zaatar, at night.

Then they'd sing:

What can I say? What has happened to Beirut?
Beirut groans and weeps. There are no longer houses there.
The rockets have destroyed the houses. Mama, Children are dying.

It was no shelter.

'If a rocket falls behind us,' Fathiya said, 'everything will be destroyed.'

The shelter was a cellar with windows near the ceiling at ground level. Part of the cellar served as a store. The main room was used as a play area for the children on rainy days.

A rocket fell in the playground outside. The earth was ripped up and the glass of the windows in the building shattered. Pipes burst and water poured into the main room. The air pressure was awful and the walls almost caved in. The air pressed on our chests and deafened us. The turbulence built up with intervals of deceptive tranquillity. Dazed, we were thrown against the walls.

A group of little ones came to me for comfort. The children hung on to us—we're their foster mothers. They clung to our bosoms, our clothes, all around us ... The planes went away only to return. Between one explosion and another, time would return to normal. Seconds went by; minutes, hours. Little Ahmad asked me, his wide black eyes fighting back tears, 'Are you scared?'

'The planes are a long way away.'

'But I'm scared ... Not for myself, but for my brother and sister here.'

Two little children were flat against the wall. The girl wasn't yet one year old and her brother was three. He held her with his arms around her. I sat down on the floor and pulled the three of them to me.

Ahmad went on talking. 'My mother and father were working in Saudi Arabia. We came back to Tyre. Then there was the air raid and they were killed. I love our home here but I'm scared they'll destroy it. If they do where can I take my little brother and sister?'

'Don't be frightened. I'm not going to leave you.'

'You mustn't die as well.'

Little Najwa pulls at me.

'It's most important. We mustn't die.'

'We're not going to die. The raid's a long way away.'

'Where is it? It might be at the camp.' We all burst into tears. 'I'm worried about Nazmi, my brother. He went to the camp yesterday to visit my grandfather and hasn't come back.'

Najwa's a big girl, eight years old. Her grandfather, a man of about eighty, brought her with her brother, Nazmi. We were standing at the gate bidding farewell to the Commander-in-Chief. Najwa crossed the ranks and stood in front of him. 'Are you Abu Ammar?' she said. 'I love you and I know you from your pictures.'

Nazmi, hardly six years old, interrupted her: 'Please, brother, take me and my sister; we don't have any parents or home.'

The grandfather added, 'I wander round offices and commando bases with them. The young men are generous, and let us eat and sleep with them.'

The children didn't stop shouting and crying. There was no let-up in the situation of total breakdown. Each of us tried in turn to calm the children's nerves, but terror was a wall of steel that we couldn't pierce. We talked a lot but it didn't help. We shouted, 'You can hear the sound of our artillery fighting back.' Then we sang a patriotic song, and that stopped the crying.

There was a change of atmosphere in this room packed with terror-stricken children. The rhythm of the song worked like magic. The words were echoed on their lips. Blood returned to faces that had been drained of colour. We were vanquishing primitive fear.

When we finally came out of the sodden shelter, it was seven o'clock in the evening. We realized that we'd absolutely have to move the children to Suq al-Gharb.* Nobody knew what tomorrow had in store.

The noise of ambulances is the real noise of death. It's what confirms its presence. The sirens of scores of cars are heard everywhere. Evening turns

---

* Suq al-Gharb is a Lebanese town in the Shouf district of the mountains of Lebanon.

into a funeral. The city turns its back on festivities. Its aspect has changed. Four hours have altered the city. It now has the appearance of a wounded hero leaving the wrestling arena. Holes, red mounds, burst pipes, and the rubble of buildings block the roads.

We turn off towards the Awza'i road. People are gathering around radio sets, or dashing to bakeries and other shops to get what's needed for the hard times ahead. Everybody's rushing around looking for wounded relations. Muhammad and Nazih are watching the raid from the balcony. Bombs fall and rip up everything that's underground, churning up the red soil with bits of metal, water, parts of destroyed buildings, and bits of human flesh. It's all burnt and the ashes are tossed sky high and then thrown down again. The city's drowned in flames and smoke. Muhammad looks at me closely. 'The war's begun, but it's not like the other wars. They'll open up the main front here.'

I don't believe him. I don't want to believe him.

There was a power cut. We had to make provision for the years of war. I took out the gas lamp and cleaned it. In the evening light coming from the kitchen balcony, I discovered that it wasn't working. I lit a candle and stood gazing at the mountain.

The evening light was a mass of white and blue. Above Beit Meri, Brummana,* and Bhamdount** it spread a translucent mantle of spring brightness. Through it twinkled the lights overlooking Beirut, announcing the beginning of the night. But it wasn't a night like other nights. There was something different about everything—even the songs that could be heard coming from radios on the balconies of our neighbours.

'We're going to sleep in the hall,' I said. 'It's safer.'

'This is a different kind of war,' he commented, 'it hasn't been defined yet. Let's go and look for our dead. They don't have any faces or names nowadays.' In the candlelight I saw his face consumed with anger. He was breathing with difficulty, as if he were going to burst.

Translated by Peter Clark & Christopher Tingley

---

* Brummana is a Lebanese town in the Matn region of the mountains of Lebanon.

** Bhamdoun is a Lebanese town in the Shouf district of the mountains of Lebanon.

Palestine

From A Mountainous Journey

Fadwa Tuqan

I was not in a position to participate actively in the kind of life necessary to a poet. My only world, in that dreadful reality, empty of any meaningful emotion, was the world of books. I lived with the ideas planted in books, isolated from the world of people, my femininity whimpering like a wounded animal in a cage, finding no means of expression.

While I was in this state of psychological siege and exile, Father often came and asked me to write political poetry. He wanted me to fill the empty place Ibrahim had left behind. Whenever a national or political occasion arose, he would come asking me to write something on the subject. A voice from within would rise up in silent protest: How and with what right or logic does Father ask me to compose political poetry, when I am shut up inside these walls? I don't sit with the men, I don't listen to their heated discussions, nor do I participate in the turmoil of life on the outside. I'm still not even acquainted with the face of my own country as I was not allowed to travel. With the exception of Jerusalem, which I came to know thanks to Ibrahim taking me in when he worked in Radio Palestine, I was not familiar with any other city beside Nablus.

One of the irrefutable laws of nature is that plants and animals cannot live and thrive without particular environmental conditions. As for me, the home environment in which I grew up was not conducive to the creation of a concern for the outside world and its struggle.

Father was demanding that I write on a subject totally removed from my interests and having no connection with the psychological struggle going on inside me. Feelings of incompetence so inundated me that, when I went to bed, I would give myself over to weeping.

When we arrive at a point where things exceeding our natural capabilities are demanded of us, the resulting shock and the difficulties we encounter often cause us psychological harm. Father thought I was capable of composing on any subject. Despite the fact that I had already planted my feet firmly in poetry, my psychological current was flowing in a direction that differed entirely from that in which Father wanted me to drift along. A poet must be familiar with the life of the world around, before dealing with it in poetry. From where was I to obtain suitable raw material required? Where was I to have the intellectual and psychological environment conducive to writing such poetry? Would I derive it from the newspaper Father brought every day at noon when he came home for lunch? Reading the papers, however important, was not enough to light the flame of political poetry within me. I was completely isolated from life on the outside. This isolation had been imposed upon me; I didn't choose it of my own free will. The outside world was taboo, forbidden to the women of the family, depriving them of any community activities or political concerns. Mother was a member of a women's charitable committee, but that didn't change the picture in any way. She seldom attended their meetings, nor was she permitted to travel to the women's conventions, as other members were. Above all, she was absolutely forbidden to participate in the women's demonstrations. Family tradition would never allow that.

A women's committee had been founded in Nablus in 1921, under the leadership of the late Mariam Hashim (died 1947). This society was, at first, of a charitable nature. Then in 1929 it united with the general Arab Women's Federation, founded in Egypt by the late Huda Sha'rawi. At this time, the Palestine Women's Federation undertook the organization of the Palestinian women's participation in the political struggle in most of the cities and sometimes in the villages. The city women's activities were confined to demonstrations, to sending telegrams of protest, and convening meetings through the women's organizations that the bourgeoisie of that era had created. Being unveiled, the country women had greater and more effective freedom of movement. They were the ones who carried arms and food to the rebels holing up in the mountains.

With this total isolation imposed upon the women of our household, it was not strange that the atmosphere in the female quarters was devoid of any political or community awareness. The house was like a large coop filled with domesticated birds, contented to peck the feed thrown to them, without argument. That was the be-all and end-all of their being. The vocation of those tame birds was confined to hatching the chicks and wasting up the days of their lives between the large brass cooking pots and the firewood burning constantly in the stoves, winter and summer.

As happens in backward societies where a woman's life revolves around trivialities, the female environment in our house did not deviate from this pattern, which prevailed in all families and all homes. Therefore, the family environment offered me nothing; rather, it only increased my burden.

I was struck with a deep hatred for politics. During this particular period, I underwent a severe psychological and intellectual conflict. I was trying to comply with Father's wishes, in order to please him and win his favour, while everything in me was protesting, refusing, and rebelling. Since I was not socially emancipated, how could I wage war with my pen for political, ideological, or national freedom? I still lacked political maturity, just as I had no social dimensions. I possessed nothing but a literary dimension that was itself still deficient.

I knew myself; I was aware that the self could not become complete, except in a community of people. But between me and the community there, outside the walls that confined me, lay the distance of many centuries of the world of the harem ...

My feelings of incompetence continued to dominate me. The ability to write poetry failed me. I even stopped composing personal poems. Poetical barrenness enveloped this whole difficult period of my life.

My keen awareness of the repression and tension I was under affected both my spiritual and physical being, making me lose more weight. I was scarcely ever without a headache; mental weariness weighed heavily upon every part of my body; at night I was bathed in sweat.

Life no longer held any meaning or relish for me. When I tried to fathom my private anxieties and personal feelings, it was as if something had been broken inside; misery inflated my consciousness of myself and my own existence. I was bleeding from the two-edged blade of that old proverb: 'If I am not for myself, who will be for me; if I am for myself, who am I?' My weak links with reality and my need for contact with the outside world remained the source of a psychological conflict which I endured for a long time. Father was the one who had sowed the seeds of this conflict, which haunted me, in other ways as well, during the subsequent stages of my poetical career.

I went on feeling completely alone, that there was no one who felt my misery except myself. It was my being that was being stretched taut, torn apart; the heart that was constricted and crushed was my heart; and the ordeal that was becoming more critical was my ordeal. There was no other being to share all this with me, no other person.

As the misery of repression and subjugation increased, my feelings of individuality and identity also increased. My existence inside the harem wing of the house made me shrink and recoil, so that I was bottled up inside myself. I got to the point where I could do nothing but stare into the reflection of that self shut up inside the cursed bottle. The poetry I published in the papers was the one social activity I could use as a bridge to link me with others, as I couched within those ancient walls. Thus my feelings of alienation deepened, and my sense of being robbed of my dreams, my desires, and my aspirations began to take the form of a sickness.

It was during this period that I swallowed the whole contents of a bottle of aspirin. The family doctor, Nadeem Salah, saved me from the death that had become my only means of escape from the torment I was in.

I did not bear any strong attachment to my father. My feelings toward him remained neutral: I did not hate him, neither did I love him. He never occupied any space in my heart, except when he was sick, imprisoned, or in exile for political reasons. To me, he was the tent that sheltered us; if we lost him we would be exposed to the storms of life. I was continually in fear of him dying and leaving us to the mercy of others. Thus my emotions see-sawed between a sense of need for his produce and a sense of estrangement and lack of any emotional relationship to him. He never manifested any sort of concern or affection for me. Whenever I fell victim to malaria in my childhood, he never came near me or asked how I was. That neglect pained me. Thus Ibrahim, with his overflowing compassion and love for me, replaced the father who never let me feel the warmth of fatherly sentiments. When Ibrahim died and Father was still living, I truly felt like an orphan. When Father passed away I was experiencing a fearful psychological crisis at the time, due to the severe emotional repression that I had endured all those years. I tried to write an elegy for him, but failed. However, I missed him severely later on when the winds of family problems began to blow our way.

I never took sides in any dispute or quarrel; I always stood apart from the disputes, seeing, hearing, and suffering. During this period, I wrote 'Life', one of the few poems I composed in a few consecutive hours. In this poem, my true feelings at the loss of my father are revealed; feelings that went very deep.

Father died amongst the tumult of the 1948 debacle.

Thousands of refugees, moving eastward in their flight, arrived in Nablus. Houses, mosques, schools, and the caves in Mounts 'Aibal and Jerzim were jam-packed with them.

Many long months passed after this first scandal on Arab soil, before I returned to writing poetry. Behind this silence, a process of preparedness and storing was going on all the time in my depths and I no longer suffered feelings of emptiness and desolation.

Eventually my tongue was loosened. I wrote the patriotic poetry to which Father had so often wished to see me dedicate myself, in order to fill Ibrahim's place. I wrote that poetry quite voluntarily, without any outside coercion.

After Father's death my reaction to politics was no longer wanting. Although it was not too strong it still swayed me at different times, but it lacked the quality of permanence. It would catch fire on certain occasions when things were inflamed, then die down when things were calm; I would flare up when there were general outbursts and cool off when there were lulls. With the status quo of the Palestinian situation, a numbness began creeping over my political sentiments. I entered into life, drinking it in large drafts, touching it and clinging to the fleeting moments, not allowing them to escape me, enjoying it second by second and minute by minute.

In the first half of the1950s, I escaped from the prison of the harem. When the roof fell in on Palestine in 1948, the veil fell off the Nablus woman's face. She had struggled for a long time to free herself from the traditional wrap and the thick black veil.

Before the final lifting of the veil, the Nablus women had succeeded in changing their outer covering, by stages, over a period of thirty years. In the 1920s they got rid of the full black flowing skirt, substituting a black or brown coat or one of some other sombre colour. At the beginning of the 1940s they got rid of the triangular bolero-like cover that was worn on the head and came down over the shoulders down to the waist, concealing the shape of the upper half of the body, and behind which the woman would fold her hands over her breast, so the men could not see her fingers. In the middle 1940s the transparent black kerchief became more transparent, revealing the face under it; and in the middle 1950s the black veil was finally lifted, allowing the beauty of their God-given faces to shyly speak for itself.

The evolution of the veil in Nablus was slow compared to Jerusalem, Haifa, and Jaffa. The path our development took was neither easy nor smooth. Nablus remained a bigoted city, clinging to the old traditions in which social changes were not easily carried out. The established moulds and patterns remained the prevailing order, despite the many well-educated young men and women. It is strange that this city, whose inhabitants are famous for their dynamism and great enterprise, remained adamantly against anything new touching their traditions. However, the inevitability of development eventually overpowers all resistance. It is life's march, impossible to check or halt.

My hunger for life was relentless. Someone who has squandered many years of her life in the desert of the Empty Quarter cannot turn her back on a green oasis when its doors are opened to her. The child of life emerged now into the life that had given her birth. Being completely sincere, she faced life with a genuine and natural frankness that society, with its stern rules and customs, insists on counterfeiting and covering up with a false mask. This child of life was not selfish; she took and she gave. Giving was her way of life, an inseparable part of her nature. Previously, when she stole out to the wheat fields, she would feel downcast and sad at seeing the gift the wheat had to offer, when she had nothing to offer. A heart filled with love suffocates if it finds no one to love.

The time arrived for this daughter of life to speak and, when a truthful woman speaks, it is life that is speaking.

Our Eastern Arab society suppressed the sentiment of love, just as it continually oppressed the woman. This beautiful human emotion, whose magic hand even touched the hearts of prophets. It was because of this emotion that the noble Prophet Muhammad (God bless him and grant him salvation!) said: 'Praise be to God! Praise be to the director of hearts!' the moment he saw Zaynab Bmt Jahsh* suddenly appear to him. In our Arab society, this beautiful human emotion is the victim of the split personality of our society and still carries connotation charged with disgrace and shame.

As far as I'm concerned, love bears a wider concept than the affirmation of a woman's femininity. To me it is the affirmation of my crushed humanity and its very salvation. All my life, I have been drawn to love, driven by a poetic sentiment difficult to explain. Just as birds respond instinctively to the magnetic field in determining the path of their flight, so have I always responded to love. It remained to me the most attractive torch that beckoned me among life's various aspects.

I am not straying far from the truth when I say that, with me, love remained a concept; an absolute world. For me the 'other' was the embodiment of that idea, whose horizons I was never able to relinquish. It became an instinct and a natural impulse, forever warm and throbbing in my heart, and I'd plunge into the warm sea of emotion that cleansed my soul of bitterness. This abstract concept had no shore or harbour where I could cast anchor. It was a vast sea where, sometimes, the waves were so high that they became a whirlpool turning me in a circle until I lost all sense of the outside world around me.

Before emerging from the harem, my adolescent emotions were on fire. I was a repressed soul who responded to the first word of love received on the page of a letter. Love by correspondence. I would fall into this sort of imaginary love and wallow in it, while the old walls of the harem lay between me and the actual experience. So that imagination and the exchange of letters were at once the length and breadth of my sphere of action. I hungered for something that did not exist; I was lost, alone, possessing nothing but this fired imagination.

The liberation came at last; I found myself merged with the 'other',

---

* One of the Prophet's wives. She was first married to his adopted son, Zayd. However, the Prophet, on seeing her once in her ordinary house clothes (as opposed to the coverings a Muslim woman world wear in the street) as he went seeking Zayd, was struck with her revealed beauty. Zayd divorced her so the Prophet could marry her. This story, about the Prophet's tenderness towards beauty, is mentioned by Tuqan here in praise of love which is denied to young people in the traditional culture in Palestine.

discovering myself through the compass of reality. My heart has ever been a fresh garden ripe for love. During moments of love a person feels his humanity intensifying. He or she leaves the far distant icy pole to travel to radiant sunshine. The 'other' becomes the bridge to a world whose scattered parts have been brought together to become one inseparable whole; a world that, by its sweetness and bitterness, its contradictions and ironic situations, paves the way to mental and spiritual well-being; it is a beautiful, harsh, tender world, just like life itself. And after all is said and done, love is proscribed like life and death, especially upon those with poetic natures. For them there is no escape from it.

There is nothing sweeter than when love touches even trivial things, transforming them into things of beauty and worth: a restaurant bill, a theatre ticket, a dried flower, a ballpoint or fountain pen. All these and similar trivial things become rare and priceless when touched by love.

My vivid imagination created a magic halo around the beloved, projecting upon him what he did not have. I would see the faults, but, in my view the faults did not stand in the way of love. Which of us searches for a Christ to love? In my opinion, the exemplary ones make poor lovers. Their idealism makes them review the affair in a manner that strips love of all its great excitement. I have always believed that love is a treasure whose worth we can never estimate until we have exhausted it or lost it in a gamble.

When time—that gigantic force of destruction—has played its role in things and relationships, I do not linger amongst the ruins. I do not remain faithful to the past, after it is over and done with. I do not allow myself to give the past permission to rob the future, for the past is a thief that takes away but does not give. It is not strange for the heart to love more than once. It is unnatural that a person's heart should be bound up in one person all its life. It is normal for more than one relationship to form and for love to recur in the heart. And each time one falls in love, the emotions are just as strong, and just as sincere and fragrant as the previous time. But there has never been a place in my heart for casual love, for frivolous relations and reckless carousing.

Frequently, I find that the past has not only gone in its physical sense, but in its psychological sense also. What is in the past bears a certain value that differs entirely from my present view, causing it to lose its psychological significance. I feel that I am another person with no connection to my former self, no longer acquainted with it except in memory.

The world of my childhood is the only one that has not lost its psychological meaning for me. It is the only world to which I return with the old warmth of heart. With that exception, everything, in my view, submits to the laws of change.

Translated by Olive Kenny

Palestine

Stone Fence

LISA SUHAIR MAJAJ

I was a small child climbing walls, defying my father's injunctions. *Who wants a tomboy for a wife?* I clambered up cherry trees, skinned my knees, rode my bike farther than I was allowed to go. On picnics I collected rocks, hoarding them in the old tin can I kept under my bed. It rattled like my mother's button box.

Daddy planted seeds, watered rosebushes. Mom weeded the strawberry patch, picked berries, juice staining her mouth and hands. Grandma gathered mint from the garden, boiled Easter eggs in onion skin, fasted two weeks each year in gratitude that my father, her baby, had lived.

That was years ago. Now they're gone, all of them. Chinks of me fill with voices like green things sprouting, wisps of life between rocks. Birds drop seed, soil collects in pockets.

I tilt toward the earth, leaning with the weather, held in place by little more than gravity and the tenacious will of someone who gathered stones from the field, placing them one atop another, trying to make something that would stay.

Bits and pieces of how many lives?

I build myself up as I go.

Yemen

Friendship

Aziza Abd Allah

We were on the verge of friendship
Until he hunted ready-made wings
While I was sculpting other wings
Which cannot be hunted

A Hailstone of Lightning

A flash
Drowning me in hailstones
Covering me with a cloak of storm
I sweat in fear
(Are there no butterflies to break it???)
I part the crowd: passers-by and racket
The cups have been drunk, the chairs are alerted
The pores of distance are shrunk, the table collapses
Did I ask for a wall for the crowd?
Did I ask them for more doubt?
Your silence folds the wall
I will depart
You are blocking my steps
You are staring: (You scattered birds)

From my horizons
Release your hands
Steps walking carefully
I walk on two pains
Count: How many days and nights

Fall on my shoulders?
Uncountable: the injuries you caused me
I shiver …
(No dove lays you a poem??)
Streets crossed by … heart beats
You are capable of silence
So why then, do the prison bars lean toward me?

I shiver
I enter the crowd … rushing … crushed
The heart's rudder moves us to and fro
You are always kinder …
I sneak love
I encourage the astonishment
No trees … no streets … no outside … everything is inside
A cloak shook off a flash and shook me off
Tens of women fell beneath it … I'm not one of them
I shook off love
Nothing between us
Except that I am not … just any one

Notes on Contributors

Aziza Abd Allah: Despite the editors' best efforts to trace information about the author, no details were available.

Laila 'Allush (b.1948) has several collections of poems that include *Spices on the Open Wound, Years of Drought* and *My Heart.* She writes in a tone of regret over Palestine's fate but her verse is also marked by some faith in the inevitability of resurgence.

Jean Arasanayagam (b. 1930) is an English language poet and fiction writer. The theme in her work is generally the ethnic and religious turmoil in Sri Lanka. Her collection of poems *Kindura* is known for its engagement with cultural hybridity.

Hanan Mikha'il Ashrawi (b. 1946), a professor of English literature and a political activist, won international recognition for her articulate defense of Palestinian national rights. Her innate eloquence is further manifested in her literary accomplishments and her critically acclaimed memoir, *This Side of Peace.*

Maria Arbatova (b. 1957) is popularly acknowledged as the ideologue of Russian feminism. She has authored numerous plays, stories and novels and is known as a non-conformist writer.

Li-ang (b. 1952) is considered one of the best Taiwanese feminist writers. Her novel, *Butcher's Wife,* won her the Union News Novel Award and has been translated into several languages. Her stories have been published in such journals as *New York Times* and the *Guardian.*

Phan Thi Vang Anh (b. 1968) works for the Youth Publishing House. Her writings raise the emerging questions of youth yearning for freedom and choices. Her father Chi Lan Bin was one of the greatest Vietnamese poets of the century.

Wong Bikwan (b. 1961) is the author of many books, some of which have won prestigious awards. Her work reflects something of the freewheeling admixture of highbrow and lowbrow elements characteristic of recent cultural production in Hong Kong.

Maria Ondina Braga (b. 1932) is a translator and writer who is known for her prize-winning novel *Nocturno em Macao* (1991) and her fictionalized autobiography, *Estatua de Sal*. She taught in Angola, Goa and Macao in the 1960s.

Ajeet Cour (b. 1934), a well-known writer in Punjabi, set up the Academy of Fine Arts and Literature and its SAARC literary wing, the Foundation of SAARC Writers and Literature. She has several collections of short stories and her autobiography *Khanabadosh* won a lot of acclaim.

Tan Mei Ching writes short stories as well as plays and has won many awards including the 'Just a Moment Writing Contest', Jason Writing Contest and others. Her novel *Beyond the Village Gate* was awarded the Singapore Commendation Prize in 1992.

Kim Chi-won (b. 1943) is a well-known short story writer who comes from a literary family. She has published many collections of stories and a novel, *Morae Shigye* (*Hour Glass*). Her writings describe the trials of Korean immigrants in the American metropolis.

Leila S. Chudori (b. 1962) is an important writer who engages with the issues of double standards in culture and how that affects women. She worked as a reporter in Jakarta for 'Tempo', until Suharto's New Order government banned it in 1994.

Lam Thi My Da (b. 1949) worked with the youth brigades during the War. She is an executive board member of the Vietnam Writers Association and the Vietnamese Women's Association. Her book of poems, *De tan mot giac mo*, won the highest honours in Vietnam.

G. Delgermaa is employed as the Advocacy Program Coordinator at the Arts Council of Mongolia. She has worked as a professional translator as well as a journalist.

Mahasweta Devi (b. 1926) is a deeply political social activist who has been working with and for tribals and marginalized communities. She has been honoured with many awards which include the Jnanpeeth Award, Sahitya Akademi as well as the Magsasay Award.

Marjorie Evasco has served as Director of Bienvenido N. Santos of Creative Writing and Research Centre for many years at De la Salle University. Her prize-winning poetry books are: *Dreamweavers: Selected Poems* and *Ochre Tones: Poems in English and Cebuano.*

Forugh Farrokhzad's (1935-67) first collection of poems, *Asir* (The Captive) was brought out in 1955 after which she published four more books of poems. She also made a film, *The House is Black,* on a lepers' colony for which she received many awards. She died in an accident in 1967.

Enchi Fumiko's (1905-86) short stories and novels focus on repressed passion and the mysterious workings of women's minds. She also wrote many stage plays. In 1932 she won the Women's Literature Prize and was given the Order of Culture by the Japanese Government in 1985.

Geyang (b. 1972) studied writing at the Lu Xun Institute in Beijing. At present she works for the Tibetan Meteorological Bureau. Her stories have won her a number of awards.

Gulnazar (b. 1945) worked as a journalist. She also wrote the lyrics for the Tajikistan National Anthem officially adopted in 1991.

Donia Gobar was born and raised in Kabul and is a doctor, artist, sculptor and writer. She was the winner of the International Poet of Merit Award 2000-01.Her book of poems, *The Invisibles,* also carries nineteen prints of her paintings.

Banira Giri (b. 1946) teaches Nepali at Tribhuvan University and she was the first woman to receive the Sajha Award, for her poetic fiction *Shabdatit Shantanu*. Her sensitive and forceful logical exposition probing the depths of human wounds is noteworthy.

Teji Grover (b. 1955) is a well known poet in Hindi. Her works include the collection of poetry *Lo Kaha Sanbari* and a novel *Neela*. She has translated Swedish poets into Hindi. In 1989 she received the Bharat Bhushan Agarwal Award for her poetry.

Oh Jung Hee (b. 1947) has very distinctly depicted the female consciousness through her skillful metaphors, lyrical style and unique form. She was awarded the Yi Sang Literature Award and the Tongin Literature Award, the most prestigious awards in Korea.

Zaheda Hina (b. 1946) is a prominent Urdu fiction writer from Pakistan who has progressive leanings. Associated with human rights and women's movements, she is an incisive journalist who has also been actively writing short stories. She is the recipient of the SAARC Literary Award.

Manju Kanchuli (b. 1951) is the author of a number of collections of short stories, including *Some Love, Some Difference.* A recipient of many awards, she has also published some collections of poems such as *My Life My World*.

Sukrita Paul Kumar (b. 1949) has published several collections of poems which include *Without Margins* and *Oscillations*. She is also a well-known literary critic with many critical books to her credit. Her special areas of interest are 'Cultural Diversity in South Asia' and 'Partition literature'.

Yangtso Kyi (b. 1963) was formerly a community educator for a local women's association and then, an official translator. She now works as a legal researcher. This is her most widely known story.

Agnes Lam (b. 1954) has taught at the National University of Singapore and is at present at the English Centre of the University of Hong Kong. This poem is from her first collection, *Woman to Woman* (1997).

Ly Lan's (b. 1957) first collection of short stories, *Singing Grass*, was followed by over twenty collections of short stories and poems. She has also worked as a journalist for a newspaper and has translated six volumes of *Harry Potter.*

Jyoti Lanjewar is a university professor writing poetry in the Marathi language and known as a prominent poet with a heightened consciousness of being a Dalit woman poet. In the hierarchy of the Hindu caste structure, Dalits belong to the lowest caste.

Savyon Liebrecht (b. 1948), born to Holocaust survivors, is an author of four collections of short stories. She has been translated into many languages and she writes television scripts. Her own stories too have been adapted for television.

Lisa Suhair Majaj is a Palestinian American who grew up in Jordan and studied in Lebanon before moving to Cyprus in 2001. In addition to her creative writing, she has also written many critical essays on Arab American literature.

Nazik al-Mala'ika (b. 1923) taught at the University of Musol in Iraq. She is acclaimed to be the first Arab to have broken away from the classical 'Qasida' and led the movement of Modern Arabic verse. Her publications include her book of poems, *Lil Salat wal Thawra* (To Prayer and Revolution).

Afagh Masud engages with the psychological constraints women face in a patriarchal culture, as in her short stories *'Tak'* (Alone), *'Izdiham'*, (Crowding) and *'Serchalar'* (Sparrows). Her work depicts women who resist social constructs.

Pollie Bith-Melander is an Associate Director, Asia-Pacific Institute of Tropical Medicine & Infectious Diseases at the University of Hawaii. She was born in the province of Battambang during the Pol Pot era. Most of her stories are about women who survive tragedies.

Kishwar Naheed (b. 1940) is an Urdu poet from Pakistan known for her pioneering feminist poetry. A former civil servant and editor of a prestigious monthly magazine, she has written extensively on women's issues, crimes against women and the images of women in media.

Taslima Nasreen (b. 1962) is an ex-physician turned feminist author who describes herself as a secular humanist. She received a number of international awards, including the Simone de Beauvoir Feminist Award 2008, in recognition of her demand for freedom of expression.

Shahrnush Parsipur (b. 1946) is a prolific fiction writer whose works have been translated into many languages. She currently lives in USA as a political refugee. Her book *Prison Memoirs* recalls her time spent in jail. Her novel *Touba va Maanayeh Shab* (*Touba and the Meaning of Night*) brought her a lot of acclaim.

Chiranan Pitpreecha (b. 1955) was a student activist who played a vital role in the October 1973 uprising in Thailand. Her collection of poems *The Lost Leaf* won the SEA Write Award in 1989.

Zong Pu (b. 1928) worked in the Foreign Literature Research Institute of the Academy of Social Sciences. This story embodies her personal experience of the persecution of intellectuals during the 'Cultural Revolution' in China.

Bano Qudsia (b. 1928) has published a number of novels, novellas and short story collections. She writes regularly for the stage and television in both Urdu and Punjabi and is a winner of many literary awards. Her novel *Raja Gidh* has received wide critical acclaim.

Pratibha Ray (b. 1943) is an academic and she writes novels and short stories in Oriya. She takes an active interest in social reform and her writings explore issues of social justice. Amongst other awards, she received the Orissa Sahitya Akademi and the Moorthi Devi Award.

Putsata Reang is currently working as the resident advisor for the Internews Network in Phnom Penh. She has written on her family's escape from Cambodia in 1975, affected by the genocide of people under the Khmer Rouge.

Rizia Rahman (b. 1939) is well known for her novels, *Rokter Okshor (Blood Words)* and *Bong Theke Bangla* which encompass the history of the nation, culture and language of Bangladesh. She has won several literary awards including the Saadat Ali Akhand Literature Award 2003.

Kunzang Choden Roder (b. 1952) writes stories drawing heavily from the oral folklore of Bhutan. She uses legends and accords them the shape of fiction.

Ma Sandar (b. 1947) is a very prolific writer who won a prize for her collection of short stories in 1982, and then in 1994 for her novel *Alwan Eikmer Pan*. She is a realist and reflects on relationships, ageing and the sexual double standard.

Zohra Saed was born in Jalalabad and now lives in USA. She keeps herself deeply connected to the country of her origin through her writings. She co-edited *Drop by Drop We Make a River: A Collection of Afghan Writings from 1978-2001*.

Tsuboi Sakae (1900-67) was awarded the Shincho Literature Prize for her first short story collection. Her stories for children carry serious messages for adults while her works for adults often criticize contemporary society from the view point of a child.

Ratna Sarumpaet (b. 1949) has been avidly supporting political causes through her writing. She suffered imprisonment towards the end of the Suharto regime for her participation in a pro-democracy meeting in north Jakarta. In her drama Sarumpaet features strong female figures who challenge social justice.

P. Sathyavathi was born in Kolakalur in Andhra Pradesh. Her writing focuses mainly on women's issues and she has published three anthologies of short stories. She has won the prestigious Chaso Spoorti award, Rangavalli award and Telugu University award.

Mona Sa'udi (b. 1945) has exhibited her sculptures in Jordan, France and other places. She has published collections of her drawings and poems together. She received the National Award for Arts in 1993 in Jordan. She is also the author of a bilingual collection of conversations with Palestinian children from the Baqa'a Refugee Camp.

Ariyoshi Sawako (1931-84) is one of Japan's most successful writers who combines literature with social criticism and women's issues. Her writing is more humanitarian than political. *The Doctor's Wife* is considered to be her best novel.

Mai Sayigh (b. 1940) was the president of the Union of Palestinian Women from 1971. Her books of poems are: *Garlands of Thorns* (1968), *Love Poems for a Hunted Name* (1974) and *Tears and the Coming Joy* (1975). She also wrote prose, *The Siege,* about the Israeli invasion and occupation of Beirut in 1982.

Hanan al-Shaikh (b. 1945) wrote her first novel, *Intihar Rajul Mayyit* (The Suicide of a Dead Man) when she was a student in Cairo. She worked as a journalist in Beirut and has published many short stories and novels. She is considered one of the Beirut Decentrists.

Benju Sharma is committed to the creation of free and vibrant poetry, giving expression to the downtrodden and seeking emancipation from economic exploitation. Emotionally sustained expression and a sure lyricism mark her poetry.

Bi Shu-min is the Vice Chairman of Beijing Writers' Association. She is a psychologist with unique insights to depict life and human beings. Her novel *Save the Breast* has come to be known as a 'psychotherapy' novel. Her experiences as a medic in Tibet inspired her to start writing.

Heng Siok Tian has published four volumes of poems: *Crossing the Chopsticks, My City, My Canvas* and *Contouring*. She also writes short stories. Her short play, *The Lift* was selected for the Third International Women Playwrights' Festival in Adelaide.

Mey Son Sotheary (b. 1977) works at Channel 3, TV Broadcasting of Phnom Penh. She is interested in women's social problems and tensions between the urban and the rural cultures.

Qian Xi Teng (b. 1983) is currently freelancing as a writer, translator and film publicist. She was part of the Simon Elvin Young Poet of the Year prize-winners' poetry course (Arvon Foundation/Poetry Society, London) in 2000 and 2001.

Maya Thakuri (b. 1946) has published many collections of poems, short stories and songs to which she has given music and voice. Her songs have been recorded by several radio stations and her writings find place in many text books for schools and colleges. She is a recipient of many awards.

Fadwa Tuqan (1917–2003) was one of the most influential poets in Modern Palestinian poetry. She took a departure from the traditional Arabic poetry and is known for taking up sensual themes. In 1990 she got the PLO's Jerusalem Award for Culture and Arts and in 1996 the Honorary Palestine Prize for Poetry.

Kamala Wijeratne (b. 1939) has five collections of poems and an anthology of short stories entitled *Death by Drowning and Other Stories*. In 2004 she was awarded the State literary award for her poetry.

Tsushima Yuko (b. 1947) has been acclaimed by Japanese critics as a 'representative writer' of the post-war generation. Her typical work takes on domestic details and gives them a powerful significance. In 1983 she was awarded the Kawabata Prize for the story included in this book.

Noraini Md. Yusof (b. 1962) won a prize for Best Fiction in 1985 for her short story 'The Monsoon'. She teaches literature at the Faculty of Language Studies, University of Kebangsaan. She explores the clashing values of different religions practised in Malaysia.

Copyright Acknowledgements

All efforts were made to contact the writers, translators and publishers of the material selected for this volume. We are very glad to acknowledge the support we received from everyone for this venture. However, in case any permissions have been left out inadvertently, kindly contact the publishers of this book.

It is with deep gratitude that we acknowledge the following for permissions received by us:

For 'One Centimetre': Bi Shu-min & translator Carolyn Choa, *Vintage Book of Contemporary Chinese Fiction*, ed. Carolyn Choa & David Su-Li-Qun, Vintage Books, New York, 2001.

For 'Melody in Dreams': Zong Pu, translator Song Shouquan & publisher Can Xui, *Seven Contemporary Chinese Women Writers*, Panda Books, China, 1983.

For 'She's a Young Woman and So Am I': Wong Bikwan & translator Naifei Ding, *Red is Not the Only Color*, ed. Patricia Sieber, Rowman & Littlefield Publishers Inc., USA, 2001.

For 'My Cerebral Child': Agnes Lam, *Woman to Woman and Other Poems*, Asia 2000 Ltd, 1997.

For 'Umbrella on a Moonlit Night': Tsuboi Sakae & heirs of the author & translator Chris Heftel, *The Mother of Dreams and Other Short Stories: Portrayals of Women in Modern Japanese Fiction,* ed. Makoto Ueda, Kodansha International Ltd, Tokyo, 1986.

For 'The Tomoshibi': Ariyoshi Sawako & translator Keiko Nakamura, *The Mother of Dreams*, Kodansha International Ltd, Tokyo, 1986.

For 'The Silent Traders': Tsushima Yuko & translator Geraldine Harcourt, *The Showa Anthology: Modern Japanese Short Stories (1929-1984)*, ed. Van C. Gessel & Tomone Matsumoto, Kodansha International Ltd, Tokyo, 1993.

For 'Boxcar of Chrysanthemums': Enchi Fumiko, *This Kind of Woman: Ten Stories by Japanese Writers, 1960-1975*, trans. & ed. Yukiko Tanaka, Elizabeth Hanson & the Board of Trustees of the Leland Stanford Jr University, Stanford Univ. Press, California, 1982.

For 'Chinatown' by Oh Jung Hee & 'A Certain Beginning' by Kim Chi-won: Translators Bruce Fulton & Ju-Chan Fulton, *Words of Farewell: Stories by Korean Women Writers*, ed. Kang Sok-Kyong, Kim Chi-won & O Chong-hui, Avalon Publishing Group Inc., Seal Press, California, 1989.

For 'The Lepers': Maria Ondina Braga, *Visions of China: Stories from Macau*, trans. & ed. David Brookshaw, Hong Kong Univ. Press, Hong Kong, 1992.

For extract from *Marsinah Accuses*: Ratna Sarumpaet & translator John H. McGlynn, Reprinted from *The Lontar Anthology of Indonesian Drama: Volume 3, Indonesian Drama During the New Order*, vol. ed. Cobina Gillit, series ed. John H. McGlynn, The Lontar Foundation, Jakarta, 2006.

For 'Flower Season': Li-ang & translator Howard Goldblatt, *Asia*, Magazine of Asian Literature, vol. 2. no. 4, Spring 2007.

For 'An Old Nun Tells her Story': Geyang, *Tales of Tibet: Sky Burials, Prayer Wheels, and Wind Horses,* trans. & ed. Herbert J. Batt, Rowman & Littlefield Inc., Maryland, USA, 2001.

For 'Journal of the Grassland': Yangtso Kyi & translator Lauran R. Hartley, *Manoa,* Univ. of Hawaii Press, vol. 12, no. 2, 2000, pp. 19-26.

For 'The Dinner Guests': Putsata Reang, *Manoa,* University of Hawaii Press, vol. 16, no. 1, 2004.

For the following pieces from *Virtual Lotus: Modern Fiction of South East Asia*, ed. Teri Shaffer Yamada, University of Michigan Press, 2002:

'My Sister': Mey Son Sotheary & translators Tomoko Okada, Vuth Reth & Teri Shaffer Yamada;

'The Purification of Sita': Leila S. Chudori & translator Claire Siverson;

'Dance of the Bees': Noraini Md. Yusuf;

'An Umbrella': Ma Sandar & translator Than Than Win.

For 'Caged Bird will Fly': Pollie Bith-Melander, *Shadow of Angkor,* ed. Frank Stewart, Univ. of Hawaii Press, Hawaii, 2004.

For 'Caravan of the Waterbearers': Marjorie Evasco, *Dreamweavers*, Aria Editions Inc., Manila, 1987.

For 'Ochre Tones': Marjorie Evasco, '*Ochre Tones: Poems in English and Cebuano*', Salimbayan Books, Manila, 1999.

For 'Sunny-side Up': Tan Mei Ching.

For 'Journal Week': Heng Siok Tian.

For 'Medusa: Stone Poems': Qian Xi Teng.

For 'The Defiance of a Flower': Chiranan Pitpreecha & translator Sudchit Bhinyoying, *The S.E.A. Write Anthology of Thai Short Stories & Poems*, ed. Nitya Masavisut Mathew, Grose Silkworm Books, Chiang Mai, 1998.

For 'Thuong': Phan Thi Vang Anh & translators Nan Son & Wayne Karlin, *Manoa*, ed. Frank Stewart, Univ. of Hawaii Press, vol. 15, no.1, 2003, pp. 113-18.

For 'Woman Wearing B!ack': Lam Thi My Da & translators Martha Collins & Thuy Dinh, Reprinted from *Green Rice* with the permission of Curbstone Press.

For 'The Ghost': Ly Lan & translator Kevin Bowen, *Manoa*, Univ. of Hawaii Press, vol. 11, no. 2, 1999, pp. 1-6.

For 'Things Cheaply Had': Taslima Nasreen & translators Mohd Nurul Huda & Carolyne Wright, *Infinite Variety*, ed. Firdous Azim & Niaz Zaman, Dhaka Univ. Press, 1994.

For 'Women Can't': Taslima Nasreen translator Fazlul Alam, *Infinite Variety,* Dhaka Univ. Press, Dhaka, 1994.

For 'Irina's Picture': Rizia Rahman & translator Radha Chakravarty, *Crossings: Stories from Bangladesh and India*, ed. Radha Chakravarty, Indialog Publications, New Delhi, 2003.

For 'Garba Lung Gi Khorlo and the Demoness of Nyala': Kunzang Choden Roder, *Voices of Asia: An Anthology of SAARC Fiction,* ed. Ajeet Cour & Pankaj Bhan, Foundation for SAARC Writers & Literature, New Delhi, 2002.

For 'Giribala': Mahasweta Devi & translator Radha Chakravarty, *In the Name of the Mother*, Seagull Publishers, 1986.

For 'Caves': Jyoti Lanjewar & translator Shanta Gokhale, *No Entry for the New Son*, ed. Arjun Dangle , Orient Longman Pvt. Ltd, 1992.

For 'Cow-dust Time': P. Sathyavathi and translator Ranga Rao.

For 'Dead-end': Ajeet Cour, *Slate of Life*, Kali for Women, New Delhi, 1990.

For 'Laila's Call': Sukrita Paul Kumar, *Without Margins*, Bibliophile South Asia, New Delhi, 2004.

For 'Silence': Teji Grover & translator Arlene Zide, *The Tree of Tongues: An Anthology of Modern Indian Poetry*, ed. E.V. Ramakrishnan, IIAS, Shimla, 1999.

For 'The Stigma': Pratibha Ray, *The Harper Collins Book of Oriya Short Stories*, trans. & ed. K.K. Mahapatra, Leelawati Mahapatra & Sudhansu Mohanty, Harper Collins, New Delhi, 1998.

For 'The Grass is Really Like Me' & 'Who Am I?': Kishwar Naheed, *We Sinful Women: Contemporary Urdu Feminist Poetry*, trans. & ed. Rukhsana Ahmad, Rupa, New Delhi, 1990.

For 'To Be or Not To Be': Zaheda Hina & translator Faiz Ahmad Faiz, *Fires in the Autumn Garden*, ed. Asif Farrukhi, OUP, Karachi, 1997.

For 'Soul-weary': Bano Qudsia & translator M. Asaduddin, *Short Stories from Pakistan*, ed. Intizar Hussain & Asif Farrukhi, Sahitya Akademi, New Delhi, 2003.

For 'A Strange Temple': Manju Kanchuli & translator Wayne Amtzis, *Manoa*, Univ. of Hawaii Press, vol. 13, no. 2, 2001, pp. 55-57.

For 'Illicit Connection' by Banira Giri, Untitled poem by Benju Sharma & 'It Has Already Been Late' by Maya Thakuri (translated by Damodar Sharma): Dr Madhav Pokhrel.

For 'Wedding Photographs' & 'Telephone Conversation': Jean Arasanayagam, *Fussilade,* Indialog Publications, New Delhi, 2003.

For 'Death by Drowning': Kamala Wijeratne, *Voices of Asia,* ed. Ajeet Cour & Pankaj Bhan, 2002.

For 'Sparrows': Afagh Masud & translator Shouleh Vatanabadi, *World Literature Today* 70, no. 3, Summer 1996, pp. 505-08. Copyright © 1996 by *World Literature Today.* Reprinted by permission.

For Untitled poem from Mongolia: G. Delgermaa.

For 'A Letter': Gulnazar & translator Sunil Sharma, *World Literature Today* 70, no. 3, Summer 1996, p. 575. Copyright © 1996 by *World Literature Today*. Reprinted by permission.

For 'What The Scar Revealed' & 'Voices: Archive of Spines': Zohra Saed.

For 'The Ugly Face of Power' & 'Ariana': Donia Gobar.

For 'I am Called A Woman': Maria Arbatova & translator Ranjana Saxena.

For 'Zarrinkolah': Shahrnush Parsipur & translators Kamran Talatoff & Jocelyn Starlet, *Women Without Men,* The Feminist Press, New York, 1989/2004.

For 'O Bejewelled Land' & 'I Will Greet the Sun Once Again': Forugh Farrokhzad & translators Hasan Javadi & Susan Sallée, *Another Birth: Selected Poems of Forugh Farrokhzad*, Middle Eastern Series No. 1, Albany Press, California, 1981.

For 'My Silence' & 'Washing off Disgrace': Nazik al-Mala'ika and translator Kamal Boullata, *Women of the Fertile Crescent: An Anthology of Modern Poetry by Arab Women*, ed. Kamal Boullata ,Three Continents Press, Washington DC, 1978.

For 'What Am I Speaking, Greek? She Said to Him': Savyon Liebrecht & translator Marganit Weinberger-Rotman, *Not just Milk and Honey*, ed. Haya Hoffman, NBT, India, 1998.

Copyright in the original Hebrew by the authors, translation © The Institute for the Translation of Hebrew Literature.

For 'A Girl Called Apple': Hanan al-Shaikh & translator Miriam Cooke, *Opening the Gates: A Century of Arab Feminist Writing*, ed. Margot Badran & Miriam Cooke, Virago, London, 1990.

For Untitled Poems from Jordan: Mona Sau'di & translator Kamal Boullata, *Women of the Fertile Crescent: An Anthology of Modern Poetry by Arab Women*, ed. Kamal Boullata, Three Continents Press, Washington DC, 1978.

From *Anthology of Modern Palestinian Literature*, ed. Salma Khadra Jayyusi, Columbia University Press, New York, 1992:

'The Path of Affection': Laila 'Allush & translators Lena Jayyusi & Naomi Shihab Nye;

For extract from 'The Diary of an Almost-Four-Year-Old': Hanan Mikha'il Ashrawi;

For extract from 'The Siege': Mai Sayigh & translators Peter Clark & Christopher Tingley;

For extract from 'A Mountainous Journey': Fadwa Tuqan & translator Olive Kenny.

For 'Stone Fence': Lisa Suhair Majaj, *World Literature Today* 78, nos 3-4, September-December 2004, p. 20. Copyright © 2004 by *World Literature Today*. Reprinted by permission.

For 'Friendship': Aziza Abd Allah, courtesy Dr Antelak al-Mutawakel, Gender and Development Studies Centre.

A large number of libraries and private collections were used to collect the material for this volume. We thank the staff of the following institutions:

Library of Congress (Washington DC), American University Library (Washington DC), Hong Kong Baptist University (Hong Kong), University of Chicago Library (Chicago), Durrell Centre at Corfu

(Greece), Rockefeller Foundation Bellagio Center, Chinese Cultural Secretary (Chinese Embassy, Delhi), Jawaharlal Nehru University Library (Delhi), Sahitya Akademi (Delhi), Cultural Centre of Iraq at Delhi, Hamdard University Library, Central Reference Library (University of Delhi), India International Centre Library (Delhi), Indian Institute of Advanced Study (Shimla).

Our heartiest thanks are due to the following for helping us connect with individuals and institutions:

Frank Stewart, Alvin Pang, David Simon, Madhav Pokhrel, Agnes Lam, Lucinda Peach, Marjorie Evasco, Radha Chakravarty and many others.

We wish to acknowledge here the contribution of our team of research associates in helping us compile this book over the last three years. We are deeply indebted to them for their dedication and readiness to work. Thank you very much, Vandana Singh, Rachna Sethi and Shyista Khan.

Sukrita Paul Kumar and Malashri Lal